VISIT US AT

www.syngress.com

Syngress is committed to publishing high-quality books for IT Professionals and delivering those books in media and formats that fit the demands of our customers. We are also committed to extending the utility of the book you purchase via additional materials available from our Web site.

SOLUTIONS WEB SITE

To register your book, visit www.syngress.com/solutions. Once registered, you can access our solutions@syngress.com Web pages. There you may find an assortment of value-added features such as free e-books related to the topic of this book, URLs of related Web site, FAQs from the book, corrections, and any updates from the author(s).

ULTIMATE CDs

Our Ultimate CD product line offers our readers budget-conscious compilations of some of our best-selling backlist titles in Adobe PDF form. These CDs are the perfect way to extend your reference library on key topics pertaining to your area of expertise, including Cisco Engineering, Microsoft Windows System Administration, CyberCrime Investigation, Open Source Security, and Firewall Configuration, to name a few.

DOWNLOADABLE E-BOOKS

For readers who can't wait for hard copy, we offer most of our titles in downloadable Adobe PDF form. These e-books are often available weeks before hard copies, and are priced affordably.

SYNGRESS OUTLET

Our outlet store at syngress.com features overstocked, out-of-print, or slightly hurt books at significant savings.

SITE LICENSING

Syngress has a well-established program for site licensing our e-books onto servers in corporations, educational institutions, and large organizations. Contact us at sales@syngress.com for more information.

CUSTOM PUBLISHING

Many organizations welcome the ability to combine parts of multiple Syngress books, as well as their own content, into a single volume for their own internal use. Contact us at sales@syngress.com for more information.

SYNGRESS®

FISMA
Certification &
Accreditation
Handbook

Laura Taylor

Matthew Shepherd Technical Editor

KEY	SERIAL NUMBER
001	HJIRTCV764
002	PO9873D5FG
003	829KM8NJH2
004	BNXXX34887
005	CVPLQ6WQ23
006	VBP965T5T5
007	HJJJ863WD3E
008	2987GVTWMK
009	629MP5SDJT
010	IMWQ295T6T

PUBLISHED BY
Syngress Publishing, Inc.
800 Hingham Street
Rockland, MA 02370

FISMA Certification & Accreditation Handbook

Printed in Canada
1 2 3 4 5 6 7 8 9 0
ISBN: 1-59749-116-0
ISBN-13: 978-1-59749-116-7

Publisher: Andrew Williams
Acquisitions Editor: Gary Byrne
Technical Editor: Matthew Shepherd
Cover Designer: Michael Kavish

Page Layout and Art: Patricia Lupien
Copy Editor: Adrienne Rebello
Indexer: Richard Carlson

Distributed by O'Reilly Media, Inc. in the United States and Canada.
For information on rights, translations, and bulk sales, contact Matt Pedersen, Director of Sales and Rights, at Syngress Publishing; email matt@syngress.com or fax to 781-681-3585.

Acknowledgments

Syngress would like to acknowledge the following people for their kindness and support in making this book possible.

Syngress books are now distributed in the United States and Canada by O'Reilly Media, Inc. The enthusiasm and work ethic at O'Reilly are incredible, and we would like to thank everyone there for their time and efforts to bring Syngress books to market: Tim O'Reilly, Laura Baldwin, Mark Brokering, Mike Leonard, Donna Selenko, Bonnie Sheehan, Cindy Davis, Grant Kikkert, Opol Matsutaro, Steve Hazelwood, Mark Wilson, Rick Brown, Tim Hinton, Kyle Hart, Sara Winge, Peter Pardo, Leslie Crandell, Regina Aggio Wilkinson, Pascal Honscher, Preston Paull, Susan Thompson, Bruce Stewart, Laura Schmier, Sue Willing, Mark Jacobsen, Betsy Waliszewski, Kathryn Barrett, John Chodacki, Rob Bullington, Kerry Beck, Karen Montgomery, and Patrick Dirden.

The incredibly hardworking team at Elsevier Science, including Jonathan Bunkell, Ian Seager, Duncan Enright, David Burton, Rosanna Ramacciotti, Robert Fairbrother, Miguel Sanchez, Klaus Beran, Emma Wyatt, Krista Leppiko, Marcel Koppes, Judy Chappell, Radek Janousek, Rosie Moss, David Lockley, Nicola Haden, Bill Kennedy, Martina Morris, Kai Wuerfl-Davidek, Christiane Leipersberger, Yvonne Grueneklee, Nadia Balavoine, and Chris Reinders for making certain that our vision remains worldwide in scope.

David Buckland, Marie Chieng, Lucy Chong, Leslie Lim, Audrey Gan, Pang Ai Hua, Joseph Chan, June Lim, and Siti Zuraidah Ahmad of Pansing Distributors for the enthusiasm with which they receive our books.

David Scott, Tricia Wilden, Marilla Burgess, Annette Scott, Andrew Swaffer, Stephen O'Donoghue, Bec Lowe, Mark Langley, and Anyo Geddes of Woodslane for distributing our books throughout Australia, New Zealand, Papua New Guinea, Fiji, Tonga, Solomon Islands, and the Cook Islands.

Author

Laura Taylor is Director of Security Certification and Accreditation at COACT, Inc, a leading provider of security compliance solutions. Additionally, Ms. Taylor is the Founder of Relevant Technologies, a security research and advisory firm. Her security research has been used by the FDIC, the FBI, the IRS, various U.S. Federal Reserve Banks, U.S. Customs, the U.S. Treasury, the White House, and many publicly held Fortune 500 companies. Ms. Taylor specializes in security audits of financial institutions and has provided information security consulting services to some of the largest financial institutions in the world, including the U.S. Internal Revenue Service, the U.S. Treasury, the U.S. Governmentwide Accounting System, and National Westminster Bank, a division of the Royal Bank of Scotland.

Formerly, Ms. Taylor was Director of Security Research at TEC. Ms. Taylor also served as CIO of Schafer Corporation and Director of Information Security at Navisite. Earlier in her career, Ms. Taylor held various positions at Sun Microsystems, where she was awarded several Outstanding Performance awards, and a CIS Security Award. Ms. Taylor has also received awards from a division of the U.S. Financial Management Services commissioner for her assistance with FISMA-compliant Security C&A of highly sensitive systems. Ms. Taylor is a Certified Information Security Manager (CISM).

Ms. Taylor has been featured in many media forums, including ABC-TV Business Now, CNET Radio, the *Boston Business Journal*, *Computerworld*, and *The Montreal Gazette*. Her research and popular security columns have been published on Web sites and in magazines, including *Business Security Advisor*, *Forbes*, *SecurityWatch*, eSecurityOnline, SecurityFocus, NetworkStorageForum, ZDNet, *Datamation*, *MidRangeComputing*, and *Securify*. Ms. Taylor has authored hundreds of research articles and papers on information security topics and has contributed to multiple books. Ms. Taylor graduated from Skidmore College with honors, and is a member of the Society of Professional Journalists, the IEEE Standards Association, and the National Security Agency's IATFF Forum.

Contributing Author

Glenn Jacobson is a Senior Certification and Accreditation (C&A) Engineer with COACT Inc. Prior to working for COACT, Mr. Jacobson worked for SysNet Technologies Inc, where he worked on various C&A activities for the FAA. Mr. Jacobson's FAA projects included security testing and planning, vulnerability analysis, remediation identification, and risk management. Prior to SysNet Technologies, Mr. Jacobson worked as a consultant for both government and civilian organizations, specializing in network and security solutions development and implementation. Currently, Mr. Jacobson is working on developing a C&A training class.

Technical Editor

Matt Shepherd (CISSP, MCSE, GCFW, GSEC) is a consultant for Project Performance Corporation of McLean, VA. Project Performance Corporation synthesizes its capabilities in security architecture, compliance, and certification and accreditation with best-of-breed tools to provide effective security solutions to customers in the public and private sectors. Matt uses his experience as a network administrator, IT manager, and security architect to deliver high-quality solutions for Project Performance Corporation's clients. Currently, he is supporting the US Patent and Trademark Office's Certification and Accreditation program.

Matt holds bachelor's degrees from St. Mary's College of Maryland and is currently working on his Master's of Science in Information Assurance. Matt would like to thank his wife, Leena, for her invaluable support and guidance throughout his career, his family for their love and support, and Olive for making every day special.

Contents

Foreword

When I was the Security Staff Director of the Federal Deposit Insurance Corporation (FDIC), the Federal Information Security Management Act of 2002 (FISMA) was not yet in existence; however, the Government Information Security Reform Act (GISRA) was. Since GISRA was signed into law on October 30, 2000, U.S. federal agencies have been paying far more attention to information security than they did previously.

In 2002, FISMA was signed into law, creating more specific regulations for U.S. federal agencies than those established by GISRA. Today, with FISMA, and the process known to support FISMA, Certification and Accreditation (C&A), agencies are far more diligent about assessing their security controls and vulnerabilities. Despite what you may read in the news, however, many federal agencies are far more secure than their commercial counterparts in the private sector.

C&A is still a nascent science, and although excellent guidance exists on how to evaluate the risk exposure of federal information systems, agencies are still working on improving their C&A programs. C&A is, however, a large endeavor. Although the process has been proven to reduce risk to federal information systems, many people new to C&A don't know where to start or how to get going on their C&A projects. Seasoned C&A experts continue to look for new ideas on how to improve their existing processes. This book is the first publication with numerous practical examples that can help you step through the C&A process from beginning to end. I wish this book had existed while I was the Security Staff Director of the FDIC so that I could have provided copies to my staff.

Federal agencies aside, the principles discussed in this book can be applied to almost any organization that cares about the security of its information technology systems and infrastructure. Cyber criminals, identity thieves, and terrorists have made information security assessments a requisite fundamental part of doing business today. Laws mandate information security compliance, and federal and private organizations are allocating budgets to ensure that their confidential information remains private and secure. Although the C&A process was first rolled out by federal agencies, I anticipate that private industry organizations will adopt C&A principles to assess their own systems going forward.

There is a lot more to securing an infrastructure of systems and applications than simply performing penetration tests and security scans. This book was written so that almost anyone can understand it. If you're interested in learning how to assess all the different security aspects of your systems, networks, and applications, this book is for you. With an abundance of pointers to outside references, this book includes almost all the resources you need to learn C&A. I hope you'll find it as easy to follow as I have.

—*Sunil J. Porter*
Former Security Staff Director of the FDIC

Preface

As the federal regulators have come to understand the risks to the U.S. national infrastructure, regulations and laws have been written to ensure that due diligence occurs in securing critical applications and systems. An outcome of the laws and regulations is a formalized process for reviewing, documenting, analyzing, and evaluating information security requirements and controls. The process described in this book, known as C&A, will assist government agencies in complying with the Federal Information Security Management Act of 2002.

Audience

The audience for this book includes those individuals currently performing information security support at U.S. Federal agencies, defense contractors that need to comply with FISMA to support government task orders, information security consultants, and anyone else who would like to learn a very thorough methodology for conducting information security audits to safeguard sensitive information, mission-critical applications, and their underlying infrastructure.

While much of the discussion in this book is geared to U.S. federal agencies, this book describes a process that can essentially be applied to any information technology organizations or infrastructure. This book does not describe the only way to perform C&A; however, it does describe a methodology that has been proven successful in assisting U.S. government agencies in obtaining near-perfect scores on the annual Federal Computer Security Report Card. All kinds of variations for performing C&A exist. This book describes one way.

Organization of This Book

This book contains 24 chapters.

Chapter 1 (*What Is Certification and Accreditation?*) explains what is meant by Certification and Accreditation and why the process is mandated by federal law. The different Certification and Accreditation laws will be cited and discussed. A brief history and chronology of the mandated laws will be included in the discussion.

Chapter 2 (*Types of Certification and Accreditation*) includes descriptions of the four primary different types of C&A: NIST, NIACAP, DITSCAP, and DCID 6/3.

Chapter 3 (*Understanding the Certification and Accreditation Process*) explains the logical steps that one goes through to prepare for a C&A audit/review. It also explains the roles and responsibilities of the audit/review team, including the role of the reviewers, the accrediting authority, and the federal auditors/inspectors.

Chapter 4 (*Establishing a Certification and Accreditation Program*) includes information on what types of tasks you'll need to do to put a C&A Program into place. This chapter explains what types of documents and guidelines you'll need to establish a C&A Program. If you already have a C&A Program, you can always make it better and refine it. You'll want to improve your C&A Program and revise it periodically as you notice what items are missing and what areas need more clarification.

Chapter 5 (*Developing a Certification Package*) includes information on what you need to do to prepare for an upcoming C&A project. This chapter tells you what documents you need to collect and have on hand in order to prepare your C&A review (e.g., the organizational security policies and procedures and the security organization structure). Information on whether to outsource the C&A review or do it in-house is also provided.

Chapter 6 (*Preparing the Hardware and Software Inventory*) includes a sample of a C&A asset inventory and how one should go about developing it and putting it together.

Chapter 7 (*Determining the Certification Level*) includes information on how to put together the *Security Categorization and Certification Level* approval letter and the *Determination Level Profile* documents.

Chapter 8 (*Performing and Preparing the Self-Assessment*) includes information on how to perform and document a Self-Assessment. The differences between management, operational, and technical security controls are explained.

Chapter 9 (*Addressing Security Awareness and Training Requirements*) includes information on how to review, analyze, and document Security Awareness, Training, and Education.

Chapter 10 (*Addressing End-User Rules of Behavior*) advises you on how to review, analyze, and document C&A requirements for *End-User Rules of Behavior*.

Chapter 11 (*Addressing Incident Response*) includes information on how to address and document Incident Response requirements. The role of the incident response manager and different incident types are discussed.

Chapter 12 (*Performing the Security Tests and Evaluation*) includes information on how to perform and document the required security tests and evaluation (ST&E). This chapter also addresses whether or not a penetration test is required. Information about how to execute a penetration test will be discussed.

Chapter 13 (*Conducting a Privacy Impact Assessment*) helps you understand under what circumstances you'll need to develop one of these types of documents and what to include in one. Individual privacy rights and responsibilities of the Senior Agency Official for Privacy are discussed.

Chapter 14 (*Performing the Business Risk Assessment*) includes information on how to perform a *Business Risk Assessment* and what types of information should be included in a *Business Risk Assessment*.

Chapter 15 (*Preparing the Business Impact Assessment*) includes information on how to prepare and perform the *Business Impact Assessment* and what types of information should be included in such an assessment.

Chapter 16 (*Developing the Contingency Plan*) includes information on how to prepare a *Contingency Plan* and what types of information should be included in a *Contingency Plan*.

Chapter 17 (*Performing a System Risk Assessment*) includes information on how to prepare and perform the *System Risk Assessment*.

Chapter 18 (*Developing a Configuration Management Plan*) explains what you'll want to include in this plan, and how to go about accumulating the information.

Chapter 19 (*Preparing the System Security Plan*) includes how to prepare and document a *System Security Plan*.

Chapter 20 (*Submitting the C&A Package*) includes information on how to put together the final Certification Package. Information on the *Security Assessment Report* prepared by the Certifying Agent is also included in this chapter.

Chapter 21 (*Evaluating the Certification Package for Accreditation*) includes information on how to evaluate a Certification Package to determine if it should be accredited. This chapter includes information on how the evaluators determine whether the package should pass or fail. Checklists and how to use them to produce the *Security Assessment Report* are discussed.

Chapter 22 (*Addressing C&A Findings*) includes information on strategies for defending your C&A review, as well as how to address any failures cited by the evaluation team. The evaluators typically require a document known as a *Plan of Action & Milestones (POA&M)* to be drafted and adhered to for the purpose of addressing failures. A sample *POA&M* is included along with recommendations on how to write one.

Chapter 23 (*Improving Your Federal Computer Security Report Card Scores*) explains what shows up in the FISMA Report Cards and how to go about improving your agency's scores.

Chapter 24 (*Resources*) includes a list of recommended resources that C&A teams can use to help understand the C&A process. A list of acromyns is also included

Conventions Used in This Book

The following typographical conventions are used in this book:

Italic is used for commands, directory names, filenames, scripts, emphasis, and the first use of technical terms.

Bold is used for emphasis.

Arrow < brackets > are used for user input.

We'd Like to Hear From You

We have reviewed and verified all of the information in this book to the best of our ability, but you may find that certain references to federal regulations have changed.

For more information about this book and others, see the Syngress Web site: www.syngress.com/solutions.com.

Author Acknowledgments

Without the help and support of many individuals, this book would not have been possible. I'd like to thank my editors, Gary Byrne and Matthew Shepherd, who helped keep me on track and polished up the rough edges. I'd also like to thank Andrew Williams for giving me the opportunity to write for Syngress. The entire Syngress team is a world-class publishing organization. I'd also like to thank my former editors at O'Reilly Media, Allison Randal and Tatiana Apandi Diaz, who helped me refine some of the earlier drafts of this book. Thank you also to Nathan Torkington of O'Reilly, who was one of the early believers in this book.

Thank you to Stephen Northcutt of SANS, who was instrumental in helping this book get off the ground.

Various C&A and security professionals whom I have worked with over the years have all contributed to my knowledge of C&A, which likely resulted in a better book. Various people provided research for this book, and some even allowed me to C&A their mission-critical systems, which no matter how many times I do it, never fails to add new learning experiences. Alphabetically by last name, I'd like to thank John Alger, Gwen Bryant-Hill, Chris Buehler, John Cowan, Tamiiko Emery, Whitney Goss, Sheila Higgs, Cindi Jansohn, Yi-Fang Koh, Dave Metler, Angela Rivera, and Angela Vessels.

Thank you to Wanda Headley at the Natural Hazards Center at the University of Colorado, Boulder, for help with research on natural hazards. I'd also like to thank Eileen McVey, of the National Oceanic & Atmospheric Administration, who contributed information on natural hazard probabilities.

Thank you to the staff at COACT for all the support and words of encouragement. In particular, I'd like to thank Jim McGehee, Lou Lauer, Randy Williams, and Glenn Jacoboson, who made contributions to Chapter 22.

Thank you to Micah Tapman of SAIC, who provided research and recommendations for Chapter 23.

Thank you to Brien Posey, Shaam Rodrigo, and Troy Thompson of Relevant Technologies. They are consistently always there when I need an extra helping hand.

Much thanks to my parents, Barbara and Robert Taylor, who made many sacrifices to help me receive the education that gave me a foundation for writing.

Last, and most of all, I'd like to thank my 13-year-old son, Sammy, who gave up numerous hours of family time with Mom to make this book possible.

—*Laura Taylor*
Columbia, MD
October 2006

## Chapter 1

What Is Certification and Accreditation?

"The law cannot be enforced when everyone is an offender."

—Chinese Proverb

Topics in this chapter:

- Terminology
- Audit and Report Cards
- A Standardized Process
- Templates, Documents, and Paperwork
- Certification and Accreditation Laws Summarized

Introduction

Certification and Accreditation is a process that ensures that systems and major applications adhere to formal and established security requirements that are well documented and authorized. Informally known as *C&A*, Certification and Accreditation is required by the Federal Information Security Management Act (FISMA) of 2002. All systems and applications that reside on U.S. government networks must go through a formal C&A before being put into production, and every three years thereafter. Since accreditation is the ultimate output of a C&A initiative, and a system or application cannot be accredited unless it meets specific security guidelines, clearly the goal of C&A is to force federal agencies to put into production systems and applications that are secure.

FISMA, also known as Title III of the E-Government Act (Public Law 107-347), mandates that all U.S. federal agencies develop and implement an agency-wide information security program that explains its security requirements, security policies, security controls, and risks to the agency. The requirements, policies, controls, and risks are explained formally in a collection of documents known as a Certification Package. The Certification Package consists of a review and analysis of applications, systems, or a site—basically whatever it is that the agency wants accredited. New applications and systems require accreditation before they can be put into production, and existing applications and systems require accreditation every three years.

> Each agency shall develop, document, and implement an agency-wide information security program to provide information security for the information and information systems that support the operations and assets of the agency, including those provided or managed by another agency, contractor, or other source...
>
> —Federal Information Security Management Act of 2002

Laws for U.S. federal departments and agencies mandate C&A; however, private organizations can also take advantage of C&A methodologies to help mitigate risks on their own information systems and networks. In fact, about 90 percent of the nation's critical infrastructure is on private networks that are not part of any U.S. federal department or agency. The nation's critical infrastructure includes those information technology systems that run electrical systems, chemical systems, nuclear systems, transportation systems, telecommunication systems, banking and financial systems, and agricultural and food and water supply systems to name only a few.

The entire C&A process is really nothing more than a standardized security audit, albeit a very complete standardized security audit. Having worked in both private industry and on government networks, my experience indicates that contrary to what you read in the news, most private and public companies do not put nearly as much time, effort, and resources into documenting their security as government agencies do. All the C&A methodologies described in this book can be adopted and used by private industry. Though federal departments and agencies seem to get repeated criticisms belittling their security initiatives, it's my experience and belief that the criticisms are largely exaggerated and that their security conscientiousness far exceeds that of private industry.

The C&A model is a methodology for demonstrating due-diligence in mitigating risks and maintaining appropriate security controls. Any enterprise organization can adopt best practice C&A methodologies. A special license is not required, and no special tools are required to make use of the model—it is simply a way of doing things related to security.

Terminology

Certification refers to the preparation and review of an application's, or system's, security controls and capabilities for the purpose of establishing whether the design or implementation meets appropriate security requirements. Accreditation refers to the positive evaluation made on the *Certification and Accreditation Package* by the evaluation team.

Different documents written by different federal agencies have their own definitions of certification and accreditation, and though the definitions are similar, they are each slightly different. NIST Special Publication 800-37[1] defines certification as:

> A comprehensive assessment of the management, operational, and technical security controls in an information system, made in support of security accreditation, to determine the extent to which the controls are implemented correctly, operating as intended, and producing the desired outcome with respect to meeting the security requirements for the system.

The guidance written by NIST is intended for information systems that process unclassified data, more commonly known as SBU data—Sensitive But Unclassified. The Committee on National Security Systems, Chaired by the Department of Defense, defines certification in the National Information Assurance Glossary,[2] Revision June 2006 as:

> A comprehensive evaluation of the technical and nontechnical security safeguards of an IS to support the accreditation process that establishes the extent to which a particular design and implementation meets a set of specified security requirements.

You can see that even experts among us don't necessarily agree on a concrete definition. However, since experts in most professions typically bring their own uniqueness to the table, I don't see the differences in definitions as being a show stopper for getting the job done. The definitions are similar enough.

An evaluation team reviews a suite of documents known as a Certification Package and makes recommendations on whether it should be accredited. The evaluation team may be referred to by different names in different agencies. You should think of the evaluators as specialized information security auditors; often they are referred to as certifying agents. Each agency may refer to their own auditors with slightly different names, so you shouldn't get hung up on what to call these folks. The main thing to know is that each agency has their own set of auditors that have the power either to pass or fail the different elements of a Certification Package, and provide a recommendation either to accredit the package or not.

The term "Certification" can be confusing because a Certification Package does not mean that any part of the infrastructure described in the package has been certified by anyone for anything. The Certification Package itself is not, and does not, get certified. However, it does get reviewed by certifying agents. A more apropos name might have been a Security Package but that isn't the name our friendly federal regulators wanted to use so we won't be using it here.

Once a Certification Package has been evaluated, a positive accreditation indicates that a senior agency official has formally made the decision that the documented risks to the agency, assets, and individuals are acceptable. Senior agency officials employ large teams of information assurance oversight staff that go over the Certification Packages with fine-toothed combs. Accreditation does not come lightly, and occurs only after each Certification Package has undergone a scrupulous review. By accrediting an information system, the senior agency official agrees to take responsibility for the accuracy of the information in the certification package and consents to be held accountable for any security incidents that may arise related to the system.

NIST Special Publication 800-37 refers to accreditation as:

> The official management decision given by a senior agency official to authorize operation of an information system and to explicitly accept the risk to agency operations (including mission, functions, image, or reputation), agency assets, or individuals, based on the implementation of an agreed-upon set of security controls.

And the National Information Assurance Glossary refers to accreditation as a:

> Formal declaration by a Designated Accrediting Authority (DAA) that an IS is approved to operation at an acceptable level of risk, based on the implementation of an approved set of technical, managerial, and procedural safeguards.

Much of the terminology that federal agencies use in developing C&A programs and processes comes from the Office of Management and Budget (OMB) Circular A-130, Appendix III (listed in Appendix B). To view this document, go to www.syngress.com. The OMB is part of the Executive Office of the President of the United States. Aside from assisting the president with the budget, the OMB's mission is also to create and oversee information and regulatory policies. The OMB was created in 1970, and essentially replaced the Bureau of Budget. The fact that the OMB plays a significant regulatory role in C&A shows just how important information security has become to our national infrastructure. It also means that C&A initiatives will have a budget and are clearly a priority to the Executive Office of the President of the United States—and that's a good thing.

Audit and Report Cards

Some agencies have two sets of auditors and a Certification Package may under go review by one evaluation team first, and another evaluation team second. The first group of evaluators ensures that the Certification and Accreditation package was prepared correctly, according to agency guidelines. The second set ensures that the first set evaluated the C&A package correctly, according to agency guidelines. Sometimes the two sets of evaluators do not always agree on whether or not certain parts of the Certification Package are acceptable. If this happens the evaluators need to discuss the discordance among each other until they reach agreement.

Once a package has been accredited, auditors from outside the agency, from the Government Accountability Office (GAO), come on site and review the Certification Packages and write up reports on how well the agency's C&A program is working. The GAO auditors are known as Inspector Generals (IGs). If the IGs find deficiencies in any accredited packages, the agency will receive unsatisfactory ratings by the GAO. (I will discuss more of how these packages are audited and reviewed in Chapter 21.) A goal for any agency is to make sure that all Certification Packages were properly evaluated and accredited so that the GAO does not find any deficiencies.

After the GAO documents its findings, these findings get reviewed by the U.S. Government House of Representatives Government Reform Subcommittee on Technology and Information Policy. When former Rep. Stephen Horn (R–CA) chaired the *House Subcommittee on Government Management, Information and Technology, Intergovernmental Relations and the Census,* he came up with the idea of issuing federal computer security report cards and the first report card was issued in 2000. Originally these report cards were dubbed the Horn Report, however, today the report cards are known as the annual *Federal Computer Security Report Cards*. Although Stephen Horn no longer chairs the subcommittee, these report cards are still often referred to as the Horn Reports, and they are based entirely on how well an agency performs C&A.

The subcommittee is now known as the *Subcommittee on Government Management, Finance and Accountability* and is part of the Committee on Government Reform. As of this writing, the URL of its Web site is http://reform.house.gov/GMFA/.

The most current *Federal Computer Security Report Cards* as of this writing can be found at http://reform.house.gov/UploadedFiles/2004% 20Computer%20Security%20Report%20card%202%20years.pdf.

A Standardized Process

C&A is standardized process. Each agency decides what their standardized security C&A process consists of, and documents it. The different U.S. federal departments and agencies develop their own unique standardized process based on guidance it has used from one of the following three organizations: the National Institute of Standards (NIST), the Committee on National Security Systems (CNSS), or the Department of Defense (DoD).

For agencies that are doing their C&A the right way, their own internal guidance that describes their repeatable process likely consists of as much material as you will find in this book. C&A is a voluminous process, and the documentation that exists to describe any one agency's C&A process can be daunting. The documentation that goes into writing and putting together a Certification Package is also daunting. The amount of security documentation that you will find in one Certification Package is easily more extensive than all the tips, suggestions, and guidance that you'll find in this book.

Typically, a well-documented C&A process consists of not just one document, but a set of documents. Of primary importance in this set of documents is the C&A handbook that describes the agency's overall C&A process. The title of the handbook varies from agency to agency, but will most likely sport a name akin to *The <Name> Agency Certification and Accreditation Process and Handbook*. Without a handbook to standardize the process, there would be a lack of cohesiveness in the different Certification Packages published by the agency.

When putting together a Certification Package for a particular agency, you will continually need to go back to the handbook and reference it. The handbook will have way too much information in it for you to read and absorb and remember in one fell swoop. However, if you are about to undertake a C&A initiative, you should try to read the handbook from front to back at least once, knowing that you won't remember everything, but you may remember better where to look to find the information you'll need when the time comes.

Templates, Documents, and Paperwork

C&A is essentially a documentation and paperwork nightmare. If you're just embarking on C&A for the first time, be prepared for that. To create some order out of the paper work nightmare, aside from a handbook, most agencies now have templates that they use for all the different types of documents that go into the Certification Package. Agencies that don't have templates should certainly strive to develop some.

Templates ensure that all the different types of documents that go into the agency-wide Certification Packages have the same look and feel, and they standardize the documentation. A good template helps to ensure that all key information is included in the Certification Package. Well-written templates also assist the auditors in finding the information that they are looking for because they will know exactly in which section of the package to find the information they are looking for. The amount of information that is required in any one Certification Package is so great, that if each Certification Package had a different format, it would be nearly impossible for the auditors to evaluate the package. When the auditors evaluate a Certification Package, they want to know where to look to find key information and they don't want to have to hunt for it. I have seen Certification Packages receive failures not because the right information wasn't in the Certification Package, but because the right information was not where it was supposed to be.

Preparing a Certification Package is very documentation intensive. If you have just gotten yourself into the C&A business for the first time, and are about to start helping an agency prepare a Certification Package, prepare yourself to write, write, and write some more. If you detest writing, you're in the wrong business. Basically, preparing a Certification Package is writing about security—extensive writing about security. When you are preparing a Certification Package, you usually don't actually perform any sort of hands-on security. You review the existing security design and architecture documents, interview various IT support and development folks familiar with the infrastructure, and document your findings. Because a lot of time is taken up in reviewing existing security and architecture documents, often the people who prepare Certification Packages are known as the C&A preparation team.

Certification and Accreditation Laws Summarized

Though FISMA is the overriding law that necessitates the need for C&A, there are other laws, regulations, and national policies that provide secondary authority. The secondary laws, regulations, and policies that C&A must also accommodate are listed here:

- The Clinger-Cohen Act, formerly known as Information Technology Management Reform Act (ITMRA) of 1996

- Homeland Security Presidential Directive (HSPD-7)

- The Government Management Reform Act (GMRA) of 1994

- The Government Performance and Results Act (GPRA) of 1993

- Critical Infrastructure Protection Act of 2001

- Homeland Security Act of 2002 (Public Law 107-296)

- OMB Circular A-123, Management Accountability and Control

- Executive Order 10865 of February 20, 1960—Safeguarding Classified Information Within Industry

- OMB Circular A-130, Management of Federal Information Resources

- Executive Order 13130 of July 14, 1999—National Infrastructure Assurance Council

- The Computer Security Act of 1987

- The Computer Fraud and Abuse Act of 1986

- The Computer Abuse Amendments Act of 1990

- Executive Order 12958 of April 17, 1995, Classified National Security Information

- The E-Government Act of 2002

- The Privacy Act of 1974

Summary

Toward the future, I anticipate that C&A will become even more important than it is today. The current trend is that as security incidents continue to wreak havoc on information systems, new laws and policies are being proposed and passed every day to create more stringent security controls. Breaches in security on both government information systems and those maintained by the private sector create millions of dollars in losses and also threaten the national security of our country, and everyone in it. According to their annual 2004 survey on cyber crime, the Computer Security Institute found that in 2004, viruses caused $55million worth of damage among 269 survey respondents.[3]

Current trends show that unauthorized intrusions are declining—probably a result of organizations showing greater due diligence when it comes to system and network security either on their own volition, or as a result of new laws and regulations. However, to be sure, threats are becoming more sophisticated and terrorists continue to use high-technology to threaten not just data and our infrastructure, but worse yet, human lives.

C&A is creating a new market for security services. As agencies try to buff up their internal C&A processes, interest in understanding how to automate these processes and track them online will start to increase. Tools that can decrease the amount of time that it takes to put together the required documents such as a System Risk Assessment will become more and more important. However, today, automated C&A tools are still remedial at best and take an enormous amount of time to set up and configure.

Notes

1. R. Ross, M. Swanson, G. Stoneburner, S. Katzke, and A. Johnson. NIST Special Publication 800-37, *Guide for the Security Certification and Accreditation of Federal Information Systems*. May 2004, National Institute of Standards and Technology.

2. *National Information Assurance Glossary*. CNSS Instruction No. 4009, Revised June 2006 (www.cnss.gov/Assets/pdf/cnssi_4009.pdf).

3. Lawrence A. Gordon, Martin P. Loeb, William Lucyshyn, and Robert Richardson. *2004 CSI/FBI Computer Crime and Security Survey*. Computer Security Institute (http://i.cmpnet.com/gocsi/db_area/pdfs/fbi/FBI2004.pdf).

## Chapter 2

Types of Certification and Accreditation

"It is common sense to take a method and try it. If it fails, admit it frankly and try another. But above all, try something."

—Franklin Delano Roosevelt, Oglethorpe University, Atlanta, Georgia, May 22, 1932

Topics in this chapter:

- The NIACAP Process

- The NIST Process

- DITSCAP

- DCID 6/3

- The Common Denominator of All C&A Methodologies

- C&A for Private Enterprises

Introduction

There are four primary C&A models that agencies use as a basis to architect their standardized C&A process. The four C&A models are the National Information Assurance Certification and Accreditation Process (NIACAP) model, the National Institute of Standards and Technology (NIST) model, the Defense Information Technology Systems Certification and Accreditation Process (DITSCAP) model, and the DCID 6/3 model.

The NIACAP model is based on a process published by the Committee on National Security Systems that documents its methodology in the *National Security Telecommunications and Information System Security Instructions,*[1] otherwise known as *NSTISSI No. 1000.* The NIST model is described in a publication known as *NIST Special Publication 800-37, Guide for the Security Certification and Accreditation of Federal Information Systems.*[2] In the past, many civilian federal agencies have used either the NIACAP or NIST's previous models; however in recent years, the trend has been to abandon the NIACAP model and adopt the NIST model. The NIST specifications are more up to date, and include a vast amount of supporting documents that complement the foundational guidelines. The DITSCAP[3] model is used primarily by defense agencies, though civilian agencies have the option of adopting any DITSCAP principles that they feel may complement their own unique C&A program. The DCID 6/3 model is used only by intelligence agencies. Although almost all federal agencies base their C&A program on one of these models, each agency's C&A program is at the same time unique to that particular agency. No two C&A programs are exactly alike.

If a private or public business wanted to adopt one of the C&A models to create their own unique security auditing program, the model that would likely be easiest and best to adopt would be the NIST model. The National Institute of Standards is constantly revising their guidelines and coming out with new and updated guidelines all the time. They also make all their draft guidelines available to review by any industry professionals, including those individuals from nonfederal enterprise organizations.

The NIACAP Process

As you recall, the NIACAP C&A model was developed by the CNSS, and its intent is to be used as guidance for the C&A of national security systems. National Security Systems are systems that contain National Security Information (NSI). Classified NSI includes information determined to be either "Top Secret," "Secret," or "Confidential" under Executive order 12958,[4] which was released by the White House office of the Press Secretary in April 1995. However, NSI may also include Sensitive But Unclassified (SBU) information. The NIACAP C&A model was developed for auditing National security systems. National security systems are those systems related to intelligence activities, equipment that is an integral part of a weapon system, command and control of military forces, cryptologic activities related to national security, or equipment that is critical to the direct fulfillment of military of intelligence missions. NIST clarified the definition of National Security Systems in August 2003 when it released, NIST SP 800-59, *Guideline for Identifying an Information System as a National Security System*.

Recall that the NIACAP process is described in *NSTISSI No. 1000*. *NSTISSI No. 1000* describes tasks, activities, and a recommended management structure to use for your C&A process. The similarities between NIACAP and NIST arise in part because *NSTISSI No. 1000* recommends that C&A activities take the NIST guidance into consideration stating,

> While developed for national security systems, the NIACAP may, at an agency's discretion, be adapted to any type of IS and any computing environment and mission subject to the policies found in OMB Circular A-130, Appendix III and the standards and guidance issued by the National Institute of Standards and Technology (NIST).

The NIACAP is endorsed by the U.S. National Security Agency and was last updated in April of 2000. Though originally intended for national security systems, any federal agency (or private enterprise) can adopt and use the NIACAP process as long as their oversight authority allows it. However, as of this writing, systems that are classified as national security systems are still required to follow the NIACAP methodology.

The NIST Process

The NIST process was designed for unclassified information, more commonly known as Sensitive But Unclassified (SBU) information. The framework for the NIST C&A methodology is described in a publication known as *NIST Special Publication 800-37, Guide for the Security Certification and Accreditation of Federal Information Systems*. A copy of it is available online at http://csrc.nist.gov/publications/nistpubs/800-37/SP800-37-final.pdf.

NIACAP and NIST Phases, Differences, and Similarities

Both NIST and NIACAP establish a framework to provide accountability for those people tasked with responsibility of the system. Both processes stipulate definitions and requirements for system characterization, risk assessment, verification and validation of security controls, and testing. Certification recommendations and accrediting decisions are also called for by both processes.

Some civilian federal agencies use the NIACAP process, however the current trend is for agencies to move away from the NIACAP process and instead use the NIST process. However, to be sure, the NIACAP and NIST models are very similar and if their own internal oversight authority allows it, an agency can use a combination-hybrid of the NIACAP and NIST models.

Both the NIACAP and NIST models describe the C&A process being done in four phases. The four phases of the NIACAP are:

1. Definition
2. Verification
3. Validation
4. Post Accreditation

The four phases of the NIST model are:

1. Initiation
2. Certification
3. Accreditation
4. Continuous Monitoring

Agencies who are working on refining their C&A process by updating and revising their process guidelines should not get hung up on the names used for the phases. Whether you call the first phase Definition, Initiation, or something of your own making is not going to affect how well the process works, and whether or not you receive an A or a B on the annual Federal Computer Security Report Card. The important thing is to make sure that whatever terminology is being used is well defined, understood by all, and is consistent throughout all the other agency C&A documents. Keep in mind that the goal of creating a C&A process is to create a well-defined repeatable process.

NIACAP and NIST Compared

The NIACAP methodology is six years old and CNSS is currently in the process of being updated. NIACAP guidelines are described in a document known as NSTISSI No. 1000, which is available at www.cnss.gov/Assets/pdf/nstissi_1000.pdf.

The NIST methodology was last released in May of 2004. Prior to updating their guidelines, NIST goes to a lot of trouble to solicit review and comments from both public and private industry, which greatly enhances the quality of their publications.

The NIST guidance is well written and easy to follow. However, it is only a 69-page document, and is just a framework—following it won't solve all your C&A problems because it leaves a lot of gray areas open to interpretation. Agencies and bureaus that embrace the NIST model use NIST Special Publication 800-37 as a guide to write their own internal C&A process and handbook customized for their own unique requirements.

In essence, NIST Special Publication 800-37 is a call to action and gives agencies a "to do" list for actions, plans, policies, procedures, training, and methodologies that need to be put into place. Putting into place the items that the NIST C&A process proposes that agencies include (without putting together any Certification Packages) is a huge undertaking in itself.

Some of the C&A guidance for NIACAP, DITSCAP, and DCID is publicly available. However, because these methodologies are related to national security systems, defense systems, and intelligence systems, it is possible that they could be made unavailable to the general public at any time. The NIST model is very current, and NIST solicits and receives feedback from a much larger community of experts. Of all four C&A methodologies, the NIST model is more "open source" than the others—if you can call a methodology open source.

DITSCAP

DITSCAP was developed for evaluating and accrediting Department of Defense systems and also includes four phases. DITSCAP was developed and is published by the Defense Information Systems Agency (DISA) and it applies to the acquisition, operation, and on-going support of any Department of Defense system that collects, stores, transmits, or processes unclassified or classified information. It is mandatory for use by all defense agencies.

The DITSCAP guidance is described in a document known as DoDI 5200.40 and is available at www.dtic.mil/whs/directives/corres/pdf/i520040_123097/i520040p.pdf.

The four DITSCAP phases are the same as the NIACAP phases and are known as:

1. Definition
2. Verification
3. Validation
4. Post Accreditation

The major areas of analysis for the DITSCAP methodology, as described in Phase II, are:

- System Architecture Analysis
- Software Design Analysis
- Network Connection Rule Compliance
- Integrity Analysis of Integrated Products
- Life Cycle Management Analysis
- Security Requirements Validation Procedures
- Vulnerability Evaluation

DISTCAP uses an infrastructure-centric approach and stresses that DoD systems are network-centric and interconnected. There are numerous DoD policies, referred to as directives that the DITSCAP must also adhere to. All the directives are named with numbers and begin with the numbers 5200. One of the most important DoD directives with which DITSCAP must be in compliance is DoDD 5200.28. The subject of 5200.28 is *Security Requirements for Automated Information Systems (AIS)*. 5200.28 is available at http://csrc.nist.gov/fasp/FASPDocs/authorize-process/d520028p.pdf.

5200.28 is a 32-page document that names numerous other directives that must be complied with while adhering to the DITSCAP process. Relatively speaking, 5200.18 is an old document released in 1988. However, it is still in effect today, and there are many concepts related to information security that have not changed over time, which is why this policy is still relevant.

DCID 6/3

DCID 6/3 is the certification and accreditation process used by federal agencies working on intelligence projects (e.g., the CIA). Specifically, information technology projects that require that anyone working on them has a Top Secret, Sensitive Compartmentalized Information (SCI) clearance use the DCID 6/3 process. DCID stands for Director of Central Intelligence Directive and 6/3 refers to the process described in section 6, part 3 of the compendious Director of Central Intelligence Directives.[5] The certification and accreditation process that the Intelligence Community (IC) used before DCID 6/3 came along was called DCID 1/16.

The DCID 6/3 model is based on certification and accreditation performed on information systems that are characterized by Protection Levels (PL), and DCID 6/3 defines five different protection levels. DCID 6/3 deals only with classified information and its PL model helps ensure that only properly cleared people have access to classified information.

Although the DCID 6/3 model was designed for classified information and intelligence work, it is publicly available for review, and any agency or private organization can adopt the methodology, and customize it according to their own unique requirements. The DCID Standards Manual, which defines the DCID 6/3 certification and accreditation process, can be found

on the Federation of American Scientists[6] Web site at www.fas.org/irp/
offdocs/dcid-6-3-manual.pdf.

The DCID 6/3 C&A process must also comply with the DCID 6/3
policy manual. The DCID 6/3 policy manual can be found on the Web at
www.fas.org/irp/offdocs/DCID_6-3_20Policy.htm.

Many of the requirements for IC certification and accreditation are based
on physical security, since classified information must always be physically
secured. Aside from physical security, the IC puts a lot of emphasis on encryption. The emphasis in these two areas is what really sets apart DCID certification and accreditation from the other C&A methodologies.

The Common Denominator
of All C&A Methodologies

The common denominator of all the C&A methodologies, and this book, is
that they are all based on three attributes: Confidentiality, Integrity, and
Availability of information and information systems. All the C&A methodologies include definitions for categorizing Confidentiality, Integrity, and
Availability qualitatively. In all four of the C&A methodologies, information
technology assets and controls must be categorized qualitatively by sensitivity
related to Confidentiality, Integrity, and Availability.

Confidentiality of information is insurance that it will not be disclosed to
unauthorized persons or systems. Integrity of information is insurance that
the information will not be altered from its original and intended form.
Availability ensures that the information will be available as planned. Though
Availability might seem so obvious at first that it is not worth mentioning, the
reason it is important is because it forces the information owner to make provisions for contingencies and outages. Because Availability is important, the
C&A requires that contingency planning is developed and tested.

All the C&A models call for accountability. Security accountability of IT
systems means that activities can be traced back to a person or a process and
that the people who are responsible will be held accountable for their actions.
One of the reasons that roles and responsibilities are clearly defined in every
Certification Package is to make it clear who is responsible for what. The

DITSCAP model in particular emphasizes accountability perhaps more so than the other C&A models.

All four of the C&A models described thus far are really very similar in numerous ways. If you read all the guidance documentation for each, you might come to the conclusion that the four methodologies are essentially the same thing written four different ways. In order to take you through the C&A process, it makes no sense for me to walk you through it in four different ways. The goal of this book is to present a methodology of simply one way to perform C&A. This is not to say that there aren't other ways to do C&A.

The C&A recommendations in this book are a hybrid of the four different C&A models. The guidance I will refer to most often will be from NIST since it is more up to date than the guidance for the other methodologies. Where the NIST guidance leaves gaps and is vague, I have used ideas from the NIACAP, DITSCAP, and DCID. I have made some small deviations from the different methodologies where I feel that certain aspects of one of the four were not made clear, or required expansion. NIST guidance is also publicly available for anyone to review, and in that sense it is the most open source of the four methodologies. Certainly, it is not my intent to republish any of the known four methodologies.

Something to remember is that every agency, bureau, and department in the government that has built a robust and thorough C&A process has their own unique requirements built into it. No two are alike, but the good ones that enable top scores on the Federal Computer Security Report Cards are all similar and will all lead to successful accreditations.

C&A for Private Enterprises

Even though C&A methodologies are well entrenched in U.S. federal agencies, there is nothing that says that these methodologies and practices cannot be adopted and used by private businesses, publicly traded corporations, and nonprofit organizations. In order to obtain new contracts under government task orders, many private defense contractors must now sign agreements that stipulate that they are in compliance with FISMA.

At the time of this writing, there is a group of industry experts that are working on transforming much of NIST's guidance used for information security management, including certification and accreditation, to documentation that fits better for private industry. NIST publishes excellent guidance on information security management, though it is directed at federal agencies. Although the C&A methodologies they describe can be adopted by anyone, private industry will more readily familiarize themselves with their guidance once the term "federal agency" has been replaced by "enterprises."

Any organization that processes sensitive information should have a methodology for evaluating and accrediting the security of their systems. To protect individuals from having their medical information exposed, Congress enacted the Health Insurance Portability and Accountability Act (HIPAA) in 1996. Sarbanes-Oxley became law in January of 2002 to regulate accounting practices and standards of publicly traded companies. Although accounting may seem like just a financial matter, keep in mind that Integrity of information can be ensured only by strict security controls. Therefore, Sarbanes-Oxley has become an information technology problem.

Sarbanes-Oxley and the HIPAA were passed to hold certain covered entities accountable for the security of their systems, but what these regulations lack are standardized methodologies. A law is one thing, and a standardized process or methodology for complying with the law is quite another. FISMA, HIPAA, and Sarbanes-Oxley are merely laws. What has evolved out of FISMA, which has not yet evolved out of HIPAA and Sarbanes-Oxley, is that standardized certification and accreditation processes now exist that enable FISMA compliance. HIPAA and Sarbanes-Oxley both need standardized certification and accreditation processes. The way that HIPAA and Sarbanes-Oxley are complied with today depends on who you ask—all organizations are attempting to comply with HIPAA and Sarbanes-Oxley differently, according to whatever way they know how. While attempting to comply with these laws is meritorious, trying to apply oversight to the compliance process will be difficult until standardized C&A processes that are unique to each law evolve.

Summary

Certification and Accreditation processes formally evaluate the security of an information system, determine the risk of operating the information system, and then either accept or not accept that risk. There are generally four different methodologies for performing C&A: NIACAP, NIST, DITSCAP, and DCID 6/3. These different methodologies were developed for four different audiences within the federal community: national security systems, nonnational security information systems, defense agency information systems, and information systems operated by the intelligence community. Despite the different nuances in these methodologies, they all have the goal of accomplishing the same task of certifying and accrediting information systems, and as such, there are many similarities between them. Although none of these models was developed for the private sector, laws such as Sarbanes-Oxley, HIPAA, and others hold certain private sector enterprises responsible for maintaining basic levels of information security. Therefore, drawing from these four models to develop private sector C&A processes can help businesses achieve compliance with these laws.

Notes

1. *National Information Assurance Certification and Accreditation Process (NIACAP).* NSTISSI No. 1000. National Security Telecommunications and Information Systems Security Committee (www.cnss.gov/Assets/pdf/nstissi_1000.pdf).
2. R. Ross, M.Swanson, G. Stoneburner, S. Katzke, and A. Johnson. *Guide for the Security Certification and Accreditation of Federal Information Systems.* NIST Special Publication 800-37. National Institute of Standards and Technology, May 2004 (http://csrc.nist.gov/publications/nistpubs/800-37/SP800-37-final.pdf).
3. *Department of Defense Information Technology Security Certification and Accreditation Process (DITSCAP) Application Manual.* DoD 8510.1-M. United States Department of Defense, July 31, 2000 (www.dtic.mil/whs/directives/corres/pdf/85101m_0700/p85101m.pdf).
4. *Executive Order 12958.* The White House Office of the Press Secretary, April 17, 1995 (www.fas.org/sgp/clinton/eo12958.html).

5. *DCIDs: Director of Central Intelligence Directives.* Federation of American Scientists Intelligence Resource Program, Updated August 28, 2006 (www.fas.org/irp/offdocs/dcid.htm).

6. According to its Web site, "The Federation of American Scientists is a non-profit, tax-exempt, 501c3 organization founded in 1945 as the Federation of Atomic Scientists. FAS is the oldest organization dedicated to ending the worldwide arms race and avoiding the use of nuclear weapons for any purpose."

## Chapter 3

Understanding the Certification and Accreditation Process

"You say it as you understand it."

—Johann Friedrich von Schiller, famous German dramatist and poet

Topics in this chapter:

- **Recognizing the Need for C&A**
- **Roles and Responsibilities**
- **Stepping through the Process**

Introduction

The Certification and Accreditation (C&A) process begins when an information system owner recognizes that either an application, system, group of systems, or site requires Accreditation. The information systems owner might be an IT operations director, an IT operations manager, a security officer, or an application development manager. When the need for C&A is recognized, it is time to put in motion a plan to carry out and oversee the C&A process.

Recognizing the Need for C&A

All general support systems and major applications are required by FISMA and the Office of Management and Budget (OMB) *Circular A-130, Appendix III* (see Appendix B) to be fully certified and accredited before they are put into production. Production systems and major applications are required to be reaccredited every three years. Going forward we will refer to systems that require C&A (e.g., general support systems and major applications) simply as information systems.

One of the primary objectives of C&A is to force the authorizing official to understand the risks an information system poses to agency operations. Only after understanding the risks can an authorizing official ensure that the information system has received adequate attention to mitigate unacceptable risks. Evaluating risk and documenting the results is something that should be incorporated throughout a system or application's system development lifecycle. NIST has defined the system development lifecycle to consist of five phases:

1. System initiation
2. Development and acquisition
3. Implementation
4. Operation and maintenance
5. Disposal

FISMA mandates that new systems and applications need to be fully certified and accredited before they can be put into production. The best time to begin the C&A of new systems and applications is while they are still in development. It is easiest to design security into a system that has not yet been built. When new information systems are being proposed and designed, part of the development should include discussions on "What do we need to do to ensure that this information system can be certified and accredited?" After a new application is built and ready to be implemented is not the time to figure out if it will withstand a comprehensive certification review.

Legacy systems that are already in their operational phase are harder to certify and accredit because it is altogether possible that they were put into production with little to no security taken into consideration. In putting together the Certification Package for a legacy system, it may be discovered that adequate security controls have not been put into place. If it becomes clear that adequate security controls have not been put into place, the C&A project leader may decide to temporarily put on hold the development of the Certification Package while adequate security controls are developed and implemented. It makes little sense to spend the resources to develop a Certification Package that recommends that an information system not be accredited. However, coming to an understanding that an information system has not been properly prepared for accreditation is precisely one reason why C&A exists—it is a process that enables authorizing officials to discover the security truths about their infrastructure so that informed decisions can be made.

Roles and Responsibilities

C&A involves a lot of different people all working together on different tasks. There are the folks who develop the C&A program, the folks who prepare Certification Packages, the folks who are held accountable for the Certification Packages, the agency auditors who evaluate the Certification Packages prior to accreditation, and the federal inspectors who audit the agency to make sure that they are doing C&A the right way.

Chief Information Officer

The agency Chief Information Officer (CIO) is the most obvious person held accountable for a successful information security program and C&A

program. It is the CIO's responsibility to make sure that an information security program, including a C&A program, exists and is implemented. However, most agency CIOs don't play a hands-on role in developing these programs. Usually the CIO will designate the development of these programs to the Senior Agency Information Security Officer. However, delegating the program development does not mean that the CIO does not need to understand the process. If the CIO does not understand all the elements of a successful C&A program there is little chance that the CIO will be able to hold the Senior Agency Information Security Officer responsible for developing a complete program. Without understanding the particulars of what a program should include, the CIO will not know if the Senior Agency Information Security Officer has left anything out.

A piece of C&A that cannot be overlooked is the need for the CIO to develop a budget for C&A. C&A is very time intensive, and a typical C&A takes on average six months to do a thorough job, replete with all the required information. The CIO works together with the authorizing official to ensure that there is enough of a budget to staff the resources necessary to put together the certification program. If CIOs do not budget for C&A, C&A may not get done. The CIO enables C&A to take place by fully understanding the federal budgetary process as documented in a publication put out by the White House known as *Circular No. A-11 Part 7 Planning, Budgeting, Acquisition, and Management of Capital Assets*. This publication is currently available at www.whitehouse.gov/omb/circulars/a11/2002/part7.pdf.

A-11 Part 7 references other budgetary guidelines that the CIO should also become familiar with, including one known as OMB Exhibit 300. OMB Exhibit 300 is currently available at www.cio.gov/archive/S300_05_draft_0430.pdf.

It is ultimately the CIO that is likely to be held responsible and accountable if the agency receives a poor grade on the annual Federal Computer Security Report Card. One of the responsibilities of the CIO is to care about the annual Federal Computer Security Report Card grade. If an agency receives a failing grade, then clearly there is something wrong with either the C&A program itself, or how the program is implemented. If an agency receives a top score on the annual Federal Computer Security Report Card, then as far as C&A goes, the process is being worked the right way. As the

Federal Computer Security Report Cards get more and more public attention each year, a poor score on the report card can be a career-limiting experience for any agency CIO.

I will discuss the Federal Computer Security Report Cards more in Chapter 23.

Authorizing Official

The *authorizing official* is a generic term for a senior management official within an agency who authorizes operations of an information system, declaring that the risks associated with it are acceptable. It is unlikely that any person would hold the title of "authorizing official," hence I am not punctuating it here with capital letters. There may be multiple authorizing officials within each agency, all responsible for their own designated areas. In many agencies, the authorizing official is referred to as the Designated Accrediting Authority (DAA).

The authorizing official usually has budgetary responsibilities for ensuring that a certain amount of resources are set aside for overseeing the C&A process. Usually the agency CIO reports to the authorizing official. However, in large agencies, where some bureau CIOs report to the agency CIO, it can be the case that a CIO is the authorizing official. In other cases the authorizing official may be the Commissioner or an Assistant Commissioner. If the authorizing official and CIO are two different people, they must work together to make sure that an adequate budget has been set aside for C&A.

The authorizing official should, according to the *National Institute of Standards, Special Publication 800-37* (May 2004), be an employee of the U.S. government and cannot be a contractor or consultant. However, the authorizing official may designate a representative to carry out the various tasks related to C&A, and the designated representative can be a contractor or consultant. However, the final security accreditation decision and its accompanying accreditation decision letter must be owned and signed by the U.S. government employee that is the authorizing official.

Senior Agency Information Security Officer

The Senior Agency Information Security Officer (SAISO) is the person that that CIO holds accountable to oversee all of the agency's information security initiatives. The SAISO is akin to a Chief Information Security Officer in private industry. It's possible that CIOs may perform this role themselves, in which case there wouldn't be a separate individual holding these responsibilities.

The SAISO works with the agency authorizing officials to ensure that they are in agreement on the security requirements of the information system as well as the key documents contained in the Certification Package such as the risk assessments and the Security Plan. In working together, the SAISO and the authorizing officials should be sure to take into consideration the mission and business requirements of the agency.

The SAISO provides management oversight to the Certification Agent and works with him or her to ensure that the C&A process is well thought out, and includes all the necessary documentation and guidance. The SAISO appoints the Certification Agent and holds them accountable for performing their duties. It is very important for the SAISO to choose their Certification Agent(s) carefully because they will need to rely on their accreditation recommendations.

The SAISO may wish to review all the Certification Packages that are processed within the agency; however, as a practical matter, it is next to impossible to do this. In most agencies, there are far too many Certification Packages for one individual to review and validate. Due to this very reason, the SAISO employs a Certification Agent (or agents) to read packages, perform evaluations, write recommendations, and produce a document called a *Security Assessment Report*. The *Security Assessment Report* is basically an evaluation summary and should justify and support the recommendation on whether or not to accredit the package. The *Security Assessment Report* should have all the information that the SAISO needs to justify signing the accreditation letter, and escalate the recommendation upward to the authorizing official as to whether or not they should sign the accreditation letter.

Senior Agency Privacy Official

Each agency is supposed to have a Senior Agency Privacy Official. For a large agency, a Senior Agency Privacy Official might be a full time job. However, for a small agency, it's possible that the responsibilities of this official may be performed by the CIO, the CIO's staff, or the SAISO. The person in this role could hold the title of Chief Privacy Officer—he or she does not necessarily have to be called the Senior Agency Privacy Official. What's most important is that someone is designated to perform the duties of safeguarding confidential and private information.

Certification Agent/Evaluation Team

The Certification Agent reviews the Certification Packages, making recommendations as to whether they warrant a positive Accreditation or not. Essentially, Certification Agents act as an auditor. They comb through the unwieldy Certification Packages looking for missing information and information that doesn't make sense. Their goal is to determine if the package is in compliance with the agency's documented C&A Handbook, process, security policies, and the information system's security requirements. In some agencies, there are so many packages to evaluate that the Certification Agent is comprised of an evaluation team. The team may have a departmental name such as Mission Assurance, Information Assurance, or Compliance. The organizational name is for the most part irrelevant as it could be different from agency to agency.

After reviewing the C&A packages, the Certification Agent, or evaluation team, makes recommendations to the internal accrediting authorities—the SAISO and authorizing official—on whether or not a package should be accredited or not. In most cases, the SAISO and authorizing official accepts the recommendation of the Certification Agent, and signs the accreditation letter based solely on a recommendation of the Certification Agent. Along with the recommendation, the Certification Agent also produces and includes the *Security Assessment Report*. The *Security Assessment Report* should justify the recommendation. I will talk more about the *Security Assessment Report* in Chapter 21.

When the Certification Agent is a team of people, they usually split up the different tasks that need to be accomplished in order to expedite the process. For example, one person might evaluate packages for the General Support Systems, another person might evaluate packages for Major Applications, another person might create and update templates, and another person might update the handbook.

The Certification Agent is also responsible for developing the internal C&A process, and all the documentation that describes this process—the handbook and the templates. The documentation that the Certification Agent develops for evaluating the packages are checklists and score cards. The checklists and score cards should be consistent with the templates and the handbook. The checklists help the Certification Agent write the *Security Assessment Report*.

It is possible that the Certification Agent and the Senior Agency Information Security Officer may be the same person since some small agencies may not have the internal resources to have two different staff members assigned to these roles. If the Certification Agent and SAISO are one in the same person, then the Certification Agent makes the accreditation recommendation to the authorizing official. The Certification Agent does not make the final decision on whether a C&A package should be accredited—he or she makes recommendations only on whether or not the package should be accredited.

In order to demonstrate objectivity, it is often the case that the evaluation team consists of outside consultants. FISMA, § 3454 states:

> Each year each agency shall have performed an independent evaluation of the information security program and practices of that agency to determine the effectiveness of such program and practices.

If an agency decides to use its own staff, it should be sure that there is a clear separation of duties between the evaluators and the organizations that are presenting the C&A packages for evaluation.

Business Owner

The *business owner* is a generic reference to the information system owner, and it is likely that there are no employees of the agency with the title "information system owner," which is why I am not capitalizing the terminology here. The information system owner could be a Program Manager, an Application Manager, an IT Director, or an Engineering Director for example. In short, it is the person who is responsible for the development and operations of the information system.

The information system owner is the one who typically gets the ball rolling for a new C&A project. Information system owners need to ensure that their information system is fully accredited before being put into production. Once an information system is in production, it needs to be recertified and accredited every three years.

It is the information system owner's responsibility to appoint someone to be the Information System Security Officer for the system requiring C&A.

System Owner

The system owner is the person responsible for administering the systems that the C&A application runs on. A system owner can be one lone systems administrator, or a systems department. In a large distributed application, it is possible that the different systems that are a piece of the application infrastructure have different system owners. When a large distributed application has different system owners, sometimes the different system owners can be different geographic locations or different buildings.

All C&A packages, whether it is a package for a Major Application, or the General Support Services infrastructure that the application runs on, should specify who the system owner is. The system owners are the folks who provide the systems support. The system owner should be indicated in the *Asset Inventory*. The contact information for the system owners should be indicated in the *Contingency Plan* and the *Business Impact Assessment*.

Information Owner

The information owner is the person who owns the data. The information owner is concerned about the integrity of the data, and communicates with the system owner about issues related to the security controls of the system or databases that the data resides on. The person, or department, that owns the data is not always the same as the system owner, though it could be. In many cases, the system owner maintains the data for the information owner. The information owner is often someone who reports to the business owner and could be a database manager, or an application manager. It is possible that in some organizations the information owner and the business owner are the same person.

It is possible that the data on the system slated for C&A falls under a different jurisdiction than that of the system owner. It is also possible that the information owner and the system owner are one in the same person. Sometimes databases may be administered and managed by someone that has expert credentials in the area. If the system owner and information owners are not one in the same people, this should be noted in the Certification Package in the *Asset Inventory*.

Information System Security Officer

The Information System Security Officer (ISSO) is responsible for managing the security of the information system that is slated for C&A. The ISSO insures that the information systems configuration is in compliance with the agency's information security policy. All the certification package documents are prepared either by the ISSO, or for the ISSO, by staff or contractors. Typically ISSOs have a large plate of responsibilities and they likely will need to augment their staff with contractors to prepare a Certification Package expeditiously. It is not uncommon for one ISSO to be responsible for the preparation of half a dozen C&A packages. Since one C&A package could easily take a year for a well-versed security expert to prepare, it is considered standard and acceptable for ISSOs to hire consultants from outside the agency to prepare the Certification Package. It also improves the objectivity of the Certification Package to have it prepared by third-party individuals that are not part of the agency's own staff.

Once a Certification Package is complete, the ISSO presents it to an evaluation team who then proceeds to validate the findings. The evaluation team is an extension of the certifying agent. If the certifying agent does not appoint or assemble an evaluation team, the certifying agent should be prepared to evaluate the Certification Package and make a recommendation on whether to issue a positive Accreditation.

C&A Preparers

The C&A preparers, sometimes referred to as the C&A review team, prepare the Certification Packages for submission to the evaluation team. In many cases, the C&A preparers are outside consultants. The C&A preparers can also be a mixed team of outside consultants and internal agency staff.

The C&A preparers work for the information system owner, but usually under the direction of the Information System Security Officer. When it comes to putting together the Certification Package, it is the C&A preparers that perform the bulk of the work. The C&A preparers need to have an expert background in information security with a breadth of understanding the various facets of security architecture, information Confidentiality, information Integrity, information Availability, security policies, and FISMA regulations.

Agency Inspectors

To prepare for visits from the GAO, all agencies, and some bureaus, have their own inspectors that come on site to agency offices to periodically assess if proper FISMA compliance is taking place. In most cases, the agency inspectors are not required to give much advanced notification and their visits can take place without warning. The agency internal inspectors come from the agency Office of Inspector General (OIG). Many agency OIG offices have their own Web sites, and you can read more about the different responsibilities of the OIG there. A short list of a few OIG Web sites is listed in Table 3.1.

Table 3.1 Agency OIG Web Sites

Agency Name	Agency OIG Web Site
Environmental Protection Agency	www.epa.gov/oigearth/
Federal Communications Commission	www.fcc.gov/oig/
Dept. of Agriculture	www.usda.gov/oig/
Dept. of Health and Human Services	http://oig.hhs.gov/
Social Security Administration	www.ssa.gov/oig/
United States Postal Service	www.uspsoig.gov/

The goal of the agency OIG is to catch any problems and resolve them so that they do not show up as deficiencies on GAO reports. The OIG offices have their own investigation and review process and different OIG offices may perform their audits in different ways. OIG offices that are more vigilant in their audit and review process are more likely to prevent the agency from being cited as deficient by GAO inspectors.

GAO Inspectors

Oversight auditors from the GAO visit federal agencies on an annual basis, and review accredited Certification Packages to make sure that they have been accredited properly. The GAO also reviews the agency's C&A process to determine if it is acceptable. If the GAO discovers that Certification Packages were inappropriately accredited, or if the agency's C&A process is deficient in any way, agency officials will document the findings and the agency will receive poor grades on the annual Federal Computer Security Report Card. The Federal Computer Security Report Card is published each year by the U.S. Committee on Government Reform.

Levels of Audit

Taking into consideration the evaluation team, the OIG inspectors, and the GAO inspectors, you can see that the FISMA process undergoes rigorous levels of audit (see Figure 3.1). Usually there are no less than three levels of audit. Some agencies may even have an additional level of audit. After the evaluation team reviews the Certification Package, it is possible that another internal compliance organization may review the Certification Package again to see if the evaluation team did their job correctly. The original evaluation team and an ancillary compliance team may not in fact agree on whether a Certification Package should be accredited, and often the two internal audit organizations will have to have numerous discussions among themselves to come to an agreement on the final Accreditation recommendation.

Having so many levels of audit can in fact seem like overkill; however, the agencies that seem to indulge in these audit redundancies, and separation of duties, often fare the best on the Federal Computer Security Report Card.

Figure 3.1 FISMA Levels of Audit for Reviewing the Certification Package

GAO Inspectors
↓
OIG Inspectors
↓
Certifying Agent
↓
Evaluation Team
↓
Certification Package

Stepping through the Process

As you recall from Chapter 2, there are four high-level phases to the C&A process. To get from one phase to another, a lot of stuff happens along the way. Let me help you understand how to get from one phase to the next.

The Initiation Phase

The Initiation Phase is usually informally managed by the information system owner and the ISSO. Although all information system owners should be aware of the fact that FISMA requires new information systems to be positively accredited, this may not be at the forefront of their minds. Therefore, it is altogether likely that the ISSO may bring the need for C&A to the attention of the information system owner. Whether the need for C&A is initiated by the information system owner, or the ISSO, some sort of acknowledgment between these two individuals that a C&A needs to take place should occur. The acknowledgment does not have to be formal, or even written. A simple hallway conversation can suffice as long as both parties come to agree that it's time to get a C&A project started.

During the Initiation Phase, the information system owner and the ISSO should agree on what resources to use to for the C&A prepare team. Decisions need to be made on whether to hire outside contractors, or use in-house staff. Since C&A, if done properly, is usually a much bigger job than most people realize, I cannot emphasize enough the value in using outside consultants. Putting together a Certification Package is a full-time job and usually the results will be insufficient if the government office tries to double-up its existing staff to perform C&A duties in conjunction with their existing daily routine.

In outsourcing the preparation of a Certification Package to outside consultants, it is important for the ISSO to ensure that he or she is hiring capable individuals with the appropriate expertise. The ISSO should ask numerous questions to a potential contract company and its staff before enlisting the Contractor Officer (COTR) to close an agreement. Questions that may assist an ISSO in determining the expert C&A capabilities of potential consultants might be:

- For what other agencies have you performed C&A?

- Do you have a track record in obtaining positive Accreditations?

- Can you name the C&A documents that you are experienced in preparing?

- Will you be able to make numerous trips on site to meet with our staff?

- Can you provide resumes for the available consultants?

- Do you have a description of your C&A preparation services?

- Can you provide references from other agencies?

Not all C&A consulting services are the same. One clear indication that a contracting company does not fully understand C&A is if they list only a few document types in their C&A service description. Some companies claim to understand C&A, but for example, will list that their C&A service consists of a Self-Assessment and a Vulnerability Assessment (which of course is only part of the picture). You really want to hire consultants that understand the entire ball of wax and can develop all the documents required for C&A.

It will only slow down and complicate the process if you hire, say, one company to develop part of the deliverables and another company to develop the other part. When it comes to C&A, finding a contracting company that offers one-stop-shopping is really the most efficient way to go. One good way to find out how well a candidate contracting company understands C&A is to ask them for a project proposal with milestones built into it. By comparing different project proposals side-by-side, it should become clear which of the candidate contracting companies offer the best expertise.

Last but not least, before preparing a Certification Package, the ISSO should have some understanding of whether or not the proposed Certification Package will result in a positive accreditation. If the ISSO knows up front that proper security controls have not been put into place, that security is improperly configured, and that security policies have not been adhered to, it is better to fix these problems before beginning the C&A process. This does not mean that C&A is optional. What I am suggesting is that if you know of weaknesses that require correction, start correcting them immediately. Don't wait for C&A time to come along before making the necessary corrections.

NIST advises that the information System Security Plan be analyzed during the initiation phase. Although there is nothing theoretically wrong with this approach, it is often the case that for a new information system, a System Security Plan does exist. In putting together the Certification Package, it is a more likely scenario that the System Security Plan will be either written for the first time, or revised and updated during the Certification Phase. During a recertification of a package that has been previously accredited, an old System Security Plan would of course already exist.

C&A Best Practices...

Initiation Phase Milestones

During the initiation phase, you should be asking these questions:

- Have C&A preparers been identified?
- Have known security weaknesses been addressed?
- Has the of the FIPS 199 security categorization been completed?

The Certification Phase

The Certification Phase is the time period in which the Certification Package is prepared. It is during this phase that the C&A preparers (or review team) gather all the supporting evidence and documentation, and develop the new documents required for the Certification Package.

If the proposed C&A is for a brand new information system, no prior Certification Package will exist. If the C&A is for an older information system, a prior Certification Package should exist and be available for review. New C&As are required every three years. Certification for an information system that previously has been accredited is referred to as a "recertification." Recertifications require the same suite of documents that new Certification Packages require. When working on a recertification, the prior Certification Package should be reviewed thoroughly to ensure that all risks previously cited in the old Certification Package have been mitigated.

The C&A review team will need to come on site to the agency's office to be available to interview the information system's development and management team. It is critical for the C&A review team to learn as much about the information system as possible and ask as many questions as necessary. The information system owner should advise his or her development staff to accommodate the C&A review team and provide them with as much information as possible about the design and configuration of the system slated for C&A.

C&A review teams may consist of anywhere from a few people, up to a dozen or more depending on the complexity of the information system slated for C&A. What should determine the number of individuals on the C&A team is the scope of the project, and timeframe of the project. As you increase the scope, and decrease the timeframe, the need for a bigger C&A review team increases. Most C&A review teams require at least three months minimum to assemble an adequate Certification Package. It would not be out of the question, however, for a C&A review team to take six months to prepare a Certification Package for a large and complex infrastructure.

C&A Best Practices...

Certification Phase Milestones

- Design and architecture documents are reviewed.
- Vulnerabilities are identified.
- Evidence of risk mitigation is identified.
- Certification documents are written.
- Analysis of acceptable risk to agency is completed.

The Accreditation Phase

The Accreditation Phase begins when the Certification Package has been completed. The evaluation team reads through the Certification Package in its entirety, and validates if the findings are accurate, and if all the required information is present. A Certification Package can easily be in excess of 500 pages. At least two to four weeks should be allotted for the Accreditation Phase.

Most evaluation teams will have already prepared checklists of particular criteria they expect to find in the Certification Package before they actually begin the evaluation. In Chapter 21 I will discuss what these checklists typically look like.

If a Certification Package passes muster with the evaluators, a recommendation will be made that the package be positively accredited. The Certifying Agent will review the recommendation, and as long as it appears justified, will sign a formal letter of Accreditation. The accreditation letter will also need to be signed by the ISSO, the information owner, the authorizing official, and then will be sent to the CIO. The CIO is supposed to acknowledge receipt of the letter by signing it.

C&A Best Practices...

Accreditation Milestones

- Submission of package to evaluators
- Review and comment resolution
- Recommendation to Accredit (or not)

The Continuous Monitoring Phase

Once an information system has been accredited, it should be continuously monitored. Configuration management changes should be an on-going and well-managed process with approval mechanisms built in. Dates of changes and versions of code changes should all be documented. Security controls should also be monitored and any changes made to them should be documented. If firewall policies are changed, the changes and reasons for the changes should be documented. If intrusion detection configuration changes are made, they should be fully described and the reasons for the changes should documented.

It is often the case that not nearly enough time is put into the Continuous Monitoring Phase, since once a positive Accreditation has been made, most ISSOs and information system owners tend to breathe a sigh of relief and seem to like to put the entire C&A process behind them. Putting together a Certification Package and obtaining an Accreditation is a daunting task and doing more of it, after the job is done, is not usually high on anyone's agenda after the fact. However, keeping the documents up to date will make any future recertifications much easier. Unless the information system is decommissioned, it in fact will need to be recertified in three years.

The documents that are a part of the Certification Package are considered live documents, and can be updated at any time. It is best to update the documents as soon as changes are made to the information systems since that is when the new information is most fresh in everyone's mind. Updating documentation never seems to be high on the list of important tasks to complete, and for that reason, I recommend that updating Certification Package documents be built into the change management process. Each time a document is updated, it should be reviewed and approved through the change control process and then archived both locally and at an offsite location.

C&A Best Practices

Continuous Monitoring Milestones

- Reconciliation of POA&M citations
- Documentation of changes to system
- Ongoing monitoring of security controls

Summary

The certification and accreditation process consists of a four-phase life cycle: initiation, certification, accreditation, and continuous monitoring. Throughout all four phases there are several roles participating in the process, and each role is responsible for the execution of specific tasks. As a C&A professional you are responsible for the execution of your tasks, but in order to accomplish them, you must ensure that all other individuals filling C&A roles are working together effectively and efficiently as well. It is critical to understand the overall process, and how all the pieces described in this chapter fit together in order to manage a C&A project.

## Chapter 4

Establishing a C&A Program

"A bad beginning makes a bad ending."

—Euripides

Topics in this chapter:

- C&A Handbook Development
- Template Development
- Provide Package Delivery Instructions
- Create an Evaluation Process
- Authority and Endorsement
- Authority and Endorsement
- Improve Your C&A Program Each Year
- Problems of Not Having a C&A Program

Introduction

If your agency or bureau doesn't already have an information security program established, chances are that it hasn't scored well on the annual Federal Computer Security Report Card. Since FISMA isn't going to go away, and senior executives will be held accountable for obtaining acceptable Federal Computer Security Report Card scores, now is the time to start putting into place an information security program. The C&A program is just a piece of the greater information security program, albeit a big piece. The information security program includes the whole ball of wax—security policies, procedures, requirements, C&A guidelines, and all the documentation that goes with it. The C&A program is a well-thought-out process with documentation to support it. It explains how C&A will be done within the agency.

If your agency already has information security and C&A programs in place, now might be a good time to start thinking about how you can improve your program. Once a C&A program has been developed, an astute agency will find the need to update and revise the program each year. The more your C&A program is used, the better it will become.

The C&A program developers are often the same folks who are part of the agency evaluation team—however, they don't have to be. There are no federal restrictions on which people within the agency can participate in developing the C&A program. The agency itself, however, may set their own policies on who is responsible for development of the C&A program. Since developing the program is a big job, whoever manages the project to develop the program should reign in participants throughout the agency to help build and document the program. To ensure a separation of duties and enforce objectivity, some agencies may opt to, or be required to, hire outside consultants or contractors to help develop their C&A program.

C&A Handbook Development

In developing the program, you'll need to write a *C&A Handbook* that instructs your agency or bureau on how to prepare a Certification Package. The idea is to standardize the development of all Certification Packages that are submitted for evaluation. Without a handbook and a specified process, the

Certification Packages will have a different look and feel. If 50 different Certification Packages all have the right information in it, but in different formats, it is going to be very difficult for the evaluators to find the information. If the packages have different types of information in them, it is going to be very hard for the evaluators to review the packages according to the same standards.

Writing the handbook is a big job. A good handbook is likely to be around 200 pages long. The handbook has to include very specific information on what your agency evaluators need to see in every Certification Package. It should instruct the folks preparing the Certification Packages on what documents they will be required to submit, and what should be included in each document. The best way to ensure that each document includes the right kind of information is to create templates.

What to Include in Your Handbook

Each agency's handbook will be somewhat different and take on slightly different organizational formats. However, it is highly advisable that all handbooks include sections in the following areas:

- Background, purpose, scope

- Regulatory citations (FISMA; FIPS 199; OMB Circular A-130. Appendix III)

- Reference to associated internal security policies

- System lifecycle information

- An overview of the process

- Roles and responsibilities

- Definition and explanation of Certification Levels

- Information on the required Certification Package documents

- How to define security requirements

- How to understand accreditation boundaries

- Threat and risk assessment guidelines

- Security controls

- Required security tests
- Evaluation checklists
- Plan of Action & Milestones
- Acronyms
- Glossary
- References and related publications
- An Appendix for each template

Who Should Write the Handbook?

There are no restrictions on who can write a C&A Handbook. An agency can use its own staff, or outside consultants. However, the development of the handbook should probably be done under the authority of the department that will oversee the evaluators. It makes sense that the Certifying Agent should designate the appropriate staff to write the handbook since he or she will need to live by its guidelines and accredit packages according to its stipulations. There is nothing that says the Certifying Agent cannot author the handbook. However, given the daily day-to-day responsibilities of the Certifying Agent, the time it takes to development the handbook may require that it be done by an appointed staff, or outside consultants.

Template Development

Certification Packages consist of a set of documents that all go together and complement one another. A Certification Package is voluminous, and without standardization, it takes an inordinate amount of time to evaluate it to make sure all the right information is included. Therefore, agencies should have templates for all the documents that they require in their Certification Packages. Agencies without templates should work on creating them. If an agency does not have the resources in-house to develop these templates, they should consider outsourcing this initiative to outside consultants.

A template should be developed using the word processing application that is the standard within the agency. All of the relevant sections that the evaluation team will be looking for within each document should be included. Text that will remain constant for a particular document type also should be included. An efficient and effective C&A program will have templates for the following types of C&A documents:

- *Categorization and Certification Level Recommendation*
- *Hardware and Software Inventory*
- *Self-Assessment*
- *Security Awareness and Training Plan*
- *End-User Rules of Behavior*
- *Incident Response Plan*
- *Security Test and Evaluation Plan*
- *Privacy Impact Assessment*
- *Business Risk Assessment*
- *Business Impact Assessment*
- *Contingency Plan*
- *Configuration Management Plan*
- *System Risk Assessment*
- *System Security Plan*
- *Security Assessment Report*

The later chapters in this book will help you understand what should be included in each of these types of documents. Some agencies may possibly require other types of documents as required by their information security program and policies.

Templates should include guidelines for what type of content should be included, and also should have built-in formatting. The templates should be as complete as possible, and any text that should remain consistent and exactly the same in like document types should be included. Though it may seem redundant to have the exact same verbatim text at the beginning of, say, each *Business Risk Assessment* from a particular agency, each document needs to be able to stand alone and make sense if it is pulled out of the Certification

Package for review. Having similar wording in like documents also shows that the packages were developed consistently using the same methodology and criteria.

With established templates in hand, it makes it much easier for the C&A review team to understand what it is that they need to document. Even expert C&A consultants need and appreciate document templates. Finding the right information to include the C&A documents can by itself by extremely difficult without first having to figure out what it is that you are supposed to find—which is why the templates are so very important. It's often the case that a large complex application is distributed and managed throughout multiple departments or divisions and it can take a long time to figure out not just what questions to ask, but who the right people are who will know the answers.

Provide Package Delivery Instructions

Your C&A program should include information on how specifically the ISSO should submit the final Certification Package to the evaluation team. The evaluation team needs to understand whether to expect the package by e-mail, CD, or to look on a protected network share. It's a good idea for agencies to require that both hardcopy and software documents be submitted to the evaluation team. Hardcopy documents should be bound together. I recommend using a three-ring binder because it is easy to update a single piece of the package and insert it easily after removing the outdated pages.

Most of these documents will contain sensitive information, and for that reason, they should not be e-mailed to anyone over the Internet unless they are protected by 128 bit encryption—either by file encryption or through a Virtual Private Network (VPN). Before e-mailing C&A documents out of the agency over any external public networks, you should really check the security policies of your particular agency to find out what the requirements are for protecting sensitive information. If outside consultants are being used to prepare a Certification Package, it may very well be that the only safe way to exchange documents with them is for them to come on site. Most agencies will not set up a VPN to outside consultants, and getting approvals to use file encryption or certificates can take more time than the time it takes to create the entire Certification Package. Though it may seem trailing-edge, sometimes exchanging documents in person using a CD or a USB flash drive is the easiest way to exchange C&A documents.

Create an Evaluation Process

The evaluation of a Certification Package should be a standardized procedure. Before going through the Certification Package, the evaluation team should know up front exactly what it is that they are looking for. Agencies that do not have a standardized methodology for evaluating Certification Packages will not score well on the annual Federal Computer Security Report Card.

The standardized process should be different depending on the security category (level) of the Certification Package. There are four possible security levels that Certification Packages can be prepared in accordance with, and these different levels have slightly different requirements. The level is determined using guidance from the U.S. Federal Information Processing Standard (FIPS) 199 (see Appendix C). I will talk more about how to determine C&A levels using levels of impact in Chapter 6.

Authority and Endorsement

It is important that a C&A program be developed and endorsed at a high level within the agency. The purpose of the program will be completely defeated if individual departments each try to create their own C&A program. The idea is to create a standard, and a standard means one process. The program should be spearheaded by the CIO or authorizing official, even if all the work is delegated to the certifying agent. That doesn't mean that the technical staff within various departments can't contribute to the program's development. Some of the best ideas often come from the technical staff that takes the most interest in a project. The development of the program, however, needs to be organized and endorsed at the level of the CIO, authorizing official, and certifying agent.

Improve Your C&A Program Each Year

Once a handbook and templates are established, they should be improved upon and refined as necessary. However, updating them every single year may be counterproductive. You want the people within the organization to gain familiarity with the C&A handbook and process. If you change the handbook, process, and templates every year, they will not become familiar with it. Once you have a handbook and process in place that has been reviewed, edited, and published, it is best not to rewrite the handbook more often than every two years. Of course if there are egregious errors, those may need to be addressed.

Developing a handbook and templates takes a long time. Once an agency has invested the time to develop these materials, they should hold training courses to train the agency's ISSOs on how to follow the requirements. Once ISSOs have been duly informed and trained, they can clearly be held accountable for their role in developing proper Certification Packages according to the agency requirements.

Problems of Not Having a C&A Program

If your agency does not have a standardized C&A program, you can expect the C&A process to become extremely confusing and overly complicated. C&A preparers will not know what should be included in each package, and evaluators will not know if anything is missing.

Missing Information

Without a C&A program, different Certification Packages will include different types of information. For example, without a prescribed and standardized C&A program, one Certification Package might have an Information Technology Contingency Plan (ITCP) and others might not. One Certification Package might include a network topology map, and others might not. When it comes time to evaluate the entire Certification Package, it is hard to fail a package for not having an information technology Contingency Plan if no policy or organizational process ever required one to exist in the first place. It is very hard to hold the information system owners and the ISSOs accountable for putting together adequate Certification Packages if your agency has not yet defined what exactly constitutes an adequate Certification Package.

Lack of Organization

Though specifying the right information to include in a Certification Package is of primary importance, the format of the package should not be overlooked. A Certification Package can be 500 pages long. Unless each one is organized the same way, it will be very cumbersome for the evaluators to wade through the voluminous information and check to see if all the right material has been included. It's best to make things easiest for the evaluators. Evaluators who can't make heads or tails out of the information presented to them, and can't find key pieces of information, are going to be reluctant to recommend that a package be accredited.

Inconsistencies in the Evaluation Process

You want each Certification Package to be evaluated the same way. One agency may have many different evaluators. Without any sort of standard for Certification Package content or format, you are leaving the entire evaluation up to the subjective opinion of one (or a small group) of people. Different evaluators may put emphasis on different areas. If each package has the same organizational format, it improves the chances that different evaluators will evaluate the packages in the same way because they will look for, and expect the same type of information.

Unknown Security Architecture and Configuration

Without a Certification Package, it may be the case that the security architecture and configuration of your information infrastructure is not known. By working through the C&A process, you will become aware of whether this is the case or not. If the security architecture is well documented, C&A serves as an opportunity to make sure the architecture diagrams and network maps are correct. If it's not well documented, or not documented at all, this is something you'll want to research and diagram. The same holds true for the security configuration. All software requires configurations. When operating systems and applications are installed, even if they are installed securely, are the security settings documented? If the security settings are not documented, they are basically unknown. Even expert and seasoned systems administrators cannot usually remember every little thing they have done to a system when configuring it because today's operating systems and applications are so feature rich. That is why security architecture and configuration documentation is critical. The C&A process is designed to find the unknowns of the security architecture and configuration settings and then resolve the unknowns by creating the necessary documentation along the way.

Unknown Risks

Federal laws aside, the primary reason for understanding the security posture of your information systems is to identify risks, understand them, and take mitigating actions. With C&A left undefined, you are leaving the risks that you want your agency to look for open to speculation. Maybe the agency ISSOs will identify all the key risks, but maybe they won't. One ISSO may put emphasis on disaster recovery planning, and another might put emphasis on system risks. It is unlikely that they all will put the same emphasis on all aspects of information security. When it comes to identifying risks, there are numerous items to take into consideration. There are business risks, system risks, training risks, policy risks, inventory risks, and so on. A well-defined C&A program ensures that all the relevant types of risks are taken into consideration.

Laws and Report Cards

You may be surprised to find out that the words "certification" and "accreditation" are not used in the *Federal Information Security Act of 2002*. However, the law very clearly states the requirement of an information security program, and also names the required elements of that program. Many of the required elements of the mandated information security program are those that have evolved to be now known as "Certification and Accreditation." Even if the agency-wide program were called something else—say "The

Security Validation Program"—all the same elements of the program would be required. You should not get hung up on the fact that you don't see the terms "certification" or "accreditation" in the written law. The named elements of the program are required by law no matter how you entitle them. Without these elements, and without an information security program, agencies are breaking the law. What's more, agencies that don't have the right elements included in their information security program will obtain poor Federal Computer Security Report Card grades. I'll discuss this more in Chapter 23, but it's almost a sure bet that if you don't have a well-defined C&A program, you won't get a good grade on the Federal Computer Security Report card.

Summary

There is no task that can be effectively accomplished using a repeatable process without having adequate documentation in place. Therefore, the first step in implementing a C&A program in an organization is developing a C&A handbook. Once the handbook is finalized it should be clear that there is a set of documents that will be created or used during the execution of each C&A task. Templates for each of these tasks should be developed to standardize the output and to reduce the work required to create them. Once these items are in place, C&A packages can effectively and efficiently be generated, but the C&A program should include mechanisms by which the process itself can be evaluated and improved. Cars are not manufactured the same way today as they were 20 years ago. Process improvements are discovered and incorporated into the process, and the same should be true of any C&A program. If an organization's C&A program is constantly evolving and improving, then by extension, the organization's security posture should be evolving and improving as well.

Chapter 5

Developing a Certification Package

"He who has begun, is half done."

—Horace

Topics in this chapter:

- Initiating Your C&A Project
- Analyze Your Research
- Preparing the Documents
- Verify Your Information
- Retain Your Ethics

57

Introduction

Before you'll be able to start putting together a Certification Package, you'll need to acquire as much information as possible about the systems or applications you'll be certifying. You need to be a good detective, and not lose faith when the details appear unclear. The more information you gather the clearer the details will become. You are about to put together an information technology jigsaw puzzle.

Initiating Your C&A Project

When you begin your C&A project, don't expect everyone who has played a role in developing and administering the application or systems you are certifying to start volunteering information for you to use. You will need to take the initiative to go out and collect as much documentation as you can, and conduct interviews with the appropriate staff. If you are a consultant, first you will need to figure out who the appropriate staff are that you need to talk to. You are going to have to ask a lot of questions. The sponsoring manager that signed you up for completing the C&A is the best person to start this. The sponsoring manager may be the system owner, the ISSO, the contracting officer, or an application development manager.

Put Together a Contact List

You first need to figure out who will have knowledge of all the security particularities of the information system. You should start by identifying the people involved. The sponsoring manager should be able to answer a lot of your questions. To find the appropriate people who understand the security of the information system or systems that require accreditation, you'll need to ask the following questions:

- Was the application developed in-house or purchased from a vendor?
- If the application was purchased from a vendor was any customization done to it?
- Who did the customization?
- If the application was developed in-house, who designed it?

- Are there design specifications and documents? Who has them?

- Is the application hosted on-site or at a remote site?

- If the application is hosted remotely, who is responsible for its operations?

These questions are the "Who?" questions. From the answers to your questions, you should be able to start putting together a contact list of the people who have been a part of the design and implementation of the information system. Include their phone numbers and e-mail addresses because you'll need to contact them often.

Some federal agencies are quite large, and due to the size of the operations, sometimes impersonal. When you contact the various people on your contact list, you'll need to explain to them who you are and why you are contacting them. Don't expect them to know that a C&A project is underway or even to know what C&A is about. If you contact them and say that you need to meet with them to discuss a C&A project, be prepared to tell them what C&A means since there is a good chance they may not have a clue what you are talking about.

Finding out all the information you will need to create a Certification Package is much like going on a treasure hunt. If you are an outside consultant, at the start of the project, it is altogether possible that no one except the sponsoring manager will know why you are on-site at the agency. It's very unlikely that someone will come up to you and say, "I hear that you are on-site to put together a Certification Package for our information system. Here are all the security policies, design documents, and the security configuration of the system that you will need." In large federal agencies, my experience has been that no one readily and quickly volunteers information about system security.

Hold a Kick-Off Meeting

Once you have found out who the key players are (the people that have been part of designing, developing, coding, and implementing the information system), you should schedule a Kick-off Meeting and invite them all. Do your best to form good relationships with these folks because you will become reliant on them for information. During the Kick-off Meeting introduce them to the C&A team, and explain to them briefly what C&A is all about. During this first meeting, you should tell them that you will need as much documentation as you can get on the particular information system that is slated for accreditation. Ask them if they can e-mail you documentation as soon as possible; otherwise they may take weeks to get it to you. You will need information on the design, development, implementation, configuration, network topology, and testing of the information system. You will need to review all this documentation to find the right bits of information to put into the Certification Package.

Obtain Any Existing Agency Guidelines

It is key to find out if the agency you are working for has a C&A Handbook. Agencies that have in the past scored well on their Federal Computer Security Report Cards probably have one. Agencies that have scored poorly on their report card may not have one. If a handbook exists, you must follow all the guidelines written in it when preparing your Certification Package—even if they are poor guidelines. If the evaluation team does its job properly, they will be evaluating the Certification Package for how well it follows the agency C&A Handbook and requirements.

If a handbook exists, and you think parts of it are so wrong that you shouldn't follow it, you need to take this up with the ISSO and package evaluation team before making any decisions. When you are preparing a Certification Package is not necessarily the best time to try to get the agency to change their regulations and policies. If you think that some parts of it are incorrect, before you go ahead and decide to go your own way and create a more "correct" Certification Package, bring the issues to the attention of the ISSO and offer justification as to why you would like to proceed differently. Some agencies will fail your Certification Package if you don't follow their handbook—even if the handbook is wrong.

All agencies are supposed to have a handbook and templates to standardize the C&A process. However, some agencies are less prepared than others, and if you embark on a C&A project, and find out that no handbook or templates exist, you'll have to do without. You can still put together a solid Certification Package without a handbook or templates, and if you do a good job, perhaps you will be enlisted as a future contributor to develop the much needed handbook and templates. If a C&A handbook is not present, then see if the parent agency has one. For example a bureau or agency department may not have their own handbook, but the parent agency might. If no C&A handbook at all exists, figure out which methodology your agency should be using (NIST, DITSCAP, NIACAP, DCID 6/3) and look to that for guidance.

Analyze Your Research

Once you have received the various documents from the information system developers and administrators, you'll need to analyze these documents to see if they include the kind of information that you'll need to include in the Certification Package. It is likely that much of the information you need for the Certification Package will not be included in the various documents you receive. If the information system(s) that are up for C&A have been previously accredited, then a prior Certification Package should exist. You should make it a point to review the prior Certification Package, and use any information from it that is still relevant. If anything appears incorrect in the prior Certification Package, you should correct it, even if it was not cited for deficiencies in the prior Accreditation.

Put together a list of questions regarding the kinds of things you still need to find out from the information system developers and administrators, and schedule meetings with the folks that you think can best answer your questions. Keep meeting with the team and contacting them on the phone and by e-mail until all your questions are answered. It often takes several rounds of inquiries before you receive all the appropriate information.

Preparing the Documents

Although there are likely no regulations that require you to put together the Certification Package documents in any particular order, I happen to think that the order in which you put the documents together is important. For example, if you put together the *Hardware and Software Inventory* up front, it will help you in writing the descriptive text about the accreditation boundaries that are required in the *System Security Plan*. In the subsequent chapters of this book, I present the various Certification Package documents in the order that I have found works well for cohesiveness in understanding the information system. In some cases, it may make sense for you to change the order of these documents when putting together your Certification Package. The main point to take away is that if a document contains information that is dependent on a prior document, develop the prior document first. It will be hard to know how to rate the outage impact of the assets listed in the *Business Impact Assessment* if you don't yet know what the assets are—if the *Hardware and Software Inventory* has not yet been completed.

It's Okay to Be Redundant

Many of the documents in the Certification Package include information that is redundant from one document to the next. The reason for this is because each document needs to be able to stand on its own. Some of the information that you find for some of the earlier documents can and should be used in subsequent documents. You want to give the impression that all the documents are consistent with each other and support each other. Though in many forms of writing being redundant is not desirable, in crafting Certification Packages, it is necessary. One of the things that the evaluators look for are inconsistencies between the various Certification Package documents. Any inconsistencies usually raise a flag and call for closer inspection.

Different Agencies Have Different Requirements

Not all agencies require the exact same documents for C&A. FISMA allows for flexibility, and one agency may require certain documents that other agencies don't require. Though it could be argued that this is inequitable, FISMA was designed to allow each agency to determine its own needs within the boundaries of the stipulation. The Certification Package documents that I will be discussing in this book are among the most frequently required C&A documents. However, there may be others that some agencies require that are not discussed in this book. If your agency requires documents not discussed in this book that are part of the stated C&A program, that doesn't mean that your agency is administering their C&A program the wrong way. However, to be sure, agencies should be able to justify to the agency Inspector Generals, and to the GAO, which documents they require and why.

Including Multiple Applications and Systems in One Package

You can include multiple applications and information systems in one Certification Package. To be sure, it makes no sense at all to create a Certification Package for each and every system that exists at your agency. You should define the accreditation boundaries of your C&A package as broadly as you possibly can. Determining the accreditation boundaries is sometimes the trickiest part of putting together a Certification Package. You need to understand where the accreditation starts and stops. In general, you should pick a boundary determination that is large and logical. For example, if you are accrediting general support systems, you may want to define your boundary by network domains. If you are accrediting major applications, you will need to include all the pieces of the infrastructure that the application touches.

Usually application infrastructure is managed by a different organization than the underlying general support systems. Operating systems and network typically have different information system owners than the applications. C&A is about holding information system owners accountable, and therefore, the boundaries need to lie within the jurisdiction over which the information system owner has control. If you are certifying an application that is depending on general support systems that the application gets installed on top of, then this should be clearly stated in the Certification Package. An underlying general support system usually has a different Certification Package than the applications that are installed on top of it. When your Certification Package and the security of your systems is in part dependent on other systems, that needs to be specifically stated. You can reference other Certification Packages and other systems that are not within your accreditation boundaries in your documentation. It would be perfectly plausible to insert a statement such as:

> **The major applications described in this Certification Package are dependent on the underlying general support systems that have been previously accredited at Level 4.**

You should list the formal Certification Package name of any other packages that you reference. If you don't know the package name, try to find it out. It's even better to obtain a copy of it if you can. In some cases, it may be against the security policies of the agency to share such information between one information owner to another. However at the very least, an outside information owner should be able to share with you the official document name and publication date of the related Certification Package.

Verify Your Information

Once you have completed a document, before submitting it to the ISSO, send it out first to the information system developers and administrators that are most familiar with the information systems you are seeking to Accredit. Ask them to review it and inform you of any factual errors. Network diagrams should also be reviewed for accuracy. If something doesn't make sense, it's probably either not well-documented or plain wrong. Certification and Accreditation is a time of ensuring that everything is accurate.

In reviewing design documents that you receive, do not just assume that information contained in them is how the application or information systems were actually developed. Designs go awry and management changes their minds about requirements halfway into a project. Just because an information system was supposed to turn out one way, doesn't mean it didn't turn out a different way. You need to take everything you read with a grain of salt, and ask questions about things that don't make sense.

Retain Your Ethics

In most agencies, all the information system owner wants the Certification review team to do is to get the information systems certified. They don't necessarily want to know how you will go about doing this as long as you get it done. Even though you should do everything possible to make that happen, by all means do not compromise your ethics.

C&A Best Practices…

Hold Fast to Your Ethics

Never compromise your ethics. Under no circumstances should you invent security controls that do not exist, or document that risks have been mitigated if they haven't. If the information owner or ISSO pressures you to document items that are obviously not true, you should refrain from doing so and report the problem to your management. If in the course of preparing the Certification documents you find that certain security controls that should have been implemented were not, report that to the ISSO and recommend that they get implemented as soon as possible. As long as they are implemented before the Certification Package is submitted, your documentation will not be incorrect. If you feel that there is absolutely no way the information systems will obtain a positive Accreditation, discuss this with the ISSO. It is not your job as a Certification document preparer to resolve security problems that should have been put in place previously. The information system owner and ISSO are likely both aware that security controls are mandated by law, and need to be in place. If they are responsible individuals with ethics of their own, they will not expect you to resolve agency security problems that you have no control over.

Most agency information systems can likely obtain a Level 1 Accreditation with a properly documented Certification Package. (I'll discuss the certification levels in detail in the next chapter.) However, if security controls on information systems appear to be so poorly implemented as to not even warrant a Level 1 Accreditation you should meet with the information system owner and the ISSO and advise them of this. Be sure to include justification as to what you feel is so terribly wrong. If a Level 1 cannot be justifiably obtained, there are really two choices:

- Stop the C&A process and put in place the necessary security controls
- Continue with the C&A process, documenting the accurate existing security information, and hope the evaluator will grant the business owner an *Interim Authority to Operate*.

An *Interim Authority to Operate* (IATO) is basically like a consolation Accreditation, and in most cases IATOs expire after six months. An IATO means that you have convinced the evaluators that the information owner is at least putting forth a good effort in trying to implement proper security controls. And for that reason, the Certifying Agent gives you six months to come into compliance. An IATO usually will include a list of security controls that will need to be in place when the IATO expires. At that time, if the requirements of the IATO have been met, the system usually will receive an *Authority to Operation* (ATO), but if not, the systems can be shut down. Without an Accreditation in hand, the GAO or the agency OIG can come in and shut your systems down. However, although the GAO or OIG could require the systems to be shut down, for practical purposes, in real life this rarely happens. Certainly an IATO is better than no accreditation at all.

Summary

Developing a Certification Package is a big endeavor. One of the biggest problems that I have noticed is that often business owners and ISSOs do not start the C&A process soon enough and do not allocate enough resources to get the job done. The first C&A package you develop for your information system will be the most challenging. After that, unless a significant architectural or configuration change occurs, continuous monitoring and updating of the package are easy enough and should not require as many resources the second or third time around.

## Chapter 6

Preparing the Hardware and Software Inventory

"The prudent heir takes careful inventory of his legacies and gives a faithful accounting to those whom he owes an obligation of trust."

—John F. Kennedy

Topics in this chapter:

- **Determining the Accreditation Boundaries**
- **Collecting the Inventory Information**
- **Structure of Inventory Information**
- **Delivery of Inventory Document**

Introduction

All Certification Packages are required to include a software and hardware inventory of the applications and systems that are being accredited. You'll also need this hardware and software inventory when you develop your *Business Impact Assessment*. Hardware and software should be thought of as assets. All key assets that make up the information system should be reported.

Determining the Accreditation Boundaries

One of the biggest problems in putting together a hardware and software inventory is figuring out which systems and applications belong in the inventory, and are within the boundaries of the information system you are certifying. It is possible that the organization that developed the information system you are accrediting never formally acknowledged or described the boundaries. However, you can still come up with clear boundaries based on certain guidelines. As a general rule, the hardware and software assets of the information system that you plan on accrediting should:

- Have the same general security requirements

- Be managed by the same information system owner

- Have a consistent organizational function or mission

- Have consistent operational characteristics (geographical locations, network zones, security zones, firewall policies, etc.)

You will also need to list all the components of major assets on which the information system is dependent. Remember, the term information system is a general term for the item that you are describing in the Certification Package—it could be a group of general support systems or an enterprise application. If the information system is an enterprise application, you will still need to list the hardware platform and operating system of the general support system on which the application resides, even if the general support system itself is not part of the Certification Package. For an enterprise application, the application cannot run without the hardware platform and operating system, which is why they must be listed in the asset inventory. If you are certifying a general support system or systems, you do not need to list the applications that reside on these systems unless they are part of the Certification Package. Most of the time, general support systems are certified and accredited separately from applications.

The following types of information should be collected about the hardware:

- Manufacturer (Dell, IBM, Hewlett-Packard, etc.)
- Model
- Serial Number
- Geographical location including address, building number, room number
- Associated signification storage devices
- Associated IP address(s) and hostname
- External storage devices

Most C&A programs do not require you to list the amount of RAM and disk space so it is safe to leave that information out, unless the Handbook specifically requires you to list such things. There are likely various physical systems that safeguard the information system (e.g., halon fire suppressant systems and temperature alarm systems), but you do not need to list these items in the asset inventory.

The following types of information should be collected about the software:

- Operating system name and version
- Patch level and version
- Application name and version
- Database names and version
- Middleware
- Backup software and version
- Software license keys

If backups are performed by a third-party provider either within the agency or by an external private company, it is not necessary to list the name of the backup application software. However, if the information system has backups built into it that are performed under the same management organization of the information system being certified and accredited, then the backup software should be listed.

Collecting the Inventory Information

There is no requirement for how you collect the inventory information. If your information system consists of a large enterprise application, it sure makes things easier if the inventory information is collected through an automated process such as some asset inventory tool. However, even if the agency or bureau you are working with has access to an automated asset inventory, the information contained in the inventory still will not necessarily tell you which of the assets are part of the information system(s) you are trying to certify and accredit.

Usually there is no fast and easy way to collect asset inventory information. You will have to have discussions with the in-house subject matter experts, developers, and management team to come to an understanding of which components should be included. It is more than likely that much of the collection will have to be done manually by asking various people to look up IP addresses, find out the patch levels, find out the version number, look on the back of systems to find the serial numbers, and so on. You may need to ask support staff who are in entirely different departments, organizational groups, or locations to help you obtain this information. Don't expect that they will know anything about your C&A project. You will have to explain to them why you are collecting the information. Due to security concerns, support staff likely will require various types of authorization before they can give you the information you are looking for. Be prepared for a lot of red tape and responses such as "I can't give this information to you. You will have to have your ISSO request it and then the request will have to be approved by my supervisor." Due to the long chain of authorizations that may be required to assist you, collecting the asset inventory information usually takes longer than you would expect.

Structure of Inventory Information

I strongly recommend that you document the hardware and software inventory into a well-organized table or spreadsheet. You can use this same tabular format later to put together your *Business Impact Assessment*. (I'll be discussing the Business Impact Assessment in Chapter 15.) The function of the asset should be listed somewhere in the asset inventory table. Aside from listing the information in a table, you will want to put a short description of the information system at the beginning of the asset inventory document. The information system description should be consistent with the description that will be used later in the *System Security Plan*. The hardware and software inventory should be a separate document that includes the following elements:

- Cover page with data classification, warnings, date of publication and version

- Table of Contents

- Record of Changes

- An overview section that describes the purpose of the document

- A brief description of the information system

- A brief description of the agency C&A program requirements for assets

- Names of related documents

- Asset inventory tables

Table 6.1 shows a sample asset inventory table. Large distributed applications may have a lengthy asset inventory table. Also, if you are including an entire network domain of general support systems in one C&A package, that may also require a lengthy asset inventory table.

Delivery of Inventory Document

If your inventory document contains IP addresses, you will want to be sure not to e-mail it to anyone over the Internet. If you are an outside consultant and are working from your company office, you may have to go on-site to deliver the inventory document or else e-mail it through secure channels such as a VPN or using file encryption. Alternatively it is usually considered acceptable to deliver documents by CD and courier. However, in case there are any security policies associated with the file delivery, you should consult that *C&A Handbook* of the agency you are working for.

Table 6.1 Sample Asset Inventory Table

Asset Description	Function	Hardware or Software	Hostname	IP Address	Manufacturer	Model or Version	Serial # License Key
Server	Hardware Platform	Hardware	NY01	64.82.2.39	Dell	PowerEdge SC410	12345-LPT22
Operating System	Operations of Server	Software	NY01	64.82.2.39	Microsoft	Windows 2003 Server	XE413-431345
Database	Data Storage	Software	NY01	64.82.2.39	Oracle	Standard Edition 10G	12345
Server	Hardware Platform	Hardware	NY02	64.82.2.40	Sun	UltraSparc IV	N3K19-RCT97
Operating System	Operations of Server	Software	NY02	64.82.2.40	Sun	Solaris 10	ST047-102759
Database	Data Storage	Software	NY02	64.82.2.40	SQL Server 2000Microsoft	Microsoft	12345

* Asset Information for **Security Application** at New York Data Center, Street Address, Building, City, State, Zip/Postal Code

Summary

Collecting hardware and software inventory information is the first big step in developing a C&A package. This inventory will define the accreditation boundary as well as the scope (and cost) of your project, so it is important to develop a complete and accurate inventory. To develop the inventory, you will need to work with many of the people in charge of day-to-day operations of an organization's information systems. These people are not always focused on information security issues, and they are usually overworked as it is. So you need to keep in mind that you should make collecting inventory information as simple and efficient as possible for them and that you need to develop and maintain a positive relationship with them. Without their timely and accurate assistance, your C&A work can suffer the negative impacts of delays and inaccuracy.

Chapter 7

Determining the Certification Level

"Don't try to figure out what other people want to hear from you; figure out what you have to say. It's the one and only thing you have to offer."

—Barbara Kingsolver

Topics in this chapter:

- What Are the C&A Levels?
- Importance of Determining the C&A Level
- Don't Make This Mistake
- Criteria to Use for Determining the Levels
- Confidentiality, Integrity, and Availability
- System Attribute Characteristics
- Determining Level of Certification
- Template for Levels of Determination
- Rationale for the Security Level Recommendation
- Process and Rationale for the C&A Level Recommendation
- The Explanatory Memo

Introduction

All Certification Packages get certified and accredited at Level 1, 2, 3, or 4. The C&A review team, information system owner, and ISSO determine the C&A level and justify this level in a document known as the *C&A Level of Recommendation*. Unless the agency has decided to use some other methodology for determining the level of recommendation, the best guidance that exists for determining the level of accreditation is a document known as FIPS 199 (see Appendix C) written by the National Institute of Standards. Although I don't plan on trying to recreate FIPS 199, I want to help you understand how to use it.

What Are the C&A Levels?

There are four different levels for which information systems can be certified and accredited. The four levels are known simply as Level 1, Level 2, Level 3, or Level 4. The information system owner is supposed to decide at what level to certify the information system, and then obtain buy-in on that level from the authorizing official. The ISSO and C&A prearation team should assist the information system owner in determining the proper level at which to certify and accredit the information system.

Level 1 is for information systems that are not sensitive, and have few security requirements. Level 2 is for information systems that are somewhat sensitive, and have some Confidentiality, Integrity, or Availability requirements. Level 3 is for systems with sensitive information that have significant Confidentiality, Integrity, and Availability requirements. Level 4 is for extremely sensitive information systems that have the highest requirements for Confidentiality, Integrity, and Availability. Most information systems will fall into the category of Level 2 or 3. Deciding at which level to certify and accredit your information systems—2 or 3—can be somewhat thought-provoking.

Level 1

A Level 1 C&A requires a minimal security review. A Level 1 Certification Package requires only a Security Plan, an Asset Inventory, and a completed

Security Self-Assessment. Additionaly, security policies must be clearly defined. A sample self-assessment can be found in Appendix D. Some agencies may have different requirements for a Level 1 and you should of course always follow the existing agency guidelines.

Information systems that typically may require a Level 1 C&A are systems that:

- Publish general public information
- Deliver courseware and training programs
- Publish information on product information
- Publish information on workplace policies
- Publish forms, maps, or charts that are nonsensitive

Level 2

A Level 2 C&A requires a basic review and analysis of the security of the information system. A Level 2 C&A requires everything included in a Level 1, plus a full set of C&A documents, and a *Security Test & Evaluation (ST&E)*, (but not test results). Security policies must be clearly defined and implemented. If an agency requires something different than what I recommend here, you should defer to the agency recommendations.

Information systems that typically may require a Level 2 C&A are information systems that:

- Are used for contracts, proposals, and legal proceedings
- Are used for Capital budget applications
- Serve office applications
- Operate benefits management applications
- Manage supply chain management transactions

Level 3

A Level 3 C&A requires a detailed review and analysis of the security of the information system. A Level 3 C&A requires everything that is required in a

Level 1 and 2 C&A, plus a network vulnerability scan, as well as tests that show that have been correctly implemented security policies. Some agencies may have different requirements for a Level 3 and you should always use the agency guidelines and follow the recommendations in their handbook.

Information systems that typically may require a Level 3 C&A are information systems that:

- Monitor information or physical security

- Manage operations of financial transactions

- Operate payroll management applications

- Transmit intelligence information

- Communicate information about dangerous substances

Level 4

A Level 4 C&A requires an extensive review and analysis of the security of the information system. All items required for Levels 1, 2, and 3 are required for a Level 4, plus a penetration test, and confirmation that all security tests were passed. Some agencies may have different requirements for a Level 4 and just as with a Level 1, 2, or 3, you should always defer to the agency guidance.

Information systems that typically may require a Level 4 C&A are information systems that:

- Operate and monitor nuclear power plants

- Make decisions on where to drop a bomb

- Monitor a patient during surgery

- Operate and monitor a large dam

- Manage and operate mass transportation facilities

- Monitor water quality and safety of public drinking water

- Manage top secret Department of Defense projects

- Prevent terrorist attacks

- Perform large monetary transactions

Importance of Determining the C&A Level

Determining the level of the Certification Package up front is one of the most often-overlooked parts of C&A. There are numerous organizations that don't perform this step until the entire Certification Package has been developed, which is the absolute wrong way to go about this. One of the reasons for determining the level up front is because the level determines what types of information need to be included in the Certification Package. The Certification Package is evidence that security risks have been understood and mitigated properly. The higher level of Certification that one seeks, the more evidence is required. For example, network vulnerability scanning is required for Level 3 Certification, but not for Level 2. If you are seeking Level 3 Certification, you need to complete a network vulnerability scan and address the resulting risks identified and include this information as part of the Certification Package.

Don't Make This Mistake

The biggest mistake you can make in categorizing the Confidentiality, Integrity, and Availability of your data is to over-classify it. Agencies do this all the time, thinking that by over-classifying the data, the information system owners are protecting themselves. Classifying data one way or another does not increase the security of it. It is the controls that you apply to the data that increase its security and preserve Confidentiality, Integrity, and Availability.

Most information system owners and systems administrators seem to think that their data's importance is greater than the importance it actually holds in real life. Upon first consideration, most people will assume that their data is mission critical. It seems that if information system owners claim that their data is mission critical, they feel that they are covering themselves in the event that something goes awry—they told everyone it was mission critical so if an incident occurs it is not their fault. However, overstatement of data classification could actually lead to unforeseen investigations, and disciplinary action for the information system owner, if a security incident really does occur. For example, if data should be protected at the highest Confidentiality, Integrity, and Availability levels, then that means that the most stringent security controls should be applied to it. If a security incident occurs for data that was characterized by the highest Confidentiality, Integrity, and Availability ratings, and it is discovered that the security controls that were put in place were minimal, there could be egregious consequences in an investigation or audit. Auditors may wonder why more stringent security controls were not applied, or they may wonder why the data was characterized to be of such high importance if that is not the case after all.

Furthermore, C&A is an expensive process and the expense goes up as the C&A level goes up. If you do not need to C&A your information system at Level 3, then don't. Obtaining a Level 3 C&A will cost more, and take longer, than a Level 2 C&A. It will also be harder to obtain. You want your C&A level to be just right—not too high and not too low—which is why you need to understand how to figure out what level to select. The information owner selects the level, and then gets approval on the recommended level from the authorizing official. The auditors will evaluate your package at whatever level you submit it for. They do not tell you what level to select. However, if you select the wrong level, and your documentation is not consistent with the level selected, they may have questions you'll have to answer, which could hold up your Accreditation.

Under-classifying data should also be avoided. Data that is not used to make critical decisions, and would have little impact if it were unavailable for a period of time, should not require expensive and elaborate security systems. C&A auditors typically are not concerned with OMB-300 budget audits; however in the last year or so, many of GAO's OMB-300 budget auditors have started asking to see C&A documentation in order to understand if large expenditures of monies on elaborate security implementations were indeed necessary. (OMB-300 audits are audits performed to verify if government funds were spent appropriately.)

Inconsistencies in your data classification and your security controls raise the brows of auditors. For example, an auditor may wonder, if your data has such low requirements for Confidentiality and Availability, why have you implemented such grandiose encryption and PKI requirements? Or if your data has such high requirements for Availability, why haven't you implemented highly available, fault-tolerant RAID systems? If your data has low Confidentiality, Availability, and Integrity requirements, why did you perform an exhaustive and expensive network vulnerability scan and penetration test? You need to be able to justify everything to an auditor and the best way to do that is to make sure that your decisions and statements are consistent with your processes.

Criteria to Use for Determining the Levels

In order to determine the level at which your information should be certified and accredited, there are seven criteria you should take into consideration:

- Confidentiality
- Integrity
- Availability
- Interconnection State
- Processing State
- Complexity State
- Mission Criticality

I am going to show you how to assign risk and impact levels to these characteristics in order to determine what level at which to C&A your information system. Some C&A programs may opt to use more than seven criteria and may vary their risk ratings, however all C&A level determinations should take a similar approach.

Confidentiality, Integrity, and Availability

Preserving the Confidentiality, Integrity, and Availability of your information systems is one of the key objectives of FISMA. FIPS 199 helps you understand how to categorize the Confidentiality, Integrity, and Availability of your information systems so you can take that information and determine a C&A level. Another document that can help you understand how to properly categorize Confidentiality, Integrity, and Availability is *Special Publication 800-60*

(SP 800-60), V2.0, Volumes 1 and 2: Guide for Mapping Types of Information Systems to Security Categories, June 2004, by NIST, available at http://csrc.nist.gov/publications/nistpubs/800-60/SP800-60V1-final.pdf.

SP 800-60 describes many different information types and presents recommendations (Low, Moderate, High) for each of their Confidentiality, Integrity, and Availability sensitivities. The different information types listed are spread over 15 Operational Areas and include both Services Delivery Support Information and Government Resource Management Information. If you are unsure of how to categorize Confidentiality, Integrity, or Availability for the different information types, I encourage you to review this well-thought-out guide.

Confidentiality

According to FIPS 199, Confidentiality is a legal term defined as:

> …preserving authorized restrictions on access and disclosure, including means for protecting personal privacy and proprietary information…

Legal terms aside, Confidentiality means that people who are not supposed to see sensitive data don't end up seeing it. Confidentiality can be breached in numerous ways, including shoulder surfing, capturing network packets with a protocol analyzer (sometimes referred to as "sniffing"), capturing keystrokes with a keystroke logger, social engineering, or dumpster diving. Confidentiality can also be breached completely accidentally, for example, if systems administrators accidentally configure an application such that people who are not supposed to see the data have login access to it.

Confidentiality typically is preserved through use of the following techniques:

- Encryption
- Roles-based access control (RBAC)
- Rules-based access controls
- Classifying data appropriately
- Proper configuration management

- Training end-users and systems administrators

Determining the Confidentiality Level

In determining the proper level at which to certify and accredit your information system, you need to determine what impact a breach of Confidentiality of the data would have on your organization. If the impact of disclosure would be of little consequence, the rating of Low should be selected. If the impact of disclosure to the wrong individuals would be disastrous, the rating of High should be selected. If the impact of adverse disclosure would be somewhere between Low and High, the rating of Moderate should be selected.

For example, data that is to be made publicly available on the Web would have a Low Confidentiality rating. Data that should be viewed by only a very small group of people, where disclosure to the unauthorized viewers would have critical consequences, would require a High degree of Confidentiality. Data that should be viewed by an intermediate amount of users, that would have a moderate adverse effect if it were disclosed to the wrong individuals, would have a Moderate Confidentiality rating.

When considering impact of disclosure, it helps if the data within your organization has a classification scheme. If it does, you can create numerical weights based on the data classification scheme that are somewhat more specific than the assignments of High, Medium, or Low. Table 7.1 offers a recommended approach to assigning Confidentiality levels according to data classification.

Table 7.1 Confidentiality Levels Based on Data Classification

Data Classification	Weight	Impact of Disclosure
Unclassified	1	Low
Sensitive But Unclassified (SBU)	2	Low
Confidential	3	Moderate
Secret	5	Moderate
Top Secret	6	High
Compartmented / Special Access	8	High

Integrity

Like Confidentiality, Integrity is also a legal term defined by FIPS 199 and reads as follows:

> ...means guarding against improper information modification or destruction, and includes ensuring information nonrepudiation and authenticity...

Preserving the Integrity of the data ensures that the information is reliable and has not been altered either by unauthorized users, or processes gone awry. After all, if data is not accurate, it is of little use and in fact can be detrimental if it is being used to make decisions where lives are at stake. Attackers may attempt to purposely alter data, but systems administration errors and sloppy programming can also create data that contains the wrong information. If input variables in programs are not checked for memory bounds, buffer overflows can occur, which have the potential to alter good data.

Integrity often is preserved through the same techniques you use to preserve Confidentiality. However, additional techniques that help ensure that Integrity of data is left in tact are:

- Perimeter network protection mechanisms
- Host-based intrusion prevention systems
- Network-based intrusion detection systems
- Protection against viruses and other malware
- Physical security of the information systems
- Adherence to secure coding principles
- Backups and off-site storage
- Contingency management planning

Determining the Integrity Level

Similar to determining the Confidentiality level, when you determine the Integrity level, you need to determine what impact a loss of data Integrity would have on your organization. If the impact of unauthorizzed data modification would be of little consequence, select the Low rating. If the impact of unauthorized data modification would be disastrous, select the High rating. If the impact of adverse and unauthorized data modification would be somewhere between Low and High, you should select Moderate.

Remember, loss of Integrity means that the data has been modified through unauthorized channels, either on purpose or by accident. If it is a company calendaring application that has its Integrity breached, this will not have anywhere near the same consequences as if it were a patient's medical record in a Veteran's Hospital. A breach of Integrity on a patient's medical record could have life or death consequences and a serious adverse affect.

Integrity levels should be assigned based on a scale that is indicative of risk to Integrity loss. Table 7.2 offers a recommended approach to assigning Integrity levels according to risk associated with data Integrity compromises.

Table 7.2 Integrity Levels, Weights, and Impact of Loss

Level of Integrity Required	Weight	Impact of Loss
Not Applicable	0	Low
Approximate	3	Moderate
Exact	6	High

Availability

FIPS 199 stipulates the legal definition of Availability to be:

> …means ensuring timely and reliable access to and use of information.

Not all data have the same requirements for Availability. Data that has an impact on human lives needs to have its Availability ensured at higher levels than data that is intended for trivial purposes (e.g., the cafeteria lunch menu). Data that has high Availability requirements needs more elaborate safeguards and controls to ensure that Availability is not compromised. Data that has low Availability requirements may need no safeguards or controls.

Determining the Availability Level

In determining Availability, you need to understand how urgent it is (or not), that the data exists in its everyday state. What would happen if the data were to become unavailable for a period of time? Would the unavailability of the data prevent critical decisions to be made? Would human lives become at stake? Would anyone even notice or care? Some C&A experts claim that risks to Availability should be concerned only with security, and not performance. However, security vulnerabilities often are exploited through attacks on performance, and therefore, I believe that taking performance into consideration is important. If a denial of service attack prevents data from becoming available due to degradation in system performance, it would be prudent to consider the performance impact caused by the attack on security. Table 7.3 offers an approach to assigning a numerical weight to the impact of a loss on Availability.

Table 7.3 Availability Requirements, Weights, and Impact of Loss

Level of Availability Required	Weight	Impact of Loss
When Time Permits	1	Low
Soon	2	Moderate
As Soon As Possible (ASAP)	4	Moderate
Permanent	7	High

How to Categorize Multiple Data Sets

If you are planning to certify and accredit multiple applications together, or applications for multiple lines of business or multiple operational areas, you will need to do some additional work to figure out your Confidentiality, Integrity, and Availability scores. However, it is much more efficient to C&A multiple applications together, and multiple lines of business together, than to develop two entirely separate C&A packages.

First you figure out the Confidentiality, Integrity, and Availability qualitative ratings individually for each application, line of business, or operational area. Once you have done that, you put the final scores for each of the individual areas into a summary table. The different individual areas may have different scores for Confidentiality, Integrity, and Availability. However, your C&A package needs to be geared toward one level. To obtain the final Confidentiality, Integrity, and Availability rating, you will want to select the highest rating in all categories and use that one. For example, if you have three lines of business, and they have Confidentiality ratings of High, Moderate, and Low, you will select High for your final Confidentiality rating. Table 7.4 shows a sample table of multiple Confidentiality, Integrity, and Availability data sets.

Table 7.4 Figuring Multiple Confidentiality, Integrity, and Availability Data Sets

Operational Area	Business Line	Information Type	Confidentiality	Integrity	Availability
Public Relations	Dept. 55	Public Comments	Low	Low	Low
Contracts	Dept. 09	Proposals	Moderate	Low	Low
IT	Dept. 22	Security Management	High	Moderate	Moderate
Highest Rating			High	Moderate	Moderate

Figuring out Confidentiality, Integrity, and Availability using the approach I have just described is the ideal way to figure Confidentiality, Integrity, and Availability scores if you have different departments that share the same server. You certainly will not want to put together three different Certification Packages for the same server. Due to the large amount of time and resources it takes to put together a Certification Package, you want to cover as many information technology assets in one package as you can.

Impact Levels and System Criticality

FIPS 199 summarizes the characterization of Confidentiality, Integrity, and Availability according to adverse impact in the event of a security incident. Low, Moderate, or High impacts are described by FIPS 199 as indicated in Table 7.5. The levels of impact described in Table 7.5 are consistent with the data classification levels for Confidentiality, Integrity, and Availability that we have already discussed.

Table 7.5 Summary of FIPS 199 Levels of Impact

Level of Impact	Description from FIPS 199
Low	The potential impact is **low** if the loss of Confidentiality, Integrity, or Availability could be expected to have a limited adverse effect on organizational operations, organizational assets, or individuals.
Moderate	The potential impact is **moderate** if the loss of Confidentiality, Integrity, or Availability could be expected to have a serious adverse effect on organizational operations, organizational assets, or individuals.
High	The potential impact is **high** if the loss of Confidentiality, Integrity, or Availability could be expected to have a severe or catastrophic adverse effect on organizational operations, organizational assets, or individuals.

What is important in following these guidelines is being able to justify the rationale behind selecting the category of Low, Moderate, or High for your information system. Questions that you will want to ask the in-house subject matter experts to help you determine the Confidentiality, Integrity, and Availability impact levels are:

- Do these information systems perform operations that put human lives at stake?

- Is the data read-only data?

- Does the data constitute executable programs?

- Who are the stakeholders of the data?

- If the data disappeared completely and forever what would be the impact?

- If the data disappeared for one hour what would be the impact?

- If the data disappeared for one day what would be the impact?

- Does the information system connect to any other systems or networks?

The final Confidentiality, Integrity, and Availability rating that you calculate to summarize all the systems in your C&A package is called the Security Profile (see Table 7.6).

Table 7.6 Example of Security Profile

System Criticality	Low, Moderate, or High
Confidentiality	Moderate
Integrity	Low
Availability	Moderate

System Attribute Characteristics

Aside from Confidentiality, Integrity, and Availability, there are four other system attributes that should be taken into consideration to determine your C&A level. Those four attributes are known as the Interconnection State, the Processing State, the Complexity State, and Mission Criticality. By assigning numerical risk levels to these attributes and tallying up the totals, you can refine your security characteristics and justify your C&A level.

Interconnection State (Interfacing Mode)

The interconnection state often is referred to as the *interfacing mode* in agency documents, and refers to the connections the information system has to other networks, devices, databases, and systems. I prefer the terminology "interconnection state" because it is more descriptive and less cryptic than *interfacing mode*. Many security experts do not know what *interfacing mode* means without doing further research. If you see *interfacing mode* in C&A publications put out by federal agencies, what the terminology refers to is the state of the interconnections of the different network components, and you should think of this as the same thing as the interconnection state.

To understand what the interconnection state is, let's take into consideration a security incident. If a security incident occurred, would the incident be contained within the single information system or would it perpetrate out to other systems? In understanding the interconnection state, you need to determine if risks can be contained. To determine if the risks can be contained, you need to know if the interconnection of network devices are nonexistent, passive, or active. A nonexistent interconnection state would indicate no physical or logical connections. A passive interconnection state would indicate logical or physical connections that are tightly controlled. For example, a system may be set up to receive only certain types of data on certain ports. An active interconnection state would indicate a direct, and relatively open, interaction with other systems, data structures, and networks.

Clearly there is more risk associated with an active interconnection state, less risk with a passive interconnection state, and no risk with a nonexistent interconnection state. Although some C&A programs may assign other numerical weights to these interconnection states, I recommend that the weights that appear in Table 7.7 be used.

Table 7.7 Interconnection Risk Weights

Interconnection State	Risk Level	Weight
Nonexistent	Low	0
Passive	Moderate	2
Active	High	6

Access State (Processing Mode)

The access state of your information system refers to the complexity by which data is accessed, transmitted, and stored. The access state often is referred to as the *processing mode* in agency C&A documents. However, I believe that *processing mode* is misleading because what we are really trying to determine is the level of user access. To understand the access state, take into consideration the level of approvals necessary to access the data. How many technical security controls and configuration parameters are implemented and manipulated in order to grant access? You need to determine the number of different levels of user privileges and the complexity of configuring and implementing those access states. Table 7.8 offers guidelines for assigning weights to the access state.

Table 7.8 Access State Weights

Level of Access	Weight
All Users	1
Few Users	3
Need to Know Only	5
Select Users	6

Accountability State (Attribution Mode)

Accountability state refers to how accountable you need your information system to be. This information state often is referred to in agency C&A documents as the *attribution mode*. However, the terminology *attribution mode* is again cryptic—no one knows what it means and it's time to replace it with more descriptive terminology. The terminology "accountability state" is less confusing. To understand accountability state, you need to take into consideration the complexity of accountability required to identify, validate, audit, and monitor system entities and configurations. Does the system undergoing C&A require simple or complex audit mechanisms? Are intrusion detection or intrusion prevention systems required? Do security events need to be correlated with a security information management (SIM) console? How many places should data be stored in? How many monitoring systems do you need? Do you need monitoring systems in multiple geographic locations? To determine the complexity state, it is worth considering who the stakeholders are for the data. Is it the president of the United States? Or are the stakeholders data entry clerks? Find out who the data stakeholders are and what they are using the data for. You may need to interview the stakeholders, the developers, and the information system owner in order to find out what they are using the data for.

To determine the complexity of the accountability required by the information system, I have set up a scale, depicted in Table 7.9. Make a qualitative decision based on information that you obtain from the stakeholders, the information system owner, and the developers.

Table 7.9 Levels of Accountability Weights

Level of Accountability	Weight
None	0
Rudimentary	1
Comprehensive	3
Sophisticated	6

Mission Criticality

One way of gauging the importance of an information system is to understand how critical that particular information system is to your business. How reliant is your business on the information system that is up for C&A? There are four categories of reliance that you should try to align your information system with:

- No reliance
- Cursory reliance
- Partial reliance
- Complete reliance

The information system owner should have a good idea of the mission criticality of the information system that is up for C&A. I caution against interviewing the end users of the information system on mission criticality because they often give exaggerated viewpoints on mission criticality. You should verify the information system owner's viewpoint with the in-house developers and subject matter experts. Table 7.10 offers recommendations on how to weight mission criticality.

Table 7.10 Mission Criticality Weights

Mission Criticality	Weight
None	0
Cursory	1
Partial	3
Complete	7

Determining Level of Certification

The way to determine the C&A level is to assign scores to the seven information system attributes that you have taken into consideration and then add them up. Based on the weights in the preceding sections, the scale that I recommend for determining your C&A Level is:

- Level 1: < 16
- Level 2: 12–32
- Level 3: 24–44
- Level 4: 38–50

Table 7.11 presents a sample summary that illustrates how weights are added up.

Table 7.11 Sample C&A Level Determination

Characteristic	Possible Weights	Recommended Weight
Interconnection State	0=Nonexistent 2=Passive 6=Active	2
Access State	1=All Users 3=Few Users 5=Need to Know Only 6=Select Users	2
Accountability State	0=None 1=Rudimentary 3=Comprehensive 6=Sophisticated	3
Mission Criticality	0=None 1=Cursory 3=Partial 7=Complete	3
Availability	1=When Time Permits 2=Soon 4=ASAP 7=Permanent	2

Continued

Table 7.11 continued Sample C&A Level Determination

Characteristic	Possible Weights	Recommended Weight
Integrity	0=Not Applicable 3=Approximate 6=Exact	3
Confidentiality	1=Unclassified 2=Sensitive But Unclassified (SBU) 3=Confidential 5=Secret 6=Top Secret 8=Compartmented / Special Access	5
Total	Level 1: <16 Level 2: 12–32 Level 3: 24–44 Level 4: 38–50	20

From Table 7.11, you could conclude that the recommended C&A Level is Level 2.

Note that there is a discretionary area where the weighting overlaps. The discretionary overlap has been set up by design in case there are unusual circumstances where you may need to make a professional judgment call. If the total weighting falls into a discretionary area, you really have a choice of which level to select. Whichever level you select, if the weighting falls into a discretionary area, you should also include a justification and description of why you selected the higher or lower of the two levels.

Template for Levels of Determination

I have developed a structure and framework that you can use as a template for authoring a *C&A Levels of Determination* document. You may need to modify certain sections of this to meet the unique requirements of your agency or organization.

Title

Recommendations by <name of organization authoring this document> for the Security Profile and Certification and Accreditation Level of <name of information system>

<date>

Introduction

Federal and <Agency Name> policies require two separate but parallel and interrelated security determinations for every <Agency Name> information system. An information system shall be construed as either a general support system, or an application.

Federal policy mandates that every federal information system be assigned a "Security Profile," which assesses three aspects of its operations: Confidentiality, Integrity, and Availability. Each of these three aspects is to be categorized as being of Low, Moderate, or High sensitivity. The documents that provide guidance for this categorization are the following.

- The Federal Information Processing Publications Standard (FIPS) 199, *Standards for Security Categorization of Federal Information and Information Systems,* December 2003, mandates the determination of the Security Profile for each Federal IS.

- The National Institute of Standards and Technology (NIST) Special Publication (SP) 800-60, *Guide for Mapping Types of Information Systems to Security Categories, Volumes I and II,* assists in the application of FIPS 199 by providing guidance based on the degree of impact resulting from the loss or misuse of an IS or its data.

The *<Agency Name> Certification and Accreditation Program Handbook, <publication date>* requires that each <Agency Name> information system be assigned a "Certification and Accreditation (C&A) Level." The process for determining the C&A Level is described on pages <page numbers> of the *Handbook.* Table 7.12 lists the four possible C&A Levels.

Table 7.12 Certification and Accreditation Levels

Certification Levels	Description
Level 1	Minimal Review
Level 2	Basic Review and Analysis
Level 3	Detailed Review and Analysis
Level 4	Extensive Review and Analysis

<Agency Name> has tasked <name of organization authoring this document> to apply this guidance to <name of information system> to make recommendations for its Security Profile and C&A Level, and to document the analysis and rationale for the recommendations they make.

<Name of organization authoring this document> conducted interviews with <information system name> management and subject matter experts (SME) during <time period of interviews>. Specifically, <name of organization or people completing this document> met with <person1> on <date> and with <person2> and <person3> on <date>. All results stated in this memorandum are the result of these interviews.

Based upon information presented by the <information system name> management and SMEs, and using the earlier guidance, <name of organization authoring this document> recommends that the Security Profile for the <name of information system> be established as:

- Confidentiality   <Low, Moderate, High, or Not Applicable>
- Integrity   <Low, Moderate, High, or Not Applicable>
- Availability   <Low, Moderate, High, or Not Applicable>
- Overall System   <Low, Moderate, High, or Not Applicable>

Based upon its assessment of the characteristics of the <name of information system> and using the earlier guidance, <name of organization authoring this document> recommends that the <name of information system> be certified and accredited at Level <number>.

Rationale for the Security Level Recommendation

FIPS 199, *Standards for Security Categorization of Federal Information and Information Systems,* December 2003, requires that a new federal information system be categorized in three aspects of its operations: Confidentiality, Integrity, and Availability. Each aspect is to be categorized as having Low, Moderate, or High sensitivity. These three determinations are referred to collectively as the information system's Security Profile.

NIST SP 800-60, *Guide for Mapping Types of Information Systems to Security Categories, Volumes I and II,* assists in the application of FIPS 199 by providing guidance based on the degree of impact that would result from the loss or misuse of an information system or its data.

<Name of organization authoring this document> conducted interviews with <information system name> representatives <names of subject matter experts> in <date range>. These interviews established that, of the <number> Information Types that were identified, only <number> are applicable to <name of information system>: <names of Information Types>.

Subject matter expert, <name of person>, emphasized that < list any rationale that was emphasized>. As a result, <name of organization authoring this document> recommends that the Information Type <name of Information Type> for Operational Area <name of Operational Area> be included in all systems analyses. In the case of <name of information system> this recommendation applies to <Confidentiality, Integrity, Availability> and not to <Confidentiality, Integrity, Availability>. <Brief description on why the recommendation is applicable to as described to Confidentiality, Integrity, and Availability.>

The Confidentiality, Integrity, and Availability summary analysis of the multiple data sets taken into consideration in this C&A package is presented in Table 7.13.

Table 7.13 Data Sets and Security Profile Recommendations That Are Applicable to <name of information system>, Showing Also the <agency name> Business Lines from the <agency name> System Security Categorization Guide

Operational Area	Business Line	Information Type	Confidentiality	Integrity	Availability
<name>	<name>	<type>	<High, Moderate, Low, or N.A.>	<High, Moderate, Low, or N.A.>	<High, Moderate, Low, or N.A.>
<name>	<name>	<type>	<High, Moderate, Low, or N.A.>	<High, Moderate, Low, or N.A.>	<High, Moderate, Low, or N.A.>
<name>	<name>	<type>	<High, Moderate, Low, or N.A.>	<High, Moderate, Low, or N.A.>	<High, Moderate, Low, or N.A.>
Highest Rating			<High, Moderate, Low, or N.A.>	<High, Moderate, Low, or N.A.>	<High, Moderate, Low, or N.A.>

(N.A. = Not Applicable)

Based upon this analysis and using the earlier guidance, <name of organization authoring this document> recommends that the final Security Profile for the <name of information system> be established as:

- Confidentiality   <Low, Moderate, High, or Not Applicable>
- Integrity   <Low, Moderate, High, or Not Applicable>
- Availability   <Low, Moderate, High, or Not Applicable>
- Overall System   <Low, Moderate, High, or Not Applicable>

Process and Rationale for the C&A Level Recommendation

The *<Agency Name> Certification and Accreditation Program Handbook, <publication date>* pages <numbers> presents the process for determining the C&A Level for <Agency Name> information systems. This process involves assessing the information system in seven distinct characteristics. Each characteristic is assessed at one of a specified set of possible weights; the C&A Level is then determined by the total of the accumulated weights. Table 7.14 summarizes this process, indicating the seven information system characteristics, the set of possible weights for each, and the weights recommended by <name of organization authoring this document>.

Table 7.14 <Agency Name> C&A Level Weighting Process

Characteristic	Possible Weights	Recommended Weight
Interconnection State	0=Nonexistent 2=Passive 6=Active	<number>
Access State	1=All Users 3=Few Users 5=Need to Know Only 6=Select Users	<number>
Accountability State	0=None 1=Rudimentary 3=Comprehensive 6=Sophisticated	<number>
Mission Criticality	0=None 1=Cursory 3=Partial 7=Complete	<number>
Availability	1=When Time Permits 2=Soon 4=ASAP 7=Permanent	<number>

Continued

www.syngress.com

Table 7.14 continued <Agency Name> C&A Level Weighting Process

Characteristic	Possible Weights	Recommended Weight
Integrity	0=Not Applicable 3=Approximate 6=Exact	<number>
Confidentiality	1=Unclassified 2=Sensitive But Unclassified (SBU) 3=Confidential 5=Secret 6=Top Secret 8=Compartmented / Special Access	<number>
Total	Level 1: <16 Level 2: 12–32 Level 3: 24–44 Level 4: 38–50 <total number>	

The right column of Table 7.14 lists the characteristic weights that <name of organization authoring this document> recommends for the <name of information system>. As a rationale for these recommendations, each of the seven characteristics is considered individually.

- **Interconnection State**. <name of information system> <interconnects, doesn't interconnect> closely with other information systems. Thus, the <nonexistent, passive, or active> weight is appropriate.

- **Access State**. <name of information system> users will be restricted to processing only <data processing restrictions>. They will be further restricted in their operations by <roles, policies, rules> assigned to them by <administrative group>. There <is a, is no> requirement for mandatory access controls or data labeling, so the <highest, lowest> weight <would be, would not be> excessive. Thus, the <*All Users, Few Users, Need to Know Only, Select Users*> *Access State* weight is appropriate.

- **Accountability State**. <name of information system> <requires, doesn't require> detailed recording of certain types of processing. <Most, Some, Few> of these needs are satisfied by <process name> mechanisms that are already an inherent feature of the <name of information system>. Specific security auditing is needed for capturing <event type, e.g., authentication, monitoring> security-relevant events such as <example>. Thus the *<None, Rudimentary, Comprehensive, Sophisticated>* weight is appropriate.

- **Mission Criticality**. In interviews conducted by <name of organization authoring this document>, <names of subject matter experts> stated that the <name of information system> <is, is not> officially deemed as either essential or critical to the missions of <information system owner department name>. Since the <name of information system> <is, is not> essential to the mission of <information system owner department name> the *<None, Cursory, Partial, Complete>* weight is appropriate.

- **Availability**. The <user group> are required to exchange information with the <user group> in a <timely, periodic, infrequent> manner and the <name of information system> is an integral part of the reporting cycle. <Information system owner department name> and the <user group> have agreed, however, that it is sufficient to keep these systems available on a <high priority, best effort, infrequent> basis, and provide backups for certain critical elements and sites such as <name of critical elements> and <name of critical sites>. The *<When Time Permits, Soon, ASAP, Permanent>* weight is therefore appropriate for characterizing Availability.

- **Integrity**. The data contained in the <name of information system> is supplied by <source of data> and is monitored <constantly, periodically, never> by both <responsible party> in the normal course of their missions. Furthermore, the <name of information system> data is routinely subject to <detailed and extensive, comprehensive and periodic, cursory and infrequent> auditing to detect accidental or malicious manipulation. The Integrity characteristic can thus be assessed as *<Not Applicable, Approximate, Exact>*.

- **Confidentiality**. <name of information system> data <is, is not> classified and is, in essence, <publicly, not publicly> available. Therefore, the weight of <*Unclassified, Sensitive But Unclassified, Confidential, Secret, Top Secret, Compartmented / Special Access*> is appropriate.

Using this process and recommended weights, the <information system> has a total accumulated weight of <number> points. This places it into Level <number>.

Based on these assessments, <name of organization authoring this document> recommends that the <name of information system> be Certified and Accredited at Level <number>. <If you decide to assign a level that is discretionary, e.g., Level 30, put the justification for your decision here.>

The Explanatory Memo

Once a *C&A Level of Determination Recommendation* has been developed, the information owner needs to submit a memo to the authorizing official that summarizes and supports the *C&A Level of Determination Recommendation*. The ISSO should review the memo before the information system owner signs it and submits it. The authoring official is supposed to acknowledge the letter with a signature and then return it to the information system owner. If the authorizing official will not accept the recommended C&A level, then the *Levels of Determination* will need to be revised until it has been found to be acceptable. The authorizing official should respond back to the information system owner during the initial phase of the C&A project so that the folks preparing the Certification Package will know at which level the package should be prepared. Although the memo does not have to be in any particular format, I have provided a template to help you understand what to include.

Template for Explanatory Memo

Memorandum

Date: \<insert date>
To: \<name of Authorizing Official>
\<Title of Authorizing Official>
                         \<bureau, agency, or organization name>

From: \<name of information system owner>
                         \<title of information system owner>
                         \<bureau, agency, or organization name>
Subject: Security Categorization and Certification Level of \<name of
                         information system>

This memorandum is to advise you on the security categorization of \<name of information system> and to obtain your approval on the appropriate certification level. The *\<Agency Name> Certification and Accreditation Program Handbook, \<publication date>* requires that each \<Agency Name> Information System (IS) must be assigned a certification level. This certification level, in turn, is determined by assessing seven characteristics of the IS and assigning a weight (point) to each one; the total points determine the certification level (although the range of levels overlap somewhat). This process is described in detail on page \<page number> of the *Handbook*.

An assessment was conducted by \<name of organization who authored *C&A Levels of Determination* document> to determine a recommended certification level for \<name of information system>. Based upon the assessment of the seven characteristics of \<name of information system> (Interconnection Mode, Access State, Accountability State, Mission Criticality, Availability, Integrity, and Confidentiality) and the resulting total weight of \<0–50> points, the recommended certification level for \<name of information system> is Level \<1,2,3, or 4>. The weights are in accordance with the definitions documented in \<Agency Name>'s most current *Certification and Accreditation Program Handbook, \<publication date>*. \<If the weights added up to a discretionary level, e.g., Level 30, put the justification for selecting the recommended level here and indicate that the total weight and level are in fact discretionary.>

In conducting this assessment, Federal Information Processing Standards Publication 199, *Standards for Security Categorization of Federal Information and Information Systems*, and National Institute of Standards and Technology (NIST) and *Special Publication 800-60 V2.0, Volumes 1 and 2: Guide for Mapping Types of Information Systems to Security Categories,* June 2004, NIST have been taken into consideration. With this in mind, I am recommending that <name of information system> be certified and accredited for operation at Level <1,2,3, or 4>.

APPROVED:_____   DATE: _____

<name of information owner>, <title of information owner>

<bureau, agency, or organization name>

DISAPPROVED: _____   DATE: _____

Attachment <attach the *C&A Level of Determination* document>

Summary

Determining the certification level for the system for which you are developing a C&A package can be the step that is most often performed incorrectly. System owners frequently feel that if they simply overclassify the sensitivity of the system that they are responsible for, thereby holding it to more stringent standards of security, they will ensure that it is secured properly. However, implementing unnecessary security controls and performing a Level 3 C&A on a system that only needs a Level 2 C&A waste time and money. This does not make good business sense.

Therefore, it is your job to make sure you fully understand the certification levels and the requirements for each. You must also have a good understanding of the confidentiality, integrity, and availability security objectives; be able to evaluate the sensitivity of each with regards to a particular system; and to elicit accurate and thorough information from the system owner on which this evaluation will be based.

Once you gather the information and make the determination about the certification level to be used, you must codify this in a formal document that will be included in the final C&A package. An example of the explanatory memo has been provided, but you should see if a template is already in use at your agency. Use this to get final signed approval of the certification level you calculated for the information system. Once you have this in writing from the information owner, you have a clear picture of the level of effort required throughout the rest of the C&A task. You can reference the requirements for how much ST&E must be performed and what documents are included in the final package. At this point, you can proceed with the rest of the C&A task.

## Chapter 8

Performing and Preparing the Self-Assessment

"True genius resides in the capacity for evaluation of uncertain, hazardous, and conflicting information."

—Winston Churchill

Topics in this chapter:

- Objectives

- Designing the Survey

- Questions for Self-Assessment Survey

Introduction

Most agencies require a security self-assessment only in the off years when C&A packages are not required for submission. Performing a security self-assessment is a process by which an agency or organization determines the current security posture of their information systems and infrastructure. A self-assessment helps give you a level of assurance as to how well the management, operational, and technical security controls are working. One of the best guides in how to perform a security self-assessment is *Special Publication 800-26, Security Self-Assessment Guide for Information Technology Systems*, November 2001, by the National Institute of Standards.

A security self-assessment is a survey-based audit that is essentially a long list of questions. The survey should be designed to be consistent with the requirements set forth in the *Federal Information System Controls Audit Manual* (FISCAM), January 1999. GAO auditors and agency inspector generals use FISCAM when reviewing the agency security program including the C&A program. FISCAM is available on the GOA Web site at the following URL: www.gao.gov/special.pubs/ai12.19.6.pdf.

FISCAM includes a significant amount of information on how to audit financial systems. Though following FISCAM guidelines for financial systems is certainly meritorious, for C&A we are more concerned with information technology than with financial statements. However, as far as audits go, many of the same principles used for financial audits apply also to information technology audits and in that regard, the FISCAM guidance is certainly applicable.

Special Publication 800-26 is a 95-page document, and *FISCAM* is a 298-page document. I mention the length of pages to give you an idea of how much there is to actually know about self-assessments. I don't plan on trying to recreate either of these well-written documents here. My objective is to give you a condensed version that offers practical applicability.

Objectives

A self-assessment is a high-level, 30,000 foot-up type of security audit. The survey should be designed to cover a broad range of requirements that are related to the management, technical, and operational controls of the information system. It's often the case that a particular survey question could fall into more than one of these three categories. Don't spend a long time deliberating which category each question should go in. Pick whatever category seems appropriate for the particular information systems that are up for C&A and simply put the survey question there. It's more important simply to ask the right questions and discover the honest answers, than to figure out which category of the survey the question should go in.

Designing the Survey

Before you start to design a self-assessment survey, check to see if your agency has a self-assessment template that already exists that they would like you to use. Since you're probably under a deadline, don't recreate a brand-new self-assessment survey if a pretty good one already exists at your agency. Also, it may be against the agency security policies to use a survey that is different than the one they provide. If your agency does not have a self-assessment survey template, you will need to develop one before you can answer the questions. Special Publication 800–26 contains a fairly comprehensive sample survey and it's a great starting point for developing one for your Certification Package. You'll likely want to modify the survey you find in Special Publication 800–26 to make it more apropos to the objectives of your agency and information system.

Special Publication 800–26 recommends that your survey be designed for five levels of compliance. However, since almost every C&A program includes four levels of compliance, from a practical standpoint, it makes more sense to build four levels of compliance into your survey. The recommendation for five levels of compliance originated from a document published on November 28, 2000 known as the *Federal Information Technology Security Assessment Framework (FITSAF)*.[1] Since most C&A programs have only four levels of compliance, it is possible that if the FITSAF had been published after FISMA was passed, it may have included only four levels of compliance.

Levels of Compliance

To keep things simple, I suggest referring to the levels of compliance on your survey simply as L1, L2, L3, and L4. These levels of compliance should be consistent with the C&A levels that I previously described in Chapter 6. We refer to each question of the survey simply as a *control*. The compliance levels are simply boxes to check off next to the survey question, and should be interpreted as follows:

- L1 indicates the security control is written into policy

- L2 indicates that the security control is implemented

- L3 indicates that the security control is tested

- L4 indicates that the security control has passed all tests and is tightly integrated

Each compliance level includes the requirements from the prior level. It makes it very easy to understand at which C&A level your information systems are able to be certified if you design your self-assessment this way. Keep in mind that even if your information systems can be certified and accredited at a higher level, and each control item complies up to L4, that doesn't mean that you should certify and accredit your information systems at the highest level. As already discussed, you should never certify and accredit your information system at a level higher than what is necessary. Table 8.1 illustrates a commonly used format for self-assessment survey questions.

Table 8.1 Self-Assessment Survey Format

No.	Question	L1	L2	L3	L4
1	Are network vulnerability assessments performed on a regular basis?	✓	✓	✓	

A checkmark in the L1 box indicates that there is a security policy that requires the control to exist, and a checkmark in the L2 box indicates that the control has been implemented. A checkmark in the L3 box indicates that tests have been performed on the implementation, and a checkmark in the L4 box indicates that all tests have been passed and that the control is tightly integrated into the information system. You're probably wondering what is meant by "tightly integrated." Tight integration is a somewhat nebulous term, and to be sure, although NIST and many security experts use this terminology commonly, there is no one agreed upon definition for what it means. My recommendation is that tight integration is something that you can justify through evidence and demonstration in one of the following ways:

- Automated technical features

- A strict change control process

- A robust configuration management process

- An online workflow process that includes levels of approvals and sign-offs

For example, if a network vulnerability assessment is performed automatically on a regular basis, according to a published schedule, it may qualify as "implemented" in compliance with L2 requirements. If all vulnerabilities are mitigated each time an automated network vulnerability assessment occurs, you could then claim that risk assessments are performed on a regular basis up to compliance level L4. If a network vulnerability assessment is performed now and then, but not on any regular schedule, and known vulnerabilities are recorded but not immediately mitigated, you could claim that risk assessments are in compliance with level L3. If network vulnerability assessments are required to be completed, and one is scheduled to occur but hasn't occurred yet, then you could claim that the information system was in compliance up to level L2. If there was simply a policy that existed for network vulnerability assessments to be completed, whether any vulnerability assessments were actually completed or not, you could justifiably claim your information system is in compliance with level L1.

Management Controls

The survey questions should be designed to discover the truths about the management controls and should be focused on the following key areas:

- Risk mitigation

- Reporting and review by management

- System lifecycle requirements

- Security planning

- Security oversight
- Documentation for managers

You want the survey questions to uncover how well the management team complies with agency security policies, and how well they manage and oversee the operational and technical controls. Management is about budgeting, tracking, reporting, communications, accountability, and analysis. Questions surrounding security management controls should be designed with these elements in mind.

Operational Controls

Operational controls focus on processes and procedures that are implemented by people. The survey questions surrounding the operational controls should be geared toward finding out if the processes and procedures designed to control security work as planned. The discoveries made from responses to operational survey questions should be concerned with how well the people who administer the systems carry out their daily duties. Survey questions related to operational security controls should be focused on the following key areas:

- Personnel security
- Physical and environmental operations and safeguards
- Administration and implementation
- Preventative maintenance
- Contingency and disaster recovery planning
- Training and security awareness
- Incident response procedures
- Preservation of data integrity (antivirus, intrusion detection, etc.)
- Network and system security operations
- Documentation for operational staff

An important part of surveying operational controls is to find out if there is a clear separation of duties between the different administrative roles. In general, duties should be separated so that access to operations is available according to the principle of least privilege—users should be given no more privileges than absolutely necessary to do their jobs.

Preservation of data integrity and confidentiality issues should be investigated by questions regarding operational controls. As one example, data integrity questions should be designed to find out how antivirus programs are managed. An example of confidentiality questions would include those questions designed to find out about background checking processes for key personnel.

Technical Controls

Technical controls refer to the security safeguards that are built into the information systems. Survey questions should be designed to find out the status of the built-in technical controls. The type of information that you are trying to uncover is to find out if technical controls exist, and if they do, whether they are effective.

The key areas that technical controls focus on are:

- Authentication and identity verification
- Logical access controls
- Secure configurations
- Interconnectivity security
- Audit mechanisms

If a *Security Self-Assessment* has been designed to fit all the information systems in a particular agency, it will likely be the case that some of the questions designed for technical control assurances will not be applicable. Not all information systems will require the same types of technical controls.

Correlation with Security Policies and Laws

When putting together the self-assessment, it can be helpful to have agency security policies and federal guidance that require the controls, to be listed with the question. An example of this is shown in Table 8.2. Controls that are required by FISCAM and OMB Circulars will be items that GAO inspectors will look for during an audit. Controls that are required by the agency are of interest to the agency OIG auditors. Guidance from NIST is also worth citing for reference purposes. OMB Circular A–130 often is used as guide for developing the self-assessment questions.

Answering the Questions

Once a survey is developed, it needs to be completed. You will need to interview the developers, subject matter experts, and management team in order to find out the answers to the questions. Interviews can be performed either in person or electronically. There are many nice survey tools that can be implemented that are designed to collect this information through a Web portal. It's often the case that some of the survey respondents may be in disparate geographic locations. By setting up the survey through a Web portal, you can simply send out an e-mail asking the required participants to login and answer the questions. Many of the online survey tools offer roll-up scores and advanced graphs that allow you to see which control areas require more attention. As organizations refine their self-assessment methodology, implementing the survey via an online portal is really the way to go.

Table 8.2 Oversight Requirements Depicted in Survey Questions

No.	Question	L1	L2	L3	L4
1	If firewalls are installed, do they comply with the required firewall policies and rules? Required by: FISCAM AC-3.2				
2	Is the privacy policy regarding the information system published and visible? Required by: OMB-99-18				
3	Are guest and anonymous accounts prohibited? Required by: <Agency Name> Security Policy 1.0				
4	Is there application documentation for in-house applications? Recommended by: NIST SP 800-18				

Self-assessments should not be done in an accusatory way that implies wrong-doing has occurred. The point of a self-assessment is to collect information designed for agency or organizational self-improvement. Respondents to the questions should not be made to feel guilty if a particular area is not in compliance. You want the respondents to give honest answers. It is very important that respondents understand up front that no negative repercussions will occur as a result of their answers. If honest answers are not provided on the self-assessment, it becomes useless.

In May of 2000, the Department of Energy released a report[2] regarding various security incidents that had occurred at Los Alamos National Laboratory. It was discovered that respondents to security self-assessments answered survey questions purposefully incorrectly because they felt pressured to give the "right" answer as opposed to the truthful answer. As a result, various security vulnerabilities were never discovered, and so nothing was ever done to mitigate them. Since the security vulnerabilities were never mitigated, security incidents occurred that exploited the vulnerabilities. Not only is it unethical to intimidate self-assessment respondents into answering the questions untruthfully, it defeats the purpose of the exercise.

Similar to what happened at Los Alamos, in September of 2003, a report[3] put out by the Office of Inspector General at the Environmental Protection Agency found that 36 percent of the responses to security self-assessments contained inaccurate information. Submission of inaccurate security self-assessments is a known problem. The intent of a self-assessment is for the ISSO and information system owner to use the self-assessment surveys internally, though auditors may try to find out if the information contained in them is accurate. As more attention is being cast on inaccurate security self-assessments, scrupulous auditors will be spending more time trying to verify the accuracy of the information contained in them. Truthfulness conveys trust, and if auditors discover that security self-assessments are not accurate, they may scrutinize other parts of the Certification Package more so than they would otherwise.

TIP

Encourage self-assessment respondents to answer questions truthfully.

Evaluators may ask questions to try to ascertain if the ISSO and information system owner actually use their own self-assessments to take corrective actions. Presumably, if an information system owner finds out from the self-assessment process that the vulnerabilities discovered do not warrant pursuing C&A, an ethically upstanding information system owner would put the C&A process on hold until proper mitigation of vulnerabilities occurs. Keep in mind that information system owners do not need to wait until a C&A deadline is looming to conduct a security self-assessment. It is probably best to get started on your self-assessment long before the three-year C&A deadline is looming overhead.

Questions for Self-Assessment Survey

The list of questions in Tables 8.3, 8.4, and 8.5 can be used to develop a *Security Self-Assessment.* The questions are based on the recommendations set forth in *Special Publication 800-26, Security Self-Assessment Guide for Information Technology Systems*, August 2001, by the National Institute of Standards. However, additional questions and categories have been added to increase the breadth of coverage. Some of the original rhetoric from NIST 800-26 has been simplified and modified in order to provide clarity. For example, I have changed NIST's reference of "Personnel Security" to "User Trust" since securing the personnel was never the intention. Some of the questions may be found in categories different than the original NIST recommendations. Federal laws and regulations, and NIST guidance are cited along with the relevant questions in Tables 8.3, 8.4, and 8.5. If a particular question is not applicable to your information system you can indicate that by inserting N.A. into any of the right-hand columns.

Management security controls refer to security controls that are required and reviewed through organizational accountability processes.

Table 8.3 Management Assurance Control Questions

No.	Questions	L1	L2	L3	L4

Risk Management

Required by: FISMA § 3541 (2)(A) and § 3544(b)(1); OMB Circular A-130 III; FISCAM SP-1
Recommended by: NIST SP 800-18; NIST SP 800-30

No.	Questions	L1	L2	L3	L4
	Are initial risk assessments performed before a system is put into production?				
	Are risk assessments performed on a regular schedule?				
	Are risk assessment reports documented and archived?				
	Are changes to the system documented in a configuration management plan or utility?				
	Is the current system configuration documented?				
	Is a topological map of the network documented and updated on a regular basis?				
	Have data sensitivity levels been determined?				
	Have natural threat sources been identified and considered?				
	Have human threat sources been identified and considered?				
	Has a list of vulnerabilities that could be exploited by threats, errors, or security weaknesses been developed?				
	Has a risk assessment that determines if security requirements adequately mitigate threats been done?				
	Has a business (mission) risk assessment been done?				
	Have final risk determinations and sign-offs been documented and approved by management?				

Continued

Table 8.3 continued Management Assurance Control Questions

No.	Questions	L1	L2	L3	L4
	When a significant change occurs to the system is a new risk assessment conducted?				

Security Controls

Required by: FISMA § 3541 (1) and § 3544 (a)(2)(D); OMB Circular A-130 III; FISCAM SP-5
Recommended by: NIST SP 800-18; NIST SP 800-30

	Questions	L1	L2	L3	L4
	Are *Security Self-assessments* conducted on a regular schedule?				
	Have adequate security controls been implemented to mitigate the identified risks?				
	Are tests of essential security controls (e.g., network scans, penetration tests) performed on a regular basis?				
	Are security incidents properly categorized?				
	Are security incidents reported to management?				
	If the system connects to other systems, have security controls been established for the interconnections?				
	Are security controls for network boundaries and interconnections reviewed periodically for vulnerabilities?				
	Have security controls of interconnections been distributed to the interconnected system owners?				
	When a significant change to the information system occurs, are the security controls and design reviewed by a third-party independent expert?				
	Are security controls of the system consistent with security controls of the adjacent IT infrastructure?				

Continued

Table 8.3 continued Management Assurance Control Questions

No.	Questions	L1	L2	L3	L4
	Are security controls supported by signed agency agreements and memorandums of understanding?				
	After new security controls are added, are they tested as required?				
	Do security controls operate as intended?				

Life Cycle Support

Required by: FISMA § 3544 (b)(2)(C); OMB Circular A-130 III; FISCAM CC-1.1
Recommended by: NIST SP 800-18; NIST SP 800-30

	Are security requirements identified during the system or application design?				
	Are design reviews and operational tests conducted prior to placing a system or application into production?				
	Do design reviews system tests and operational tests include a test for security requirements?				
	Are all test results documented?				
	Does the information system have written authorization to operate?				
	Have planned corrective actions been implemented as scheduled?				
	Is the sensitivity (confidentiality, integrity, availability) reviewed during each lifecycle phase?				
	Are security requirements developed and evaluated before procurement occurs?				
	Are adequate budget provisions made for security?				
	Are security resources justified by business requirements?				

Continued

Table 8.3 continued Management Assurance Control Questions

No.	Questions	L1	L2	L3	L4
Authorization					

Required by: FISCAM CC-1.2
Recommended by: NIST SP 800-30

No.	Questions	L1	L2	L3	L4
	Are authorizations for software modifications documented and maintained?				
	Do solicitation documents (e.g., RFPs and product evaluations) include security requirements?				
	Do solicitation documents require and permit that security controls (e.g., patches) be updated and implemented as required?				
	Does management review and approve all security documents?				
	Is the system authorized to operate by full ATO or IATO?				
	Is the system certified (or recertified) every three years as required?				
	Have all system interconnections, agreements, and memorandums of understanding been authorized by management?				
	Has management verified that the existing security controls are consistent with data sensitivity?				
	Does management correct deficiencies (e.g., Plans of Action & Milestones) in a timely manner?				
	Has the *Security Plan* been approved by management?				
	Have all users been authorized for system access by management?				

Continued

Table 8.3 continued Management Assurance Control Questions

No.	Questions	L1	L2	L3	L4
Security Plan					

Required by: OMB Circular A-130 III; FISCAM SP 2-1
Recommended by: NIST SP 800-18; NIST SP 800-30

	Questions	L1	L2	L3	L4
	Has a *Security Plan* been developed and distributed for review?				
	Is the *Security Plan* updated on a regular basis?				
	Does the *Security Plan* include a general description of the system?				
	Does the *Security Plan* include a diagram of the system or network components (e.g., network map)?				
	Is the purpose of the system noted in the *Security Plan*?				
	Are all security controls documented in the *Security Plan*?				
	Does the *Security Plan* include laws, regulations, and policies that the system must adhere to?				
	Does the *Security Plan* include documentation of physical and environmental safeguards?				
	Are the system interconnections described in the *Security Plan*?				
	Does the Security Plan provide rationale and justification of the sensitivity (confidentiality, integrity, availability) levels?				
	Is information about backups (e.g., schedule, storage location) documented in the *Security Plan*?				

Operational security controls refer to installations, configurations, and mitigating actions performed by operations staff.

Table 8.4 Operational Assurance Control Questions

No.	Question	L1	L2	L3	L4

User Trust

Required by: FISMA § 3543 (a)(2) & 3545(f); OMB Circular A-130 III, FISCAM SD-1, 1.2, 2, 3.2
Recommended by: NIST SP 800-18; NIST SP 800-30

No.	Question	L1	L2	L3	L4
	Is suspicious activity investigated and appropriate action taken?				
	Have *Rules of Behavior* been established and agreed to by all users?				
	Are *Rules of Behavior* available for personnel to reference on an on-going basis?				
	Are all positions reviewed for user trust levels?				
	Are background investigations performed as required?				
	Do separation of duties exist according to requirements?				
	Do job descriptions accurately reflect levels of experience, responsibilities, and expertise?				
	Are processes in place to hold users accountable for their actions?				
	Does an enrollment process exist for issuing user accounts?				
	Do termination procedures exist for closing user accounts?				
	Are regularly scheduled vacations and job rotations required?				
	Are privileged users (authorized to bypass security controls) screened at a higher level of risk (e.g., credit checks)?				
	Are security clearances issued and enforced as required?				

Continued

Table 8.4 continued Operational Assurance Control Questions

No.	Question	L1	L2	L3	L4

User Trust

Is security awareness training given on an annual basis?

Do users receive periodic training to ensure that they understand their responsibilities?

Are training classes documented and is attendance taken?

Do employees have access to the agency (and bureau) security policies?

Are security awareness materials (e.g., posters, signs, booklets) distributed and displayed?

Are users recertified on a regular basis?

Does a Help desk or user support resources exist?

Do user manuals exist for applications that users are required to use?

Physical and Environmental Safeguards

Required by: FISMA § 3545 (f); FISCAM AC-3 & SC-2.2
Recommended by: NIST SP 800-18, NIST SP 800-30, NIST SP 800-37

Is access to buildings controlled by guards, badges, smart cards, biometrics, or other entry devices?

Is access to the computer room controlled by an automated entry device?

Is access to facilities tracked through sign-in books and audit trails?

Are entry codes to buildings and computer rooms changed periodically?

Are visitors signed-in and escorted as necessary?

Continued

www.syngress.com

Table 8.4 continued Operational Assurance Control Questions

No.	Question	L1	L2	L3	L4
	Are visitors provided badges that are publicly viewable?				
	Are wiring closets locked with access controlled?				
	Are fire suppression devices installed and working?				
	Are fire risk sources (old wiring, improper storage materials) reviewed periodically?				
	Are heating, air conditioning, and ventilation systems operational and regularly maintained?				
	Is a backup air-conditioning system in place for the computer room?				
	Is the temperature and humidity of computer rooms monitored with alarms?				
	Is preventative maintenance performed on electrical power distribution and circuit breakers?				
	Are circuits documented including information about locations and power capabilities?				
	Is an uninterruptible power supply installed and operational?				
	Are plumbing, sewage systems and lines operational and regularly maintained?				
	Are plumbing lines documented with their whereabouts indicated?				
	Have environmental safeguards been put into place to protect against natural disasters?				
	Are mobile systems stored securely?				
	Do emergency exit and re-entry procedures exist?				

Continued

Table 8.4 continued Operational Assurance Control Questions

No.	Question	L1	L2	L3	L4

Software, Hardware, and Network Maintenance

Required by: FISMA § 11331 SEC 305; OMB Circular A-130 III; FISCAM SS-3.1, CC-1.2, 2.1, 3.2, 3.3
Recommended by: NIST SP 800-18

	Are all hardware serial numbers documented?				
	Are all software licenses documented?				
	Are unused or nonissued keys stored securely?				
	Are controls in place to ensure that repairs and maintenance are conducted only by authorized personnel?				
	Are there separate maintenance procedures for on-site and off-site services?				
	Are maintenance personnel given access to systems on a least privilege basis?				
	Are system components tested prior to being put into production?				
	When maintenance personnel make changes to the system are the changes tested and documented prior to being put into production?				
	Has the operating system been configured to prevent circumvention of security settings and controls?				
	Do detailed hardware systems specifications exist?				
	For new installations, are default security settings set to the most restrictive settings?				
	Before changes are made to a system, are changes requested, reviewed, and approved by management?				

Continued

Table 8.4 continued Operational Assurance Control Questions

No.	Question	L1	L2	L3	L4
	Are procedures documented for using system maintenance and monitoring utilities?				
	Are processes in place to track version control of operating systems?				
	Are processes in place to track version control of hardware?				
	Are processes in place to track version control of applications?				
	Is licensed software labeled and stored securely?				
	Is licensed software inventoried either manually or automatically?				
	Does a policy exist to prohibit the use of nonlicensed software (that is not freeware or shareware)?				
	Does a policy exist to explain how freeware and shareware should or should not be used?				
	Does a process exist to allow for expedited emergency change procedures?				
	When new versions of software are installed, are the versions tested prior to being put into production?				
	Do procedures exist to test and install new software patches?				
	Are operating systems hardened and are unnecessary services turned off?				
	Are systems scanned for known vulnerabilities on a regular basis?				
	Are vulnerabilities reviewed and mitigated?				
	Does all purchased software and hardware include vendor supplied documentation?				

Continued

Table 8.4 continued Operational Assurance Control Questions

No.	Question	L1	L2	L3	L4
	Does documentation exist for custom and in-house developed applications?				
	Do procedures for testing security configuration exist?				
	Are router and switch configurations documented?				
	Does an up-to-date topological map of the network exist?				
	Are the firewall rules documented?				

Data Integrity

Required by: FISMA § 3544 (c)(2)(G); OMB Circular A-130 III; FISCAM SP-1, SS-2.2
Recommended by: NIST SP 800-18; NIST SP 800-30

No.	Question	L1	L2	L3	L4
	Has data integrity been characterized?				
	Have threats to data integrity been reviewed?				
	Have safeguards been implemented to preserve data integrity?				
	Is sensitive information encrypted as required?				
	Are PKI certificates issued securely?				
	Are PKI certificates distributed only to authorized users?				
	Have safeguards been put into place to protect systems from viruses, worms, and Trojans?				
	Are antivirus signatures updated on a regular basis?				
	Is virus scanning automatic?				
	Are reconciliation routines (e.g., hashes, checksums) used for programs and files as required?				

Continued

Table 8.4 continued Operational Assurance Control Questions

No.	Question	L1	L2	L3	L4
	Are passwords audited for compliance?				
	Are intrusion detection (and prevention) tools installed and operational?				
	Are firewall logs reviewed for dubious network traffic?				
	Are intrusion detection logs reviewed for dubious behavior?				
	Are intrusion prevention heuristics updated regularly to safeguard against new exploits?				
	Is network traffic monitored to detect performance (availability) problems created by denial of service attacks?				
	Are message authentication codes (MACs) used in accordance with security policies?				
	Are Virtual Private Network (VPN) configurations documented?				

Media Controls

Required by: FISMA § 3544 (b) AGENCY PROGRAM (2)(D)(iv); FISCAM AC-3.4
Recommended by: NIST SP 800-18

No.	Question	L1	L2	L3	L4
	Is access to stored media controlled and documented?				
	Are data files backed up on a regular schedule?				
	Is the backup schedule documented with files, directories, and filesystems noted?				
	Are backups stored off-site through a rotation basis?				
	Is the location of stored backups identified?				
	Are procedures documented on how to back up and restore files?				

Continued

Table 8.4 continued Operational Assurance Control Questions

No.	Question	L1	L2	L3	L4
	When files are restored, are the particulars documented?				
	Is media properly sanitized before reuse and disposal?				
	Are electronic records properly archived or disposed?				
	Is digital media properly stored and disposed of?				
	Are paper records properly archived or shredded?				
	Are logs kept regarding who disposes or archives records, documents, and media?				
	Do procedures exist for mailing (or transporting) sensitive printed materials and digital media?				
	Do audit trails exist for receipt of sensitive printed materials and digital media?				
	Are media audit trails available for inventory management?				
	Are there controls to ensure that unauthorized users are not able to access sensitive printed materials and digital media?				
	Are only authorized users allowed to obtain and deliver sensitive printer materials and digital media?				
	Does an inventory of all archived media exist?				
	Is damaged media properly disposed of or destroyed?				
	Is all media properly labeled?				
	Are data classifications and handling instructions clearly marked on all media?				

Continued

Table 8.4 continued Operational Assurance Control Questions

No.	Question	L1	L2	L3	L4
Contingency Planning & Disaster Recovery					

Required by: FISMA § 3542-44; OMB Circular A-130 III, FISCAM SC1.1,
1.2, 1.3
Recommended by: NIST SP 800-18, NIST SP 800-34

No.	Question	L1	L2	L3	L4
	Does a *Contingency Plan* exist?				
	Does the *Contingency Plan* include a business impact assessment?				
	Are critical assets identified?				
	Is a current copy of the contingency plan stored off-site in a secure location?				
	Has the *Contingency Plan* been distributed to appropriate personnel?				
	Are roles and responsibilities for recovery assigned?				
	Have relative priorities for recovery been established?				
	Have notification and activation processes been established?				
	Are there detailed instructions for restoring operations?				
	Does an alternate processing site exist?				
	Is the alternate processing site in a different geographic location than the primary site?				
	Does the *Contingency Plan* and recovery documentation exist at the alternate processing site?				
	Are key personnel trained in recovery operations?				
	Is the *Contingency Plan* periodically tested?				
	Has the *Contingency Plan* been reviewed and approved by management?				

Continued

Table 8.4 continued Operational Assurance Control Questions

No.	Question	L1	L2	L3	L4

Incident Response Capabilities

Required by: FISMA § 3546 (2), OMB Circular A-130 III, FISCAM SP-3.4
Recommended by: NIST SP 800-18, SP 800-61

	Question	L1	L2	L3	L4
	Are security incidents and alerts analyzed and documented?				
	Are remedial actions taken as required when a security incident occurs?				
	Is there a documented process for reporting security incidents?				
	Is training provided to key personnel on how to handle security incidents?				
	Do key personnel respond to security incident alerts and advisories?				
	Are security incidents monitored and tracked until they are resolved or closed?				
	Does *an Incident Response Plan* exist?				
	Is the *Incident Response Plan* updated as required?				
	Has management reviewed and approved of the *Incident Response Plan*?				
	Is information about security incidents appropriately shared with owners of interconnected systems?				
	Are security incidents reported to the agency CSIRC, FBI, and US-CERT,[4] and local law enforcement as required?				
	Are security vulnerabilities and threats listed on the US-CERT Web site reviewed on a regular basis?				

Technical security controls refer to controls that are executed by systems, products, and technologies.

Table 8.5 Technical Assurance Control Questions

No.	Question	L1	L2	L3	L4
Identification and Authentication					
Required by: FISMA § 3542-44, 3547; OMB Circular A-130 III; FISCAM AC-2, .32					
Recommended by: NIST 800-18					
	Are users uniquely identified (e.g., unique usernames/logins) before being allowed to access sensitive systems and data?				
	Are users required to provide proof of identify (e.g., passwords, tokens, two-factor authentication) before being allowed to access sensitive systems and data?				
	Is identification and authentication information protected from unauthorized access? (How are passwords and usernames safeguarded on the backend?)				
	Is authentication information protected from replay attacks (e.g., logon credentials are protected during network transmission of packets)?				
	Are digital signatures used?				
	Do digital signatures comply with FIPS 186-2?[5]				
	Are access scripts, programs, and applications with hardcoded passwords prohibited?				
	Does a list of authorized users exist and is it kept up to date?				
	Is temporary and emergency system and network access authorized?				
	Are there procedures for handling lost and compromised passwords?				

Continued

Table 8.5 continued Technical Assurance Control Questions

No.	Question	L1	L2	L3	L4
	Are login processes set up so that passwords are not displayed when entered?				
	Has automatic password expiration been configured and put into place?				
	Are users required to change their passwords at the minimum every 90 days?				
	Have login processes been configured (e.g., eight or more alphanumeric characters, upper- and lowercase) to require passwords to be difficult to guess?				
	Are inactive user accounts automatically expired?				
	Have users been informed about password disclosure policies and social engineering attacks?				
	Are passwords distributed or disclosed in a secure manner?				
	Do friendly termination procedures exist for closing user accounts?				
	Do unfriendly termination procedures exist for closing user accounts?				
	Are passwords encrypted and stored using secure protocols and algorithms?				
	Are vendor and default passwords immediately replaced or disabled?				
	Are accounts locked after a specified number of invalid access attempts?				
	Are user logins recorded by the system?				
	Are data owners consulted for access authorizations?				
	Is access to security software and tools restricted to authorized security administrators?				

Continued

Table 8.5 continued Technical Assurance Control Questions

No.	Question	L1	L2	L3	L4
	Are guest and anonymous accounts authorized and monitored?				
	Do biometric devices comply with appropriate false acceptance rates?				
	Do biometric devices comply with appropriate false reject rates?				
	Are biometric false reject and false acceptance rates tracked and documented?				

Logical Access Controls

Required by: FISMA § 3542-44, 3547; OMB Circular A-130 III; FISCAM AC-3.2
Recommended by: NIST 800-18

	Are unauthorized access attempts recorded in log files?				
	Do screensavers lock systems after a period of inactivity?				
	Is there a separation of duties between administrators who provide access and incident response engineers?				
	Are remote logins disconnected after a period of inactivity?				
	Is the user access list documented and is it updated on a regular basis?				
	If encryption is used, are there procedures for key recovery?				
	If encryption is used are there procedures for key distribution?				
	Do encryption algorithms comply with FIPS 140-2?[6]				
	Are insecure protocols (e.g., NETBIOS) used with safeguards or else disabled?				
	Are firewalls, secure gateways, or security appliances installed?				

Continued

Table 8.5 continued Technical Assurance Control Questions

No.	Question	L1	L2	L3	L4
	Are controls in place to monitor and authorize access to telecommunications hardware and devices?				
	Have vendor-supplied default configurations been reviewed for security weaknesses?				
	Do all firewalls comply with the prescribed firewall policies?				
	Are router access lists (ACLs) documented?				
	Is access to router ACLs restricted?				
	Are router ACLs changed only by authorized administrators?				
	Are data transmissions encrypted as required?				
	Are sensitive Web transmissions encrypted (e.g., SSL) as required?				
	Do network devices disconnect (users) at the end of logon sessions?				
	Are procedures for authorizing remote access documented?				
	Are procedures for configuring accounts for remote access documented?				
	Are remote access accounts authorized?				
	Is remote access restricted so that it can take place only through specific ports of entry and terminals?				
	Is a login banner that warns users about unauthorized access displayed?				
	Is a privacy policy posted in a public place for all users to review?				
	When the system and network is scanned is a report generated that classifies vulnerabilities as high, medium, or low risk?				

Continued

Table 8.5 continued Technical Assurance Control Questions

No.	Question	L1	L2	L3	L4
	Does the CIO or CISO review the agency's security posture on an annual basis?				
	Has the agency had an independent objective security audit?				

Audit and Monitoring

Required by: FISMA § 3546 (2); OMB Circular A-130 III; FISCAM AC-4.1
Recommended by: NIST 800-18

	Do host-based audit log files (e.g., syslog) exist?				
	Do host-based audit log files trace user actions?				
	Are host-based audit logs properly time-stamped?				
	Is dial-in and remote access monitored?				
	Are trust relationships between interconnections and domains monitored?				
	Do network-based log files (e.g., firewall logs) exist?				
	Do network-based log files trace network traffic?				
	Are network-based log files properly time-stamped?				
	Is access to time-stamp modifications controlled?				
	Is access to audit logs controlled?				
	Are host-based audit logs reviewed on a regular schedule?				
	Are network audit logs reviewed on a regular schedule?				
	Are audit logs stored on backup tapes?				
	Are audit log archives stored off site?				
	Are automated tools used to monitor audit logs?				

Continued

Table 8.5 continued Technical Assurance Control Questions

No.	Question	L1	L2	L3	L4
	Is suspicious activity documented?				
	Is suspicious activity investigated?				
	Are security incidents documented?				
	Are security incidents investigated?				
	Is keystroke monitoring used? If so, are users notified?				
	Is there a separation of duties between staff that administers user access control and staff that reviews audit logs?				

Summary

Although a formal C&A package attempts to assess and document the security of an information system at a fine level of detail and using rigorous verification and validation, a self-assessment is a less rigorous tool used to assess the security of the information in the years between formal certification and accreditations. Instead of bringing in outside agents to assess the security of a system, the self-assessment relies on people within the agency to perform the assessment. Self-assessments should be questionnaires that cover a range of technical, management, and operational controls that should be in place for information systems, so although the assessment questions do not need to replicate every control you would cover in a formal C&A, there should be some overlap. This way, you end up with a C&A package that reflects an outside auditor's assessment of the security for a system and a "gut check" performed by agency personnel. Comparisons between the two evaluations can then be drawn.

Notes

1. "Federal Information Technology Security Assessment Framework." National Institute of Standards and Technology's Computer Security Division, System and Network Security Group. November 28, 2000 (www.cio.gov/archive/federal_it_security_assessment_framework.html).

2. "Summary Report on Inspection of Allegations Relating to the Albuquerque Operations Office Security Survey Process and the Security Operations' Self-Assessments at Los Alamos National Laboratory." United States Department of Energy. May 30, 2000. (www.fas.org/sgp/othergov/doeig_0471.html).

3. "EPA's Computer Security Self-Assessment Process Needs Improvement." Report Number 2003-P-00017. United States Environmental Protection Agency. September 30, 2003 (www.epa.gov/oigearth/reports/2003/2003p00017-20030930.pdf).

4. United States Computer Emergency Readiness Team (US-CERT) (http://www.us-cert.gov/).

5. "Digital Signature Standard (DSS)." FIPS Publication 186-2. United States Department of Commerce/National Institute of Standards and Technology. January 27, 2000 (http://csrc.nist.gov/publications/fips/fips186-2/fips186-2-change1.pdf).

6. "Security Requirements for Cryptographic Modules." FIPS Publication 140-2. Updated December 3, 2002. National Institute of Standards and Technology's Computer Security Division (http://csrc.nist.gov/cryptval/140-2.htm).

## Chapter 9

Addressing Security Awareness and Training Requirements

"The ultimate value of life depends upon awareness and the power of contemplation rather than upon mere survival."

—Aristotle

Topics in this chapter:

- **Purpose of Security Awareness and Training**
- **Security Training**
- **The Awareness and Training Message**
- **Online Training Makes It Easy**
- **Document Your Plan**
- **Security Awareness and Training Checklist**
- **Security Awareness Material Evaluation**
- **Security Awareness Class Evaluation**

Introduction

All Certification Packages that are Level 2 and above require a *Security Awareness and Training Plan*. The *Security Awareness and Training Plan* has to include accurate information about training that has taken place in the past, and any training that will take place in the future. Probably one of the most oft-overlooked pieces of a security program, security awareness and training is paramount to improving your agency's security posture. A *Security Awareness and Training Plan* is simply a documented description of the security awareness and training program.

In October 2003, the National Institute of Standards published[1] recommendations for security awareness and training programs. The document, informally known as NIST Special Publication 800-50, describes four critical elements that all security awareness and training programs should include:

1. Design and planning of the awareness and training program
2. Development of the awareness and training materials
3. Implementation of the awareness and training program
4. Measuring the effectiveness of your program and updating it

Purpose of Security Awareness and Training

Many end-users simply don't understand how rampant security threats are. A security awareness and training program forces end-users to become aware of these threats. By participating in security awareness and training, end-users come to realize that your agency cares about security.

Security awareness and training are two different things. Security awareness refers to the marketing and promotion of security inside your agency. Security awareness programs put in place signs, booklets, posters, and electronic reminders. Awareness programs serve as constant reminders that your agency or organization takes information security seriously and are motivational in nature.

Security training refers to actual security coursework. The course can take place in a classroom or via an online training program. Most users enjoy having the opportunity to learn new things. By assisting users in increasing their actual knowledge of security they will naturally use this knowledge to help protect the enterprise infrastructure. Your best security stewards are really your employees. Your employees use and administer the systems that need to be secured. They understand how the systems are used, how they operate, and know them more intimately than anyone else. Even though you can hire expensive outside consultants to come in and secure your network, your employees have invested more time in your organization, and will likely care more about doing the right thing. By training your own employees, you empower them to assist you in security certification and accreditation.

Since there are practical limitations to the amount of employee time you can take up, your information security and training program needs to be keenly focused. The focus of your security awareness and training program should be to protect the confidentiality, integrity, and availability of your organization's information.

Security Training

Security training should be mandatory for all end-users including contractors. A written record of all training classes, and the users that participated in them, should be documented and archived. By making security training mandatory, end-users get the message that your agency is serious about security. If you advise your end-users of your expectations in regards to security, you can much more easily hold them accountable.

In implementing a training program, you need to take into consideration your employee's roles and responsibilities. There should be an overall basic training course that all employees participate in, and you will want to give advanced security training course to the personnel that have actual security responsibilities. The following types of individuals should participate in at least one or more advanced security training courses per year:

- Information System Security Officers
- Network engineers

- Security engineers
- System administrators
- Chief Security Officers
- Mission assurance staff

To find out how well the training programs are, it is a good idea to present the employees with a quiz at the beginning and end of each course. If the class is a good one, at the end of each course their score on the quiz should be much higher than it was before they took the course. You should also ask the employees to fill out an evaluation of the course after it is over. You'll want to try to find out how appropriate your employees felt the training material was and if they thought the instructor understood the material and was able to present it in a manner that was understandable.

Security Awareness

Reminders work and that's what security awareness is about. However, security awareness requires some management. For the system that is undergoing C&A, the ISSO needs to ensure that awareness materials are made available. The awareness material may be e-mail reminders, pamphlets, or even *tchotchkes*. Security awareness materials should be attention getting. They need to be prominently displayed in highly trafficked areas. People notice awareness materials more easily if they are colorful and pleasing to look at. If an auditor walked through the user community offices, security awareness materials should be in plain sight.

The Awareness and Training Message

Since information security is a very broad topic, you will clearly not be able to train your employees in all aspects of it. Except for your information security engineers and staff, most of your end users have much work to do that is likely unrelated to security. Therefore, you need to selectively pick and choose the security topics you want your users to learn about. You will want to hone in on security topics that will have the greatest impact on improving the security posture of your infrastructure. Make your employees aware of the greatest threats, and how to most easily mitigate them.

Items that I recommend that you include in your security awareness and training program are the following:

- Ensure that your users have read and understood the ten most important security policies.

- Explain the dangers of social engineering and instruct your users how you would like them to handle suspicious phone calls.

- Advise your users to update their anti-virus software on daily basis. Users should also be educated about the dangers of opening attachments.

- Describe to your users what constitutes a safe password. Some users may not realize how easy it is to launch dictionary attacks. Remind users that good passwords include mixed-case characters and numbers.

- Advise your users how they should report suspicious activity including viruses, denial of service attacks, and possible break-ins.

- Expectations for laptop security should be discussed. Should users lock them in their desks if they leave their laptops in the office overnight? Are there any security requirements for laptops when taken on business travel?

- Expectations for handhelds should also be specified. Are users allowed to connect them to the corporate network? What type of handheld is allowed?

- Personal firewall requirements should be discussed. Are they required or optional? Which ones are supported and who do users call for assistance with them?

- The expectations for security patch installation on laptops and desktop systems needs to be stated. Do users have to install and patch their own systems? Where should they obtain the patches? Is the patching process automated?

- Explain any requirements for encryption. Are certain files supposed to be stored only in an encrypted state? Does your agency allow the use of algorithms that have not undergone FIPS 140-2[2] validation testing?

■ Personal use of laptops and desktops should be stated. Are employees allowed to send personal e-mails from agency accounts?

Chances are your agency has unique security requirements for users. New employees are joining the agency every day. Time goes by and people forget what they learned last year. You need to enlist your users in training on a regular schedule.

Online Training Makes It Easy

With widespread use of intranets, most agencies will find it easy to distribute a basic security training course electronically. A good online training course will quiz the user at the end of the course, and offer the user feedback on missed questions. Some agencies require users to retake the course if they do not achieve a certain threshold of correct answers. You'll want an online course to track the users who have logged on and completed it. Users should be given a deadline to complete the course by a certain date, or have their access removed.

Document Your Plan

Your *Security Awareness and Training Plan* is simply a document that describes how security awareness and training works for the information system that is undergoing C&A. Your plan might simply be a write-up that references a broader agencywide plan. Or it may include reference to the agencywide plan as well as a detailed description of specific security training requirements for a unique application.

The fact that you are already doing excellent security awareness and training is not enough. As far as C&A is concerned, if it is not documented, it doesn't exist. You need to indicate who is responsible for updating the plan, and who is responsible for implementing security awareness and training initiatives. For example, who makes the security awareness posters? Is it done in-house, or does your agency use an outside graphic design company? Who puts up the posters? Who teaches the courses, and where are they held? If it sounds simple, that's because it is.

Security Awareness and Training Checklist

The following checklist will help you ensure that you have not forgotten to note anything in your plan:

- Is the type and frequency of training noted?

- Are training classes for security personnel described?

- Are training classes for basic end-users described?

- Are instructors for the training classes noted?

- Is it noted that security training is tracked and logged?

- Is it noted that all courses are evaluated by the users?

- Are roles and responsibilities for security awareness noted?

- Are roles and responsibilities for security training noted?

- Does the plan indicate that a record is kept of user training participation?

- Does the plan indicate that users are assessed for their security knowledge after they undergo training?

Security Awareness Material Evaluation

Here is an example of an evaluation form for a security awareness initiative.

Topic: _____   Date: _____

Name: (Optional) _____   E-mail: _____

Strongly Disagree	Disagree	Neutral Opinion	Agree	Strongly Agree
1	2	3	4	5

Using the scale shown in the preceding example, please evaluate the awareness material by circling the most appropriate response.

I have seen/received information on the current IT security awareness topic.	1	2	3	4	5
The information was clear and easy to understand.	1	2	3	4	5
The information was useful in helping to understand the topic covered.	1	2	3	4	5
Information was included that I was not aware of or previously knowledgeable about.	1	2	3	4	5
The information was useful to me in helping me to understand my security responsibilities.	1	2	3	4	5
The information grabbed my attention.	1	2	3	4	5
I would benefit from more information similar to this.	1	2	3	4	5
The information effectively explained the topics.	1	2	3	4	5
Did you have questions about the material presented?	Yes	No			
If yes, have you received a response to your question?	Yes	No			
If no, please explain:					
Are there any other topics on information security that you would like to see covered? What topics?	Yes	No			

Security Awareness Class Evaluation

Here is an example of an evaluation form for a security awareness class.

Class Name: _____   Date: _____

Name: (Optional) _____   E-mail: _____

Strongly Disagree	Disagree	Neutral Opinion	Agree	Strongly Agree
1	2	3	4	5

Using the scale shown in the preceding example, please evaluate the awareness class by circling the most appropriate response.

I recently took a class on information security awareness.	1	2	3	4	5
The class material was easy for me to understand.	1	2	3	4	5
The information presented grabbed my attention.	1	2	3	4	5
The information helped me to understand my security responsibilities.	1	2	3	4	5
The instructor seemed knowledgeable on the subject material.	1	2	3	4	5
The instructor was interesting and held my attention.	1	2	3	4	5
The instructor responded to questions.	1	2	3	4	5
The training material was the right level of detail for me.	1	2	3	4	5
Did you have questions about the information presented?	Yes	No			
If yes, have you received a response to your questions?	Yes	No			

Continued

If no, please explain:

Are there any other classes on information security that you would like to see covered? What classes?	Yes	No

Summary

Security awareness and training are important parts of any information security program, and a *Security Awareness and Training Plan* is required for Level 2 or higher C&A packages. In essence the training and awareness program serves to facilitate and improve the C&A process and the overall security posture of the organization by disseminating important security information to the units that support the organization's day-to-day operations. Security training needs to be targeted at the variety of audiences within that overall group (such as developers, ISSOs, and the network operations support group), and feedback from the individuals undergoing training helps to refine and improve the overall program. The methods by which the awareness and training program will be executed need to be documented in the security awareness and training plan.

Notes

1. Mark Wilson and Joan Hash. "Building an Information Technology Security Awareness and Training Program." *NIST Special Publication 800-50*. National Institute of Standards and Technology, October 2003.
2. "Transition Plan for the Use of Key Sizes and Security Strengths by Federal Agencies." *NIST Special Publication 800-57 Part 1*. National Institute of Standards and Technology, 2006 (http://csrc.nist.gov/cryptval/).

## Chapter 10

Addressing End-User Rules of Behavior

"Rules are made for people who aren't willing to make up their own."

—Chuck Yeager

Topics in this chapter:

- Implementing Rules of Behavior

- What Rules to Include

- Consequences of Noncompliance

- Rules of Behavior Checklist

Introduction

End-User Rules of Behavior are policies that your users agree to abide by before they are allowed access to whatever it is that you are certifying and accrediting. Your *End-User Rules of Behavior*, and your plans for implementing them, have to be clearly articulated in the Certification Package. Although a Level 1 Certification Package usually doesn't require an official *End-User Rules of Behavior*, it is still a good idea to put one into place if you have systems that are processing sensitive information.

The *End-User Rules of Behavior* are the rules that end-users have to agree to before they are allowed access to the information system. Clearly, end users need to know what these rules of the road are before they can agree to them. The agreement should be verified before giving the user access. All end users of the information system being certified, including contractors, should agree to the rules.

End users may already have access to the agency network, or have other logins to other applications. Therefore, the rules of behavior should be unique and specific to the information system that is being certified and accredited. Just because an end user has agreed to the rules for other applications doesn't mean they have agreed to the rules for the application that is up for Accreditation.

Implementing Rules of Behavior

The rules of behavior can be implemented either on a paper form or online. In some cases where you are giving a user access to a general support system, and they do not yet have an account at all, a paper form may be the only possibility. If a user already is set up on the enterprise network, and has a private key from an internal Certificate Authority, you can have the user sign rules for access to a new application with their private key. There are administrative advantages to having users sign the rules online. By signing the rules online, administrators can more easily track who has signed them. If paper forms are used, they should be collected and archived in a central and secure place with limited access. The ISSO for the information system that the rules apply to is responsible for either keeping the rules secure, or designating an appropriate staff person to store and secure them.

What Rules to Include

Each information system will require a unique set of rules, and rules that apply to one system may not apply to another. Database systems may require different rules than, say, an application for handhelds. Systems that process financial transactions may require an entirely different set of rules. Rules for a desktop system and the enterprise network may be vastly different than, say, rules for an Employee Resource Processing (ERP) system.

Although some rules are redundant because they simply agree to abide by specific citations of the agency security policy, it is worth listing them to emphasize their importance and to create an accountability log in the form of a user signature. To help you understand the types of rules that should be listed, some sample rules are listed in Tables 10.1 through 10.4.

Rules for Applications, Servers, and Databases

Different applications may require different rules. The rules in Table 10.1 can be adapted to most applications, servers, and databases. Some rules from Tables 10.2 through 10.4 may also be apropos for applications, servers, and databases.

Table 10.1 Rules of Behavior for Applications

End-User Rules of Behavior for \<Name of Information System\>
I agree to:
Use an eight-character password that includes mixed cases, characters, numbers, and letters
Protect my user ID from unauthorized disclosure
Refrain from sharing my password with others
Refrain from trying to subvert the security of any application
Refrain from trying to use any other account except my own
Refrain from representing myself as somebody else
Refrain from disclosing data presented by the application to unauthorized individuals

Continued

Table 10.1 continued Rules of Behavior for Applications

End-User Rules of Behavior for <Name of Information System>
Report any bugs to the information system owner
Report any vulnerabilities discovered to the information system owner
Report suspicious activity or use of agency IT resources
Use the application for its stated purpose
Follow the stated logon and logoff procedures
Change my password every 90 days
Complete training and education classes as required
Retrieve all hard-copy printouts in a timely fashion
Abide by security awareness notices and reminders
Abide by all agency security policies
Challenge unknown personnel who do not display an identification or visitor's badge

Additional Rules for Handhelds

Many of the rules in Table 10.1 also apply to handhelds—for example, the rules for passwords—and are not repeated in Table 10.2. Additional rules that handhelds may require are listed in Table 10.2.

Table 10.2 Rules of Behavior for Handhelds

End-User Rules of Behavior for <Name of Handheld>
I agree to:
Disable HotSync/ActiveSync when not using it
Ensure that any sensitive information that I put on my handheld is encrypted
Protect Classified Information with data wiping software
Run agency-approved antivirus software on my handheld
Keep the antivirus signatures on my handheld up to date
Refrain from connecting to public networks that use Wi-Fi

Continued

Table 10.2 continued Rules of Behavior for Handhelds

End-User Rules of Behavior for \<Name of Handheld\>
Connect only to approved wireless networks
Report any handheld security incidents that I become aware of
Use the approved secure remote access VPN to connect to the corporate network

Additional Rules for Laptops and Desktop Systems

Many of the rules in Table 10.2 also apply to laptops—for example the rules for antivirus software. Additional rules that laptops may require are listed in Table 10.3.

Table 10.3 Rules of Behavior for Laptops

End-User Rules of Behavior for \<Name of Laptop\>
I agree to:
Make sure I do not leave my laptop unattended in a public place
Use an approved cable lock to lock my laptop to my desk
Make sure that approved laptop recovery software is installed on my laptop
Turn on the screenlock when I step away from my laptop or desktop system
Run an agency-approved personal firewall on my laptop and desktop
Refrain from installing unapproved hardware (e.g., Wi-Fi card) on my laptop
Refrain from disabling mandatory antivirus software
Connect to the agency network using the approved remote dial-in procedure
Abide by the agency limited personal use policy
Refrain from using my system to access pornography
Refrain from using my system for illegal activities
Refrain from using my system for commercial profit-making activities
Comply with all IT audits
Abide by all federal copyright laws
Refrain from violating any software license agreements

Continued

Table 10.3 continued Rules of Behavior for Laptops

End-User Rules of Behavior for <Name of Laptop>
Report any security incidents I become aware of
Refrain from disclosing my private keys
Report the loss of my private key
Protect agency resources from unauthorized disclosure, modification, and deletion
Refrain from downloading freeware and shareware without authorized permission

Additional Rules for Privileged Users

All the rules in Table 10.3 apply to Privileged Users; however, there are additional rules that Privileged Users should agree to, some of which are listed in Table 10.4. Rules from Table 10.1 also apply to Privileged Users and are not repeated in Table 10.4.

Table 10.4 Rules of Behavior for Privileged Users

End-User Rules of Behavior for <Name of Information System>
I agree to:
Refrain from programming login IDs or passwords into scripts or routines
Refrain from disclosing account or login information without proper approvals
Refrain from disclosing the *administrator* and *root* passwords
Disclose user passwords in accordance with the agency security policy
Terminate user accounts according to the agency security policy
Ensure that all system configuration changes are documented
Make sure configuration changes are submitted through the change management configuration change approval process
Install all security patches as required
Monitor and review firewall, intrusion detection, and system logs in a timely manner
Configure systems to abide by the agency security policies

Continued

Table 10.4 continued Rules of Behavior for Privileged Users

End-User Rules of Behavior for <Name of Information System>
Ensure that *groups* and *netgroups* are properly registered with the LDAP server
Assist end users with security help as required
Ensure that servers log appropriate security events
Refrain from altering data except in accordance with my job responsibilities
Refrain from disclosing the remote login procedures to unauthorized users
Ensure that I configure systems to be in compliance with agency security policies

Consequences of Noncompliance

Somewhere in the rules of behavior, consequences for noncompliance should be described. Possible consequences might be:

- Disciplinary action (unspecified)
- Mandatory security awareness training
- A supervisory warning
- Revocation of a security clearance
- Termination

The noncompliance consequences should be well thought out. For example, it may not be in the best interest of the agency to terminate key personnel for leaving a paper document overnight on a printer. Each case of noncompliance should be evaluated individually to determine the magnitude of the risk to the agency.

Rules of Behavior Checklist

To ensure that your rules of behavior is deemed acceptable by auditors, use the following checklist to ensure that you have not forgotten anything:

- Have all users of the information system undergoing Certification signed a statement agreeing that they have read and understand the rules of behavior?

- Are the consequences of noncompliance stated in the rules of behavior?

- Are signed rules of behavior archived?

- Does the ISSO know where to find the archived Rules of Behavior?

- Are paper-based rules of behavior protected from fire and flood threats?

- Are the rules of behavior published in a place where they can be reviewed by the end users after they have been previously agreed to?

- Are noncompliance breaches of rules of behavior treated as a security incident?

- If private keys are used for signing an online rules form, are the private keys properly protected?

- Are end users required to report if their private keys are lost or stolen?

- Have privileged users been identified?

Summary

End-User Rules of Behavior are important to any organization because they formally sets the standards by which users are expected to conduct themselves. These rules of behavior also set forth the consequences of noncompliance. Without a document outlining rules of behavior, users cannot be held accountable for their actions, making it impossible to expect that they are employing basic principles of security while using the organization's information resources. End users need to be informed of the rules of behavior, and they need to understand that by using the information system, they are agreeing to abide by them.

Chapter 11

Addressing Incident Response

"It has long been a grave question whether any government...can be strong enough to maintain its existence in great emergencies."

—Abraham Lincoln

Topics in this chapter:

- **Purpose and Applicability**
- **Policies and Guidelines**
- **Reporting Framework**
- **Roles and Responsibilities**
- **Definitions**
- **Incident Handling**
- **Forensic Investigations**
- **Incident Types**
- **Incident Response Plan Checklist**
- **Security Incident Reporting Form**

Introduction

Although an *Incident Response Plan* is required only for certifications Level 2 and up, all IT organizations that take security seriously should have an Incident Response Plan whether their systems are undergoing C&A or not. When it comes to C&A, the goal of the *Incident Response Plan* is to describe the incident response process by which the information system undergoing C&A is required to abide.

Due to its unscheduled nature and its potential for damage, a security incident can predispose an otherwise competent staff into immediate anxiety and frustration. A well thought out Incident Response Plan helps retain order and efficient organizational processes during a stressful situation. Every Incident Response Plan should contain certain key instructional elements and the C&A audit team may fail your Incident Response Plan if any of these elements are missing. Though your plan can include more information than the required key elements, be sure at the very minimum to include a section on each of the following:

- Purpose and applicability
- Policies and guidelines
- Reporting framework
- Roles and responsibilities
- Definitions
- Incident handling
- Incident types
- Incident reporting form

If time permits, you may also want to include information on how to detect incidents and how to proceed with forensic investigations.

Purpose and Applicability

Even though it may seem obvious that your document should include a stated purpose, it is important not to forget this section. If you don't say what information system(s) the Incident Response Plan is for, the C&A auditors could come to the conclusion that an Incident Response Plan for the system that is up for C&A does not exist. The name of the Incident Response Plan should be consistent with the name of all the other document plans in your Certification Package, and it is a good idea to state the information system in the document title. For example, if you are certifying and accrediting an information system known as System ABC, make sure your Incident Response Plan is titled *Incident Response Plan for System ABC*.

Policies and Guidelines

In the policies and guidelines section, you will want to cite the agency security policies, standards, and guidelines that the incident response team follows and adheres to. You should list the formal policy document names in their entirety and where these documents can be found (e.g., the Web URL on the agency intranet). Do not confuse policies with incident handling procedures. The policies describe what the rules are, and the incident handling procedures describe how to follow those rules. If your agency has an *Incident Response Manual* or handbook, you will want to list this document as reference material in this section.

You should also include any of the following federal mandates that you follow:

- The Office of Management and Budget (OMB) Circular A-130, Appendix III, *Security of Federal Automated Information Resources*, specifies that federal agencies will "Ensure there is a capability to provide help to users when a security incident occurs in the system and to share information concerning common vulnerabilities and threats."

- Critical Infrastructure Protection (CIP): Presidential Decision Directive 63 (PDD-63) directs that each department and agency shall develop plans for protecting its own critical infrastructure. Accordingly, the <Agency Name> has created the <Agency Name> CSIRC to provide a 24 X 7 single point of contact (POC) for computer security incidents detected within the <Agency Name>.

- The <Agency Name> Security Manual <official document name> directs the <Agency Name> and the <Agency Name> Inspector General to establish a capability that will "serve as the first tier of incident response and the investigative and reporting body…" for the <Agency Name>.

- The CSIRC is sponsored by the <Agency Name> Deputy Commissioner for Modernization and Chief Information Officer and is designed to be proactive in preventing, detecting, and responding to computer security incidents targeting <Agency Name>'s enterprise Information Technology (IT) assets.

Reporting Framework

Your incident response reporting framework establishes who should be contacted and the order in which escalation occurs. Depending on the agency requirements, it may be necessary to establish timeframes for escalation. If your agency does not require specific incident escalation timeframes, you can still establish these thresholds in your Incident Response Plan if your information system owner and ISSO require it. Timeframes for escalation often are based on the severity of the incident and the extensiveness of the damage— the more systems that are impacted, the more resources you will need to resolve the incident.

Most federal agencies have a Computer Security Incident Response Center (CSIRC). The agency CSIRC provides centralized incident response services and coordinates incident response activities agencywide. In developing an Incident Response Plan for C&A, you'll need to make sure that the Incident Response Plan is consistent with the processes already established by the CSIRC. The Incident Response Plan developed for the C&A package does not replace the process already established by the CSIRC—it augments it and embellishes it with the particulars relevant to the information system undergoing C&A. Essentially, the Incident Response Plan for the C&A package should be an extension of the agencywide incident response plan.

Agency CSIRCs are required to report significant security incidents to the United States Computer Emergency Readiness Team (US-CERT).

However, before that occurs, the incident should be reported up through the bureau, and agency CSIRC, as depicted in Figure 11.1.

Figure 11.1 C&A Incident Response Plan as an Extension of Agency CSIRC

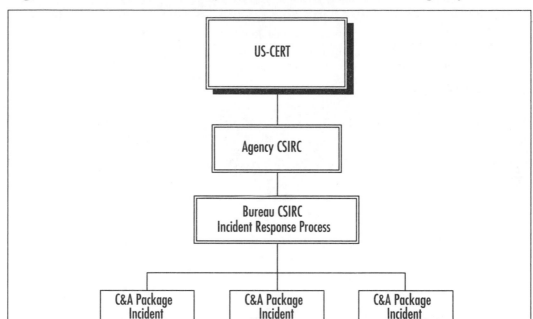

It's important to describe an escalation process in your Incident Response Plan that uses your described response framework. An incident could occur at night when some of the staff is unavailable, and sometimes people do not respond to e-mail or cell phones. The person who detects the incident needs to know who to report it to and how long to wait to escalate it if there is no response. Even with a quick response, security policies may require your incident response team to escalate high impact incidents up through the escalation framework according to particular time frames. If escalation time frames are required by your security policy and *C&A Handbook*, be sure to include them.

Roles and Responsibilities

In the roles and responsibilities section of the Incident Response Plan, you'll want to state specifically what the expected responsibilities are for the different levels of the response framework. You should include as an appendix to your Incident Response Plan, a contact list that includes every person, and each organization, that has documented responsibilities in the plan.

Agency CSIRC

Each agency CSIRC will have unique responsibilities. You should list high-level bullets of the expected responsibilities of your agency CSIRC in your C&A Incident Response Plan. Typical CSIRC responsibilities are as follows:

- Develop and maintain the agency computer security incident response capability policy and procedures

- Maintain an incident response capability to ensure timely reporting of security incidents

- Provide implementation guidance for processes and procedures

- Establish procedures to ensure timely reporting of security incidents

- Report significant computer security incidents to US-CERT as soon as possible but no more than one hour after detection with a follow-up report every four hours thereafter until the incident is resolved

- Report minor incidents in a monthly incident report to agency CIO

- Report all planned penetration testing and vulnerability assessments to the CIO

- Write lessons learned and follow-up reports on agency computer security incidents

- Implement tools and processes supporting the agency computer security incident response capability and procedures to collect and safeguard evidence for use in legal or administrative functions

- Distribute advisories and vulnerability bulletins received from the CSIRC to appropriate agency CSIRC personnel and designated points of contact (POC) at their respective sites

Information System Owner and ISSO

Typical responsibilities of the information system owner usually are managed by the ISSO. While processing a security incident, the ISSO should keep the information system owner apprised of the status incident. The C&A Incident Response Plan should list the names of the information system owner, and the ISSO on the contact page. Typical responsibilities of the information system owner include the following:

- Assign a computer security incident response team (CSIRT) that interacts with the CSIRC to resolve security incidents

- Ensure that the CSIRT has implemented procedures to reduce the risk of, and minimize the damage of, a computer security incident

- Ensure that the CSIRT operations comply with:
  - Agency Computer Security Incident Response policies
  - Agency Security Awareness Training
  - Agency security auditing and record retention procedures
  - Agency IT standards
  - The agency security program
  - OMB Circular No. A-130, Appendix III
  - The Federal Information Security Management Act of 2002

- Use guidance from the National Institute of Standards and Technology, Special Publication 800-61, *Computer Security Incident Handling Guide*

- Ensure that the information system undergoing C&A has a formal computer security incident response plan to include the timely identification, detection, management, containment, capture, and safeguarding of evidence

- Ensure that users of the information system are required to report all suspected security incidents to the information system security incident point of contact

- Ensure that security incident information will be logged and tracked by reporting, completing, and submitting the agency *IT Security Incident Reporting Form to the CSIRC*

- Assign a CSIRT point of contact that acts as a central coordination point for the agency CSIRC

Incident Response Manager

The computer security incident point of contact (POC) for the information system under C&A often is known as the Incident Response Manager. The ISSO may designate someone as the Incident Response Manager; however, the ISSO may also choose to act as the Incident Response Manager. The Incident Response Manager should coordinate notification and escalation and ensure that the incident response team is properly assembled. The Incident Response Manager typically holds responsibilities such as:

- Evaluate known threats and vulnerabilities to ascertain if additional safeguards are needed and brief the ISSO as appropriate

- Develop procedures to receive information on security incidents and common vulnerabilities from the agency CSIRC

- Determine the incident priority level of the security incident for the information system under C&A and its computing environment

- Determine incident impact to the information system under C&A

- Perform appropriate and immediate investigation of every security incident, whether the event was detected by the system or reported by a user

- Establish and implement tools and processes supporting the computer security incident response capability's procedures to ensure timely reporting of security incidents

- Fill out the *Security Incident Reporting Form*

- Report security incidents in accordance with agency security policy and standards to the ISSO and agency CSIRC as appropriate

- Report minor computer security incidents in a monthly security incident report to the agency CSIRC on a regular monthly basis

- Forward reports and documents pertaining to computer security incidents such as incident summary, lessons learned, and follow-up reports, to the CSIRT upon the receipt of the information

- Appoint a backup POC to take their own place in the event of absence

- Notify the CSIRT and ISSO when the Incident Response Plan changes.

Definitions

Your Incident Response Plan should include a section on definitions, and in it you should define any significant terms used in the plan. Some definitions that you'll want to include are incident, threat, exposure, vulnerability, event, and incident severities.

Incident

If your agency has its own unique definition of a security incident, you should use it. Other definitions I have seen used in reputable Incident Response Plans are as follows:

- **Definition 1** A security incident is a violation of a security policy for a system, network, telecommunications system, or facility.

- **Definition 2** A security incident is any real or suspected adverse event in relation to the security of computers or computer networks

- **Definition 3** A security incident is any compromised or suspected compromised system; any type of attack or pre-attack reconnaissance levied on or from a computer resource; or misuse of IT resources (such as chain letters, unauthorized access, virus hoaxes, etc.), or any other anomalous activities detected.

The National Institute of Standards and Technology makes a distinction between computer security events and computer security incidents. NIST defines a security event as follows:

> A violation or imminent threat of violation of computer security policies, acceptable use policies, or standard computer security practices.[1]

If your agency has a *C&A Handbook*, there should be a section in it on incident response. You should refer to that section when documenting your definitions and follow the recommended guidance from the handbook.

Impact, Notification, and Escalation

Although all security incidents should be taken seriously, they may not all have the same severity. Your Incident Response Plan should define how incident severities will be determined and what this means in terms of incident handling. Some of the things that you will want to take into consideration when recommending severity levels are the following items:

- Number of sites or networks affected

- Importance of systems affected

- Number of agency systems affected by this incident

- Number of other agency systems vulnerable to the same exploit

- Consistency with the latest vulnerability scan of the target system

- Known countermeasures and existence of tested vendor patches/ hot-fixes

- Entry point of the incident (e.g., network, telephone line, router, application)

- Potential damage resulting from the incident

- Estimated time to close out the incident

- Resources required to handle the incident

- Business impact of system(s) involved

- Exposure to agency data
- Potential of incident to spread to multiple sites/systems

NIST has defined severity categories and escalation thresholds in the publication, *Computer Security Incident Handling Guide*, NIST Special Publication 800-61, January 2004. Many agencies may elect to use the NIST guidelines verbatim from pp. 3–15 of this document. I have taken the NIST guidelines and made a few modifications as depicted in Table 11.1. The timeframes listed in Table 11.1 should be interpreted as the maximum amount of time allowed to pass before action is taken.

The severity of a computer security incident can be designated as High, Medium, or Low, according to the type of system compromised, and the extent of the network penetration. In general, unauthorized access to security systems such as firewalls is more critical than unauthorized access to user workstations. Therefore, unauthorized access to firewalls may be considered High priority and unauthorized access to a user workstation may be considered Low priority. However, if the unauthorized access to user workstations is networkwide, and in multiple geographic locations, this type of compromise in fact might be considered High priority. The combination of the type of system compromised, and the extent of the compromise, is vast. Due to all the possible combinations of compromise, it is difficult to describe the severity of impact for every situation. Deciding on the severity of impact is a qualitative decision and a judgment call at best. In general, if the impact to the business mission is low, the severity of the impact is low. Similarly, if the impact to the business mission is high, the severity of the impact is high.

Providing guidelines for escalation and response speeds up the decision-making process when administrators are challenged with an anxiety-provoking security crisis. In conjunction with the time frames, your plan should also establish what sort of action should be taken as far as notification to a higher authority goes. When do the information system owner, data owners, and CIO get notified? Are they notified at the same time as the agency CSIRC? If your agency security policies do not offer guidelines on reporting, the information system ISSO will need to make the appropriate recommendations.

You need to be clear as to who is part of the CSIRT. The CSIRT should be described in your plan with key personnel identified. Security incidents are never convenient and some members of the incident response team might not be immediately available. Your *Incident Response Plan* should include detailed contact lists that include home phone numbers, cell phone numbers, pagers, and e-mail addresses for everyone that is part of the CSIRT.

Table 11.1 Incident Response Escalation Time Frames

Recommended Time Frames for Response to Security Incidents (Based on Importance of System Compromised and Impact)

Current Impact or Likely Future Impact	High Importance System	Medium Importance System	Low Importance System
Root or administrator access	15 minutes	30 minutes	1 hour
Unauthorized data modification	15 minutes	30 minutes	2 hours
Unauthorized access to sensitive data	15 minutes	1 hour	1 hour
Unauthorized access to user data	30 minutes	2 hours	4 hours
Services unavailable	30 minutes	2 hours	4 hours
Annoyance	30 minutes	As required	As required

Incident Handling

Incident handling refers to the operational procedures used to actually manipulate the incident and purge it from your systems. If your agency already has detailed instructions for incident handling, it is acceptable simply to republish those instructions in this section. If you republish agencywide incident handling instructions, be sure to state what publication or document these instructions come from, and that your incident response team is required to follow these instructions. If agencywide incident handling instructions do not exist, you will need to develop some for your plan.

Something that is very important to keep in mind while processing a security incident is that once a system has been compromised, you cannot trust any of the information on it. A compromised system has lost its integrity. Systems that have been compromised will ultimately have to be rebuilt.

Detecting an Incident

Your agency may require that you include some information on how to detect a security incident. Suggestions on what to put in this section of your document are listed as follows.

Suspicious accounts and logins are often characterized by:

- Single or multiple unsuccessful login attempts
- Unexplained or suspicious entries in system log files
- Questionable user permissions on accounts
- Multiple successful login attempts in a short amount of time, on multiple systems

Suspicious activities related to data and files often are characterized by:

- Unexplained modification or deletion of data
- Unauthorized creation of new user accounts
- User accounts with unauthorized increased privilege
- Accounts without passwords
- Activities that breach existing security policies
- Unexplained discovery of new files or unfamiliar filenames
- Recurring viruses
- Modification of file lengths and/or dates without permission
- Unauthorized or unexplained attempts to write to system files

- Unexplained attempts to make changes in system files

- Detection of unauthorized mirrored sites

- Domain Name System (DNS) cache corruption

- Documents that contain malicious code or unauthorized macros

- Unauthorized modification of Web sites

- Unauthorized Access Control Lists (ACLs) on routers

- Unauthorized ports open on firewalls

- Unauthorized source or destination addresses for authorized ports

- Connectionless Transmission Control Protocol (TCP) traffic

- Missing data, files, or applications

- Unexpected processes running

- Activation of a system alarm or similar indication of an intrusion

- Denial of service on an otherwise available system

- Multiple users logged into a single account

- Entire system failures or reboots

- Unsatisfactory system performance (e.g., system is slow or locking up)

- Unauthorized operation of programs or processes

- Appearance of new files on the system, without knowledge of users or administrators

- Applications that do not execute properly, or as usual

- Suspiciously high network traffic

- E-mail server functionality loss or complete e-mail system failure

- Unusual network, system, or user activity occurring at "abnormal" operating hours

Containment and Eradication

Upon discovery of a security incident, it is very important to prevent it from spreading to other systems and networks. You should always try to contain an incident before you try to eradicate it. Somewhere in your Incident Response Plan you should state that you have a containment strategy, and describe what it is based on.

Each type of security incident may require a completely different containment strategy. Various measures that can be used to contain security incidents and eradicate the intruder include:

- Blocking all incoming network traffic on border routers
- Blocking networks and incoming traffic on firewalls
- Blocking particular services (e.g., ftp, telnet) and ports on firewalls
- Disconnecting infected systems from the network
- Shutting down the infected system
- Locking compromised accounts
- Changing passwords on compromised systems
- Isolating specific network segments

Before you attempt to remove and overwrite files associated with an incident, decisions need to be made on whether the evidence should be saved for forensic investigation. The incident response team should report the facts to the agency legal department and take into consideration their advisement. Usually, it is not worth the time and expense it takes to find out who the perpetrator is. However, before conceding that the intruder will not be caught, the question should at least be asked if evidence preservation is required.

During the containment and eradication process, the CSIRT will need to make various decisions on how to proceed. You may want to stipulate in your Incident Response Plan that the CSIRT will make the following determinations while processing the incident:

- Determine which systems, applications, and networks have been affected

- Determine whether to inform users that a security incident has occurred

- Determine to what extent the affected systems should remain operational

- Determine the scope, impact, and damage to the compromised systems

- Determine if the prescribed course of action will destroy the evidence

- Determine if other ISSOs should be informed of the incident

Recovery and Closure

As mentioned earlier, all compromised systems need to be rebuilt. Whether they will be rebuilt on the originally compromised system, or built on a new system is one of the decisions that will need to be made. Before rebuilding the system, if the decision has been made not to proceed with a forensic investigation, a regular backup should be performed. The operating system should be reinstalled, hardened, and have relevant patches installed prior to installing any applications.

When an incident is closed, both the CSIRT and CSIRC should be in agreement that the incident has been completely resolved and the affected systems have been recovered and restored. The Security Incident Reporting Form should be updated to indicate the incident has been closed.

After an incident has been closed, the CSIRT should have a meeting to discuss lessons learned. It is always worthwhile to document the lessons learned. The types of questions to be answered and documented in the lessons learned meeting include:

- Exactly what happened, and at what times?

- How well did the CSIRT perform in dealing with the incident?

- Was the CSIRC responsive to the CSIRT's needs?

- Were the documented procedures followed? Were they adequate?

- What information was needed sooner?

- Were any steps or actions taken that might have inhibited the recovery?

- What would the CSIRT do differently the next time a similar incident occurs?

- What is the monetary estimate for the amount of damage the incident cost?

- How many hours did it take to resolve the incident?

- What corrective actions can prevent similar incidents in the future?

- What additional tools or resources are needed to detect, analyze, and mitigate future incidents?

Documenting lessons learned can help improve the ability to more efficiently handle security incidents in the future. It may also provide justification for the information system owner's security budget to procure new assets like intrusion detection systems and security incident management consoles.

Forensic Investigations

Not all security incidents will require forensic investigations. In the event that a forensic investigation is required, it will expedite the process if the course of action is planned out up front. Forensic investigations require that the evidence be preserved in its original state. Any modifications made to the system containing the evidence could be construed as tainting of the evidence.

The way to preserve the evidence is to perform a bitstream backup. A bitstream backup is a special kind of backup that replicates the evidence exactly without making any changes to the original data. When preserving evidence, it is important not to change the timestamps of the data that indicate the access times. You don't want to change the read access of the data because it might have been the intruder who last read the data and created the last read access timestamp. You also want to preserve the file slack, which is the data stored in swap files or memory buffers. Therefore, if a forensic investigation is to take place, you need specific policies and procedures. If a forensic investigation should occur, you may want to stipulate that the CSIRT follows these policies:

- Only tools that create evidence grade backups (bitstream backups) can be used to access the compromised system

- Forensic investigations must be done by staff who have prior experience or training in this competency

- A chain of custody documenting who has access to the evidence must be established

- The obtained evidence must be submitted to the agency legal team along with a report of evidence findings

- Send evidence preservation request letters to ISSOs in charge of systems that are connected to the information system being investigated

- Follow all U.S. Department of Justice search and seizure guidelines

When performing forensic analysis, you'll need to use fresh software tools that are not currently installed on the tools where the incident has occurred. Any forensic tools on the breached system could have been replaced with Trojan programs; therefore you can't trust their integrity. A good example is to take into consideration the output of the **ps** program that you run on a UNIX system to view the process table. The **ps** program displays a list of the UNIX daemons currently running on the system. However, certain Trojan programs have been designed to display everything except the hacker backdoor daemons. Since you also need to preserve the evidence and integrity of the breached system, it is best that the fresh software you use to provide forensic analysis is installed on an entirely different system or drive such as a portable flash disk. Though operating systems contain some built-in programs that are useful for collecting evidence, there are also powerful commercial off-the-shelf tools designed just for this purpose.

Some of the commercial off-the-shelf tools have advanced features for preserving evidence that are above and beyond the capabilities of most operating systems. Tools that are currently being used by various federal agencies and law enforcement include products made by some of the following vendors:

- Access Data (www.accessdata.com)

- Digital Intelligence, Inc. (www.digitalintelligence.com)

- Guidance Software (www.guidancesoftware.com)

- New Technologies, Inc. (www.forensics–intl.com)

- Paraben (www.paraben-forensics.com)

Some of the things that you'll want to look for and retain for evidence and analysis are:

- Suspicious IP addresses and their geographic locations

- Open ports that should not be open

- Open files that should not be open

- File slack, RAM slack, and drive slack

- Timestamps and dates

- Services running that should not be running

- Unauthorized port listeners

- World-writeable files with new timestamps

- Aberrant packet behavior

There are some UNIX–based forensics tools available for free on the Internet that are very good at collecting and analyzing forensic evidence. Popular UNIX tools for security forensics include:

- **awk** Good to use for formatting log files to look for trends.

- **egrep and grep** Good to use in conjunction with **awk** to perform searches in log files to look for trends.

- **find** Finds and identifies files and directories that have changed since their last timestamp.

- **dd** Used for converting and copying a file to another media device.

- **dig** Similar to nslookup. Performs DNS lookups

- **lastcomm** Displays process accounting records and execution times

- **lsof** Displays list of open files

- **netcat** A port listener (also used as a popular hacker backdoor)

- **netstat** Displays current network connections, interface information, routing tables, multicast memberships, and masquerade connections.

- **nmap** A port scanner (good for finding which ports are open on your systems)

- **nslookup** Used to investigate hostname resolution or suspicious DNS anomalies

- **ps** Displays the current process table

- **tcpdump or winpcap** Used for packet forensics

- **traceroute** Displays routes that packets take to reach their destination

Incident Types

If security incidents are thoughtfully categorized, it can speed up the ability to respond to incidents by establishing a uniform understanding among the incident response team. It is certainly possible for a security incident to consist of multiple types of violations. If a security incident consists of multiple violations, all violation types should be noted on the incident reporting form.

Your agency CSIRC may already have the different types of security incidents categorized with identification numbers. If incident categories do not exist, or are not acceptable to the information owner or the ISSO, the C&A preparation team may need to develop its own categories. Table 11.2 lists a sampling of security incidents. This table is by no means exhaustive, however, it is comprehensive and most security incidents will fit in one of these categories. Before developing your own categories of security incidents for your Incident Response Plan, you should inquire with the evaluation team if this is acceptable or if you are required to use the CSIRC definitions. It is reasonable and acceptable to ask questions of the evaluation team along the way when you require clarification. If you want your package to be accredited, you're usually better off following the direction of the evaluation team even if you don't completely agree with it.

Table 11.2 Types of Security Incidents

ID No.	Incident Name	Incident Description
1	Adverse Mission Impact	Any type of circumstance that prevents agency missions, functions, or lines of business from being achieved
2	Annoyance	Any type of circumstance that creates an unprecedented annoyance that may impact the ability to perform daily job functions (e.g., hoaxes, chain letters)
3	Buffer Overflow Attack	Any circumstance that results in massive memory flooding
4	Data Modification	Unauthorized modification of files or data
5	Data Removal or Deletion	Removal of files or data where that removal has not been properly authorized
6	Denial-of-Service Attack	Any type of circumstance that degrades system performance of normal functions when overwhelmed from activity from one or more sources
7	Failed Access Attempts	Any failed attempts of unauthorized access to accounts
8	Identity Fraud	Any type of access to information technology resources where an individual (either outside the agency or within the agency) masquerades as another individual
9	Infrastructure Outage (including natural disasters)	A power loss, flood, natural disaster, or other occurrence that results in the loss of service, data, or security of the information technology infrastructure
10	Insider Threat—Misuse of Privileges	Any unauthorized use of data or systems in which the user has an authorized account

Continued

www.syngress.com

Table 11.2 continued Types of Security Incidents

ID No.	Incident Name	Incident Description
11	Insider Threat—Unauthorized Access	Any type of unauthorized use of an account outside the account's authorized levels of privilege for normal usage
12	Insider Threat—Administrator Error	An unintentional security breach that occurs due to an administrative error (e.g., incorrect configuration)
13	Installation of Unlicensed Software	Installation of software that is not approved or licensed by the agency (includes commercial software, custom code, freeware, and media)
14	IP Address Spoofing	An attack where an unauthorized user gains access to a computer or a network by making it appear that a message or packet has come from a trusted machine by "spoofing" the IP address of that machine
15	Java or ActiveX Exploitation	Any circumstance that creates exploitation of Java or ActiveX
16	MAC Address Spoofing	An attack where an unauthorized user gains access to a computer or a network by making it appear that a message or packet has come from a trusted machine by "spoofing" the MAC address of the trusted machine
17	Malicious Code	Indication of a computer virus, worm, or Trojan whether destructive, or harmless
18	Loss or Theft	An indication that a computer, system, or media has been lost or stolen
19	Man-in-the-Middle Attack	An attack where a malicious party intercepts and/or alters a legitimate communication between two friendly parties without the knowledge of the original sender or recipient

Continued

Table 11.2 continued Types of Security Incidents

ID No.	Incident Name	Incident Description
20	Network Bandwidth Attack	An unusual and unauthorized increase in network traffic (possibly induced by a user downloading excessive amounts of data, or using unauthorized tools that reserve large amounts of bandwidth)
21	Other Attacks	All other circumstances in which a security incident occurs but cannot be identified by any other predefined category
22	Packet Sniffing / Network Wiretap	A circumstance where a malicious user gathers, monitors, or analyzes data communications traveling between two or more systems
23	Reconnaissance Scans	Indication of a network probe by an unauthorized user (possibly gathering information such as open ports, running services, operating systems, or configuration information)
24	Security Attack	Any circumstance where a system or network's security support infrastructure fails, and the data on that system or network is left open to security attacks (e.g., failure of a host- or network-based intrusion detection system)
25	Sensitive Compromise	Any theft of sensitive resources (e.g., passwords; protected, classified, or restricted data; licensed applications or software; restricted applications, software or code)
26	Stolen or Misplaced Equipment	A circumstance that results in stolen or misplaced agency hardware, equipment, or media
27	Unauthorized Web Surfing	Web surfing by employees to untrusted and potentially dangerous or inappropriate Web sites

Continued

Table 11.2 continued Types of Security Incidents

ID No.	Incident Name	Incident Description
28	Unauthorized Access	Any type of unauthorized use of a valid account by someone who is not an employee of the agency
29	Unauthorized Access and Modification of Access Control Lists	Any circumstance where an unauthorized user changes the configurations of access control lists located on critical network infrastructure such as routers or firewalls
30	User Data Breach	Any type of circumstance that creates unauthorized loss, theft, alteration, or compromise of user data or private user information
31	Web Site Defacement	Any activity that causes, or attempts to deface, or create unauthorized modification of internal or external agency Web sites

Incident Response Plan Checklist

Once your Incident Response Plan is finished, use this checklist to make sure you didn't forget anything:

- Does your plan accurately describe the systems it applies to?
- Does your plan include a contact list of key personnel?
- Does your plan include information on roles and responsibilities?
- Does your plan include a diagram of the escalation framework?
- Does your plan include how to contact the agency CSIRC?
- Does your plan list the members of the CSIRT team?
- Does your plan list the members of the CSIRC team?
- Does your plan include a description of incident types?
- Does your plan include guidance on severity levels?

- Does your plan include information on agency security policies?
- Does your plan include incident handling guidelines?
- Does your plan include a section on information forensics?
- Does your plan include a *Security Incident Reporting Form*?

Security Incident Reporting Form

Every incident response program should have an *Incident Reporting Form* to standardize and track the collection of security incident information. The *Incident Reporting Form* that applies to the information system undergoing C&A should be included at the end of your Incident Response Plan. The information contained on the *Incident Reporting Form* should be consistent with the information described in the Incident Response Plan. For example, if you include a section on the form that calls for a severity classification, be sure that severities are defined in the Incident Response Plan. A sample Incident Reporting Form is shown in Figure 11.2.

Figure 11.2 Sample Security Incident Reporting Form

SECURITY INCIDENT REPORTING FORM

Incident Report Number:

Date and Time: _____

Incident Response Manager:_____ Alternate POC:_____

Name: _____

Phone: _____

Fax:_____

Pager: _____

Incident Geographic Location:

Building: _____Cubical/Room: _____

Incident Type, Name(s) and ID:

Incident Type Identification Numbers (from list):

  Data: ☐ Classified   ☐ Unclassified

System Information: (Report operating system name, version, and patch level/Service Pack)

Platform: ☐ Workstation   ☐ Server   ☐ Laptop

Asset Identification Bar Code Number: _____

Networks and Domains Affected:

Incident Summary: (Be specific. List dates and times. Include how incident was detected and resolved and describe what forensics tools and programs were used.)

Incident Status:

Open

Closed

Law Enforcement Contacted (List reasons if law enforcement was not contacted.)

Summary

An Incident Response Plan formally documents the agency's strategy for responding to security breaches. By its very nature, a security incident is a time of crisis to some degree, and during this time, more so than any other time, you need to ensure that decisions being made are levelheaded and based on sound judgments. The best way to do this is to define clear procedures and protocols for responding to the crisis before the crisis ever hits and then to train employees about these procedures and protocols. This is why the Incident Response Plan is such a vital document.

The Incident Response Plan should cover all foreseeable security events, and it should lay out the rules and triggers by which agency personnel are to take action in response to the event. Although it may be impossible to predict when and where a denial-of-service attack will strike, it is somewhat easier to determine what the appropriate response should be. If this response is documented and agency employees are trained on the response, then cooler heads will prevail when and if the possibility of the attack ever becomes a reality.

Additional Resources

This section provides you with information about organizations involved with incident response. It also includes lists of books and other material related to incident response and forensics.

Incident Response Organizations

The organizations listed in Table 11.3 offer valuable information on computer security incidents, vulnerabilities, and response activities.

Table 11.3 Incident Response Organizations

Organization and Web site	Description
CERT Coordination Center http://www.cert.org	A federally funded research and development center operated by Carnegie Mellon University

Continued

Table 11.3 continued Incident Response Organizations

Organization and Web site	Description
Common Vulnerabilities and Exposures http://cve.mitre.org	A list of standardized names for vulnerabilities developed by the MITRE Corporation
Forum of Incident Response and Security Teams http://www.first.org/	An organization that specializes in computer security incident response
SANS Top 20 http://www.sans.org/top20	A security vulnerability list maintained by SANS and development with the FBI
X-FORCE Alerts and Advisories http://xforce.iss.net/xforce/alerts	Information on Internet threats and vulnerabilities operated by Internet Security Systems
United States Department of Defense CERT http://www.cert.mil	A central DoD Web site offering current information on security vulnerabilities and incidents
United States Computer Emergency Readiness Team http://www.us-cert.gov/	Coordinates defense and response against cyber attacks on the U.S. infrastructure
United States Department of Homeland Security http://www.dhs.gov/dhspublic/	Publishes threat information to the U.S. infrastructure

Additional Resources

The following books offer useful information on computer security incident response:

> Farmer, Dan and Wietse Venema. *Forensic Discovery.* Addison–Wesley, December 2004. ISBN: 020163497X.

> Jones, Keith J. Real *Digital Forensics: Computer Security and Incident Response.* Addison–Wesley, September 2005. ISBN: 0321240693.

Kruse, Warren G. and Jay G. Heiser. *Computer Forensics: Incident Response Essentials.* Addison-Wesley, September 2001. ISBN: 0201707195.

Lucas, Julie and Brian Moeller. *The Effective Incident Response Team.* Addison-Wesley, 2004. ISBN: 0201761750.

Mandia, Kevin and Chris Prosise. *Incident Response, Investigating Computer Crime.* Osborne/McGraw Hill, 2001. ISBN: 0072131829.

Northcutt, Stephen. *Computer Security Incident Handling.* SANS Institute, March 2003. ISBN: 0972427376.

Schweitzer, Douglas. *Incident Response, Computer Forensics Toolkit.* Wiley, 2003. ISBN: 0764526367.

Van Wyk, Kenneth R. and Richard Forno. *Incident Response.* O'Reilly & Associates, 2001. ISBN: 0596001304.

Articles and Papers on Incident Response

Various useful articles and papers on computer security incident response are listed here:

Computer Security Incident Handling Guide. NIST Special Publication 800-61, January 2004 (http://csrc.nist.gov/publications/nistpubs/800-61/sp800-61.pdf).

"Digital Evidence: Standards and Principles (Draft)." Forensic Science Communications, April 2000 (www.fbi.gov/hq/lab/fsc/backissu/april2000/swgde.htm).

FCC Computer Security Incident Response Guide. United States Federal Communications Commission, December 2001 (http://csrc.nist.gov/fasp/FASPDocs/incident-response/Incident-Response-Guide.pdf).

Handbook for Computer Security Incident Response Teams (CSIRTS). The Software Engineering Institute, April 2003 (www.sei.cmu.edu/publications/documents/03.reports/03hb002.html).

"Responding to Intrusions." CERT Coordination Center (www.sei.cmu.edu/publications/documents/sims/sim006abstract.html).

Taylor, Laura. "Incident Response Planning and Management." *Intranet Journal*. Jupiter Media, January 28, 2002 (http://intranetjournal.com/articles/200201/se_01_28_02a.html).

Taylor, Laura. "Old-school UNIX tools help track down hackers." *TechRepublic,* June 19, 2002 (http://insight.zdnet.co.uk/hardware/servers/0,39020445,2123102,00.htm).

Taylor, Laura. "Read Your Firewall Logs." *ZDNet*, July 5, 2001 (http://techupdate.zdnet.com/techupdate/stories/main/0,14179,278 2699,00.html).

"U.S. Department of Justice Search and Seizure Guidelines." United States Department of Justice, November 10, 2005 (www.usdoj.gov/criminal/cybercrime/searching.html).

Wotring, Brian "Host Integrity Monitoring." SecurityFocus, March 31, 2004 (www.securityfocus.com/infocus/1771).

Notes

1. Kent Kim Grance. *Computer Security Incident Handling Guide*. NIST Special Publication 800-61. National Institute of Standards and Technology, January 2004, p. D-2.

## Chapter 12

Performing the Security Tests and Evaluation

"No law or ordinance is mightier than understanding."

—Plato

Topics in this chapter:

- **Types of Security Tests**

- **Types of Security Controls**

- **Testing Methodology and Tools**

- **Who Should Perform the Tests?**

- **Documenting the Tests**

- **Analyzing the Tests and Their Results**

Introduction

A *Security Test & Evaluation*, known among security experts as an *ST&E*, is a document that demonstrates that an agency has performed due diligence in testing security requirements and evaluating the outcome of the tests. The ST&E is a C&A document that tends to give agencies a lot of trouble. It's not clear to many agencies what tests they should be doing, who should be doing them, and what the analysis of the tests should consist of. The ST&E is supposed to convince the C&A package evaluators that the agency understands the security requirements, enough so, that they can create tests to ensure that the security controls uphold the requirements.

It is the responsibility of the information system owner to ensure that the testing actually takes place. However, the information system owner may choose to designate this responsibility to the ISSO. The federal guidance on what to include in your ST&E is somewhat vague, and though this leaves lots of room for flexibility, it leaves many information system owners, C&A package preparers, and C&A package evaluators wondering what a good ST&E should include.

Types of Security Tests

Keep in mind that you are trying to certify and accredit an information technology implementation, not a product. That being said, any implementation likely uses many products. Figuring out where to draw the line in the sand on where a product ends and where an implementation begins is half the battle. If you are using commercial off-the-shelf products, presumably due diligence was already done in selecting that product. You are not trying to justify the actual purchase of the product. You are trying to justify that the product was correctly installed and configured.

Refreshing your memory from Chapter 2, C&A is based on certifying Confidentiality, Integrity, and Availability (CIA). Therefore, your tests should be designed to determine if Confidentiality, Integrity, and Availability are preserved by the security controls that are in place. Within each CIA category, some of the tests will pertain to management controls, some of the tests will pertain to technical controls, and some will pertain to operational controls.

Confidentiality Tests

Confidentiality tests determine if unauthorized disclosure is possible. When you perform confidentiality tests, you are trying to determine if data is disclosed to people that it is not intended for. You are also trying to determine that data is readable and executable by the people it is intended for.

Before you can set up tests to ensure confidentiality, you have to understand a bit about confidentiality risks and vulnerabilities. Data traveling in plaintext over communications lines is vulnerable to sniffing. Weak passwords can be compromised using password crackers. Confidentiality tests look to ensure that authentication and encryption mechanisms work according to the security requirements. It's also important to ensure that the authentication and encryption mechanisms have not just been implemented, but that they have safeguards built around them to protect them from being sabotaged.

If you have reason to believe "shoulder surfing" is a risk, then a security policy should be written that requires all users to be partitioned from other users. If you have reason to believe social engineering (tricking a user into revealing information to unauthorized individuals) is a risk, you should be sure to address that in your *Security Awareness & Training Plan*. If you believe that cryptographic algorithms may not have been implemented correctly, you should use only products that have passed FIPS 140-2 testing performed using the Cryptographic Module Validation Program (CMVP).[1]

If password files exist, you may want to perform a test to ensure that the passwords are properly encrypted and the encrypted passwords are not easily discovered using a dictionary password cracker. You'll also want to ensure that the permissions on the password files are set correctly and are not writeable to the world.

If you are using biometric devices, you will want to be sure to test the False Acceptance Rates (FAR), the False Reject Rates (FRR), and the Cross-over Error Rates (CER). A biometric device is more accurate and reliable as the CER goes down and you will want to establish acceptable thresholds in your test plan. Other metrics to take into consideration for biometrics include the Failure to Enroll (FTE) rate and the Failure to Acquire (FTA) rate. FTE denotes the amount of people who are not able to use the system due to some sort of incompatibility and FTA denotes the number of users who are not able to render an acceptable enrollment image to use the device.

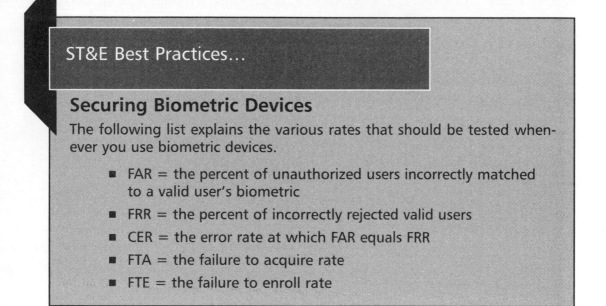

ST&E Best Practices...

Securing Biometric Devices

The following list explains the various rates that should be tested whenever you use biometric devices.

- FAR = the percent of unauthorized users incorrectly matched to a valid user's biometric
- FRR = the percent of incorrectly rejected valid users
- CER = the error rate at which FAR equals FRR
- FTA = the failure to acquire rate
- FTE = the failure to enroll rate

If VPNs are a part of the infrastructure that you are certifying, you'll need to devise some tests to ensure that the VPN has been properly configured and cannot be penetrated by unauthorized users. You'll also need to clearly describe whether the VPNs being tested are secure remote access VPNs (used by remote users) or end-to-end VPNs that encrypt all traffic that goes between designated sites. VPNs can be configured to pass packets in *tunnel mode, transport mode,* or both. Which modes does your security policy require? You'll need to ensure that VPNs are configured in accordance with your security policy.

Confidentiality problems that you'll want to check for include:

- Passwords that do not comply with the security policy
- Authentication systems that are not properly configured
- Use of algorithms that do not comply with the security policy

- Secure implementations of encryption products (VPNs, PKI, etc.)
- Implementations that do not produce logging capabilities

To help you understand how to test for confidentiality, construct questions regarding confidentiality security controls. For example:

1. What security controls ensure that passwords comply with the security policy?

2. What security controls ensure that authentication systems are properly configured?

3. What security controls ensure that algorithms comply with the security policy?

4. What security controls check for proper configuration of encryption products?

5. What security controls ensure that authentication and encryption systems produce log files that comply with the security policy?

By answering these questions, you can put together a list of security controls that address confidentiality mechanisms. Your confidentiality security controls can be managerial, operational, or technical in nature. Once you have developed your list of security controls, you can devise tests for them.

Integrity Tests

Integrity tests answer the question, "Is the data adequately protected to prevent unauthorized modification?" A goal of any information technology implementation is to preserve the integrity of the data. You need good data and you need to determine if it is possible for someone to inadvertently, or purposefully, generate bad data. For example, buffer overflow attacks are designed to breach the integrity of the system. Testing the integrity of the implementation allows you to determine if secure coding principles were adhered to and if all the right patches are in place.

Coding gaffes that you'll want to check for are:

- Buffer overflow vulnerabilities
- Extraneous lines of code

- Race conditions
- Temporary files writeable by the world
- Hard-coded passwords

To clarify how you would test for each of these five coding gaffes, construct a question related to security controls that checks and prevents the listed vulnerability. For example:

1. What security controls protect against buffer overflow attacks?
2. What security controls protect against extraneous lines of code?
3. What security controls protect against race conditions?
4. What security controls protect against temporary files writeable by the world?
5. What security controls protect against hard-coded passwords?

From your list of questions, you should be able to put together a list of security controls that address each question. Your security controls can be managerial, operational, or technical in nature. Once you have developed your list of security controls, you can devise tests for them.

Availability Tests

Availability tests ensure that availability is preserved. The tests should verify that availability exists as required by the initial design requirements. On a high-level, the kinds of tests that apply to availability are:

- Testing of the configuration management system
- Testing of the Contingency Plan
- Testing of backups
- Testing of fault-tolerant disk arrays (striping, mirroring, and duplexing)
- Testing of load-balancers
- Testing of high-availability mission critical systems (e.g., firewalls, DNS servers)

Similar to how you test for integrity tests, you should be able to construct a question related to security controls that checks for and prevents vulnerabilities related to availability. For example:

1. What security controls protect the configuration management system?

2. What security controls protect the Contingency Plan?

3. What security controls protect the backups?

4. What security controls protect high-availability and mission critical systems?

5. What security controls protect fault-tolerance?

6. What security controls protect load-balancers?

Again, from your list of questions, you should be able to put together a list of security controls that address each type of availability concern. Your security controls can be managerial, operational, or technical in nature. Once you have developed your list of security controls, you can devise tests for them.

Types of Security Controls

NIST provides an excellent listing of various security controls in Special Publication 800-53, Recommended Security Controls for Federal Information Systems (SP 800-53) available at the following URL: http://csrc.nist.gov/publications/nistpubs/800-53/SP800-53.pdf.

If you need ideas for security controls that you may want to test, a long list of different security controls begins on p. 40 of this SP 800-53. The security controls you choose to test should also be consistent with the security controls that you include in your Self-Assessment (discussed in Chapter 8).

Management Controls

The testing of management controls looks at whether or not the current information technology environment of the information system being certified holds management accountable and has built-in escalation thresholds. Planning controls ensure that the management team has ascertained the risks involved and have either accepted them, or mitigated them before authorizing operation. For example, ensuring that systems get properly certified and accredited every three years is a management control.

A test that checks to see if a risk is mitigated through existence of a written security policy in place is a management test. Typically the management team is responsible for ensuring that appropriate security policies exist.

Operational Controls

Operational tests are those that test if the actual operations of the system undergoing C&A works as expected—according to the intended design. For example, when you press a Submit button to submit a form, is the form actually submitted as planned? If you a schedule a file to be sent to another computer at 2 A.M., does the file get sent on schedule? Operational tests answer the question, "Does it work as intended according to the design requirements?" For example, ensuring that the backups work as documented is an operational control.

Technical Controls

Configuration tests determine if the configuration of all the components of the installation are correctly configured. If the products you have implemented are not configured correctly you could be setting yourself up for incredible security risks. For example, ensuring that firewalls and intrusion detection systems monitor and log all significant security events is a technical control.

Testing Methodology and Tools

Your tests can be manual or automated, or a combination of both, as long as they get the job done. Either way, you'll still have to document how the tests were conducted. If you use a software test management package, you should describe it, and how it works, in the ST&E. An example of testing procedures and results are listed in Table 12.1. You'll want to be sure to include the date and version number for every test you perform. For each test performed, you'll need to describe the *expected results* and the *actual results*. If the actual results do not match the expected results, the test has failed.

There are different testing tools you may want to employ depending on what you're going to test. Since every implementation is different, not every type of test may apply to all situations. You need to describe what was tested, and how—and how you came to the conclusion that the test passed or failed. If you use tools to perform your tests, you'll want to document your tests in a similar fashion to how you document manual tests.

Table 12.1 Sample Description of Testing Procedures

Date and Version Number Test Objective	Procedures	Pass/Fail
Verify that security events are generated	Confirm that Event Viewer is turned on Set security properties to filter all 5 even types Generate a security event in each category and verify that Event Viewer creates a record for it	P
Verify that passwords use at least 8 characters with both letters and numbers	Logon as initial user Try to change password to new password that has less than 8 characters Try to change password to new password that has 8 characters but does not use numbers Try to change password to new password that has 8 characters but does not use letters Ensure that password field will accept an 8-character password with letters and numbers	P
Verify that the system requires user to change the initial password before accepting initial password	Logon as initial user Check to see if system instructs user to change their password Don't change the initial password and see if logon is possible Change the initial password and ensure that user can logon	P

Continued

Table 12.1 continued Sample Description of Testing Procedures

Date and Version Number Test Objective	Procedures	Pass/Fail
Verify that Rules of Behavior are displayed before initial logon and before being prompted for password	Logon as initial user Look for Rules of Behavior Ensure that you can view them before you are prompted for your password Ensure that there is an acceptance box that can be checked and that it is working properly	P
Ensure that initial password is not accepted if user does not check box to agree to Rules of Behavior	Logon as initial user Look for Rules of Behavior and check acceptance box Don't check the acceptance box and see if you can still logon Check the acceptance box and ensure you can logon	F Can logon even if user does not accept Rules of Behavior
Verify that you can restore a file from the backup media	Obtain backup media from one week ago, one month ago, three months ago Attempt to restore the admin (or root) password file from each of the three archives Verify that the password file accepts the known admin (or root) password	F Could not restore password file
Verify that the only port open on the messaging server is TCP port 25	Scan the messaging server with a port scanner Verify that the only port found open is TCP port 25	P
Verify that no modems are connected to network .49	Scan network .49 with a modem scanner Verify that no modems are discovered	F A modem was found connected to John Doe's PC

Algorithm Testing

The biggest problem with encryption algorithms is that about 25 percent of the time encryption algorithms are not implemented correctly in security products. As a result of this problem, there are now laws and standards that specify how encryption algorithms need to be implemented.

If an information system implementation includes encryption products, it is a federal law that the encryption products be FIPS 140-2[2] compliant (unless they have been approved and validated for classified use). Originally passed as FIPS 140-1 in 1995, FIPS 140-2 is a Federal Information Processing Standard (FIPS) that was instituted as a result of the Information Technology Reform Act of 1996 (Public Law 104-106) and the Computer Security Act of 1987 (Public Law 100-235). FIPS 140-2 was published in May of 2001 and now supersedes FIPS 140-1. Encryption products are not supposed to be procured and implemented unless they have been officially certified and validated through the Cryptographic Module Validation Program (CMVP).

Through the CMVP program, Cryptographic Module Testing (CMT) labs use a tool called the Cryptographic Algorithm Validation System (CAVS) that can only be obtained from NIST and is used exclusively for testing encryption products. CAVS generates correct algorithm vectors that CMT labs use to ensure that encryption algorithms are correctly implemented. If an encryption product has compliant algorithms, the CMT validates the findings and submits the results to the CMVP program for accreditation.

Since all encryption products are supposed to be FIPS 140-2 compliant before they ever get implemented, a test to check for that is simply to ensure that each and every encryption product in the implementation under C&A has a valid FIPS 140-2 certificate. FIPS 140-2 certificates are considered public information and you can see all of them for every product ever validated under this program at http://csrc.nist.gov/cryptval/.

The only way to get around not using FIPS 140-2 products is for the head of the agency, or a senior agency designated officially, to apply for a waiver. There are only two reasons considered acceptable for applying for a waiver:

1. Compliance with FIPS 140-2 adversely affects the business mission

2. Compliance with FIPS 140-2 will create a major adverse financial impact

To apply for a waiver, a letter justifying the request for waiver should be sent to:

FIPS Waiver Decision

Information Technology Lab

100 Bureau Drive, Stop 8900

Gaithersburg, MD 20899-8900

Because FIPS 140-2 exists, there should never be any need to test if cryptographic algorithms were implemented correctly in a product. Products that are not FIPS 140-2 compliant should never be implemented on the systems that are being certified. Therefore, as far as algorithm testing goes, you have two options: find out if there is a FIPS 140-2 certificate for any encryption products used and if there is, document that in the ST&E. If you find encryption products without a FIPS 140-2 certificate, check to see if a waiver is on file. A waiver should have been applied for before the product was actually procured. However, if a waiver is not on file, the ISSO should advise the CIO to apply for a waiver expeditiously.

Keep in mind that FIPS 140-2 only requires that algorithms be correctly implemented in the product. It will not tell you if the encryption product has been correctly installed and correctly configured within the agency infrastructure.

Code and Memory Analyzers

If your information system undergoing C&A uses code that is custom written and is not associated with any commercial off-the-shelf product, it is a good idea to scan your source code for coding gaffes and vulnerabilities. Code and memory analyzers can help you uncover source code vulnerabilities and memory leaks. The following code and memory analyzers have helped shore up many applications:

- CodeAssure Workbench by Secure Software (www.securesoftware.com)

- Rational Purify by IBM (www306.ibm.com/software/awdtools/purify/)

- TotalView by Etnus (www.etnus.com)

- Dynamic Leak Check by DMS (www.dynamic-memory.com)

Some code analyzers are geared just for Web applications and specialize in checking for Java and ActiveX problems, SQL injection vulnerabilities, CGI problems, and cross-site scripting vulnerabilities. Products that check for Web application problems include:

- Jtest by Parasoft (www.parasoft.com)

- Shadow Web Analyzer by Safety-Lab (www.safety-lab.com)

- WebKing by Parasoft (www.parasoft.com)

- Nikto by Cirt.net (www.cirt.net/code/nikto.shtml)

Many network scanners also scan for Web site vulnerabilities as well as network and operating system vulnerabilities.

Network and Application Scanners

Once configured and set up, network scanners run automated scans of your systems and networks looking for well-known security vulnerabilities. Nonintrusive network scanners do not try to exploit the vulnerabilities they find. Intrusive network scanners find vulnerabilities and then try to exploit them, and therefore are a bit more risky to use since they could potentially cause damage to your systems. Most scanners can be configured to scan an IP address, a range of IP addresses, a domain, or a Web site. High-end scanners have the ability to generate a network map.

Some scanners specialize in scanning applications where instead of looking for operating system vulnerabilities, their goal is to uncover vulnerabilities in Web sites, cgi scripts, databases, and database applications.

Popular network and application scanners include the following:

- Internet Scanner by Internet Security Systems (www.iss.net)

- IP360 by nCircle (www.ncircle.com)

- Foundstone Enterprise by McAfee (www.foundstone.com/)

- Nessus open source network scanner (www.nessus.org)

- QualysGuard by Qualys (www.qualys.com/)

- Retina Network Security Scanner by eEye Digital Security (www.eeye.com)

- Security Auditor by Cisco (www.cisco.com)

- STAT Guardian by Harris (www.harris.com)

- AppScan by Watchfire (www.watchfire.com)

After scanning systems or networks, penetration testing is the process whereby one tries to exploit the discovered vulnerabilities. When performing penetration testing, a security engineer may use additional tools to try to penetrate the application, network, or system.

Before performing scanning or penetration testing, it is very important to obtain permission in writing from the agency, bureau, or department that owns the systems being scanned. An agreement should be established on specifically what will be scanned, and when the scanning will occur. Whether the person performing the scanning or penetration test is an agency employee or a consultant, it is important to obtain a signature on the agreement to protect yourself from liabilities so that you are not accused of being an unauthorized intruder or a malicious insider.

Port Scanners

Port scanners simply scan for open ports. The reason to use a port scanner is to find out if the open ports comply with your security requirements and your security policy. It is a security risk to have more ports open than necessary. Often hackers scan for open ports to see which open ports they may want to exploit. Once a hacker finds an open port, they often use particular hacker programs that are uniquely coded to exploit a particular port. When doing a port scan, you'll want to scan both the TCP and UDP ports. Many network scanners also scan for open ports.

By a long shot, the most popular port scanner is an open source tool called **nmap**. However there are some commercial port scanners available as well. Various port scanners that you may find useful include:

- Atelier Web Security Port Scanner (www.atelierweb.com/)

- GFiLANguard (www.gfi.com)

- Nmap (www.nmap.org)

- Port Scanner ActiveX Control by Magneto Software (www.magnetosoft.com)

- Strobe (www.packetstormsecurity.org/UNIX/scanners/ strobe-1.04.tgz)

Port Listeners

Probably the most popular port listener available is **netcat**, and since it is open source, it is free to use. You can obtain netcat from the PacketStorm Web site, http://packetstorm.linuxsecurity.com/.

A good test of your firewall is to run netcat on one of your mission critical servers that is protected by the firewall. Have netcat listen on a port that is supposedly being blocked by the firewall and see if an attacking machine can connect to this port—if it can, the firewall is being circumvented. You can also use netcat to see if the port banner can be grabbed for the purpose of finding out the version number of the operating system that is running.

Websnarf is a port listener written in perl that is made just for Web sites. You can use this tool to find out local and remote IP addresses that are trying to connect through port 80. If your firewall is blocking port 80, then no one should ever be able to connect through port 80. If websnarf logs any connections to port 80, then someone is getting around the firewall. You can obtain websnarf from the following URL: www.unixwiz.net/tools/websnarf-1.04.

Modem Scanners

Modem scanners often are referred to as "war dialing" tools. The purpose of modem scanners is to find out if there are any modems (or FAX machines) that are connected to systems in violation of your security policy. The following products offer the ability to find unauthorized modems that could create security vulnerabilities:

- ModemScan by Michael McCobb (www.wardial.net/default.html)
- Phonesweep by Sandstorm (www.sandstorm.com)
- THC-SCAN by van Hauser (www.thc.org/releases.php)

Wireless Network Scanner

Wireless network scanners are sometimes referred to as "war-driving" tools or wireless protocol analyzers. These tools are good for detecting open wireless networks in your facility. If you have a policy that prohibits wireless networks, you may want to walk around the facility with a wireless network scanner to see if you detect any unauthorized Wi-Fi networks. Popular wireless network scanners are available at the following URLs:

- Netstumbler, an open source tool (www.netstumbler.com)
- WiFiScanner, an open source tool (http://wifiscanner.sourceforge.net)
- CommView for WiFi by Tamosoft (www.tamos.com)
- iStumbler for Max OSX wireless network discovery (www.istumbler.net/)
- Sniffer® Wireless Intelligence by Network General (www.networkgeneral.com)
- Wireless Recon by Helium Networks (www.heliumnetworks.com)
- AiroPeek SE by WildPackets (www.wildpackets.com)

StumbVerter is an open source tool for mapping the results of a wireless network scan and is available at www.sonar-security.com/sv.html.

Wireless Intrusion Detection Systems

Wireless intruders can be detected through various host-based intrusion detection systems available at the following URLs:

- Wi-Fi Defense by OTO Software (www.otosoftware.com/)

- AirSnare by Digital Matrix (http://home.comcast.net/
  ~jay.deboer/airsnare/index.html)

- Surveyor by AIRMAGNET (www.airmagnet.com)

- Kismet by the open source community (www.kismetwireless.net/)

Wireless Key Recovery

Wireless key recovery tools are basically wireless key crackers. Although they
can be used to recover lost keys, they are more often used to find out if the
wireless keys that are being used are easy to crack. Wireless networks often are
secured by the Wireless Equivalent Privacy (WEP), which isn't that secure;
however, it's certainly better than no security at all. Using these popular open
source tools, you can find out how easy your wireless network's WEP keys
and keystreams are to crack:

- WEPCrack (http://sourceforge.net/projects/wepcrack)

- WEPWedgie (http://sourceforge.net/projects/wepwedgie/)

- AirSnort (http://airsnort.shmoo.com/)

Password Auditing Tools

Password auditing tools, sometimes referred to as *password crackers*, can be used
to help you find out if your users are complying with the password security
policy. You can run the password file through leading password crackers to
find out if users are choosing easy-to-guess passwords that use words that are
commonly found in dictionaries. Password auditing tools that can help you
determine weak passwords include:

- Proactive Password Auditor by Elcomsoft (www.elcomsoft.com)

- John the Ripper by the Openwall Project
  (www.openwall.com/john/)

- Revelation by Snadboy (www.snadboy.com)
- Password Recovery Toolkit by AccessData (www.accessdata.com)

Database Vulnerability Testing Tools

Database vulnerability discovery tools help you discover vulnerabilities in leading databases. Popular database vulnerability discovery tools include:

- OScanner is an Oracle assessment scanner (www.cqure.net/wp/?page_id=3)
- SQL AT finds vulnerabilities in SQL databases (www.cqure.net/wp/?page_id=6)

One of the best guides for understanding how to lock down databases is the Department of Defense database Security Technical Implementation Guide for databases available at http://iase.disa.mil/stigs/stig/database-stig-v7r2.pdf.

Test Management Packages

Test management software organizes your testing initiatives. These types of software packages are not required for C&A, but you may find that they help you more easily manage your testing program. Test management packages help you create a controlled test environment, automate tests, and create test script scenarios. Popular test management packages include:

- SilkCentral Test Manager by Seque (www.seque.com)
- WinRunner by Mercury (www.mercury.com)
- QMTest by CodeSourcery (www.codesourcery.com)
- TestTrack Pro by Seapine (www.seapine.com)

Test management packages are especially useful for tracking lifecycle changes in an application or implementation that stands to be around for a long time to and will evolve over the years.

Who Should Perform the Tests?

The security tests can be done in-house or using outside consultants. There are no OIG or GAO requirements on who performs the tests. In the security world, separation of duties is always important, and to that end, the ST&E will certainly appear to be more ingenuous if the analysis of the tests is written by someone other than the people who perform the tests. To show the C&A evaluators that a clear separation of duties has occurred, you should be sure to indicate who performed the tests, and who wrote the analysis— documenting the professional credentials for the individuals involved.

Documenting the Tests

The tests must be fully described in the ST&E and the following items should be included and described:

- Test objectives
- Test methodology
- Test environment (version number, physical location, hardware platform)
- Test procedures including test execution instructions
- Expected results
- Actual results
- Pass / Fail criteria

It helps if the tests are numbered so that they can easily be referred to in the test analysis section of the ST&E.

Analyzing the Tests and Their Results

Although the tests themselves should be considered factual information, the analysis is a subjective and detached expert opinion on the validity, integrity, and plausibility of the tests. Whether the tests are performed in-house or by outside consultants, the folks who write the analysis should be different than those who conduct the tests.

The analysis should include an expert opinion on whether the objectives of the tests adequately tested the security controls. A checklist, and relevant questions that folks who analyze the tests will want to discuss in their analysis, follows:

- Do *expected results* of tests appear to be accurate?

- Do *actual results* of tests appear to be accurate?

- Have members of the test team been described?

- Has a test failure been indicated if *expected results* do not match *actual results*?

- Are the tests conducted in a controlled setting?

- Are tests conducted according to the test plan?

- Are the tests indicative of the security requirements?

- Do all tests have a unique test number?

- Are version numbers included in the ST&E?

- Are test dates included in the ST&E?

- Is the use of all test tools documented?

- Is the test methodology documented?

- Has a security policy reference number for each test been cited?

- Where tests failed, were recommendations made to reconcile the failures?

- Are the tests well organized, either by Confidentiality, Integrity, and Availability or by the controls (e.g., management, technical, operational) they are designed to test?

- Are tests designed to ascertain if systems, networks, and applications are configured in accordance with the agency security policy

Summary

During this chapter we discussed a lot of different tools, techniques, and areas of coverage with regards to security testing and evaluation. Don't get bogged down trying to figure out how a port listener differs from a port scanner. There are three important high-level concerns when conducting ST&E: the three security objectives, types of controls, and types of testing. Your ST&E methodology should provide broad coverage in all of these areas.

When considering the triad of security objectives—Confidentiality, Integrity, and Availability—you need to include tests that assess the security of the system in terms of each of these objectives. These objectives are achieved by implementing technical, operational, and management controls, and your ST&E needs to be sure to test all three types of controls. Technical controls can be tested using technical tools. However, operational and management controls are often policies and procedures that do not lend themselves well to technical tests. Therefore, your ST&E methodology must employ interviews of personnel and examination of documents in some cases. So be sure that your ST&E covers the Confidentiality, Integrity, and Availability objectives; that it tests technical, operational, and management controls; and that it uses technical, interview, and examine test procedures. It your ST&E covers all these areas, you will have a robust, effective ST&E component to your C&A.

Additional Resources

This section provides you with a list of books and articles to refer to for more information on security testing.

Books Related to Security Testing

The following books offer useful information on testing the security of your systems:

> Doar, Matthews B. *Practical Development Environments*. O'Reilly Media, September 2005. ISBN: 0596007965.

> Graff, Mark G. and Kenneth van Wyk. *Secure Coding: Principles and Practices*. O'Reilly Media, June 2003. ISBN: 0596002424.

Hoagland, Greg and Gary McGraw. *Exploiting Software: How to Break Code.* Addison-Wesley, 2004. ISBN: 02017865958.

Howard, Michael and David LeBlanc. *Writing Secure Code.* Microsoft Press, December 2002. ISBN: 0735617228.

Long, Johnny et al. *Penetration Tester's Open Source Toolkit.* Syngress Publishing, November 2005. ISBN: 1597490210.

Oakes, Scott. *Java Security, Second Edition.* O'Reilly Media, May 2001. ISBN: 0596001576.

Splaine, Steve. *Testing Web Security.* Wiley, 2002. ISBN: 0471232815.

Viega, John and Matt Messier. *Secure Programming Cookbook.* O'Reilly Media, July 2003. ISBN: 0596003943.

Whittaker, J., H. H. Thompson, and H. Thompson. *How to Break Software Security.* Addison-Wesley, May 2003 ISBN: 0321194330.

Articles and Papers Related to Security Testing

Various useful articles and papers that may be useful for understanding how to test the security of your systems and applications include:

Chillarege, Ram. "Software Testing Best Practices." IBM Research, April 26, 1999 (www.chillarege.com/authwork/TestingBestPractice.pdf).

Fong, Derek. "Build Extra Secure Web Applications." IBM's developerWorks Web Site, November 1, 2005 (www-128.ibm.com/developerworks/web/library/wa-wapprotect/).

Faught, Danny. "Software Testing FAQs." Testingfaqs.org (www.testingfaqs.org/).

"Security and the Java Platform." Sun Developer Network (http://java.sun.com/security/).

Howard, Michael. "Reviewing Code for Integer Manipulation Vulnerabilities." Microsoft, April 28, 2003 (http://msdn.microsoft.com/library/default.asp?url=/library/en-us/dncode/html/secure04102003.asp).

Taylor, Laura. "Secure Coding Principles 101." Jupiter Media, January 20, 2004 (www.intranetjournal.com/articles/200401/ij_01_20_04a.html).

Taylor, Laura. "Security Scanning 101." Jupiter Media, September 23, 2002 (www.intranetjournal.com/articles/200209/ij_09_23_02a.html).

Taylor, Laura. "Understanding IPSec." Jupiter Media, June 13, 2002 (www.intranetjournal.com/articles/200206/se_06_13_02a.html).

Wack, John, Miles Tracy, and Murugiah Suoppaya. "NIST Special Publication 800-42, Guideline on Network Security Testing." National Institute of Standards and Technology, October 2003 (http://csrc.nist.gov/publications/nistpubs/800-42/NIST-SP800-42.pdf).

Notes

1. ""Transition Plan for the Use of Key Sizes and Security Strengths by Federal Agencies." NIST Special Publication 800-57 Part 1. National Institute of Standards and Technology, 2006 (http://csrc.nist.gov/cryptval/).
2. "Implementation Guidance for FIPS PUB 140-2 and the Cryptographic Module Validation Program." National Institute of Standards and Technology Communications Security Establishment, March 28, 2003. Last Update: October 5, 2006 (http://csrc.nist.gov/cryptval/140-1/FIPS1402IG.pdf).

## Chapter 13

Conducting a Privacy Impact Assessment

"Civilization is the progress toward a society of privacy."

—Ayn Rand

Topics in this chapter:

- Privacy Laws, Regulations, and Rights

- PIA Answers Questions

- Personally Identifiable Information

- Persistent Tracking Technologies

- Determine Privacy Threats and Safeguards

- Decommissioning of PII

- System of Record Notice

- Posting the Privacy Policy

- PIA Checklist

Introduction

A *Privacy Impact Assessment* (PIA) is the process that one goes through to determine if personally identifiable private information is being appropriately safeguarded. Aside from financial losses and losses to life, there are also privacy considerations for information technology systems. Some federal agencies have databases with highly sensitive information such as medical records, tax records, and information about private citizens. The Privacy Act of 1974 requires each federal agency to establish:

> …appropriate administrative, technical and physical safeguards to insure the security and confidentiality of records and to protect against any anticipated threats or hazards to their security or integrity which could result in substantial harm, embarrassment, inconvenience or unfairness to any individual on whom information is maintained.[1]

Agencies need to establish rules of conduct for systems developers as well as penalties for noncompliance. Privacy Impact Assessments of public Web sites and sensitive systems need to be conducted to ascertain if individuals' social security numbers, gender, race, date of birth, and financial status are subject to exposure. The point of a Privacy Impact Assessment is to determine if systems, Web sites, and applications comply with all federal laws, regulations, and security policies. Threats to privacy and mitigating factors should also be noted in a PIA. The assets that store the data subject to privacy policy provisions and laws should be determined and understood.

Privacy Laws, Regulations, and Rights

On May 22, 2006, after it was thought that private information of 26 million U.S. Veterans was stolen on a USB flash drive, Clay Johnson III, the Acting Director of the OMB, issued an important memorandum on privacy to heads of departments and agencies. The memo can be viewed at www.whitehouse.gov/omb/memoranda/fy2006/m-06-15.pdf.

The memorandum reminds heads of departments and agencies about their responsibilities to safeguard private information. The OMB has published other memorandums on privacy management as well.

OMB Memoranda

Various memoranda have been published by the Whitehouse Office of Budget and Management (OMB) and contain a wealth of information on privacy concerns and what to include in a Privacy Impact Assessment. You'll find the following five OMB Memoranda very helpful:

- *OMB Memorandum 01-05, Guidance on Inter-Agency Sharing of Personal Data–Protecting Personal Privacy* (December 20, 2000) provides a set of privacy principles in conducting interagency data sharing.[2]

- *OMB Memorandum 00-13, Privacy Policies and Data Collection on Federal Web Sites* (June 22, 2000) requires that agencies comply with the Web site privacy policies that they post following the guidance of OMB Memorandum 99-18 and specifically prohibits the use of persistent "cookies" on Federal Web sites.[3]

- *OMB Memorandum 99-05, Instructions on complying with President's Memorandum of May 14, 1998 'Privacy and Personal Information in Federal Records'*, includes what actions agencies must take for compliance and requirements for agencies to track disclosure of private information.[4]

- *OMB Memorandum 99-18, Privacy Policies on Federal Web Sites* (June 2, 1999) provides guidance and model language for Federal Web site privacy policies.[5]

- *OMB Memorandum 03-22, Guidance for Implementing the Privacy Provisions of the E-Government Act of 2002*, includes when to conduct a PIA, what elements to include in one, and definitions, and PIA reporting requirements.[6]

Laws and Regulations

Aside from the Federal Information Security Management Act of 2002, other laws bestow the necessity of privacy rights management as well. These laws include:

- 5 U.S.C. § 552, Freedom of Information Act (FOIA) of 1966, as Amended by Public Law No. 104–231, 110 Stat. 3048

- 5 U.S.C. § 552a, Privacy Act of 1974, as Amended

- Public Law 100–503, Computer Matching and Privacy Act of 1988

- Section 208 of the E-Government Act of 2002

- Section 5 of the Federal Trade Commission Act

- Children's Online Privacy Protection Act of 1998 (COPPA)

- OMB Circular A-130, Management of Federal Information Resources, 1996[7]

- The Health Insurance Portability and Accountability Act of 1996[8]

With so many laws and regulations governing privacy, and because privacy information disclosures by public and private entities are making headlines, noncompliance is clearly a liability to any agency, company, or nonprofit organization.

PIA Answers Questions

A Privacy Impact Assessment usually is designed in a survey format. It is acceptable to ask different people in the organization to answer the different questions. It is also acceptable to hold one person accountable for answering, or finding out the answers to, all of the questions. You should work with the ISSO to discuss the best approach. The best approach is the one that will help you obtain accurate answers in an acceptable amount of time. It is acceptable to conduct in-person interviews or use an e-mail or online survey. At the very minimum, a *Privacy Impact Assessment* should answer the following top ten questions:

1. What information is collected?
2. How is the information collected?
3. Why is the information collected?
4. What is the intended use of the information?
5. Who will have access to the information?

6. With whom will the information be shared?

7. What safeguards are used to protect the information?

8. For how long will the data be retained/stored?

9. How will the data be decommissioned and disposed of?

10. Have Rules of Behavior for administrators of the data been established?

If the answers to these questions result in new questions, the new questions should be asked. For example if it is discovered that the data will be retained for 50 years, you'll want to ask why. Use your common sense and good judgment in developing the questions and evaluating their answers. If the answers you receive don't sound reasonable, then they probably won't pass muster with the C&A package evaluators either. It's possible you may need to go ask a different person the same question. What you are looking for are facts. If you come up short no matter who you ask, don't be afraid to simply put down "unknown" for your answer. You definitely don't want to invent answers simply because the ones you were given sound questionable. After all, one of the reasons you're completing a PIA is to find out if private data is being appropriately protected so that mitigating actions can be enlisted if necessary.

It helps in obtaining accurate answers from the respondents if you do not convey a confrontational manner. You may need to explain to them the value of the PIA and how their responses will help agency officials put together a Privacy "To Do" list. Expound the virtues and responsibilities of being data stewards of confidential information. It helps put respondents at ease if they feel their time spent answering the PIA questions will serve to benefit people just like themselves—you may want to convey that to them in a conversation, or through e-mail.

Personally Identifiable Information (PII)

In considering what information is collected, of utmost importance should be what's known as Personally Identifiable Information (PII). PII includes information that is associated with the identity of a person. A Privacy Impact

Assessment should determine if PII is collected and should list all types of PII that are collected. Some types of PII that may be in use at your agency are:

- Name
- Home Addresses
- E-mail Addresses
- Social Security Numbers
- Telephone Numbers
- Addresses
- Passport Numbers
- Bank Account Information
- Driver's License Numbers
- State Identification Numbers
- Account Numbers
- Biometric Fingerprints
- DNA
- Photographs

Since PII includes data that is attributable to a person's identity, the data would not exist if that person did not exist. Essentially, an individual owns the attributes of the PII. Therefore, it's necessary that all PII applications include a process for individuals to correct inaccurate PII whether the inaccuracy was created by unauthorized access, an administrative error, or a change in circumstances.

You should be able to map the PII to specific applications. An example of how to do this is illustrated in Table 13.1.

Table 13.1 PII Mapped to Applications

PII	Applications That Collect PII			
	Online Tax Submission	**Payroll System**	**Building Access**	**Health Records**
Social Security No.	•	•		•
Credit Card No.	•			
Bank Account No.	•	•		
Driver's License No.			•	
PIN		•	•	
Biometric Fingerprint				•
DNA				•
Photograph			•	•

Persistent Tracking Technologies

Since persistent tracking technologies are often the biggest violators of privacy, they deserve special mention. Persistent tracking technologies record and maintain information about Web site visitors after the user leaves the Web site. The most commonly used tracking technologies are persistent cookies and Web beacons. Cookies maintain information about Web site visitors after they have left the site. Web beacons are typically a one-by-one graphic pixel placed in e-mails or Web sites that send visitor information to another destination—perhaps a server, a database, or even directly to a person in the form of an e-mail. A Web beacon can be completely invisible since the pixel can be "clear," matching the background color of the Web site. If any persistent tracking technologies are used, a good PIA will fully describe the usage and ascertain if it is in compliance with the agency privacy policy.

Determine Privacy Threats and Safeguards

A section of your PIA should include information on privacy threats, safeguards, and assets that store private information. This information can be neatly summarized in a table similar to Table 13.2.

Table 13.2 Summary of Privacy Threats and Safeguards

Privacy Threat	Asset That Stores Private Information	Type of Safeguard	Description of the Privacy Controls
Intentional physical threats from external entities	The DB-01 database in building 12, room A-2; part of an IBM cluster	Physical protection	Physical controls of the facility include guards, locks, and surveillance cameras that prevent entree by unauthorized entities.
Intentional and unintentional threats from authorized (internal and external) entities	The DB-12A5 database in building 12, room A-5	Authorization and access control systems	Enforced by Authorization Manager role-based access control system.
Systems administration errors	All databases and servers on the secret domain	Training and systems and database administration documentation	System admins and database admins undergo training once a year. Documentation is updated bi-annually.
Viruses that seek to obtain PII	All databases and systems in the Pensacola facility	Enterprise anti-virus software	Enforced by automated signature updates and regular virus scans.

Continued

Table 13.2 continued Summary of Privacy Threats and Safeguards

Privacy Threat	Asset That Stores Private Information	Type of Safeguard	Description of the Privacy Controls
Loss or theft of laptop containing sensitive information	Access database on Linda Parker's laptop	Encryption	The database is encrypted using a FIPS 140-2 validated encryption product and keys are stored securely in a locked safe in the Privacy Officer's office.

Decommissioning of PII

With the advancements in technology occurring at such a rapid rate, it is understandable that databases get merged, systems get upgraded, old systems get decommissioned, and disks with confidential PII on them are turned off never to be used again—in theory. However, in reality, old systems sometimes end up in inadvertent places. To prevent the disclosure of confidential and private information, PII should be properly decommissioned according to the agency security policy. Depending on how sensitive the data is, old disks that contain PII may require bit wiping, a degausser, or destruction by a disk crusher that drills through the spindles.

A draft document on media sanitation known as *Special Publication 800-88, Guidelines for Media Sanitation*, was published by NIST on February 3, 2006. You may find the NIST guide to be a useful resource for understanding if the appropriate measures are being undertaken when a system reaches the end of its System Development Life Cycle (SDLC); however, keep in mind that this document is still in draft form, and is therefore not yet considered official guidance. Nonetheless, you can access Special Publication 800-88 at http://csrc.nist.gov/publications/nistpubs/800-88/NISTSP800-88_rev1.pdf.

System of Record Notice (SORN)

A System of Record Notice (SORN) is a public notice that states what groups of records are under an agency's control. Whereas a PIA includes only information technology records, a SORN includes both paper and electronic records. To clarify further, a SORN is not a PIA and a SORN is not required by FISMA. The Privacy Act of 1974 established the requirement of a SORN, though that was before so much information was stored in computers. Some agencies require that a SORN be included in the PIA, though this really goes above and beyond FISMA and the E-Government Act of 2002.

Unless your agency specifically states that a SORN needs to be included in your PIA, it's not necessary to include one. However, just because your PIA and C&A package may not require a SORN, that doesn't mean your agency is exempt from posting them. It's altogether possible that a SORN and a Privacy Policy may include duplicate information.

SORNs are published in the Federal Register and PIAs are not. The Federal Register is part of the National Archives and Records Administration (NARA). You can view the Federal Register online at www.gpoaccess.gov/fr/index.html.

Posting the Privacy Policy

All public Web sites that collect information on citizens, veterans, staff, and military personnel require privacy policies. Additionally, any transaction-based system that performs financial transactions requires privacy policies. The privacy policy should list laws and regulations that it claims to comply with. Once a Privacy Policy has been established, it should be posted for end-users and administrators to see. For Web sites, it should be posted right on the front page. For systems and applications that require logins, the Privacy Policy should be posted in the banner before a user logs in.

PIA Checklist

Use the following checklist to help you ensure that you haven't forgotten anything in your PIA:

- Is the name(s) of the individual(s) who completed the PIA noted?

- Is the C&A Package name listed on the PIA?

- Is the method of collecting the information (e.g., interviews or e-mail) noted?

- Are the privacy threats and safeguards included?

- Are privacy controls noted?

- Have risks to privacy been determined?

- Are high privacy risks mitigated?

- Do the PII data stewards have access to the Privacy Policy?

- Is the Privacy Policy published on all online Web sites and logon banners?

- Has Personally Identifiable Information (PII) been identified?

- Is PII mapped to applications?

- Do procedures to correct inaccurate PII exist?

- Has the purpose of the system or application been described?

- Is there a compelling need to collect the PII?

- Is the PII consistent with the application requirements?

- Is unnecessary PII collected?

- Are system administrators aware of their privacy responsibilities?

- Is PII appropriately decommissioned?

- What happens to decommissioned PII?

Summary

In this day and age, preserving privacy is a fundamental requirement for maintaining the positive reputation of an organization. There is a balance that we try to strike between sharing information for communal use and preserving information that is so personal and descriptive of an individual, that the data owner is really the individual. Unfortunately, preserving privacy often languishes on the bottom of the C&A and information security to-do list. As soon as your own private information is disclosed against your wishes, privacy becomes far more important. However, as data stewards of other people's private information, we are ethically obligated to act responsibly to preserve that information.

Books on Privacy

The following books offer useful information on information technology privacy:

> Garfinkel, Simson. *Web Security Privacy and Commerce, 2nd Edition*. O'Reilly Media, 2001. ISBN: 0596000456.
>
> Garfinkel. Simson. *Database Nation: The Death of Privacy in the 21st Century*. O'Reilly Media, 2000. ISBN: 0596001053.
>
> Tynan, Dan. Computer Privacy Annoyances. O'Reilly Media, 2005. ISBN: 0596007752.
>
> Windley, Phil. *Digital Identity*. O'Reilly Media, 2005. ISBN: 0596008783.

Notes

1. The Privacy Act of 1974. United States Department of Justice. Updated September 26, 2003 (http://www.usdoj.gov/foia/privstat.htm).
2. Jacob J. Lew. "Guidance on Inter-Agency Sharing of Personal Data—Protecting Personal Privacy." *Memorandum for Heads of Executive Departments and Agencies. United States Office of Management and Budget*. December 20, 2000 (http://www.whitehouse.gov/OMB/memoranda/m01-05.html).

3. Jacob J. Lew. "Privacy Policies and Data Collection on Federal Web Sites." *Memorandum for Heads of Executive Departments and Agencies.* United States Office of Management and Budget. June 22, 2000 (www.whitehouse.gov/omb/memoranda/m00-13.html).

4. Jacob J. Lew. "Instructions on Complying with President's Memorandum of May 14, 1998, 'Privacy and Personal Information in Federal Records.'" *Memorandum for Heads of Executive Departments and Agencies. United States Office of Management and Budget.* January 7, 1999 (www.whitehouse.gov/omb/memoranda/m99-05.html).

5. Jacob J. Lew. "Privacy Policies on Federal Web Sites." *Memorandum for Heads of Executive Departments and Agencies.* United States Office of Management and Budget. June 2, 1999 (www.whitehouse.gov/OMB/memoranda/m99-18.html).

6. Joshua B. Bolten. "OMB Guidance for Implementing the Privacy Provisions of the E-Government Act of 2002." *Memorandum for Heads of Executive Departments and Agencies. United States Office of Management and Budget.* September 26, 2003 (http://www.whitehouse.gov/omb/memoranda/m03-22.html).

7. "Management of Federal Information Resources." *Memorandum for Heads of Executive Departments and Agencies. Circular No. A-130 Revised.* United States Office of Management and Budget (www.whitehouse.gov/omb/circulars/a130/a130trans4.html).

8. "Medical Privacy—National Standards to Protect the Privacy of Personal Health Information." United States Department of Health and Human Services. Office for Civil Rights (www.hhs.gov/ocr/hipaa/).

## Chapter 14

Performing the Business Risk Assessment

"Have I not walked without an upward look
Of caution under stars that very well
Might not have missed me when they shot
and fell?
It was a risk I had to take—and took."

—Robert Frost

Topics in this chapter:

- Determine the Mission

- Create a Mission Map

- Construct Risk Statements

- Describe the Sensitivity Model

- Make an Informed Decision

Introduction

A *Business Risk Assessment* reviews the risks to the agency mission and determines if they are acceptable or not. If the risks are not acceptable, a determination of how to mitigate them should be described. Business risks are examined at a high level and are not concerned with the particularities of information technology. The reason that business risks are important is to give some perspective on why the information technology infrastructure exists in the first place.

First, it's worth noting that not all agencies require a *Business Risk Assessment* for their C&A packages. Before you begin trying to figure out how to develop one, make sure a *Business Risk Assessment* is required. Some agencies may require only a *System Risk Assessment* that focuses on the technology of the systems and applications rather than the mission. However, to be sure, the Business Risk Assessment is related to the *System Risk Assessment*. If you develop the *Business Risk Assessment* correctly, the System Risk Assessment will look like an extension of it and you will be able to see the relationship between the two. Likewise, you will also see consistencies between the *Business Impact Assessment* and the *Business Risk Assessment*.

Discussion of the *Business Impact Assessment* occurs in Chapter 15, and discussion of the *System Risk Assessment* occurs in Chapter 16. These three related documents are presented in this order purposefully since a *Business Impact Assessment* and a *System Risk Assessment* are extensions of a *Business Risk Assessment* as depicted in Figure 14.1.

Figure 14.1 Extensions of *Business Risk Assessment*

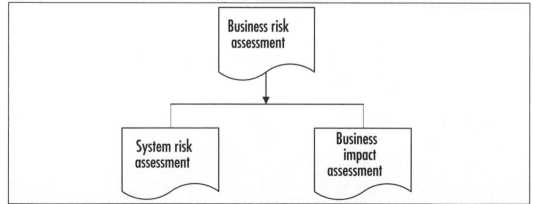

It will be easiest for you to write the subsequent document if you write them in the recommended order:

1. *Business Risk Assessment*
2. *Business Impact Assessment*
3. *System Risk Assessment*

Before you can determine the risks to your agency's mission, you need to first understand what the mission is. The process of determining the risks to the mission is in part designed to force you to understand the mission. Your agency, and its different bureaus and divisions, probably has multiple missions. You need to be able to state what the primary mission functions are before you can determine the business risks—the risks to the mission.

Determine the Mission

Business risks affect the ability to get a job or a task done. All agencies will have different mission risks depending on the mission. Chances are your agency or bureau has multiple missions. For any particular C&A project, you should be concerned only with the missions that correlate to the particular C&A package that you are putting together. Some examples of business missions are:

- Analyze and record the annual budgetary appropriation from Congress
- Provide retirement benefits to war veterans
- Prepare the nation for natural disasters
- Process enrollment information for Medicare recipients
- Enable law enforcement officials to access information on terrorists
- Provide online access of navigational charts to mariners
- Process patent applications
- Monitor budgetary requirements for an Air Force base Child Development Center
- Provide clerical support to Probation Officers

- Track gasoline-powered vehicles deployed for work on public lands
- Analyze domestic flu infections
- Compile economic statistics
- Track administration of medications in a hospital
- Procure auxiliary generators and air compressors
- Monitor compliance of visitor rules in national parks
- Document and track evidence chain of custody

Noticing the business mission takes the information technology out of the equation so you can remember why the information technology infrastructure exists to begin with. Understanding the business mission is a process of taking a momentary step backward to look at the bigger picture. In some regards, conducting a *Business Risk Assessment* is a way of looking at the critical business functions from a legacy point of view and seeing things the way business processes were accomplished on paper, years ago, before computers came into existence. Sometimes we get so entrenched in the granularity of the information systems that we fail to see how all the computer infrastructure came to be in the first place. You need to know what the essential functions are of the agency's business in order to determine what the risks are to the functions, the likelihood that the risks may occur, and their potential impact.

Questions that may help determine your agency's mission are:

- What is the largest percentage of the agency's annual budget dedicated to?
- Does your agency produce tangible assets? What are they?
- Are large financial transactions conducted by your agency?
- Is there a large central communications command center in your agency?
- Is your agency responsible for the health and safety of people?
- What do other agencies depend on your agency for?
- What vital records are being created?

- What are the key projects that are underway in the agency?
- Why was your agency originally established by the government in the first place?

Create a Mission Map

Once you have determined the primary mission or tasks related to the mission, set up a mission map that shows the relationships between agency functions and the role that systems and networks play in carrying out the mission. This is one of the best ways to figure out the relationship between the agency mission and the IT infrastructure. An example of a mission map is depicted in Figure 14.2. As you can see from this illustration, both the forecasting and budget process, and the time and attendance process, are dependent only on one geographic location, and one network. The user enrollment process is dependent on two networks and two geographic locations. Therefore, determining the risks associated with the user enrollment process is bound to be more complex. As far as natural hazards go, the user enrollment process has to worry about both hurricanes in Houston, and heavy snow in New York. The forecasting and budgetary process has fewer natural disasters to take into consideration because Washington, D.C., has milder weather than either Houston or New York.

Figure 14.2 An Example of a Mission Map

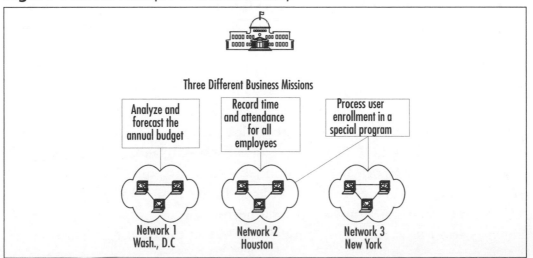

With dependencies on two networks, you'll have to look at the risks for both. One risk that could be cited might even be that the user enrollment process is dependent on two networks. If the Houston facility gets flooded by a hurricane and loses power, then the user enrollment process will stop working—even if the New York site remains operational. Clearly, one way to mitigate this risk would be to migrate the functionality of the user enrollment process entirely to the New York site. However, that may not be possible for all kinds of different reasons. Instead, it may be easier to build a failover system in Washington, D.C., that automatically picks up the user enrollment functionality provided by Houston if there is an outage in Houston. When developing a *Business Risk Assessment*, you have to take into consideration various different scenarios that could affect the business process. There are, of course, other risks aside from natural disasters. In taking into consideration the different scenarios, you need to construct risk statements.

Construct Risk Statements

Risk statements are assertions that connect a possible circumstance to a forecasted impact. A common format for a risk statement is:

If <this threat circumstance occurs>, **then** <this will be the impact>.

Once risk statements have been developed, the impact can be forecasted and the potential likelihood of the threat can be determined. Risk statements state the presumed threat, and the impact in the form of damage that could occur. The potential impact can then be factored with the probability of its occurrence to find out just how great the risk exposure is in actuality. Some threats will create a more severe impact to the business process than others.

When you are creating risk statements for business risks, knowing the technical details of the IT infrastructure is not really necessary. Save that for the *System Risk Assessment*. It shouldn't matter whether the firewall is a Cisco firewall or a Juniper firewall. It also shouldn't matter if the database is an Oracle or Microsoft SQL Server database. Likewise, whether the operating system is Sun Solaris or Microsoft Windows doesn't matter. *Business Risk Assessments* look at things from a high level. In the *Business Risk Assessment* you want to focus on business processes necessary to the organization to be able to carry out its mission(s) and the impact that the loss or degradation of one of those business processes would have. The low-level, more technical and granular risks to the information systems that support those business processes will be evaluated in the *System Risk Assessment*, discussed in Chapter 16.

Examples of risk statements for a *Business Risk Assessment* are:

- If the Houston facility gets flooded, then it won't be possible to enroll new users. (This is an availability threat.)

- If the Houston facility gets flooded, then it won't be possible to process time and attendance for any employees. (This is an availability threat.)

- If an unauthorized user gains access to the Washington, D.C., network, then the integrity and confidentiality of the annual budget could be compromised. (This is an integrity and confidentiality threat.)

- If an employee accidentally misspells a user's name, then the misspelling could be propagated to two different locations. (This is an integrity threat and most likely a relatively minor one.)

- If a disgruntled systems administrator purposefully and maliciously creates a backdoor account into the user enrollment system, it could be propagated to two different locations. (This is an integrity, confidentiality, and availability threat.)

- If a terrorist destroys the New York facility, then it won't be possible to enroll new users into the special program. (This is an availability threat.)

- If an intruder breaks into the budgeting system and changes some of the numbers in an Excel spreadsheet used for forecasting, too much, or too little money may be allocated to certain programs. (This is an integrity threat.)

- If a system administrator erroneously configures a firewall rule for the Houston firewall, then access to both user enrollment, and time and attendance, might be blocked. (This is an availability threat.)

- If a virus proliferates throughout the Houston network, both the user enrollment system and the time and attendance system could be damaged. (This is an integrity threat, and possibly an availability threat as well.)

- If an intruder breaks into the user enrollment system they could steal a database of private user information. (This is a confidentiality threat.)

- If security patches are never applied to the time and attendance systems, then intruders may gain access to the attendance systems and damage them. (This is an integrity threat, and possibly an availability threat as well.)

Once we know what the threats are, if we have a sensitivity model to measure their likelihood and impact, we can determine the risk exposure.

Describe the Sensitivity Model

According to the American Heritage Dictionary of the English Language, *risk* is the "possibility of suffering harm or loss; danger."[1] Risk analysis can be performed in a variety of different ways. One of the goals of a C&A program is to have some consistency from one C&A package to another. Therefore, it's important to pick a risk analysis methodology, describe it, and use it as described for each C&A package you develop.

A sensitivity model takes into consideration the impact of a threat, and the likelihood of its occurrence, so that you can rank the risks according to their sensitivity for the purpose of prioritizing them. In any given organization there is a limited amount of time and resources. If you were able to determine all of the risks to your organization, would you have enough time and resources to address each and every one? Probably not. Therefore, a goal is to describe the most obvious and likely risks and then further predict the probability of their occurrence. The objective is to think of what situational hazards and threats are most likely to occur, determine the risk exposure, and then either mitigate, transfer, or accept each risk based on priority.

Your sensitivity model should consist of a process for determining the risk exposure. (We already categorized the levels of Confidentiality, Integrity, and Availability of the data in Chapter 6 so we are not going to repeat that here.) In business risk assessment, risk exposure is a value that is calculated to determine the degree of risk that the mission is exposed to. The purpose of determining the risk exposure is so you can understand which business processes and missions require additional safeguards. You'll want to mitigate the most severe risks to business missions first.

It's possible to use simple equations to determine risk exposure. You don't have to be a math genius to do this. The equations we use will multiply the likelihood of a threat by the potential impact to the organization. However, before you can set up these equations, you need to create an impact scale and a likelihood scale so you know what to multiply.

Impact Scale

In qualitative risk analysis, the impact of a threat to the mission is measured in relative terms. The values that are used to measure the impact are perceived values, and are not actual values. Since a threat actually has not occurred yet, it is not possible to use actual values. If your *C&A Handbook* already has threat impact values defined, you should use those values (unless you think they are significantly flawed). Table 14.1 shows an example of an impact measurement scale with five measurements. This same scale could be set up to have more, or fewer, levels of impact to fit the unique requirements of your agency or department.

Table 14.1 An Example of an Impact Scale

Threat Impact	Impact Value	Description of Impact
None	0	The threat poses absolutely no risk to the mission.
Very Low	20	The threat poses very little risk to the mission. Safeguards currently provide near complete protection of the mission.
Low	40	The threat poses some risk to the mission. The current safeguards provide adequate protection though it is conceivable that the mission could be impeded.
Moderate	60	The threat poses a moderate risk to the mission. The safeguards that are in place provide some protection, though it is possible for the mission to be thwarted.

Continued

Table 14.1 continued An Example of an Impact Scale

Threat Impact	Impact Value	Description of Impact
High	80	The threat poses a high risk to the mission and the current safeguards provide few protections.
Severe	100	The threat may completely thwart the mission and the current safeguards provide no protection.

Likelihood Scale

The likelihood that a threat will occur is a probability expressed in relative terms. Table 14.2 lists probability levels based on likelihood of occurrence.

Table 14.2 An Example of a Likelihood Scale

Probability of Loss to Mission Expressed as a Percentage	Probability of Loss to Mission Expressed as a Decimal	Description	Likelihood
0% – 10%	.1	There is little to no chance that the threat could thwart the mission.	Low
10% – 50 %	.5	There is a moderate chance that the threat could thwart the mission.	Moderate
50% – 100 %	1.0	There is a high chance that the threat could thwart the mission.	High

Calculating Risk Exposure

In qualitative risk analysis, risk exposure is determined by multiplying the probability of mission loss (the likelihood it will occur) by the potential severity of the impact to the agency due to that loss. If we represent probability with P, and impact severity with S, our risk exposure equation looks like this:

P x S = Risk Exposure (RE)

We can also write the expression a different way to more clearly indicate we are talking about the probability of loss (L) multiplied by the severity of the loss (L):

P (L) x S (L) = R (E)

P (L) represents the likelihood. S (L) represents the impact. The probability that loss will occur is another way of referring to the likelihood. The severity of the loss is another way of referring to the impact. Therefore:

Likelihood x Impact = Risk Exposure

Now for a particular threat, we take the impact values from Table 14.1 and multiply them by the probability of loss values from Table 14.2. All the possible outcomes of multiplying the likelihood by the impact are listed in Table 14.3.

Lead the Team to Obtain the Metrics

For the purpose of C&A, when putting together your risk exposure metrics, it is important to interview the support, development, and management staff to obtain their input. It is not possible to determine the impact and likelihood of a threat to a business process in a vacuum. You need to sit down with the folks that run the business. I recommend holding a business risk assessment meeting and getting everyone together in a room. While it may seem unimportant to list risks that are so obviously low likelihood or low impact, the reason for doing so is so that you can record all the issues that are raised by the staff. It is important to record the issues raised by all the participants. Remember, C&A is a format for holding people accountable. When you develop the business risk assessment, it's not your job to determine the likelihood and impact on your own. You should take on the role of a facilitator of the process and should use the values for impact and likelihood that the team gives you in order to determine the risk exposure.

Analyze the Risks

Once you have determined the risk exposure, it is time to analyze the risks to prepare for making an informed decision. There are multiple reasons for analyzing risks. When a threat is exploited, otherwise competent staff are often

left flustered not knowing what to do first. Analyzing risk is about antici-
pating the incident in order to prevent it, and also to prepare for how to
respond in the event it does occur. Determining business risk exposure helps
you understand what risks to address first.

Even in the absence of malicious attackers, disgruntled users, and administrative errors, power outages still occur and natural disasters wreak havoc.
Understanding risks, and applying safeguards to mitigate those risks not only
prevent loss to the mission, but also helps maintain the flow of order by potentially reducing the amount of circumstances that may create disorder. You analyze risks so you can prioritize them for the purpose of managing them. Once
the risk exposure is determined and ranked from high to low, the findings
should be presented to the business owner. The business owner and ISSO
should engage in discussions with the business risk assessment team that originally assisted you in putting together the list of risks, their impact, and likelihood. Analyzing the risks means discussing the possible outcomes before
making a decision on what action to take. Table 14.3 lists risk exposure metrics.

Table 14.3 Risk Exposure Metrics

Likelihood x Impact	Risk Exposure
.1 x 0	0
.1 x 20	2
.1 x 40	4
.1 x 60	6
.1 x 80	8
.1 x 100	10
.5 x 0	0
.5 x 20	10
.5 x 40	20
.5 x 60	30
.5 x 80	40
. 5 x 100	50
1 x 0	0
1 x 20	20

Continued

Table 14.3 Risk Exposure Metrics

Likelihood x Impact	Risk Exposure
1 x 40	40
1 x 60	60
1 x 80	80
1 x 100	100

Another way of presenting the information in Table 14.3 is shown in Table 14.4.

Table 14.4 Risk Exposure Determination Table

Impact and Values	Likelihood Low (.1)	Medium (.5)	High (1.0)
None (0)	0 x .1 = 0	0 x .5 = 0	0 x 1 = 0
Very low (20)	20 x .1 = 2	20 x .5 = 10	20 x 1 = 20
Low (40)	40 x .1 = 4	40 x .5 = 20	40 x 1 = 40
Moderate (60)	60 x .1 = 6	60 x .5 = 30	60 x 1 = 60
High (80)	80 x .1 = 8	80 x .5 = 40	80 x 1 = 80
Severe (100)	100 x .1 = 10	100 x .5 = 50	100 x 1 = 100

Source: Chapter 10, *HIPAA Security Implementation 2.0*, SANS Press, 2004.

Make an Informed Decision

Once risks have been identified and analyzed, a decision can be made on what action to take. Your choices are to accept the risk, transfer the risk, or mitigate the risk. You should be able to justify your reason for whatever decision you make.

Accept the Risk

If the risk exposure is extremely low, and the cost to remove such a small risk is extremely high, the best solution may be to accept the risk. Keep in mind that for the purposes of C&A, it is up to the business owner to accept the risk. The business owner usually will accept the risk or not based on the recommendation from the ISSO and the staff that prepares the *Business Risk Assessment*. The business owner usually always wants a recommendation on whether to accept the risk or not so be prepared to make one.

Transfer the Risk

When you transfer the risk, you make another entity responsible for it. When you buy insurance, you are transferring the risk to a third party who has agreed to assume the risk for an agreed upon cost. In a federal agency, in many situations it may not be possible to buy insurance to transfer risks. However, there are other ways to transfer risk. It's possible that you may not have the appropriate personnel to support a business function. A business owner could possibly negotiate with another department to take on the responsibility of supporting the business function.

If you know something is at risk, and you know another department could manage the risk better, you might be able to transfer the risk to the other department. For example, if one of the risks to your business process is that you don't have a UNIX Systems Administrator to manage a business process that runs on a UNIX system, you may decide to transfer the management of the business process to the department that provides UNIX systems administration. The business owner will be looking for recommendations on transferring risks. A business owner is not preserving any sort of managerial territory or integrity by insisting on retaining a substantial risk that they know they cannot mitigate. A smart business owner will want to get rid of all substantial risks. A risk to a business process puts the business owner's career at risk. Imagine the outcome if an expensive security incident occurs and in the process of resolving the incident it becomes known that the business owner knew all along that a substantial risk was present, and yet did nothing about it.

Mitigate the Risk

To mitigate the risk means to either remove it completely, or reduce it to an acceptable level. If the risk exposure is very high, you'll want to consider mitigating the risk. You can mitigate risks by putting safeguards in place, or reconfiguring existing safeguards. You can also remove the factors that contribute to the risk (e.g., move the business to a location that is not prone to hurricanes), or remove some of the dependencies of the business process. Typically the more dependencies that a business process has, the more risks there are. When a business process is dependent on multiple systems, multiple software packages, and multiple locations, there most certainly will be multiple risks.

TIP

Remember the following risk monikers:

L = Likelihood
I = Impact
RE = Risk Exposure
Probability of loss = P (L) = Likelihood
Severity of loss = S (L) = impact

Multiple physical locations can go either way when it comes to risk. Two locations mean that there are two facilities to protect, which doubles the necessary safeguards. However, if the reason you have two facilities is so that one can serve as a backup site in the event of a natural disaster, you may not be mitigating risks by consolidating to one location. Every situation is unique and you should keep in mind that each business unit may have risks that are incomparable to another agency, bureau, or line of business.

For the purpose of tracking and managing your decision, you can summarize you risk statements and risk exposure metrics in a table. Table 14.5 shows a sample risk summary table.

Table 14.5 Risk Summary Table with Decision

Risk Statement	L	I	RE	Decision
If an unauthorized user gains access to a veteran's hospital enrollment system, then the intruder could remove patients from the system and impede treatment.	.1	80	8	Mitigate the risk by installing a host-based intrusion detection system on the enrollment system.

Continued

Table 14.5 Risk Summary Table with Decision

Risk Statement	L	I	RE	Decision
If John Smith (who has cancer) dies, then we won't have anyone to administer the enrollment database.	.5	60	30	Transfer the risk by getting the platform engineering department to provide the database support.
If the levees in New Orleans are not repaired, then large loss of life could occur during the next hurricane.	1	100	100	Mitigate the risk by allocating $10 billion to have the Army Corps of Engineers repair the levees.
If an unauthorized user gains access to an FAA system used to track cargo on passenger planes, then suitcases bound for Atlanta could be rerouted to Chicago.	1	80	80	Mitigate the risk by installing an additional security access control system.
If an unauthorized user gains access to an FAA system used for routing airplanes, lives could be lost if a plane is purposefully routed into a shopping center.	0	100	0	Accept the risk. Although this sounds like a legitimate concern, there are so many controls in place that there is zero chance of this happening.
If an unauthorized user gains access to a certain U.S. federal court system used for preserving evidence, then evidence and chain of custody could be altered and prosecution of a hacker could be thwarted.	.1	80	8	Accept the risk. The evidence system is locked in a security room that requires two-factor authentication for entrance. There are surveillance cameras in every corner of the room, which mitigates the small risk.

Summary

Before you take the time to implement security controls, it's important to find out where your risk exposure lies. A Business Risk Assessment examines risk from a high-level global view. By determining business risk first, you will be better able to determine system risk. During the business risk analysis process you will come to understand your organization's business mission, and see how those functions are related to your information technology infrastructure. After determining your business risk exposure, once you come to understand which functions are prone to the greatest risk, you can more accurately focus your system risk assessment on the most highly exposed functional areas. You may not have the time and resources to perform a penetration test on all of your systems; however, you may have time to perform one on your most highly exposed functional areas.

Performing a business risk assessment helps you to understand that business that you are supporting. Sometimes IT professionals lose sight of the forest and see only the trees. By understanding the business mission, and its vulnerability exposures, you can more easily justify your decisions. For example, an auditor may ask you why you decided to scan only one network domain for vulnerabilities, and not a different one. Or perhaps you scanned all your networks with one scanning tool, and then you scanned a particular high risk network segment with two other scanning tools. An auditor may ask why you scanned only the first network with one scanner, and the other network with three different scanners. Auditors are looking for you to justify your reasons for your decisions. A Business Risk Assessment serves to help justify your decisions, and make appropriate choices on security controls.

Additional Resources

The following list includes books that have sections on risk assessment and various articles that might be useful for understanding business risk assessment:

Bragg, Roberta. *CISSP Training Guide.* Que Publishing, 2002. ISBN: 078972801X.

Iheagwara, Charles. "More Effective Risk Management," *Computer Security Journal*, Volume XIX, 2003.

Taylor, Laura. *Risk Analysis Tools and How They Work*. Relevant Technologies, 2002.

Taylor, Laura. "Security Scanning is Not Risk Analysis," *Intranet Journal*. Jupiter Media Corp., 2002. (www.intranetjournal.com/articles/200207/pse_07_14_02a.html)

Notes

1. *American Heritage Dictionary of the English Language, Fourth Edition*. Boston: Houghton Mifflin. 2000. New York: Bartleby.com. 2000. (http://www.bartleby.com/61/)

Chapter 15

Preparing the Business Impact Assessment

"Business? It's quite simple: it's other people's money."

—Alexandre Dumas, French dramatist

Topics in this chapter:

- **Document Recovery Times**

- **Establish Relative Recovery Priorities**

- **Define Escalation Thresholds**

- **Record License Keys**

- **BIA Organization**

Introduction

A *Business Impact Assessment (BIA)* articulates the component restoration priorities that an interruption in service may have on an information system, application, or network. If you have a group of systems that include Web servers, directory servers, application servers, file servers, firewalls, DNS servers, and authentication servers, and your facility suffered an unprecedented disaster, which one would you try to restore first? Do you know?

An interruption in service could be as minor as a power outage, or as catastrophic as a bomb. In either case, at that time you, the system, and network support group will have enough anxiety without having to think about which system to restore first. A BIA is all about removing some of that anxiety, so that systems administration staff can just go down a list of relative priorities and get to work without having to spend time figuring out which systems should be restored first. By planning for a recovery before you need to orchestrate one, you can more efficiently manage your recovery effort. Planning for a recovery up front also more effectively provides assurances for the continuity of your agency's mission.

In a C&A package, most of the time the evaluation team expects to see the BIA as one of the appendices of the Contingency Plan. When I write a Contingency Plan, I often like to have the BIA in front of me as a snapshot of what's important, and therefore I find that it works best to write the BIA before writing the Contingency Plan. Similarly, when I write the BIA, I find that the *Business Risk Assessment* helps me establish the priorities that I need to document in the BIA. Therefore, you may want to have your Business Risk Assessment handy when you work on your BIA.

Document Recovery Times

In Chapter 6 I discussed how to put together a Hardware and Software Inventory. You should have the systems you want to recover already identified by way of that inventory. Now you need to figure out how long it will take to rebuild each of those systems. In your BIA you should document estimated recovery times. The estimated recovery time should be made by trained support staff that typically administer the systems and build them on a routine basis.

You are not trying to figure out what the management team wants the recovery times to be, you are trying to figure out what the recovery times actually are. If an IT manager wants a server to be recovered within two hours, but a systems administrator tells you that under the best possible conditions it takes four hours to build the server, it makes little sense to document the recovery time as two hours. Go talk to the systems administrators, the application administrators, the database administrators, and the backup support staff to find out the recovery times.

The reason that recovery times are important to know is because in the event of a disaster, management may need to make decisions based on recovery times. For example, it may be necessary to hire additional temporary staff to help with the recovery, and staffing decisions may need to be made based on recovery time information. If it takes too long to recover a particular server—so long that it impacts the business mission—management may make the decision that an already built standby system be available at all times at an alternate facility.

Establish Relative Recovery Priorities

In thinking about establishing recovery priorities, you need to take two things into consideration—the importance of the system to the mission and the dependencies of each system. If a particular application server is the most important system to the agency mission, but it won't work without a DNS server and router, in the event of a disaster it does little good to rebuild the application server and get it up and running before the DNS server is operational. Of course it is altogether possible that both systems could be built in parallel. However, one of the reasons for establishing recovery priorities is that there may not be enough staff available to build everything in parallel.

Each of the systems named in the Hardware and Software Inventory should have a relative restoration priority of High, Moderate, or Low assigned to it. The priorities should take into consideration the risk exposure metrics you calculated in the Business Risk Assessment, as well as the dependencies the hardware and software has on other assets listed in the inventory. Keep in mind that your systems may have dependencies on systems that are not named in the C&A package you are working on. Don't include those systems in the BIA. The systems that you include in the BIA are the same ones you listed in the *Hardware and Software Inventory*.

If there are systems or applications that your systems are dependent on, but are not part of your C&A package (e.g., are not listed in the *Hardware and Software Inventory*), simply document a statement that describes that. You can refer to that section of the BIA in a variety of ways such as:

- External dependencies
- Dependencies on general support systems
- Dependencies on network segment 45
- Dependencies on other agencies
- Dependencies on the Information Systems department assets
- Outside dependencies

Your relative recovery priorities can be defined simply as:

- High: Recover these systems and applications first
- Moderate: Recover these systems and applications second
- Low: Recover these systems and applications last

Every line item in your *Hardware and Software Inventory* should have a relative recovery priority associated with it.

Telecommunications

In the event of a disaster, in most cases the very first item that you'll want to have restored is the telecommunications system. However, if the telecomm system is not part of the C&A package that you are developing, you won't need to include it. Telephones are necessary to reestablish services provided by vendors, contactors, other agencies, and employees. Today, many employees have cell phones, smart phones, or Personal Digital Assistants (PDAs), which all can serve as backup phones in the event that the telecomm switch goes down. Keep in mind, though, that if you don't have someone's cell phone number on hand, you won't be able to call them. Additionally, in some facilities cell phones don't function well due to interference from the building and lack of signal.

Infrastructure Systems

After telephone services are restored, usually the most important pieces of the IT operations are the infrastructure systems, since all other systems usually depend on these systems for connectivity purposes. Infrastructure systems consist of:

- DNS servers
- Routers, switches, hubs
- Firewalls
- Gateways
- Connectivity provided by managed service providers (Internet connectivity)
- Domain Controllers
- Directory Servers (LDAP*, Active Directory, NIS+, etc.)

*LDAP stands for Lightweight directory Access Protocol, an IETF standard.
    It may not be necessary to include information about the infrastructure servers in your C&A package because these systems might have a different Business Owner that includes them in an altogether different C&A package. If infrastructure systems were not listed in the *Hardware and Software Inventory*, you won't need to include recovery priorities for them in your BIA.

Secondary Systems

Secondary systems include any of the types of systems that would not be able to function properly without the infrastructure systems. A secondary system cannot function on its own. It needs the infrastructure systems for routing and connectivity purposes. Examples of possible secondary systems that may exist on your network are:

- Messaging servers
- Web servers

- Database servers

- File and print servers

- Application servers

- Mainframes

Define Escalation Thresholds

Escalation thresholds are predecided-upon timeframes for notifying the right people about an outage. You can set up your escalation thresholds to whatever you want them to be, taking into consideration the importance that the systems have to the business mission. Define your escalation thresholds by unique and pertinent names. You'll also want to decide who to notify when the defined escalation timeframe is reached. For example:

- Prior to Level 1: Monitor the situation, take no action

- Level 1: Notify users and stakeholders

- Level 2: Notify developers, management, and CSIRC

- Level 3: Notify a higher authority (FEDCIRC, FBI, FEMA, local police)

Each level of escalation should have an associated timeframe. Some organizations will want to use more granular timeframes than others. If your agency has predefined escalation timeframes that have been standardized across the agency, use those. If no escalation timeframes have been previously defined in an agency C&A handbook, by policy, or by management, simply use what makes sense given the mission at hand. Possible escalation timeframes you may want to consider are:

- 15 minutes

- 1 hour

- 2 hours

- 4 hours

- 8 hours

- 24 hours

- 3+ days

- Never

- Undecided

Generally speaking, the systems and applications that need to be installed first should have the shortest escalation thresholds. It is altogether possible that two different systems, both assigned a Level 1 priority, may have different escalation thresholds depending on their usage, mission, and the number of other systems that are dependent on it. If many systems are dependent on a key server, you'll want to decrease the time of the escalation threshold (on the key server) and increase the priority. An example of escalation thresholds and priority levels are shown in Table 15.1.

Table 15.1 Escalation Thresholds and Priorities

Server Role	Level 1	Level 2	Level 3	Priority
Application Server	1 hour	4 hours	3 days	Moderate
Database Server	15 minutes	8 hours	3 days	Moderate
DNS Server	15 minutes	1 hour	24 hours	High
File Server	1 hour	4 hours	3 days	Moderate
File Server	4 hours	8 hours	Never	Low
Production Web Server	1 hour	4 hours	Never	Moderate
Test Web Server	8 hours	3 days	Never	Low

Record License Keys

Almost all software products require licenses. Software license are typically long strings of numbers mixed with letters—something like:

LTP24-W9SJT-A4BMQ-CAWZ5-71XV3

Without a license key, it's likely and possible that the software won't run. Although backup media should have all your systems' and applications' license keys stored safely, there is no substitute for having a list of all the license keys documented together in one easy-to-find location. As systems are restored, there are numerous reasons why it may be quicker to copy a license key off of document than to find it on backup media. Since the BIA is a document that you would ostensibly use during a recovery endeavor, it makes sense to record the license keys in the BIA.

If you think it is a nuisance to track down all these license keys and record them, you're right, it is. Just think of how much of an anxiety-provoking-nuisance it would be in the face of a disaster. That's why you want to find out this information up front. Chances are you'll have to resort to simply talking to folks and asking around to get the right people to give you the license keys. Some may even question your motives about asking for the keys. Simply explain why you're asking for the keys, and what you plan on doing with them. You'll want to obtain license keys primarily for operating systems, databases, and applications. Any of the following types of IT support staff may be good sources of license keys:

- Systems administrators
- Database administrators
- Network administrators
- Application support staff
- The Helpdesk

You'll want to call or e-mail them and ask them to look on the back of CD cases to look up these keys. If support personnel e-mail you the keys, be sure to advise them not to e-mail them out unprotected over the Internet. If you are working from a remote location, and there is no Virtual Private Network (VPN) between your system and the person sending you the keys, it is better to obtain the keys over the phone, by FAX, or by having them encrypt the keys using a file encryption program.

BIA Organization

In your BIA, it makes it very easy for the evaluators if you put all the information you've accumulated on priorities, escalation time frames, and such in a summary table.

It is okay to submit the BIA as two documents—the Excel summary table and a separate document that provides explanatory text. In the primary BIA document that contains the explanatory text, be sure to indicate that a summary table exists as a separate file. If you don't like the idea of submitting two files, you can embed a table into the primary BIA document.

Aside from what I have already discussed in this chapter, other items that you'll want to include on your BIA summary table (or spreadsheet) are:

- Server Role (Directory server, Web server, authentication server, file server, etc.)

- Hostname (the name known by the network and the DNS server)

- Manufacturer (e.g., HP, Sun, Dell, etc.)

- Model number (the number you would need to order a new replacement)

- Location (e.g., building, room, street address, data center)

- Description (e.g., Solaris 8 database server, Windows Domain Controller)

- Asset tracking number (often this is on a sticker with a bar code on it)

- Primary point of contact (e.g., the sysadmin who keeps it running and builds it)

- Secondary point of contact (e.g., who you call when the primary is out sick)

- Contact phone numbers and e-mail address for points of contact

Summary

A BIA helps you prepare for a unscheduled outage. It should be submitted as an appendix to your Contingency Plan; however, I have found it works out best to write the BIA before you write your Contingency Plan. If done properly, your BIA is almost like an abbreviated Contingency Plan—a cheat sheet if you will. If you take the time to figure out the escalation thresholds, recovery times, and priorities in the BIA, you can more easily document the contingency operations process in the Contingency Plan.

Aside from recovery timeframes and priorities, your BIA contains a record of essential information that you will need during recovery operations. Points of contact, license keys, make and model numbers of equipment, and so on is information that is critical to recovering your systems in a timely fashion should the need arise.

Additional Resources

Books related to business impact assessment include the following titles:

Fulmer, Kenneth L. and Philip Jan Rothstein. *Business Continuity Planning: A Step-by-Step Guide with Planning Forms on CD-ROM.* Third Edition. Rothstein Associates, October 2004. ISBN: 1931332215.

Hiles, Andrew. *BCM Framework CD-ROM for Business Continuity Management.* Rothstein Associates, September 2000. ISBN: 0964164876.

Hiles, Andrew. *Business Continuity—Best Practices.* Rothstein Associates, December 2003. ISBN: 1931332223.

Hiles, Andrew. *Enterprise Risk Assessment and Business Impact Analysis: Best Practices.* Rothstein Associates, March 2002. ISBN: 1931332126.

Chapter 16

Developing the Contingency Plan

"O to be self-balanced for contingencies, to confront night, storms, hunger, ridicule, accidents, rebuffs, as the trees and animals do."

—Walt Whitman

Topics in this chapter:

- List Assumptions
- Concept of Operations
- Roles and Responsibilities
- Levels of Disruption
- Procedures
- Line of Succession
- Service Level Agreements
- Contact Lists
- Testing the Contingency Plan
- Appendices
- Contingency Plan Checklist

Introduction

The *Contingency Plan* is one of the most important documents in the C&A package. You may need to use it someday. IT systems and networks are vulnerable to disruptions due to a variety of reasons—power outages, natural disasters, and terrorist attacks to name a few. The nature of unprecedented disruptions can create confusion, and often predisposes an otherwise competent IT staff toward less efficient practices. Confusion and inefficiency create risk. Contingency planning and testing enable you to eliminate some of that risk.

You'll never be able to plan for all the contingencies that may come your way. That being said, you still need to plan for some of them. How many? A *Contingency Plan* (sometimes referred to as an *IT Contingency Plan*) should be described in general terms in order to cover as many adverse situations as necessary. Some of the objectives of your *Contingency Plan* should be to:

- Maximize the effectiveness of contingency operations through an established plan
- Provide a road map of actions for continuing operations
- Reduce the complexity of the recovery effort
- Minimize loss of, and damage to, assets
- Identify resources to be used in the recovery operations
- Facilitate the coordination of recovery tasks
- Establish management succession and escalation procedures
- Minimize the duration of the disruption
- Assign responsibilities to designated personnel
- Provide guidance in recovering operations
- Identify an alternate site

List Assumptions

When it comes to planning for contingencies, there are various assumptions you'll need to make based on your information system and application requirements. You can't plan for every possible scenario, but you can plan for some things. Listing assumptions explains to the reader that you intend to count on certain things being a particular way if the *Contingency Plan* is to work as documented—it defines a starting point. Assumptions are circumstances that exist whether the *Contingency Plan* gets activated or not. Examples of assumptions are:

- Key staff have been correctly identified and are appropriately trained.

- The Kansas City data center will be available as an alternate recovery site.

- The off-site storage site where backup media is stored will be operational.

- Current backups of the systems are intact and available at the off-site storage location.

Concept of Operations

The concept of operations section of your *Contingency Plan*, sometimes referred to as the CONOPS (or ConOps), should describe in dialogue how the information systems and major applications that make up your C&A package work and interoperate. Three key subsections of your CONOPS are the System Description, Network Diagrams and Maps, and Data Sources and Destinations.

System Description

Include a description of the information systems and major applications to which the *Contingency Plan* applies. Your description should be consistent with the system description that you document in your *Systems Security Plan* (discussed in Chapter 19). If there are three major applications, include a summary of each of them. If there are two network domains, describe their architecture and connectivity requirements.

Network Diagrams and Maps

Network diagrams and maps are extremely helpful in understanding how a failover scenario is supposed to work, and how the network components should connect to each other. Every *Contingency Plan* should have at the very least one high-level network architecture map that shows each system listed in the *Hardware and Software Inventory*. Aside from what's listed in your *Hardware and Software Inventory*, you'll also want to include on your diagram some of the key infrastructure devices such as routers, firewalls, domain controllers, and directory servers.

You should also include logical diagrams of how major applications, Web sites, and databases interact with each other. Such diagrams are often very useful in plotting the data source and destinations.

Data Sources and Destinations

Data that is stored on information systems have sources and destinations. The sources are the inputs. It is where the data comes from originally. It might come from a user typing it in from their desktop, or it might come from another system through a secure file transfer process or a VPN. Similarly, the data has a destination. The destination is its final resting place—where it's stored.

In taking into consideration contingency planning, you need to know the source and destination for your data. In the event of a disaster, you are going to want to be able to continue to obtain data from your sources. If you can't connect to your sources, your system is not entirely operational. It's altogether possible that your source and destination system is the same system. Users might input data right into the database over the Web, and the stakeholders might view it from that same database over the Web. However, the systems in your C&A package might have different sources and destinations.

You need to understand how the data gets from the source to the destination. Is a secure file transfer tool used? Do users input the data from their desktops over the Web? Are files distributed from a central distribution server? The technology pipe that is used for getting the data from the source to the destination—the data conduit—should also be documented. In order to restore your infrastructure in the event of an outage, you'll need all this information. You can document the sources and destination of your data in a table similar to the one depicted in Table 16.1.

Table 16.1 Data Sources and Destinations

Source	Data Conduit	Destination
Users typing in data from different locations over the Web	Internet using HTTPS and SSL	SQL Database #5 on the network segment 12
IBM Mainframe #1 in Washington, D.C.	Connect:Direct	Oracle Database #2 in the Seattle field office
Sun Solaris System #5 in Dallas Datacenter	Cisco VPN	Sun Solaris System #6 in the Boston datacenter
Windows Server 2003 #2 in the Vanguard Building.	Secure FTP	Linux Server in the Test Lab on the 7th floor of the Jackson Building
Legacy Windows 2000 server in Detroit	Microsoft SMS	Windows 2003 Server #8 in the Los Angeles datacenter

Roles and Responsibilities

The *Contingency Plan* should establish roles and responsibilities designed to recover operations. Depending on the outage or disaster that has occurred, the recovery operations ostensibly could be at the original facility, or at an alternate facility. Because there are so many different recovery scenarios, you'll want to have the roles and responsibilities defined in general terms so that they can be applied to as many different types of situations as possible.

Depending on the size of your organization or department, some of your staff may provide support for more than one role. Typically, the roles of the recovery team are additional roles to a staff member's regular and ordinary duties. For example, the ISSO may act as the Contingency Planning Coordinator and an IT manager may act as the Information Systems Operations Coordinator. It is also conceivable that two people could act as a team in assuming the responsibilities of a particular role. For example, the Damage Assessment Coordinator has such an extensive list of duties that it might make sense to assign two people to this role. The names of the particular staff who will be assuming each role should be documented. An example of how to document these roles is depicted in Table 16.2.

Table 16.2 Recovery Roles Noted

Name	Regular Job Title	Recovery Team Role
Barbara Williams	ISSO	Contingency Planning Coordinator
Stan Armstrong	Contracting Officer	Logistics Coordinator
Cindy Bishop	IT Manager	Information Systems Operations Coordinator
Bill Weintraub	Development Team Lead	Damage Assessment Coordinator
Amit Franghali	Security Team Lead	Security Coordinator
Godfred James	Director of Applications	Emergency Relocation Site Advisor
Terry McDuffy	Telecomm Engineer	Telecommunications Coordinator

Roles, and the associated responsibilities of the recovery team, that seem to work well for many *Contingency Plans* are included in the sections that follow. However you should not limit your *Contingency Plan* to what is documented in these sections. Your plan may require additional or altogether different roles depending on your operations and your business mission.

Contingency Planning Coordinator

The Contingency Planning Coordinator has the following responsibilities:

- Establishes personnel rosters and maintains staff location information
- Evaluates supporting information for accuracy and correctness
- Ensures that supporting information is consistent with requirements
- Receives status reports from recovery staff
- Prepares and keeps current recovery team status reports
- Keeps the staff at remote locations advised of the situations
- Advises the Logistics Coordinator on new equipment that should be ordered

- Identifies and coordinates alternate processing location and requirements
- Coordinates annual testing of the *Contingency Plan*

Damage Assessment Coordinator

The Damage Assessment Coordinator has the following responsibilities:

- Assesses damage to the assets
- Determines the cause of the disruption
- Determines the level of the disruption
- Determines if key personnel have been lost or have perished
- Determines if there has been a violation of classified information
- Determines assets requiring replacement
- Determines if personnel are in danger
- Makes recommendations on whether or not to relocate to an alternate site
- Estimates the recovery time
- Estimates level of backup personnel required
- Contacts outside service organizations for additional support (if necessary)
- Ensures the security of the primary (original) site
- Alerts vendors of the situations and requests their assistance as necessary
- Makes recommendation on whether to relocate to alternate site
- Briefs team members on recovery duties and responsibilities
- Reports status and recommendations back to the Contingency Planning Coordinator

Emergency Relocation Site Adviser and Coordinator

The Emergency Relocation Site Adviser and Coordinator has the following responsibilities:

- Notifies team leaders of relocation arrangements and plans
- Ensures that all backup media is transported to the alternate site
- Coordinates transportation of employees to alternate site
- Ensures complete restoration of resources upon return to primary site
- Reports status and recommendations to back the Contingency Planning Coordinator

Information Systems Operations Coordinator

The Information Systems Operations Coordinator (ISOC) has the following responsibilities:

- Assists in testing of applications prior to putting into production at alternate site
- Initiates restoration of services
- Provides technical support to recovery staff as need
- Overseas operations between primary site and alternate site
- Reports status and recommendations to back the Contingency Planning Coordinator

Logistics Coordinator

The Logistics Coordinator has the following responsibilities:

- Initiates standby procurement actions
- Coordinates the delivery of equipment, supplies, parts, and software
- Expedites the acquisition of supplies and equipment
- Maintains communications with vendors providing equipment

- Documents estimated delivery times for new equipment

- Retains copies of all service level agreements and provides them to team

- Retains any encryption keys that are escrowed

- Reports status and recommendations back to the Contingency Planning Coordinator

Security Coordinator

The Security Coordinator has the following responsibilities:

- Ensures that security safeguards are restored to primary site after reconstitution

- Ensures the security of the secondary (alternate) site

- Ensures that only approved personnel have access to alternate facility

- Maintains list of all approved personnel who have access to facilities

- Reports status and recommendations to back the Contingency Planning Coordinator

- Ensures that all encryption keys are properly restored and recovered

- Maintains a checklist of security configuration restoration activity

- Verifies that security safeguards are in place before bringing alternate site into production

Telecommunications Coordinator

The Telecommunications Coordinator has the following responsibilities:

- Initiates alternate communications arrangements

- Coordinates the need for new telecomm equipment with the Logistics Coordinator

- Expedites the acquisitions of communications facilities and services

- Supervises all telecomm installations and configurations

- Overseas access to telecomm wiring closets

- Works with ISOC to restore connectivity between systems and networks

- Oversees testing of alternate communications

- Reports status and recommendations to back the Contingency Planning Coordinator

In some cases, an organization may have a separate team whose soul responsibility is to return the primary site back to operational status. This team usually is referred to as the Reconstitution Team. While operations is on-going at the alternate site, the Reconstitution Team works at the primary site cleaning up, repairing equipment, and preparing everything to return to normal operations so that a clean cut-over back to the original site can be made.

Levels of Disruption

Disruptions to systems, networks, and major applications occur in varying degrees of magnitude. In order to clearly communicate the magnitude of a disruption, it helps to have disruption levels defined up front. By defining disruption levels up front, it makes it much easier for the Damage Assessment Coordinator to assess and communicate the type of disruption so that the recovery team can get prepared. The following levels of disruption serve as examples for your *Contingency Plan*:

- A *Limited Disruption* consists of a temporary disruption not associated with damage or loss of assets (e.g., disruption due to a power failure).

- A *Serious Disruption* consists of reparable damage to equipment or a facility that can be resolved by replacing equipment or software (e.g., a blown circuit board).

- A *Major Disruption* consists of irreparable damage to a facility, or loss of key personnel, data, or software (e.g., destruction of a computer room by water or fire).

- A *Catastrophic* Disruption consists of irreparable damage to equipment or a facility, or loss of a facility, its assets, or operations staff (e.g., disruption due to a tornado or a bomb)

You may decide to define the levels of disruption using different names. For example, a Level 1 disruption may be used in lieu of Limited Disruption and a Level 2 disruption may be used in lieu of a Serious Disruption.

Procedures

Your *Contingency Plan* should contain detailed guidance and procedures for key restoration and recovery operations. Imagine that a prolonged outage or a disaster has occurred. You have the backup media in your hand. Now what should you do with it? With the backup media in hand, you need to be able to recreate the entire business. Good procedures include low-level file execution instructions such as what command line interface (CLI) commands to run and what graphical user interface (GUI) parameters to click on. The various types of procedures you should include are described in the following sections.

Backup and Restoration Procedures

Backup and restoration procedures for restoring systems and major applications from backup media needs to be thoroughly documented. The procedures should include the name of the off-site storage facility, its address, phone number, and which employees are authorized to obtain backup media from it.

You'll want to describe the backup and restoration architecture so that the reader can understand the backup and recovery process enough to completely recreate it from your description. The restoration procedures should indicate if any particular software recovery programs (and their version number and patch level) are used to recover files. Are backups done locally on servers or is the data backed up over the network? Are files restored over the network or is file restoration done locally? If backups are done over the network, what system is the backup server? Are backup agents deployed on the systems that are being backed up? All these questions should be answered.

You'll also need to document the backup rotation schedule. What file systems are backed up on what night of the week or day of the month? How often are full backups performed and how often are incremental backups performed? Include the backup schedule in a table.

When files need to be recovered, what are the commands that are used to recover these files? In restoring data, it should be very clear precisely which commands are to restore one file, a directory of files, or an entire file system. Should the administrator performing the restore launch a GUI? What should they click on? It helps to provide screenshots. If the restoration is done using a command line interface, what are the commands that need to be typed?

Procedures to Access Off-Site Storage

It's most often the case that not just anyone can walk into the off-site storage facility and obtain a copy of the backup media. Typically, the people who are allowed to access the backup media are authorized in advance. The people who are authorized to obtain the backup media may need facility access cards and a PIN to get into the off-site storage facility.

The names of the people who are authorized to obtain backup media should be documented. It's also a good idea to document their supervisors' names in case any one of them are out on vacation, out sick, or have perished in the disaster. At least two people should have access to the off-site storage facility and their full contact information needs to be documented.

Operating System Recovery Procedures

Procedures for recovering operating systems should be documented. You'll want to indicate whether systems are restored from an image file, or whether they should be rebuilt from scratch. If multiple operating systems are used (e.g., Windows and UNIX), you'll need multiple procedures. If operating system procedures are already documented in another document, it is sufficient to simply name the document and attach it as an Appendix. When naming the document, you need to provide its official name with version and data. An example of an official document name would be:

Solaris 8.0 Installation and Configuration Guide, Version 2.0,
April 7, 2006

One of the things you'll want to be sure to document is what size the file systems should be. At the time you are trying to recover systems in a hurry is not the time to have to figure all this out. You may even want to include a screenshot of the disk partition table.

If a separate document exists on how to harden and lockdown the operating system, that document name should be recorded as well. It is not sufficient to simply say, "Lock down the operating system to secure it." All the operating system hardening procedures need to be documented. If there is a section in the installation and configuration guide on hardening and securing the operating system, that is acceptable.

You will need to be sure to include information on auditing records. Where is auditing information kept? Name the auditing files and directories including the full and absolute pathnames.

Application Recovery Procedures

Application recovery procedures should include anything that is required to restore the major applications once operating systems have been recovered. This section should include information about what services are supposed to be running, and how to restore the databases. Database configuration parameters should be listed. Do databases need to be synchronized with other databases? If all this information already exists in another document, it is acceptable to simply name that document using its official and formal name and then attach it as an appendix.

If this information does not already exist, you will need to take the time to gather it all, and document it. You'll want to talk to the support staff, developers, and database administrators.

Connectivity Recovery Procedures

You need to document what sort of connectivity requirements are necessary to reconnect your systems at an alternate site in the event that moving to an alternate site becomes necessary. Do your systems and major applications require any sort of throughput? Are VPNs required? Are dedicated telephone lines to managed service providers required? Are T-1 lines required? Who are the current service providers? If systems are simply plugged into an Ethernet port and obtain their IP addresses from DHCP, that should be documented as well. If there are requirements to connect your network to any other networks, this should be indicated.

Part of the connectivity recovery procedures should include documenting the particulars of important infrastructure files such as DNS zone maps, messaging server configuration files, routing tables, and firewall rule-sets. Document what ports should be open and closed on the firewalls. If routers are included in your *Hardware and Software Inventory*, then you should either document the router ACLs, or be able to point to some other document that stipulates what these ACLs are.

Key Recovery Procedures

A list of what encryption keys will need to be recovered should be documented. For example, your systems and major applications may use encryption keys for any of the following reasons:

- Hash functions in authentication mechanisms
- Digital signatures
- File encryption applications
- Disk encryption applications
- Public Key Infrastructure (PKI) applications
- Encryption keys for VPNs
- Wireless encryption keys

You should say what keys are needed and what they are used for. You should also document where the keys are kept and who has access to them. If the keys are on the backup tapes, you can simply say that. However, sometimes keys are stored by the systems administrators on separate media. Keys may even be kept on pieces of paper locked in a safe.

If your infrastructure doesn't use encryption keys for any reason, simply say so. It's better to include a section on key recovery, and then in the section, say "not applicable," than to leave the section out completely.

Power Recovery Procedures

In the event of an electrical failure, it is possible to run your infrastructure on an uninterruptible power supply (UPS) for a short length of time. If your current operation is reliant on a UPS for any length of time, this should be described. The type of UPS (make and model number) should described, and how long your systems can expect to continue to run off of UPS power should also be noted.

Do you know the power requirements for your systems? What are the amps and voltage requirements? In order to provide for protection with a UPS, you need to understand the associated amps and voltage requirements. Your *Contingency Plan* should also make note of when the last time the UPS was tested—provide the date.

Alternatively, if your systems are reliant on a generator, or if a generator can be brought on site from an outside provider, this should also be documented. For example, should you require the use of a generator, who would you call? How long can your systems run on generator power? What sort of generator will be used?

Recovering and Assisting Personnel

Don't forget about the people. Although most of this book describes how to plan for information technology scenarios, it goes without saying that people are more important than computers. You should include a section on recovering and assisting personnel. This section should include information on how to contact local fire, ambulance, and paramedic services. If a particular staff member is certified in CPR or first aid, this should be noted as well.

Notification and Activation

It's important to define under what conditions the *Contingency Plan* will be activated and how the recovery team and general support staff will be notified. For example, it might be the case that the *Contingency Plan* should be activated only for either a Major or Catastrophic Disruption. Or there could be a specific time frame associated with the activation criteria. For example, it could be that the *Contingency Plan* is activated if major applications are unavailable for more than 48 hours. Whatever the criteria is for activating the *Contingency Plan*, it should be spelled out and agreed upon ahead of time. The business owner, in discussions with support staff and the ISSO, should make a decision ahead of time under what conditions the *Contingency Plan* should be activated. Examples of activation criteria are:

- The plan is activated if high priority systems (from BIA) are not recovered within three hours.

- The plan is activated if water starts to come through the ceiling.

- The plan is activated at the CIO's request.

- The plan is activated if the military installation comes under hostile attack.

- The plan is activated if all the high priority systems fail at the same time.

- The plan is activated if the building is bombed.

- The plan is activated if cyber attacks result in complete corruption of data.

- The plan is activated if a denial of service attack continues for more than seven days.

- The plan is activated if snow threatens to cause the roof to cave in.

- The plan is activated if all climate control systems fail for more than 48 hours.

- The plan is activated if health records cannot be accessed for more than three days.

- The plan is activated if a Category 4 or 5 hurricane is scheduled to hit the location within the next 48 hours. Upon determination that the plan will be activated, your document should specify how support staff and the recovery team will be notified. Will people be called on cell phones? Will e-mail be sent to BlackBerry devices? If e-mail, landline telephone, and cell phones are all considered acceptable methods of contacting staff, the section on notification and activation should specifically say this. In some environments, where classified information is at stake, the method of notification can be more important.

Line of Succession

A management line of succession should be stipulated in the event that key personnel are lost in a disaster or cannot be located. Some of these people might very well have roles on the recovery team. For example a line of succession might look like the one shown in Figure 16.1.

Figure 16.1 A Management Line of Succession

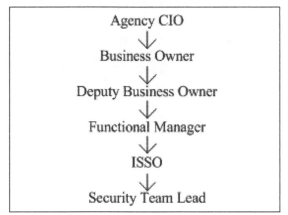

The line of succession should include names and a primary and alternate phone number for each person listed.

Service Level Agreements

Are there service level agreements (or memorandums of understanding) that pertain to the information systems and applications in your C&A package? If there are, you should include such agreements as an appendix to your *Contingency Plan*. If your department or agency uses a managed service provider, in lieu of a service level agreement there may be contracts. Any agreements or contracts that stipulate what type of service you should expect for another organization, department, or company should be attached as an appendix.

Contact Lists

One of the most important pieces of your *Contingency Plan* is the contact list. You'll want include a staff contact list, and contact lists for the vendors that make the equipment and software listed in your *Business Impact Assessment* and *Hardware and Software Inventory*. If your infrastructure spans two geographic locations, you'll want to include phone numbers for the staff in both locations. Many federal agencies employ contractors that are essential to their operations. Some of contractors have been on site for years and are more familiar with the infrastructure than some of the government employees. Be sure to include contact information for essential contractors in your contact lists.

Once your *Contingency Plan* is written, the contact list will probably be the section you will need to update most often. Staff come and go, and even for the staff that remains the same, phone numbers change more often than you'd think. Contacts listed on a *Contingency Plan* should be updated at least once every six months. When you are about to submit a new C&A package, be sure that all the contact lists are up-to-date.

Testing the Contingency Plan

Last but not least, the *Contingency Plan* should be tested at least once a year, and the testing date needs to be recorded in the *Contingency Plan*. *Contingency Plan* testing is not that high on the popularity list of C&A activities—therefore it is often overlooked. However, it's almost a given that if your *Contingency Plan* is not tested, you will be cited for it by the auditors.

Some organizations perform live failover tests where they cut over their entire infrastructure to a warm stand-by site, and other organizations simply do a table-top scenario where a fictional disaster is described and response activities are played out. You simply need to be able to justify why your *Contingency Plan* was tested in a particular fashion.

The higher the level you certify your systems at, the more involved your *Contingency Plan* testing should be. For example, if in determining the Certification Level you decided that you were going to certify and accredit your information systems at a Level 4, auditors will expect to see detailed information on how you tested the failover of your systems to a live stand-by site. If you don't believe such involved *Contingency Plan* testing is necessary, and you elected to certify and accredit your systems at a Level 4, you may want to revisit your reasons for selecting your certification level. With a high C&A level such as a 3 or 4, auditors certainly scrutinize the *Contingency Plan* in much more depth.

Auditors look for consistency across documents. A Level 4 C&A will require highly available and redundant systems, a hot-standby site, and far more detailed recovery procedures. It's not reasonable to state that the risk to your systems is so high that a Level 4 C&A is required, and then not perform detailed contingency preparations. Similarly, it makes little sense to C&A your systems at a Level 1 and then state that highly available RAID systems and hot standbys are required for all the systems listed on your inventory.

Appendices

A *Contingency Plan* is known for its numerous appendices. The Business Impact Assessment should always be an appendix of the *Contingency Plan*. Other items to include as appendices are:

- An occupant evacuation plan
- Standard operating procedures
- Contact lists
- Service level agreements or contracts

Contingency Plan Checklist

Use the following checklist to make sure you haven't forgotten anything.

- Has the *Contingency Plan* been tested?
- Does the staff that has been assigned contingency operations tasks have the authority to carry out these tasks?
- Has the staff that has been assigned tasks been given an opportunity to read the *Contingency Plan* and provide input and comments?

- Does a contact list exist and is it up-to-date?

- Are roles and responsibilities defined?

- Are procedures on recovering systems and major applications included?

- Is the off-site storage contact information and address listed?

- Is it clear who is authorized to retrieve media from the off-site storage site?

- Are restoration procedures from backup media described?

- Has a line of succession been indicated?

- Are requirements for temporary power (UPS or generator) described?

- Are necessary service level agreements (SLAs) documented?

- Has the Logistics Coordinator been given a copy of the SLAs?

- Does your *Contingency Plan* reference other pertinent and related documents?

- Has an alternate site been indicated?

- Is your *Contingency Plan* testing information that is provided consistent with the C&A level that you indicated?

- Are emergency phone numbers for local fire, police, and ambulance services noted?

- Does the plan contain a Record of Changes to record updates?

Additional Resources

The following books may be helpful to you in understanding *Contingency Plan* development:

> *Administrator's Guide to Disaster Planning and Recovery, Volume 2.* TechRepublic, CNET Networks, 1995–2003. ISBN: 1931490651.

Barnes, James C. *A Guide to Business Continuity Planning.* John Wiley & Sons, LTD, July 2001. ISBN: 0471530158.

Myers, Kenneth N. *Manager's Guide to Contingency Planning for Disasters: Protecting Vital Facilities and Critical Operations.* John Wiley & Sons, September 7, 1999. ISBN: 047135838X.

Toigo, Jon William. *Disaster Recovery Planning: Strategies for Protecting Critical Information Assets.* Prentice Hall, August 2002. ISBN: 0130462829.

Wallace, Michael, and Lawrence Webber. *The Disaster Recovery Handbook: A Step-by-Step Plan to Ensure Business Continuity and Protect Vital Operations, Facilities, and Assets.* AMACOM, July 2004. ISBN: 0814472400.

## Chapter 17

Performing a System Risk Assessment

"One of the functions of intelligence is to take account of the dangers that come from trusting solely to the intelligence."

—Lewis Mumford

Topics in this chapter:

- Risk Assessment Creates Focus

- Determine Vulnerabilities

- Threats

- Qualitative Risk Assessment

- Quantitative Risk Assessment

- Qualitative versus Quantitative Risk Assessment

- Present the Risks

- Make Decisions

- Checklist

Introduction

The *System Risk Assessment* focuses on risks to systems, applications, and facilities. The same risk exposure principles that you learned in Chapter 14 apply also to systems, networks, and applications. In Chapter 14, I mentioned that a *System Risk Assessment* can be thought of as an extension of the *Business Risk Assessment*. However, instead of thinking about the business mission, in a *System Risk Assessment* you take into consideration the systems and applications that churn the gears that drive the business.

When performing a *System Risk Assessment*, consider both technical and natural threats to applications, systems, or networks. Technical threats are for the most part invoked by people who act as a threat agent—sometimes intentionally, and sometimes unintentionally. (One could argue that some computer programs act as threat agents; however, for understanding C&A, it's not really necessary to debate that here.) Since natural disasters are always unintentional, we think about them in a different light. We don't have to take into consideration that a hurricane, flood, or tornado can be intentionally created. Though natural disasters are not technical, they do pose risks to your systems.

Your *System Risk Assessment* can be based on either qualitative or quantitative methods, or some of both. Later in this chapter I'll be explaining the differences between the two risk assessment methodologies. Whatever methodology you use in your *System Risk Assessment*, you are going to need to explain your methodology so that the evaluation team will understand how you obtained your results and your recommendations.

Risk Assessment Creates Focus

When you performed your ST&E, you performed tests on your security controls. You likely found various vulnerabilities as an outcome to the different tests you performed. The focus on the ST&E is on how to perform tests and document the results. You'll notice that the checklist items at the end of Chapter 12 are mostly a check on the concept, "Were the tests good ones and did you document the testing process and relevant information correctly?"

The *System Risk Assessment* creates focus for understanding the effect that the vulnerabilities discovered from the results of your ST&E will have on your information systems and major applications. Go back and look at the results of your tests. What do you think the vulnerabilities are? Vulnerabilities work in concert with threats to create risk. You are going to use your findings from the ST&E process to help put together a list of vulnerabilities. An illustration of the *System Risk Assessment* process is depicted in Figure 17.1.

During the development of the *System Risk Assessment*, you will:

- Consider results from your ST&E
- Determine your system and application vulnerabilities
- Level your vulnerabilities reported from scanners taking into consideration the importance of the system to the business mission
- Determine the likelihood that the vulnerabilities will be exploited
- Describe your risk assessment methodology
- Determine your risk exposure
- Present your risks in an easy to understand table
- Make decisions on what to do about the risks

Figure 17.1 *System Risk Assessment* Process

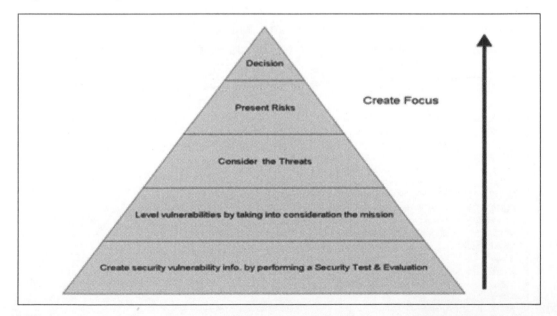

Determine Vulnerabilities

Determining vulnerabilities to your information systems is key to keeping them secure. There are different levels of granularity you should apply in looking for vulnerabilities. The higher your C&A level, the deeper and more involved your process should be for determining vulnerabilities. Review the section called "What are the C&A Levels?" in Chapter 7. Scanning for vulnerabilities was recommended for a Level 3 and 4 C&A. Additionally, a penetration test was recommended for C&A Level 4. If you feel that an auditor may question your decision that your systems warrant a Level 2 C&A (instead of a Level 3) you can potentially head-off any concerns with auditors by including the results from a vulnerability assessment even if your agency doesn't normally require a vulnerability assessment for a Level 2 C&A.

The tools today that scan for system, network, and application vulnerabilities are very advanced. These tools are indispensable for security risk assessments. Most of the leading vulnerability assessment scanners have teams of security engineers that are populating the scanner engine on a daily basis with new signatures, similar to the way anti-virus engines can be loaded with new anti-virus signatures daily. We talked about those scanners in Chapter 12, and you may have used some of them when performing your ST&E.

Most vulnerability scanning tools use qualitative rankings and automatically classify risks as high, medium, or low. Figure 17.2 shows an example of how the popular scanner QualysGuard depicts vulnerabilities.

Figure 17.2 Screenshot from the QualysGuard Security Scanner

www.syngress.com

You should, however, use the stated vulnerability ranking (high, medium, or low) taken directly from a vulnerability scanning report with caution. You will want to take into consideration something that does not show up in an automated vulnerability scanning report; that is, the importance of the system to the overall business mission. Therefore, in automated scanning tools, vulnerability rankings may show up that are inappropriate rankings for your C&A purposes. For example, if a scanner ranks a vulnerability as high, but it has been found on a system that has a relatively low importance to the business mission, there may be little justification to rank the vulnerability as 'high' in your *System Risk Assessment*. Figure 17.3 shows a vulnerability found on a Microsoft SQL Server with a criticality rating as 4 out of 5, according to the scanner.

Figure 17.3 Vulnerability Ranking from a Leading Scanner

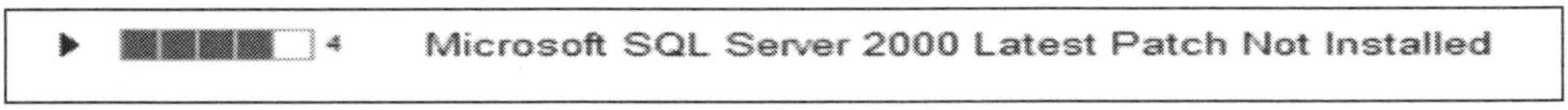

A criticality rating of 4 out of 5 sounds fairly significant. However, if this database has been purged of all data and is about to be decommissioned, and was used only to store the online cafeteria menu, then it probably isn't as significant of a vulnerability as it appears to be. Therefore, once you have a vulnerability assessment report in hand that came from an automated scanner, you should go through it and review each reported vulnerability, and then make a decision on the ranking of the vulnerability that should actually be applied based on the importance of the system. The more important the system is to the agency, the greater the severity of the loss. I refer to the process of reevaluating and reclassifying vulnerabilities found by automated scanners as "leveling the vulnerabilities." You may decide that many of the vulnerabilities in fact should retain the same risk classification reported by your scanner, and that others merit lowering or increasing their rank. Create a summary list of all the vulnerabilities from network and system scanning, and your ST&E process, level the vulnerabilities, and then create a final vulnerability list. Use the final "leveled" value when you determine your risk exposure.

Threats

A threat is something that subjects an organization to risk by acting upon a weakness (or a vulnerability) to create risk. It's important to understand fundamental concepts on threats because when you present the risks, you will use this understanding to justify and make recommendations on whether or not you think risks should be mitigated, accepted, or transferred.

Threats can lead to security incidents. Refer to Table 11.2 to review some of the more common types of security incidents. In some cases, a threat might also be defined as a security incident. For example, a denial of service attack might be thought of as both a threat and a security incident. Don't spin your wheels trying to figure out if something is a threat, or an incident. Check to see if your agency may have specific guidelines on threats that they'd like you to follow.

For C&A purposes, the threats to take into consideration are:

- Threats initiated by people
- Threats initiated by computers (or other network devices)
- Threats from natural disasters

Threats Initiated by People

It is easy to understand how a hackers or cyber criminals can intentionally threaten your systems. However, threats can be caused by unintentional human errors as well. An untrained firewall engineer could pose a threat to your systems and networks by accidentally configuring a firewall rule to open a port instead of closing it. The number of ways that your own staff can unintentionally create threats to your systems is infinite, which is one of the reasons that such a large number of checks, balances, and accountability features are built into systems (e.g., separate accounts, logging capabilities, separation of roles and responsibilities).

Threats Initiated by Computers or Devices

Sometimes, devices themselves can create threats and even security incidents. Years ago I worked at a networking company where there were various models of Hewlett Packard printers that on various occasions sprayed the net-works with enough broadcast packets to create a denial-of-service attack to the other systems on the network. We thought someone was attacking the network until we put a network analyzer on some of the network segments and traced the broadcast storm back to printers that had buggy software in them.

Threats from Natural Disasters

Many IT professionals, in the past, have not given enough credence to the possibility of natural disasters. However, recent natural disasters such as Hurricane Katrina, which took place in the New Orleans area in August 2005, have raised the awareness of natural disasters. Threats from natural disasters include, but are not limited to:

- Floods and heavy rains
- Earthquakes
- Fire
- Hurricanes and wind
- Snow and ice
- Lightning
- Tornadoe
- Volcanoes
- Tsunamis, typhoons, and tidal waves

When you take natural disasters into consideration, you can use the same principles that you use when you consider threats to systems and applications. You need to know how likely it is that a natural disaster will occur, and esti-mate the impact that it will have on your operations. You can use the fol-lowing URLs to do more research on natural disasters, their anticipated impact, and the likelihood that they will occur in a given area:

- Advanced National Seismic System Earthquake Maps and List www.ncedc.org/anss/maps/

- Federal Emergency Management Agency
  www.fema.gov/index.shtm

- Hazards Research Lab at University of South Carolina
  http://go2.cla.sc.edu/hazard/db_registration

- Natural Disaster Hotspots: A Global Risk Analysis
  http://sedac.ciesin.columbia.edu/hazards/hotspots/synthesisreport.pdf

- Natural Disaster Reference Database
  http://ndrd.gsfc.nasa.gov/

- National Geophysical Data Center Natural Hazards Data
  www.ngdc.noaa.gov/seg/hazard/hazards.shtml

- Natural Hazards Center: All Hazards
  www.colorado.edu/hazards/resources/web/all.html#indices

- National Oceanic and Atmospheric Administration Central Library
  www.lib.noaa.gov/

Qualitative Risk Assessment

When you use relative concepts to determine risk exposure, you are using qualitative risk analysis. Relative classification systems compare one component to another, allowing you to rank a classification as high, medium, or low. It's useful to rank risk exposures caused by vulnerabilities so you can more easily make decisions on what to do about them.

You can use the same qualitative risk exposure matrix listed in Table 14.4. A more simplified version of that table is shown in Table 17.1. Once you have established what the vulnerabilities are, you need to determine their likelihood of being exploited, and the severity of the loss. You determine the risk exposure by multiplying the severity of the loss by the likelihood. As a reminder:

Risk Exposure = Likelihood x Impact

$R(E) = P(L) \times S(L)$

$P(L)$ = Probability of loss (likelihood)

$S(L)$ = Severity of loss (impact)

Table 17.1 Qualitative Risk Exposure Determination Table

Impact Values S (L)	Likelihood P (L)		
	Low	Medium	High
High	Low	Medium	High
Medium	Low	Medium	Medium
Low	Low	Low	Low

(Table 17.1 is very similar to Table 3.6 in the NIST Special Publication 800-30, Risk Management Guide for Information Technology Systems, July 2002.)

Quantitative Risk Assessment

Quantitative risk assessment associates loss with a financial value. The goal of understanding financial loss is to give you more information in making decisions about the procurement and implementation of safeguards. Quantitative risk assessment is essential if you want to perform cost benefit analysis to figure out if implementing a particular safeguard is financially worth the cost. If the anticipated annual loss is less than the annualized cost of the safeguard, then it is usually not worth it to implement the safeguard.

I will use a natural disaster example to show you how to figure out financial loss based on quantitative risk assessment methods. If you look at Figure 17.4, you will see that in Florida alone there are different probabilities throughout the state for hurricanes with wind speeds greater than 100 knots. To calculate the risk of a hurricane occurring in Miami, Florida, you need to understand the likelihood of one occurring each year. If a hurricane occurs once every 20 years (1 out of 20), then it has a 5 percent chance of occurring yearly since $1/20 = .05$, which equals 5 percent.

Figure 17.4 Probabilities of Hurricanes in Florida Localities

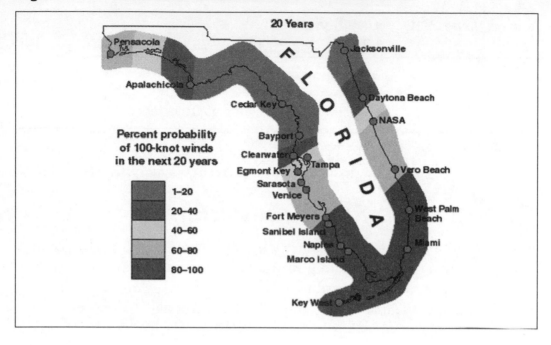

Source: U.S. Geological Survey

The frequency of Florida hurricanes with wind speeds greater than or equal to 100 knots is mapped in terms of the probability of occurrence during a 20-year exposure window. These probabilistic estimates, based on 1006 years of observations, illustrate that hurricanes with 100 knot winds occur more frequently in southern Florida, and gradually decrease in frequency towards northern Florida.[1]

The threat frequency (or likelihood) for natural disasters can be calculated by using an Annualized Rate of Occurrence (ARO). An ARO is a constant number that tells you how often a threat might occur each year. AROs can be broken down into subvalues known as Standard Annual Frequency Estimates (SAFE) and Local Annual Frequency Estimates (LAFE). The SAFE value is the number of times a specific threat is expected to occur annually in a large geographic region such as North America. The LAFE value is the number of times a specific threat can be expected to occur annually in a smaller, local geographic region such as Miami, Florida. For the purpose of C&A, it is more appropriate to use LAFE values. (If we were going to C&A all the systems in

North America in one C&A package, we might use SAFE values for that. Such a C&A package of course would be a Sisyphean exercise.)

ARO values (SAFE and LAFE) typically are represented as rational numbers, or as a decimal value as shown in Table 17.2. (A rational number is a number that can be expressed equivalently as a fraction.)

Table 17.2 Threat Values for Annualized Rates of Occurrence

ARO (LAFE) Values Expressed as a percent	Expressed as a decimal	Expressed as a fraction	Frequency of Occurrence
1%	.01	1/100	Once every 100 years
2%	.02	1/50	Once every 50 years
5%	.05	1/20	Once every 20 years
10%	.10	1/10	Once every 10 years
20%	.2	1/5	Once every 5 years
100%	1	1/1	Once a year
1000%	10	10/1	10 times a year
10,000%	20	20/1	20 times a year

The reduction in value of an information system from one threat (or incident) is referred to as a Single Loss Expectancy (SLE). If one of the systems in your hardware and software inventory is valued at $100,000, and a hurricane destroys 90 percent of it, the value of the system has been reduced by $90,000, which is the SLE.

SLE = Original Total Cost – Remaining Value
SLE $90,000 = $100,000 – $10,000

It is possible that instead of a hurricane, a hacker might destroy 90% of the system and the same SLE formula would apply. Once you know the SLE, you can determine an Annual Loss Expectancy (ALE). ALE is a risk exposure standard that is computed by multiplying the probability of a loss from a threat (or incident) by the reduction in value of the information system.

> **NOTE**
>
> ALE is a metric that was developed by the National Bureau of Standards in 1979. In the mid-1980s, the National Bureau of Standards became part of the National Institute of Standards and Technology.

ALE values are useful to perform cost benefit analysis so you can figure out if spending money on a particular safeguard is worth it or not. ALE values can be determined for any type of threat whether it is a threat launched by a cyber criminal, or a natural disaster. To determine the ALE for this same $100,000 system, use the formula:

ALE = LAFE x SLE

R (E) = P (L) x S (L)

The LAFE value is the probability of potential loss, or P (L). The SLE, or the loss from a one-time occurrence of the incident, is the severity of the loss, S (L).

If the system is located in Miami, Florida and hurricanes have a 5% chance of occurring yearly:

ALE = .05 x $90,000 = $4,500

Every year, the one information system located in Miami, Florida is being exposed to an annual loss expectancy of $4,500 from hurricanes alone. If there are 1000 systems at this facility in Miami, all with the same ALE, that would come to a whopping cumulative ALE of $4,500,000. Even if moving the facility to a different location costs $1,000,000, in this case it would be worth it since the safeguard (e.g., the move) would be far less expensive than the Annual Loss Expectancy.

An additional resource that explains quantitative risk assessment is an article titled "Security Scanning is not Risk Analysis" in the Intranet Journal (www.intranetjournal.com/articles/200207/se_07_14_02a.html).

Qualitative versus Quantitative Risk Assessment

When you use ALE values to determine cost benefit analysis, you are performing quantitative risk analysis. When you use high, moderate, and low rankings that are relative to each other, you are performing qualitative risk analysis. Whether the threat is a hurricane or a hacker, you can use either method to determine risk exposure. There are advantages and disadvantages to both methods of determining risk.

Whether you use qualitative or quantitative methods to determine your risk exposure, you should state in your *System Risk Assessment* which methodology you are using and why. Your reasons for selecting one methodology over the other might be straightforward and simple. Perhaps you decided to use qualitative risk assessment because that's what your agency requires. To use quantitative risk assessment effectively, you need to know the current dollar value of an asset. If your agency does not track that kind of information, quantitative risk assessment presents many challenges. If you are able to use quantitative risk assessment, it is an indispensable tool for determining whether an expensive safeguard is worth purchasing or not.

Qualitative risk assessment has the following attributes:

- A faster process
- Emphasizes descriptions
- Findings are simple and expressed in relative terms
- Values are perceived values, not actual values
- Requires less training

Quantitative risk assessment has the following attributes:

- Very time intensive
- Yields results that are financial in nature
- Used for cost benefit analysis
- Good for justifying the procurement of safeguards
- Requires tracking the financial value of assets

Today, most C&A packages use qualitative risk assessment methods simply because it's usually faster to perform than quantitative methods. However, as C&A programs evolve over time, it is likely that quantitative methods will gain more traction. The more expensive the safeguards are that your agency is taking into consideration, the more valuable quantitative risk assessment can be.

Present the Risks

In order to make decisions on risks, you need to present the risks in an easy to follow table. For a qualitative risk assessment, create columns for the following fields:

- ID number
- Vulnerability name
- Description
- Likelihood
- Impact
- Risk Exposure
- Recommendation

Some risk assessments also include columns for security control identifiers, policy and oversight citations, threat descriptions, CVE numbers (see http://cve.mitre.org), and other related information. Find out if your agency already has a template that they'd like you to use for your risk table. For a quantitative risk assessment, you should also create a column for ALE. Table 17.3 shows an example of an easy-to-follow format to present your risks.

Table 17.3 Risks to Systems and Recommendations

ID No.	Name	Vulnerability Description	Likelihood	Impact	Risk Exposure	Recommendation
1	SSH Vuln on erp02 host	Due to a buffer overflow vulnerabilities and design flaws in SSH1, an attacker could gain root shell access to erp02 on the network 5.	Medium	High	Medium	Mitigate the risk by disabling SSH1. Since we now use Connect:Direct for security file transfers, nobody uses SSH1 anymore anyway.
2	NetBIOS Vuln on account belonging to James Smith, Martha Doyle, and Will Jones	Due to a NetBIOS vulnerability, a brute force attack enabled a penetration tester to obtain logins and passwords for 3 different users	High	High	High	Mitigate this risk by advising users to change passwords, and implement a password complexity requirement that requires complex passwords with 10 characters, including 1 numeric and 1 uppercase letter. Implement password aging. Disable NetBIOS.

Continued

Table 17.3 continued Risks to Systems and Recommendations

ID No.	Name	Vulnerability Description	Likelihood	Impact	Risk Exposure	Recommendation
3	Administration of User Provisioning Database	There is no database administrator's guide. If our database administrator becomes ill or ends his employment, it will be difficult to understand how to administer the database.	Medium	Medium	Medium	Mitigate the risk by developing a database administration guide that includes information on how to perform all database administration functions. Include information on database configuration in the guide.
4	No separation of duties	One of the users at Office 2 has admin access to all systems in Office 2.	Low	Low	Low	Accept the risk. Office 2 is a small office with only 2 users. It doesn't make sense to hire a systems administrator for 2 people.

Make Decisions

Once you have gathered the pertinent facts about the risk exposure to your systems, you are armed with all the right information to formulate decisions. One of the objectives of the decisions that you make will be to balance the impact of threats with safeguards. Safeguards mitigate risk; however, there is a cost involved in applying safeguards. The cost of safeguards should not only include the up-front cost of procuring the safeguard, but also the yearly maintenance costs of implementing it. For example, a set of firewalls may cost $30,000 to purchase and install, but it also requires the hiring of a full time firewall administrator. Be sure to consider these hourly costs in labor rates as well as in the cost of a product.

Mitigating risks means reducing them to acceptable levels, which of course is different than mitigating risks at all costs. Most information technology risks can be reduced. Sometimes a high risk item can be reduced by simply checking a box in a GUI to enable a particular security feature. Other times, reducing a risk can be complex, very involved, and very expensive.

Since there is usually a price to pay for mitigating risks, the price is something that perceptive IT managers will want to take into consideration. Sometimes that price might be only an hour of a systems administrator's time. Other times it could be hundreds of hours of many systems administrators' time, or it may mean purchasing an enterprise product that costs several million dollars. When it comes to reducing risks, one of the first questions your business owner and ISSO should be asking is, "What will it cost?"

Consistent with the options in Chapter 14, your options are either to accept the risk, transfer the risk, or mitigate the risk. Generally speaking, high risk items that don't cost much should always be mitigated. Moderate risk items that don't cost much should also be mitigated. Low risk items may not be worth reducing at all, particularly if it costs a lot to do so.

Checklist

Upon completion of the *System Risk Assessment*, use the following checklist to make sure you haven't forgotten anything:

- Have you explained your risk assessment methodology?

- Did you integrate findings from your ST&E into your *System Risk Assessment*?

- Did you take into consideration natural disasters?

- Are the risks presented in an easy-to-follow table?

- Did you make recommendations on what to do about the risks?

- Did you provide an explanation to justify each recommendation?

Summary

The fundamental concepts for your *System Risk Assessment* should be similar to the concepts you used to develop your *Business Risk Assessment*. However, the vulnerabilities that you discuss will likely be more technical and more specific. Include enough information about the vulnerability so that the evaluation team can understand what the weakness is. Make a recommendation on whether to mitigate the risk, accept the risk, or transfer the risk and justify your recommendation. If you don't list any vulnerabilities and claim your systems, major applications, and networks don't have any, the evaluation team will likely come to the conclusion that you don't know what you're doing. You can always find some vulnerabilities. Listing vulnerabilities and making intelligent decisions about them shows more savvy than claiming that there are none. Don't forget to take into consideration natural disasters—particularly if your agency has offices and systems in areas that have a history of weather-related disasters.

Additional Resources

Books that may help improve your understanding of *System Risk Assessment* are listed here:

> Bidgoli, Hossein. *Handbook of Information Security, Volume 3, Threats, Vulnerabilities, Prevention, Detection, and Management.* John Wiley & Sons, January 2006. ISBN: 0471648329.

> Jones, Andy, and Debi Ashenden. *Risk Management for Computer Security.* Butterworth-Heinemann, March 15, 2005. ISBN: 0750677953.

> Landoll, Douglas J., CRC. *The Security Risk Assessment Handbook.* December 12, 2005. ISBN: 0849329981.

> Long, Johnny and Chris Hurley, with Mark Wolfgang and Mike Petruzzi. *Penetration Tester's Open Source Toolkit.* Rockland, MA: Syngress Publishing, December 1, 2005. ISBN: 1597490210.

> Long, Johnny and Ed Skoudis. *Google Hacking for Penetration Testers.* Rockland, MA: Syngress Publishing, 2005. ISBN: 1931836361.

McCumber, John. *Assessing and Managing Security Risk in IT Systems.* Auerbach, June 15, 2004. ISBN: 0849322324.

McNab, Chris. *Network Security Assessment.* O'Reilly, March 1, 2004. ISBN: 059600611X.

Rogers, Russ, Ed Fuller, Greg Miles, Matthew Hoagberg, Travis Schack, Ted Dykstra, and Bryan Cunningham. *Network Security Evaluation.* Rockland, MA: Syngress Publishing, August 2005. ISBN: 1597490350.

Notes

1. *Natural Disasters—Forecasting Economic and Life Losses.* U.S. Department of the Interior. U.S. Geological Survey (http://pubs.usgs.gov/fs/natural-disasters/figures/fig7.html).

## Chapter 18

Developing a Configuration Management Plan

"ISC remains deeply apologetic that prior versions of BIND did not properly catch the configuration error that you appear to have built your business on."

—Paul Vixie, author of various RFCs

Topics in this chapter:

- Establish Definitions

- Describe Assets Controlled by the Plan

- Describe the Configuration Management System

- Define Roles and Responsibilities

- Establish Baselines

- Change Control Process

- Configuration Management Audit

- Configuration & Change Management Tools

- Configuration Management Plan Checklist

Introduction

A *Configuration Management Plan* shows evidence that software changes, including code, operating systems settings, and application configurations, are known and tracked. The settings and configurations that are known and tracked should include the technical security controls. The *Configuration Management Plan* is a living document and should be updated through the life cycle of the systems that it references.

Some agencies may have one global *Configuration Management Plan* for the entire agency, and other agencies may develop *Configuration Management Plans* at the bureau or project level. If your organization actively contributes to an agencywide *Configuration Management Plan* by sending in regular updates, you can likely use that *Configuration Management Plan* for your C&A package.

Before starting to write a *Configuration Management Plan*, find out if your group or department already participates in updating an existing one. If one does exist, you can use it for your C&A package as long as assets from your hardware and software inventory of your C&A package are named and tracked in that plan. If you are unsure if an existing *Configuration Management Plan* will be acceptable, schedule a meeting with the evaluation team and present them with your questions. They should be able to give you guidance before you start working on your *Configuration Management Plan* as to what they consider to be acceptable or not.

Establish Definitions

To ensure that the configuration management terminology that you use in your *Configuration Management Plan* will have consistent definitions to those used by the evaluation team, establish your definitions up front and list them near the beginning of your document. Table 18.1 includes some commonly used configuration management terms. It's possible that these terms may be defined slightly differently by different agencies. What's important is that these terms mean the same thing to you as they do to the evaluation team. If your agency already has configuration management terms defined through policies, use them and republish them in your *Configuration Management Plan*.

Table 18.1 Common Configuration Management Terms

Term	Description
Baseline	The set of hardware and software configuration items formally reviewed during a system's lifecycle that completely comprises the functional, logical, and physical characteristics of a system.
Change Control	The systematic evaluation, coordination, and implementation of all approved changes for an established system, application, or code.
Change Management	The methodology that integrates change into the business.
Change Request	The formal documenting of a desire to modify an existing system (or code) due to the need to augment the system or because an anomaly, discrepancy, or bug has occurred in the system.
Configuration Auditing	An evaluation of change integrity for controlled assets.
Configuration Identification	The determination and naming of assets to be controlled.
Configuration Identifier	A number or reference ID used to catalogue a document or asset in the configuration management system.
Release Management	The process by which one identifies, packages, communicates and delivers changed or new elements of a hardware or software asset.
Regression Testing	The selective testing and retesting of a software system to ensure that (1.) bugs are discovered and fixed and that (2.) no previously working functions have failed as a result of the introduction of new code.

Describe Assets Controlled by the Plan

One of the first things you'll want to include in your *Configuration Management Plan* is a description of the hardware and software assets that the *Configuration Management Plan* pertains to. You can obtain this information quickly from your *Hardware and Software Inventory*. You should also include a brief system description about the system or major application that the *Configuration Management Plan* is associated with. Using the same system description that you included in your *Hardware and Software Inventory* is perfectly acceptable. The *Configuration Management Plan* should be able to stand alone as its own document, which is why it is necessary to include this background information, even though it is somewhat redundant when considering the C&A package as a whole. Always remember that most of the documents that you work on are not only parts of the C&A package you are developing, but are working documents that the team managing the system uses on a daily, weekly, or monthly basis as well.

Describe the Configuration Management System

Most agencies, bureaus, or their departments have a configuration management system. The configuration management system is the storage and retrieval mechanism for baseline configurations, documents, products, and code. Some configuration management systems might be simple databases, and others might be products designed specifically for configuration management tasks. Whatever system your agency uses, describe it, make note of who uses the system, and note who has access to it. If a particular product or open source tool is used to perform configuration management, you will want to note the product and vendor name or the open source download location. Be sure to include the version numbers of software that's installed on the configuration management system.

Additionally, you should describe the security controls that protect the configuration management system. Include discussion about the authentication mechanism, access to the system, perimeter protection (firewalls and routers), and host– or network-based intrusion detection systems that are used.

Finally, you should be sure to include information about how the configuration management system is backed up. Who is responsible for the backups? What programs are used to perform the backups? Where is backup media stored and who has access to it?

Define Roles and Responsibilities

One of the first items you'll need to discuss is to identify the folks who are actually performing configuration management. Describe their roles and responsibilities and list their names and contact information. Typical configuration management responsibilities are listed in Table 18.2. If you have a small agency, it is possible that some of these roles are consolidated into one role. Additionally, it is possible that the names of the roles found in Table 18.2 could vary from agency to agency.

Table 18.2 Configuration Management Roles and Responsibilities

Role	Responsibilities
Director of Configuration Management (Director of CM)	Develops and maintain CM plans, policies, and procedures
	Works with CM Analysts and CM Coordinators to ensure that configuration duties are understood
	Presides over Change Control Board (CCB) activities and meetings
	Designates a scribe to take notes or minutes during each CCB meeting
	Makes minutes available to all team members
	Approves or disapproves change requests discussed in the CCB meeting
	Maintains local records, databases, and libraries (repositories) to ensure compliance
	Authorizes access to the configuration management system
	Conducts configuration audits to ensure that CM activities are being performed correctly
	Reports compliance information to auditors as necessary
	Notifies CM Analysts and CM Coordinators about CM tools, CM policies, and procedures
	Leads the agency configuration management team
	Ensures that introduction of the proposed changes will not have a negative impact on current operations

Continued

Table 18.2 continued Configuration Management Roles and
Responsibilities

Role	Responsibilities
Configuration Management Administrator (CM Administrator)	Administers the configuration management system Receives new or updated documents and enters them into the configuration management system Receives all baselines and enters them into the configuration management system Catalogues change requests into the configuration management system Administers change request notifications and closes change request tickets Ensures that backups are performed of the configuration management system Ensures that an off-site backup of the configuration management exists Attends Change Control Board meetings Sends monthly report to the Director of CM
Configuration Management Analyst (CM Analyst)	Ensures that all software is baselined Administers the release engineering system Performs release engineering activities Maintains source code and version control Assists in software integration and bug fixing Manages the software build process and controls the migration of software throughout the life-cycle Maintain records, databases, and software libraries (repositories) Notifies developers and testers of configuration management status and policies Coordinates project configuration control activities Ensures that introduction of changes will not have a negative impact on current operations Maintains open communication with the CM Administrator Attends Change Control Board meetings Sends monthly report to Director of CM

Continued

Table 18.2 continued Configuration Management Roles and Responsibilities

Role	Responsibilities
Configuration Manager Coordinator (CM Coordinator)	Develops and maintain CM plans, policies, and procedures for operating systems and applications Oversees generation of functional and product baselines Coordinates release of product components (hardware, software, interfaces, and documentation) Maintains records, databases, and libraries (repositories) to ensure compliance Maintains system integrity by performing configuration control Conducts training in CM tools and CM policies and procedures for project Ensures that introduction of changes will not have a negative impact on current operations Maintains open communication with the CM Administrator Attends Change Control Board meetings Sends monthly reports to Director of CM

Establish Baselines

Discuss your configuration management process for establishing baselines. A baseline identifies and defines all the configuration items that make up a system at a particular moment in time. Baselining is a formal process, which occurs infrequently. The configuration management system should always have the current updated baseline available for review. There are three types of baselines:

- Functional Baseline
- Software Baseline
- Product Baseline

A Functional Baseline contains all agreed-upon documentation for an information system or major application. Each document should be assigned a document ID number and include a publication date and the author name(s).

A Software Baseline contains all of a system's software. A Software Baseline includes the source code for each software configuration item and a software baseline document that provides a listing of the software and any other pertinent information such as developer, version, or software libraries. A Software Baseline locks in a version, build number, or release number at a particular moment in time.

A Product Baseline is the combination of the Functional Baseline and the Software Baseline. A product is not a product without documentation that explains how it works. A product could be an application that has been developed in-hour or a commercial off-the-shelf application. Whether the product has been developed in house or not, it should include installation and configuration information pertinent to the actual implementation. For a product developed in-house, the configuration management system should include the design and requirements documents. It's not necessary to include design requirements for commercial off-the-shelf products since companies will likely not give that out.

If any license keys are used in the baselines, you will want to state how license keys are archived and preserved. You should also include the agency security policies against using unlicensed software. What method is used to ensure that software license keys are not installed on systems that have not paid for the keys?

CM Analysts and Coordinators should establish new baselines at the end of the design and build phases in the system development life cycle and again at the end of the test phase. All baselines should be entered into the configuration management system. New baselines should be continuously sent to the Director of Configuration Management, or the designated individual that updates the configuration management system.

Change Control Process

The *Configuration Management Plan* should clearly describe the configuration management process. You'll need to explain how configuration changes are requested, approved, disapproved, and implemented. Sometimes inserting a flow chart of the configuration management process is the best way to show how it works. Figure 18.1 depicts an example of a change control process flowchart.

Change Request Procedures

Discuss the change request procedures in the *Configuration Management Plan*. Change requests typically go through the following phases:

- Initiation
- Review and analysis
- Approval or disapproval
- Notification that change will or will not occur (including the date for change)
- Implementation of change
- Closure of the change request

Change requests usually are initiated by filling out either a paper form, a web form, or sending in an e-mail request. You'll want to describe what the procedure is in your agency for initiating a change request. If there are particular timeframes that the initiator can anticipate as the change request passes through steps 1 through 6, you should indicate those time frames in the *Configuration Management Plan*.

Emergency Change Request Procedures

Your agency should have an expedited change request process for emergency change requests. You'll want to find out what that process is and devote a small section to it in your *Configuration Management Plan*. There are often valid reasons for emergency change requests such as new code to fix a bug that is hampering operations, or installing a patch to mitigate a security vulnerability.

Change Request Parameters

Each change request should have certain parameters that are required when submitting an initial change request. An example of a *Change Control Request Form* that includes typical change request parameters is found in Figure 18.1. Figure 18.2 provides a flowchart depicting the Change Control process.

Configuration Control Board

The Configuration Control Board (CCB) is the forum where change requests should be discussed. An agency may have multiple CCBs, each acting on behalf of its own business unit. In your *Configuration Management Plan*, you should identify the key information about the CCB that is relevant to the hardware and software assets for your particular C&A package as well as general information about how the CCB operates. Questions that you should answer in your discussion about the CCB are:

- When do CCB meetings take place?
- Who runs the CCB meetings?
- Who are the members of the CCB?
- Are there CCB members from the C&A package's business owner's department?
- Is information about the CCB posted on an internal Web site that you can point to?
- Does the CCB generate a monthly report?
- Where can monthly CCB reports be found?
- Is there a group e-mail address for the CCB members?
- Is there an e-mail address for submitting change requests to the CCB?
- Is there a Web form for submitting change requests to the CCB?

Figure 18.1 Example of a Change Request Form

Change Request Form

Select severity:
  Critical: A change request considered essential to the system.
  Very Important: A change request that would enhance performance or
operations.
   Important: A change that would be beneficial to system users
   Non-Critical: A change that is desirable to implement as time permits.

Initiator of request:
E-mail address of initiator:
Telephone of initiator:

Type of change (select all that apply):
  Software code change
  Operating system configuration change
  Application configuration change
  Security configuration change

Explain reason for change request:

Anticipated impact of change:

  Approved
  Disapproved (explain why):

If approved, scheduled date of change:

Date of change request closure:

Figure 18.2 Change Control Process

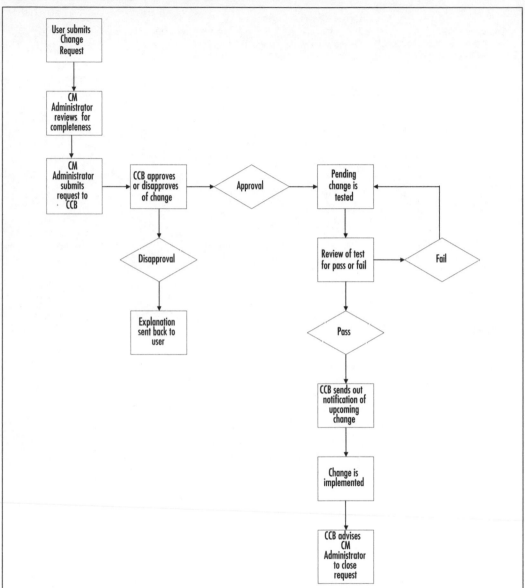

Configuration Management Audit

Include a section that explains how the Configuration Management Director ensures that the configuration management system archives the latest baselines. It is likely that auditing the configuration management system requires interviews and discussions with the configuration management staff. If the Configuration Management Director uses any sort of checklist to collate findings during the staff interviews, state that in the audit section. Discuss how often the audit interviews take place.

Configuration and Change Management Tools

There are numerous tools made to assist with configuration management duties and track version changes to code and documents. Some of these tools are licensable products and others are well-respected open source tools. Some products that are marketed as Business Continuity Tools offer useful configuration management features. If your agency uses particular tools or products to assist with change control and configuration management, you should name these products in your *Configuration Management Plan*. Popular tools that can be used for configuration management include:

- Concurrent Versions System (CVS), an open source tool
  www.cyclic.com/cyclic-pages/CVS-sheet.html

- Configuresoft's Enterprise Configuration Manager
  www.configuresoft.com/Products/ecm.aspx

- Component Software Inc.'s CS-RCS Pro
  www.componcntsoftware.com/csrcs/

- IBM's Rational
  www-306.ibm.com/software/rational/offerings/scm.html

- MKS' MKS Integrity
  www.mks.com/products/integrity

- NetIQ's Change Administrator
  www.netiq.com/products/nca/default.asp

- Strohl Systems' LDRPS
  www.strohlsystems.com/Software/LDRPS/LDRPS10.asp

- SunView Software Inc.'s Change Gear Configuration Management
  www.sunviewsoftware.com/products/cmdb.aspx

- Telelogic's SYNERGY / CM
  www.telelogic.com/Products/synergy/synergycm/index.cfm

Configuration Management Plan Checklist

Upon completion of the *Configuration Management Plan*, use the following checklist to make sure you haven't forgotten anything:

- Have you described the configuration management roles and responsibilities?

- Have you described the configuration management system and tools?

- Have you described the security controls that protect the CM system?

- Is a copy of the change management request form included?

- Have you described the change control process?

- Are procedures for making emergency changes addressed?

- Have you defined the baselines that you track?

- Have you described how license keys are archived and tracked?

- Have you described your process for establishing baselines?

- Are configuration management terms listed for reference?

- Is there a discussion about configuration management audits?

Summary

A *Configuration Management Plan* demonstrates that your organization understands how to handle change, and can track all changes to your system including the settings for security controls. An effective *Configuration Management Plan* provides audit trails and traceability as to why change has occurred. The baselines stored in the configuration management system enable your organization to understand what the given configuration of your systems and major applications are at any given point in time. Tracking configuration changes and requests enables support staff to better troubleshoot security incidents since they will have a known good configuration for reference if the integrity of the current configuration ever comes into question.

Additional Resources

The following books and articles might help you improve your understanding of configuration management and help you to create an informative *Configuration Management Plan*:

Bounds, Nadine, and Susan Dart. "CM Plans: The Beginning to Your CM Solutions." Carnegie Mellon, Software Engineering Institute. http://www.sei.cmu.edu/legacy/scm/papers/CM_Plans/CMPlans.MasterToC.html

Brad Appleton's Software Configuration Management Links. http://www.cmcrossroads.com/bradapp/links/scm-links.html#Free_CM_Tools

Dreilinger, Sean. "CVS Version Control for Website Projects." April 13, 1998. http://durak.org/cvswebsites/howto-cvs-websites.pdf

"IEEE Standard 828-1998 for Software Configuration Management Plans." IEEE Standards Association. http://standards.ieee.org/reading/ieee/std_public/description/se/828-1998_desc.html

Jonassen Hass, Anne Mette. *Configuration Management Principles and Practice.* Addison–Wesley Professional, December 30, 2002. ISBN: 0321117662.

Leon, Alexis. *Software Configuration Management Handbook, Second Edition.* Norwood, MA: Artech House Publishers, December 30, 2004. ISBN: 1580538827.

Moreira, Mario, E. *Software Configuration Management Implementation Roadmap.* Hoboken, NJ: John Wiley & Sons Inc., June 25, 2004. ISBN: 0470862645.

Chapter 19

Preparing the System Security Plan

"We spend our time searching for security and hate it when we get it."

—John Steinbeck

Topics in this chapter:

- Laws, Regulations, and Policies

- The System Description

- Security Requirements and Controls

- ISSO Appointment Letter

- System Security Plan Checklist

Introduction

The *System Security Plan* is probably the most important document you will prepare for your C&A Package. If the evaluation team is pressed for time (which sometimes happens) and elects to scrutinize only one document in your entire C&A package, skimming through the others, it is likely that that the one document they will sift through with a fine-toothed comb will be the *System Security Plan*. Some federal agencies use a *System Security Authorization Agreement* (*SSAA*) in lieu of a *System Security Plan*. The SSAA historically has been used by agencies that make use of the DITSCAP C&A methodology.

The *System Security Plan* sums up the security requirements, architecture, and control mechanisms in one document. In the *System Security Plan*, you should also list pointers to the related C&A documents that are part of the same C&A package in your *System Security Plan*. For example, you can say, "Contingency Planning is described in the *<System Name> Contingency Plan, Revision 3, April 7, 2006*." Though you don't want to rewrite the other C&A documents in the *System Security Plan*, you will want to restate certain pieces of key information contained in other documents. For example, it is worth restating the C&A Level at which the C&A package is going to be submitted—the level that you calculated using the methodology described in Chapter 6.

Laws, Regulations, and Policies

Near the beginning of your *System Security Plan*, you should include a list of all laws, regulations, and policies with which systems that are undergoing C&A are expected to comply. Your agency probably has hundreds of security policies. You don't need to republish all of them. Simply state the formal policy document name and the location where this document can be found; for example, *<Agency>, Security Policies, Revision 4, October 27, 2006*. The only reason to list policies singularly is if they are not contained in the overriding agency security policy document.

Likely your agency is responsible for compliance with many laws and regulations other than FISMA. List them all alphabetically. Here is an example of a list of laws, regulations, and policies similar to what you may want to include in your *System Security Plan*.

An Example of Laws, Regulations, and Security Policy Descriptions

The systems described in this *System Security Plan* are subject to the laws, regulations, and policies set forth by the federal government as follows:

- Computer Security Act of 1987

- Critical Infrastructure Protection Act of 2001

- Federal Information Security Management Act (FISMA) of 2002

- Government Management Reform Act (GMRA) of 1994

- Homeland Security Presidential Directive (HSPD-7)

- Information Technology Management Reform Act (Clinger-Cohen Act)

- OMB Circular A-130, Management of Federal Information Resources

Additionally, the systems described in this *System Security Plan* are subject to the following agency security policies:

- PIV Security Policy 1000.67, June 14, 2006

- Security Enrollment Account Policy, 1000.94, September 04, 2006

- <Agency Name>, Security Policies, Revision 4, October 27, 2006

The System Description

The system description section of the *System Security Plan* should describe, in prose, all the components of the information systems or major application as defined by the accreditation boundary as discussed in Chapter 7. For the purpose of the system description, the "system" refers to everything included in the C&A package—the whole ball of wax. Depending on how you define your information system, it could consist of anything from one computer to a large infrastructure of multiple computers and applications. Each C&A package is owned by the business owner (see Chapter 3). Therefore, if major applications and general support systems have different business owners, this means that there should be different C&A packages. If the general support systems have the same business owner as the major applications, you can, in fact, include all these items together in one C&A package.

A business owner can choose to include as many, or as few, major applications or general support systems into a C&A package as desired. Sometimes deciding where to draw the line in the sand on what to include and not include in your system description takes some thought and various decisions will need to be made. Many of these decisions were likely made when you put together the *Hardware and Software Inventory*. However, since you have not yet submitted your C&A package for review, you do have the liberty to go back and revise your *Hardware and Software Inventory* by taking systems out and adding new ones, if while writing your system description you notice that adjustments should be made. Keep in mind that if you add new systems, applications, or network devices, it could affect the C&A level that you originally calculated if for example you add a system that is high sensitivity to a level one or two C&A package. If you find that you need to add a new device or system while writing your *System Security Plan*, you will need to make sure that the addition is reflected in all your C&A documents. If the system or device was never tested, you will need to test it and include those results in your ST&E.

In your description, you should be sure to differentiate between general support systems and major applications. General support systems are those systems that provide the underlying infrastructure support for major applications, including file and print services.

Major applications usually get installed on top of operating systems and provide clearly defined functions. For example, some applications have server components and agent components that run on different systems. According to *NIST Special Publication 800-18, Revision 1*, February 2006:

> Major applications are systems that perform clearly defined functions for which there are readily identifiable security considerations and needs (e.g., an electronic funds transfer system).

System Boundaries

In defining your system boundaries, you need to figure out where your system begins and ends. You have some flexibility in doing this, but it should all be based on logic. For example, possible system boundaries could be defined by such things as:

- Windows domains
- Solaris NIS+ objects
- LDAP directories
- UNIX netgroups
- The DMZ
- Firewalls
- Routers and switches
- VPNs
- VLANs
- Network segments
- Major applications
- Business mission
- Business ownership and management

This list should not be considered exhaustive by any means. There may very well be other devices, whether logical or physical, that can be appropriately described as system boundaries.

When describing system boundaries, keep in mind that your description should be inclusive of, and should discuss the systems you described in your *Hardware and Software Inventory* (see Chapter 6). Systems delineated by your boundary definition should be owned by the business owner that owns your C&A project. You want to be careful not to take perceived ownership of another business owner's systems by going into lengthy detail about systems not included in your inventory in your system description. However, it is okay to refer to systems owned by other business owners for the purpose of describing your own systems. For example, you could say, "The major applications reside on network segment 21, which is bounded by Cisco firewall #2 and Check Point firewall #6. Both firewalls are owned by the Information Systems group and are reviewed in a separate C&A package."

It can be helpful to describe your boundaries in terms of network zones. Network zones are segments of network infrastructure that are separated by firewalls. Different network zones often have different security levels associated with them. However, sometimes different network zones are separate from each other simply to separate the administration of duties between two different business units or administrative groups. Since you should include a network topology map of the assets included in your C&A package, it is useful to describe the network zones and to label these zones on your network topology map. A simple, yet effective way of describing network zones is found in Table 19.1.

Table 19.1 A Sample Description of Network Zones

Zone Number	Zone Name	Description
0	Public Zone	Open to the public. Subject to privacy regulations.
1	Internal Zone	Not open to the public. Protected internal network.
2	High Security Zone	Extra secure internal network (e.g., classified network).
3	Unattached Zone	Not connected to other zones (e.g., a test network).

System Mission

You will also want to describe the general mission of the systems in your system description. You should have a good idea of the mission at hand from having worked previously on your *Business Risk Assessment*. Since the evaluation team will be looking for consistency across your documents, using some of the same mission terminology that you used in your *Business Risk Assessment* is a good idea.

You'll want to state whether the items undergoing C&A are general support systems, major applications, or both. A general support system typically consists of parts of the network infrastructure used to support general operations of your business. According to *NIST Special Publication 800-18, Guide for Developing Security Plans for Information Technology Systems*:

> A general support system is interconnected information resources under the same direct management control which shares common functionality. A general support system normally includes hardware, software, information, data, applications, communications, facilities, and people and provides support for a variety of users and/or applications.

For a general support system, the mission could be to provide a platform for major applications. It also could be simply to provide a communications network for e-mail, file sharing, development, and collaboration. There may be multiple missions and if there are, you should describe all of them. In fact, most general support systems likely have multiple functions.

Major applications are most often software applications that reside on top of operating systems of general support systems. However, it is altogether possible that a major application could also consist of hardware devices. Unlike general support systems, major applications usually have one primary purpose. For example, a smart card system usually has both software and hardware devices. The hardware devices for a smart card system could include card readers, card issuing systems, and the cards themselves. According to *NIST Special Publication 800-18, Guide for Developing Security Plans for Information Technology Systems*:

> A major application might comprise many individual programs and hardware, software, and telecommunications components. These components can be a single software application or a combination of hardware/software focused on supporting a specific mission-related function. A major application may also consist of multiple individual applications if all are related to a single mission function (e.g., payroll or personnel).

Data Flows

You are going to want to describe how the data flows from one place to another in your system descriptions. If files are transferred either manually or automatically by a scheduler, you'll want to list the file names and state the times and under what conditions they are transferred. In Table 16.1, data sources and destinations were listed. You are going to want to describe those data sources and destinations more fully as part of the system description. In each of the examples (each row) listed in Table 16.1, you should describe in prose how the data gets from its source to its destination. You may want to indicate a legend on your network topology map with numbers or letters so that you can more easily describe the data flows. An example of data flow prose used in conjunction with the fictitious network segment shown in Figure 19.1 is the following:

> System administrators in Dallas use an automated **cron** job to distribute patches from the Dallas datacenter to the Boston datacenter via a Cisco VPN every Friday between 5 and 6pm CST so that the Boston facility can receive a copy of tested patches from the Patch Master system in Dallas.

Figure 19.1 Example of a Data Flow Diagram

Security Requirements and Controls

It's not possible to evaluate the security controls without first understanding the security requirements. The requirements describe the need, and the controls satisfy that need. As you recall from Chapters 8 and 12, for the purposes of C&A, there are three types of security controls: management controls, operational controls, and technical controls. The purpose of these controls is to meet the security requirements by preserving the Confidentiality, Integrity, and Availability of the systems and applications.

In describing the security controls, you'll want to differentiate between security controls currently in place, and those controls that are planned for future implementation. In C&A, you get credit for planning. If you don't have particular controls in place yet, but they will be implemented in two months, you should document that in your *System Security Plan*. Keep in mind though that if the *System Security Plan* says that controls have been planned, your business owner and ISSO will be on the hook for actually implementing the controls. Auditors at some point in the future may verify that the "planned controls" have been put into place. Therefore, if controls have not been planned, don't say that they have been.

NOTE

The National Institute of Standards and Technology has done a lot of research on, and has published much information on security controls in *NIST Special Publication 800-53, Recommended Security Controls for Federal Information Systems*, February, 2005, found at http://csrc.nist.gov/publications/nistpubs/800-53/SP800-53.pdf.

In March 2006, the National Institute of Standards and Technology published a document titled *FIPS Publication 200, Minimum Security Requirements for Federal Information and Information Systems* (FIPS PUB 200). NIST Special Publications are generally thought of as guidance, but the Federal Information Processing Standards (FIPS) series of publications are considered mandatory. The FIPS standards, however, point you to the Special Publications, and section 8 of FIPS PUB 200 says:

> Federal agencies must meet the minimum security requirements as defined herein through the use of the security controls in accordance with NIST Special Publication 800-53,

Recommended Security Controls for Federal Information Systems, as amended.

Therefore, you are on the hook to use the recommended security controls in Special Publication 800-53 as they apply to your information systems. FIPS PUB 200 can be found at http://csrc.nist.gov/publications/fips/fips200/FIPS-200-final-march.pdf#search=%22FIPS%20200%22.

It is certainly possible that not all the guidance in Special Publication 800-53 will apply to the systems and applications listed in your *Hardware and Software Inventory*. Certainly you have flexibility. In fact, FIPS PUB 200 further states:

> Organizations must meet the minimum security requirements in this standard by selecting the appropriate security controls and assurance requirements as described in NIST Special Publication 800-53, *Recommended Security Controls for Federal Information Systems*.

To understand what security controls are appropriate, you need to understand your security design requirements, which should be based on your agency requirements. Your agency security requirements should be documented in a manual of IT Baseline Security Requirements—often referred to in federal agencies as the BLSRs. Though I certainly can't verify that all agencies have BLSRs, there is a strong chance that yours does. The security requirements for the design of the items undergoing C&A should be based on a subset of these overriding BLSRs. It is altogether possible that the evaluation team may ask to see a copy of the security requirements for the systems undergoing C&A. You should be able to refer to a formal and separate document containing these requirements in the *System Security Plan*. For example, you could say:

> This *System Security Plan* describes the security controls established to comply with the security requirements set forth in *Federal Information System (FIS) Security Requirements, Revision 2.0,* June 10, 2006.

It certainly will not hurt your C&A package to attach the security requirements as an appendix to the *System Security Plan*.

It is altogether possible that for some legacy systems, the original security requirements cannot be located. Although that certainly is not an optimal situation, for the purpose of C&A, you may have to temporarily put the cart before the horse and document *ex post facto* what you believe were the intended security requirements. Documenting security requirements can be very time consuming; be sure to schedule plenty of time to create *ex post facto* security requirements. If you are trying to develop a *System Security Plan* at the same time, you may need to enlist another resource to help you out. Examples of security requirements are found in Tables 19.2, 19.3, and 19.4.

For every security requirement, you should be able to map a security control to it that satisfies that requirement. The test results that you documented in your ST&E (see Chapter 12) should have tested the controls to see if they met the requirements. In theory, by the time you are writing the *System Security Plan*, your requirements, controls, and the implementation of the controls should already be in place such that your *System Security Plan* becomes merely an exercise in documentation. However, when doing C&A, it's altogether possible that the order of events has not been as efficient as you may have hoped. Don't despair—since you have not yet submitted your C&A package, you can go back and make modifications to your ST&E while you are developing your *System Security Plan*. You may also need to add in a requirement, and have the ISSO expeditiously implement another control, while the *System Security Plan* is still being developed. Use the Self-Assessment questions from Chapter 8 to help you better understand what security controls to document in the *System Security Plan*.

Table 19.2 Example of a Brief List of Technical Security Requirements

Security Requirements for Federal Information System, Revision 2.0		
#	Technical Requirements	SP 800-53 Control No.
001	The Authorizing Official must approve the use of group IDs.	AC-2
002	Guest and anonymous accounts are not permitted.	AC-1
003	Access control shall follow the principle of least privilege.	AC-6

Continued

Table 19.2 continued Example of a Brief List of Technical Security Requirements

#	Technical Requirements	SP 800-53 Control No.
004	Privileged account access shall follow the principle of separation of duties.	AC-5
005	Accounts that have not been activated shall be removed after 60 days.	AC-1
006	Privileged users (admin, root, etc.) must be recertified semi-annually.	CA-1
007	The information system must be protected by firewalls and virtual private networks (VPNs).	SC-7
008	Sessions shall automatically terminate after 3 minutes of inactivity.	AC-12
009	The information system must have built-in audit logging capabilities.	AU-1
010	User interfaces must be separate from system administration interfaces.	SC-2
011	All devices must be identified by their MAC and IP addresses before establishing a connection.	IA-3

Table 19.3 Example of a Brief List of Operational Security Requirements

Security Requirements for Federal Information System, Revision 2.0		
#	Operational Requirements	SP 800-53 Control No.
012	Incident response and reporting shall be centrally managed.	IR-1
013	Accounts of terminated personnel shall be removed from the system.	PS-4
014	All users must receive security awareness training.	AT-2

Continued

Table 19.3 continued Example of a Brief List of Operational Security
Requirements

#	Operational Requirements	SP 800-53 Control No.
015	A copy of backup media must be stored in an off-site location.	CP-6
016	An alternate processing must be identified and be ready 24 x 7 for disaster failover operations.	CP-7
017	The information system must be protected from malicious code by an EAL4 anti-virus product.	SI-3
018	Changes to the system must be made in accordance with the agency configuration change control process.	CM-3
019	The system hardware must undergo regular preventative maintenance support from an authorized vendor.	MA-6
020	All removable information storage media for the information system must be labeled with external labels.	MP-3
021	The information system must be housed in a facility where physical access is controlled and documented.	PE-3
022	Events on the system must be monitored by a host-based intrusion detection system to detect attacks.	SI-4

Table 19.4 Example of a Brief List of Management Security Requirements

# No.	Security Requirements for Federal Information System, Revision 2.0 Management Requirements	SP 800-53 Control
023	The information system and its major applications must undergo C&A prior to being put in production.	CA-1
024	A security budget for the information system must be established.	SA-2
025	Statements of Work (SOW) must identify how sensitive information is handled.	SA-9
026	Contracts for outsourced operations must include facility security requirements.	SA-9
027	Contracts and SOWs must stipulate that contractors will protect sensitive information.	SA-9
028	The information system life cycle must include decommissioning of data.	SA-3
029	All documentation for the system shall be marked *Sensitive But Unclassified* (SBU).	MP-3
030	The information system must be scanned for security vulnerabilities quarterly.	RA-5
040	Failure to comply with the Rules of Behavior shall be considered a security incident.	PL-4
041	Private keys shall contain a minimum of 8 characters with mixed case letters, and at least one number.	IA-5
042	The information system shall run only licensed operating systems and applications.	SA-6

Your *System Security Plan* should describe the security controls in prose. Providing a list of bulleted control names is not good enough. Use words and explain how the controls work in simple and easy-to-understand English. At the minimum, you should include discussion of the security controls described in the following sections (which are the same security controls discussed earlier in Chapter 8).

Management Controls

Management security controls help ensure that management requirements are adhered to. By clearly describing the management controls, you should be able to convince the evaluation team that the business owner's management team understands their responsibilities, are following through with these responsibilities, and are being held accountable for them.

Risk Mitigation

In the section on management controls, you should include a summary of how your agency or department mitigates risk. Risks are mitigated by reducing them to a level that is acceptable to the business owner. Clearly, before they can be mitigated, they need to be identified. In the section on risk mitigation, you should, in summary fashion, briefly describe your overall risk mitigation strategy. You may want to include diagrams or flowcharts that help visualize the strategic relationships of your risk mitigation processes. An example is shown in Figure 19.2.

Figure 19.2 Risk Mitigation Strategy

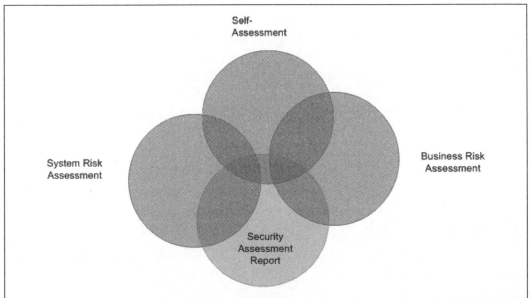

You will learn more about the *Security Assessment Report* in Chapter 21. The *Security Assessment Report* is put together by the evaluation team (after reviewing the entire C&A package) and it includes a summary of all the vulnerabilities. You'll want to point out that any vulnerabilities identified in the *Security Assessment Report* are mitigated by either reducing them, accepting them, or transferring them. While the *System Security Plan* is in development, the *Security Assessment Report* does not yet exist. However, by stating the business owner's intentions on how risks noted in the *Security Assessment Report* will be handled in the future, it assures the evaluation team that you agree up front that any reported risks will be appropriately mitigated. You need to convince the evaluation team that all risks are, and will be, appropriately mitigated. Explaining that your risk mitigation strategy includes reducing risks found in their final *Security Assessment Report* makes the evaluators feel as though you are on-board with their counsel.

Additional items that you ought to mention in this section (even if you have already mentioned these items in other C&A documents) include summary discussions about the following:

- How often you perform network- and host-based vulnerability scanning

- The fact that your C&A Level is determined by a FIPS-199-based process

- The fact that you recognize that OMB A-130 requires risk assessments every three years

- Threat sources are taken into consideration when assessing risk

- The fact that you hold external third parties (service providers) accountable for vulnerabilities

Reporting and Review by Management

There are multiple stipulations in FISMA that call for reporting and review by management. For example, in FISMA §3543(a)(5), it says:

> **The Director shall oversee agency information security policies and practices, including—reviewing at least annually, and**

approving or disapproving, agency information security programs required under section 3544(b)....

Additionally, in FISMA §3544 (c), it says:

Each agency shall - (1) report annually to the Director, the
Committee on Government Reform and Science of the House
of Representatives, the Committees on Government Affairs
and Commerce, Science, and Transportation of the Senate,
the appropriate authorization and appropriations committees
of Congress, and the Comptroller General on the adequacy of
information security policies, procedures, and practices, and
compliance with the requirements of this subchapter....; (2)
address the adequacy and effectiveness of information security policies, procedures, and practices in plans and reports...

This simply means that there are requirements to review your own security controls and reports, to create new reports on your findings, and to
submit them to various congressional committees.

In discussing how you report and review security controls, you should
summarize the process that the business owner's management team uses to
review security controls. The business owner's management team needs to
show evidence that they have reviewed security controls. The C&A process
itself is one way that the management team typically reviews security controls
since the business owner, and typically their associated managers, are required
to review and sign the C&A documents that pertain to their role and responsibility. Therefore, in the *System Security Plan*, although this may seem circum-
locutory, you are allowed to state that your C&A process fulfills the reporting
and review requirements.

In the reporting and review section, provide a summary list of all the documents in the C&A package that you are working on, and also include the
reaccreditation date for the package. If there are other documents that are not
included in the C&A package that have been reviewed by the business
owner's management team or ISSO and are related to security compliance,
you should list those documents as well, including information on who
reviewed them and when. Generally speaking, in most cases you won't want
to list documents that are more than three years old. Other than the C&A
package itself, auxiliary documents can include initial design documents,

architecture documents, security standards, security policies, checklists, or even descriptive e-mail messages.

System Life-Cycle Requirements

Your discussion of system life-cycle requirements first and foremost should acknowledge that your agency has system life-cycle requirements. The life-cycle methodology for the systems undergoing C&A should include discussions about how the systems undergoing C&A evolved. Before these systems were put into production, there must have been requirements, planning, procurements, and a need for them. As depicted in Figure 19.3, system life-cycle requirements generally include the following phases:

- Requirements identification and analysis
- Planning and procurement
- Development and testing
- Implementation
- Operations, production, and on-going maintenance
- Terminal and disposal

Figure 19.3 System Life-cycle Process

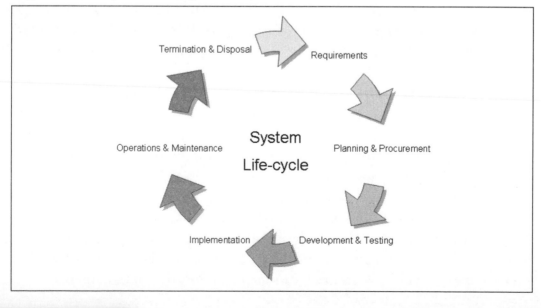

It's possible that your agency has life-cycle requirements and processes documented in a *System Development Life-Cycle* (SDLC) manual or handbook. If that is the case, you can obtain much information on what to include in the lifecycle requirements section from the handbook. If you are unable to find any evidence that an SDLC methodology exists, or that life-cycle requirements were ever taken into consideration, you'll need to create these requirements *ex post facto*. Creating requirements *ex post facto* is never ideal, but it does show that going forward your business owner acknowledges the importance of such phases. In some cases, it may be that life-cycle requirements were followed, but never documented. In the eyes of the C&A evaluation team, if something is not documented, it doesn't exist. It is possible that your agency's SDLC methodology includes four or five phases, instead of six. It may also include seven phases. Don't get hung up on the number of phases since some agencies may combine a couple of phases. Use the life-cycle support questions from Chapter 8 to help you make sure you have covered all the bases.

Security Planning

Security planning includes controls planned for future implementation, as well as resources planned for future use. Resources include personnel, contractors, equipment, software, and budgetary allocations. If you have security controls that are in the planning process, but will not be implemented until some point in the future, you should describe those controls in the section on security planning. If you plan on hiring a security administrator or a security engineer, and have allocated budgetary funds for the next fiscal year to do that, indicate this intent. If you plan on implementing new intrusion detection systems, antivirus software, single sign-on systems, or anything that will remediate existing vulnerabilities, be sure to mention this. Security planning refers to security initiatives that will improve the security posture of your organization at some point in the future. In C&A, you get credit for planning.

Documentation for Managers

To provide adequate guidance on security controls, management needs to understand the controls, and therefore needs documentation to read and review. Name the security documents that management reviews, comments on, and approves of. You need to list formal document names that include the revision number and the publication date. The documents described in this section should include any C&A documents, as well as any other documents related to security (e.g., security configuration guides and security architecture documents). Describe the review and approval cycle indicating the names of the staff that signed off on the various documents. You can summarize this information in tabular form as shown in Table 19.5.

Table 19.5 Documentation Review and Approvals

Document Name	Review and Approval Team
"Security Requirements, Version 3.0," May 1, 2006	William McKnight, ISSO Lynn Pfeiffer, Director of Application Engineering
"System Security Plan, Version 2.1," June 10, 2006	William McKnight, ISSO Gregg Sokolowski, C&A Team Lead

Operational Controls

Operational security controls help ensure that operational requirements are adhered to.

Personnel Security

Information about personnel security should include information about background investigation. Most U.S. federal agencies require background investigations. Provide as much information as you can about the background investigation and screening process. It is very possible that your agency has a security screening branch that carries out all background investigations. The security screening branch may not make all of its processes and procedures available to everyone in the agency. If that is the case, simply state the name of the department that carries out the background investigations. Also describe how the background investigation department can be contacted and where they are located. If there are policies that require background investigations, it is worth noting these policies.

Additionally, the section on personnel security should include information on how both staff and contractors are kept safe. For example, if evacuation routes are posted in hallways, or if there are formal Emergency Response Procedures, be sure to note that in the section on personnel security. In some agencies, staff (including contractors) are offered disaster preparedness training and are given disaster preparation kits that include items like flares, whistles, and food rations. Whatever measures your agency takes to ensure that their staff is safe and secure are worth stating in this section.

Physical and Environmental Controls and Safeguards

Physical and environmental safeguards protect the facilities that host information systems. Provide descriptions that support the fact that the systems listed in the *Hardware and Software Inventory* are hosted in an environment that is conducive to continuous operations. In the section on physical and environmental operations and safeguards, describe the facilities and their warning systems.

Physical and environmental safeguards include such things as facilities access, emergency power, emergency lighting, fire suppression systems, fire alarms, circuit breakers, plumbing, surveillance cameras, and temperature and humidity controls. The *System Security Plan* should specifically describe whether uninterruptible power supplies (UPS) or generators are used, and what make and model each are. Describe the type of fire suppression system including any preventative maintenance required to test it on an annual basis. Describe emergency lighting systems and where emergency lights are located. Include information about how often emergency lights are tested.

Describe the use and positioning of any surveillance cameras. For example, specify if surveillance cameras are mounted at building entrances, server rooms, or hallways. Additionally, the type of surveillance cameras should be specified as well as whether or not active monitoring is performed using the cameras, or whether they are passive cameras that simply record events that are then stored.

Information should be given about electrical circuits, voltage requirements, circuit breakers, and wiring closets. If this information is documented in a separate facilities manual, and you list the formal name of that manual, the evaluation team will likely accept this information in lieu of reprinting it all separately in your *System Security Plan*.

It is necessary to describe any physical access systems to buildings and data centers. Note the location and operation of card readers. Describe the card readers' make and model numbers. Additionally, you need to describe in general terms how the card readers work. For example, do they use magnetic stripes or RFID chips? Do they require personal identity numbers (PINs)? Describe the use of smart cards and badging systems. If smart cards are used, discuss a little bit about the type of cards used and the application system used to program them. The process of how an individual obtains an identification badge requires description. Provide an explanation of whether Personal Identity Verification (PIV) credentials or PINs are used. Describe the visitor registration process. For example, it should be noted who signs visitors in and if visitors require escorts while in the building.

Administration and Implementation

Administration and implementation refers to the installation, configuration, and administration of your systems and applications. Create a discussion about the systems and database administrations that perform the installations and configurations. Who are these folks? What is the experience level of the systems and database administrators? Do they have any technical certifications that may help a C&A package auditor have faith in their abilities? The systems and database administrators may be part of an organization that is separate from the organization of the business owner. Describe any pertinent facts about the administration organization and management team. An example of a discussion that describes the capabilities of the administration and implementation team follows:

> The enterprise resource planning systems are administered by the Information Services (IS) department, which is managed by Barbara Davidson. IS provides administrative operations and support for over 500 systems. The systems listed in the *Hardware and Software Inventory, Version 2.0, February 24, 2006* are administered by Rafael Sanchez, Tajuan McDuffie, Bruce Higgs, and Kiri Porter.
>
> Mr. Sanchez has been administering Solaris systems for six years and is a Sun Certified Systems Administrator. Ms. McDuffie has administered Microsoft Windows systems for five years, and recently obtained a Microsoft Certified Systems Engineer (MCSE) certification for Windows Server

2003. Mr. Higgs has been administering Oracle databases for two years, and before that, administered Microsoft SQL databases for five years. Ms. Porter specializes in Web site administration. She is knowledgeable about IBM Websphere and has written half a dozen articles on the how to secure Web-based applications. The IS administrators currently document their installation, configuration, and operations process, and these documents are available for review. All the administrators carry cell phones, and if they are not reachable, the call will automatically be transferred to the Network Operations Center (NOC), which is staffed 24/7, 365 days a year.

The objective of this particular section is to convince the evaluation team that the staff that administers the systems and applications on a day-to-day basis is competent and capable.

Preventative Maintenance

Preventative maintenance refers to the maintenance required to keep equipment and hardware running. Maintenance activities include performing diagnostics on circuit boards, changing boards, performing diagnostics on memory, and BIOS and any other parts of the hardware. It's possible that certain computers at times may need a new power supply or a new fan. Who are the folks who would make this determination and perform the installation? Preventative maintenance may be done by your agency's in-house staff, or it might be contracted out to a third-party organization. Whatever the case may be, document who performs preventative maintenance and whether it is performed on any sort of regular schedule. If an outside third-party performs these tasks, you'll need to include the name and contact information of the person or department responsible for managing the third-party.

A thoughtful argument can be made that preventative maintenance also includes the detection of software problems. However, I prefer to see information about the detection of software problems in the technical controls section that discusses preservation of data integrity. System diagnostics related to file system errors and file systems filling up belong in the preventative maintenance section. Some systems run scheduled diagnostics on a regular schedule to check the size of the file systems to ensure that they do not fill up. If the systems in your C&A package run any regularly scheduled diagnostics on the file systems, or are regularly defragmented, be sure to indicate this.

Contingency and Disaster Recovery Planning

The Contingency Plan was discussed in Chapter 16. It is not necessary to recreate all that information in the *System Security Plan*. However, the *System Security Plan* should include a brief summary indicating that the *Contingency Plan* exists, providing the formal name of the *Contingency Plan* document and its publication date. If there are any other documents that are related to contingency planning that you would like the evaluation team to take into consideration, be sure to name those documents in this section. For example, if your C&A package describes a major application that resides on top of general support systems, it is likely that there is a separate contingency plan for the general support systems and such a contingency plan would be worth mentioning.

In addition to noting the existence of the plan and where to find it, the *System Security Plan* should indicate vital information on the organizational requirements surrounding the maintenance and support of the plan. The SSP should indicate who is responsible for maintaining the plan, the frequency with which it must be reviewed and updated, whether key personnel with duties in implementing the plan are trained on the plan, and what type of *Contingency Plan* testing is conducted.

Training and Security Awareness

We already discussed the *Security Awareness and Training Plan* in Chapter 9. However, in the *System Security Plan* you should state that a Security Awareness and Training Plan exists, and provide the formal document name. A Security Awareness and Training Plan is considered a type of operational security control, which is why you should make reference to it in the *System Security Plan*.

Additionally, the SSP should indicate key information on the organizational requirements regarding the implementation of security training, such as the levels of training employees must go through, what training records are kept, how often employees must participate in the training, and who is responsible for overseeing the program.

Incident Response Procedures

Your Incident Response Plan should serve as an in-depth description of your incident response process. Don't recreate that plan in the *System Security Plan*. However, you should provide a brief summary of the *Incident Response Plan* and be sure to indicate that a detailed *Incident Response Plan* is available, stating the formal document name, date, and version number. The Incident Response Plan is a type of operational control, which is why you need to mention it in the *System Security Plan*.

In addition to noting the existence of the plan and where to find it, the SSP should indicate who is responsible for maintaining the plan, the frequency with which it must be reviewed and updated, whether key personnel with duties in implementing the plan are trained on the plan, and what type of incident response testing has been conducted.

Preservation of Data Integrity

You need to present information that serves as evidence that data integrity is preserved. Data integrity refers to the fact that the data is pure, and represents what it is supposed to represent—it hasn't been tainted or changed either by error or intentional malicious activity. Discuss anti-virus software, host-based intrusion detection systems, security behavioral analysis products, file encryption, and patch management. Be sure to also discuss any customized scripts used to preserve file integrity. For example, if the information system uses scripts that check for data integrity breaches using MD5 hash functions, be sure to describe what is checked and how often. In talking about the implementation of security products that ensure data integrity, such as anti-virus products, your discussion should answer the following questions:

- What is the product name and version number? Who performed the installation?
- Is there a third party (vendor or reseller) that provides ongoing product support?
- On what systems is the product implemented?

- Does it include both server and client software?

- Under what conditions do the clients interact with the server?

- Does it use agents? Where are the agents deployed?

- Is there a management console?

- Are files or databases encrypted?

- For anything that is encrypted, have you named the encryption tool and key sizes?

- Does it rely on signatures that require updating? How often is it updated?

- How are updates installed (e.g., downloaded, distributed, etc.)?

- Does it require configuration rules? If so, what are the rules?

Network and System Security Operations

The termetwork and system security operations refers to the security of the network and its associated devices and monitoring systems. Unless your agency is extremely small, it likely has a network operations center (NOC). Describe how your systems and network devices provide monitoring information back to the operations center. Are agents installed on host systems to monitor them? How would the NOC know if a mission critical system went down? It's possible that your agency may use any one of many different applications and tools to monitor their systems, in which case you will want to describe what application is used for monitoring, and how it works. For example, if used within your agency, you will want to describe the general implementation of the following network monitoring applications:

- HP Openview

- BMC PATROL Dashboard

- IBM Micromuse

- CA eHealth LiveHealth

- NETSCOUT nGenius Analytics

- CiscoWorks Hosting Solution Software

If your department is dependent on a separate network operations group that manages the networks on which your information systems reside, you will need to communicate with them to find out which tools they use to monitor your systems and applications. You'll want to ask them specific questions that will lead to information that you can include in your *System Security Plan*. It is sometimes hard to draw the line of how much you should document and how detailed you should get. You may not have time to include every last detail. However, try to include enough information so that it will be clear to the evaluation team that the business owner is well aware of who they would need to go to in order to obtain all the rest of the nitty-gritty details. For example, you could include a statement on your network monitoring system such as the following statement that includes basic information, with a pointer on where more details can be found:

> The department of memorial flags has two networks that are monitored by the Network Management Group (NMG). NMG monitors both networks using IBM's Micromuse. The configuration and operations of NMG's Micromuse system is detailed in the *Network Management Group's Network Operations Guide, V 3.1, February 24, 2006*. This guide is maintained and updated by the Director of Information Technology, Daniel Puckett, whose contact information is listed in the phonebook on the agency intranet.

State your firewall rule-set configuration strategy. For example, a common strategy is to deny all protocols and ports unless they are explicitly allowed. If approvals are required to allow an additional service, state what the approval process is. It's possible that the approval process may be as simple as "All approvals go through the agency Change Control Board, which is described in *Change Control Policies, Version 4.2*, August 29, 2005." If your department or agency is small, and you don't have a Change Control Board, you should state what individuals approve of the changes and include their names and qualifications (e.g., lead firewall engineer). Describe the workflow process from the initial request, through the final approval and actual change. It's often helpful to include a flow chart with the description of the workflow process.

Technical Controls

Technical security controls ensure that technical requirements are met. It is often the case that the evaluation team scrutinizes the technical controls more rigorously than the management or operational controls—something you'll want to keep in mind when describing these controls.

Authentication and Identity Verification

Identification and authorization (I&A) controls enable your information system and applications to prompt users for logon information and verify that they are who they say they are.

Discuss the user enrollment and registration procedure. An example of a user enrollment and registration process is illustrated in Figure 19.4. Your discussion should provide answers to the following questions:

- How are systems administrators informed that a new user should be added?

- Before an account is established, is there either a paper form that a supervisor fills out with a signature or some sort of online registration system that requires a supervisor's approval?

- Is the enrollment process manual, automated, or semi-automated?

- Are background investigations performed before user accounts are established?

- Who decides what role and user group the user should be a part of?

You also need to describe how the identification and authorization system works. Most authentication mechanisms are based on either something the user knows, something the user has, or a physical trait of the user. Examples of these three methods and their inherent risks and problems are listed in Table 19.6. Describe what is done to accommodate the potential risks or problems that may occur during usage.

Table 19.6 Authentication Methods and Potential Risks and Problems

Method	Example	Potential Risks and Problems
Something user knows	Password PIN	Can be guessed Can be shared Can be stolen
Something user has	Certificate Smart Card Token	Can be borrowed Can be stolen Can be lost
Physiological characteristic	Fingerprint Hand geometry Iris scan Retina Scan Signature	Perceived violation of privacy False positives False negatives

Figure 19.4 diagrams the user registration and enrollment process.

Figure 19.4 User Registration and Enrollment Process

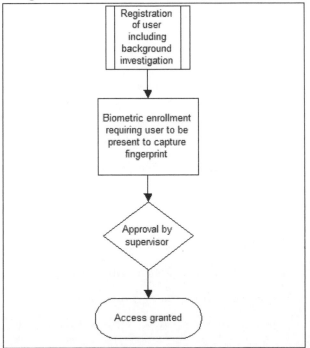

If your agency uses two-factor authentication tokens that require a password and a PIN, you should describe the product that is used to provide

these capabilities. Similarly, if biometrics mechanisms or smart cards are used, you'll want to describe how the technical delivery of the authentication process works. For any authentication products or mechanisms that your information system uses, be sure to include information on the following:

- Product name, version number, patch level
- Vendor name and vendor contact information
- Whether there is an existing support contract through a vendor or reseller
- Strength of any encryption keys used
- Name of encryption algorithms used
- Information on digital certificates used for authentication
- Logical data flow of the authentication process
- Information on how authentication credentials are stored and protected
- Single sign-on capabilities
- Session time-out rules after periods of inactivity
- Strength and complexity of password rules
- Password aging requirements
- Account lockout thresholds (how many attempts allowed)
- Account removal procedures for friendly and unfriendly terminations of staff
- Procedures for handling forgotten passwords
- Usage of LDAP and Directory Services
- Kerberos policies and settings (if you use Kerberos)
- User recertification and how often unused accounts are purged
- Whether mechanisms used have a FIPS 140-2 validation certificate

Logical Access Controls

Logical access controls are the features of your system that enable authorized personnel access to resources. To many folks, distinguishing between logical access control and I&A is confusing. Logical access controls are those controls that either prevent or allow access to resources once a user's identity already has been established. Once a user is logged in, they should have access only to those resources required to perform their duties. Different user groups usually have access to different resources, which ensures a separation of duties. Describe how the separation of duties occurs. A good portion of this discussion should be about account management. User accounts are usually part of a role-based group. Describe the names of each role and what resources each role has access to. The resources that you will want to take into consideration include systems, directories, network shares, and files. You can summarize this information in a table similar to Table 19.7.

Table 19.7 Role-Based Group Accounts Mapped to Resources

Group Name	Role	Resource Access
sysadmin	Systems Administrator	Root access to all systems on .fed domain
dba	Database Administrator	DBserver1: db001, db002, db003
dev	Development Engineer	C:/user/general (read-only) D:/dev/apps (read, write, execute)
assist	Administrative Assistant	C:/user/general (read-only)

Discussion of anonymous and guest accounts, whether they are allowed or not, should be described. Group accounts, whether they are allowed or not, should be described. System accounts—accounts set up for the purpose of accommodating system processes and programs—may or may not be allowed. If system accounts are allowed, you'll need to give justification as to why they are allowed, and what processes and programs use these accounts.

Secure Configurations

Secure configurations refers to how well information systems, their applications, and databases are hardened and locked down. Section 3544(b)(2)(D)iii of FISMA stipulates that agencies must ensure compliance with minimally acceptable system configuration requirements, as determined by the agency.

Right out of the box, most operating systems are not as secure as they could be. Administrators typically need to turn off unneeded services and modify configuration files to tighten up the security on servers. To satisfy the FISMA requirement on secure configurations, you'll need to describe how systems are locked down. Most of the systems in place at federal agencies are based either on UNIX or a Microsoft operating system. For UNIX systems, you should discuss key configuration files that affect access, or launch critical scripts. Examples of the sort of UNIX files that you should discuss include:

> /etc/hosts.equiv
>
> /etc/hosts.all
>
> /.rhosts
>
> /.netrc
>
> /etc/services
>
> /etc/ftpusers
>
> /etc/syslog.conf
>
> /etc/cron.d/cron.allow
>
> /etc/cron.d/cron.deny
>
> /etc/default/login
>
> /etc/system
>
> /etc/sulog
>
> /etc/issue
>
> /var/adm/loginlog
>
> /etc/default/login
>
> /etc/dfs/dfstab
>
> /etc/dt/config/Xaccess
>
> /etc/default/inetinit

/usr/local/etc/

/dev/ip

If you use **chmod** or **chown** commands to change file or ownership permissions to tighten security, list the names of the files that are modified and
indicate their permissions. A good resource for understanding how to lockdown a Sun Solaris UNIX system is the *Guide to the Secure Configuration of
Solaris 9*, published by the National Security Agency, July 16, 2004. You can
find that guide at http://www.nsa.gov/snac/os/sunsol_9/I331-007R-2204.pdf.

On Microsoft Windows' operating systems, if you use security templates
(.inf files), describe the security settings that the templates use, and if you have
time, include screenshots. It's always nice to throw in a few screenshots of
your security settings to show evidence that your configuration is set up the
way you claim it to be. An example of a screenshot for a password-aging
policy setting is depicted in Figure 19.5.

Figure 19.5 Screenshot That Depicts Password-Aging Setting

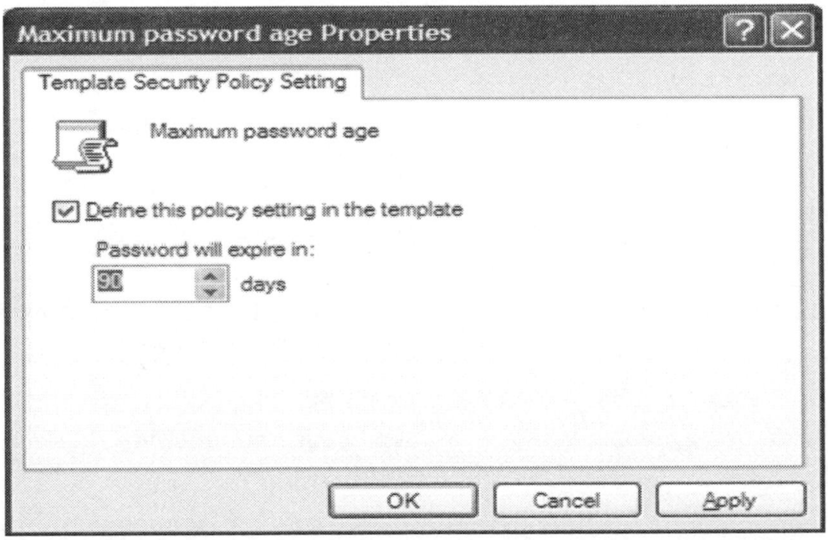

If you have existing documents that describe how operating systems are
locked down, instead of reprinting everything that is listed in that guide in
your *System Security Plan*, it should be sufficient simply to list the formal
names of these secure configuration guides (e.g., *Windows Server 2003 Security*

Configuration and Lockdown Guide, Version 2.7, October 27, 2006 or *Solaris 10 Security Hardening Procedures, Version 7.1,* November 11, 2005). It is possible that auditors from the evaluation team may ask to see any secure configuration guides that you list, so don't list any documents that you feel would be inappropriate to show an auditor.

If no security configuration guides exist that document your operating system security settings, and you have nothing to refer the evaluation team to along those lines, you are going to have more work to do. You'll have to document those settings in your *System Security Plan.*

Some useful articles on various aspects of Windows security that may help with you document Windows operating system security settings include:

- Posey, Brien. "Using the Secedit Tool to Work with Security Templates." *TechRepublic,* September 14, 2006 (http://articles.techrepublic.com.com/5100-6350_11-6107195.html?tag=sc).

- *Windows Server 2003 Security Guide.* Microsoft, updated April 26, 2006. www.microsoft.com/technet/security/prodtech/windowsserver2003/w2003hg/sgch00.mspx).

- Taylor, Laura. "It's Easy to Secure Windows 2000 Servers, Part 1." *Intranet Journal,* January 4, 2005. www.intranetjournal.com/articles/200501/ij_01_04_05a.html).

Interconnectivity Security

Interconnectivity security refers to the measures taken to secure the connection of one system to another, and can be achieved through a variety of mechanisms including VPNs, firewalls, proxy servers, gateways, routers, and secure file transfer mechanisms. In discussing interconnectivity between systems, talk about how boundary protections work. Discuss how domains and networks are separated from each other and include diagrams about the trust relationships between them.

If end-to-end link encryption is used, describe how it works. Most VPNs use certificates. Note the key length and the servers that the certificates are installed on. Describe where the VPNs are IPSec VPNs or SSL VPNs. If you are using an IPSec VPN, is it operating in transport mode or tunnel mode?

The following information should be included in your discussion about interconnectivity security:

- How denial-of-service attacks are prevented

- What type of firewalls and proxy servers are used and where they are deployed

- What type of VPNs (SSL, IPSec) are used and where they are deployed

- What type of routers and gateways are used and where they are deployed

- What type of secure file transfer mechanisms are used and how they work

- The period of idle time after which a network session is terminated

- PKI systems used that protect data in transit

- Transport Layer Security (TLS) mechanisms

- How threats to mobile code (ActiveX, JavaScript, JAVA) are mitigated

- How threats to Voice over IP (VoIP) are mitigated

- How critical single points of failure are eliminated (e.g., using two DNS servers)

- How session authenticity is maintained

- How man-in-the-middle attacks and unlinked session vulnerabilities are mitigated

- How TCP sequence number attacks are mitigated

- What ports are open and closed on firewalls

- Whether wireless networks are used, and the locations of the access points

- How wireless networks are protected (WEP, WPA, WPA-PSA, TKIP, etc.)

Audit Mechanisms

It's important to have a section of your *System Security Plan* dedicated to auditing. When you describe audit mechanisms, you essentially want to describe how security events are recognized, recorded, stored, and analyzed. Therefore, you should describe what is being audited, where the audit files reside, how the audit files are being protected, and how often the audit files are reviewed. When reviewing audit log files, systems administrators look for suspicious events that indicate a security violation has occurred, or may occur in the future. Indicate what types of circumstances or events the systems administrators (or security engineers) look for to determine potential security violations. To obtain this information, you will likely have to talk directly to the systems administrators (or security engineers or network engineers).

Additionally, you should describe how audit log files are viewed. For example, are audit files viewed from a central Security Information Management (SIM) system or a central log server? Or do systems administrators need to log on to individual remote servers to manually read through individual system syslog files? You cannot go too far in depth in documenting audit mechanisms. This is one area that the C&A evaluation team will likely not gloss over. Examples of the types of files, events, and processes that you will want to be sure to discuss include:

- Files that store failed logon attempts of all users

- Logon records of root, admin, and powerful users

- How users are traced to actions

- Startup and shutdown of the actual audit system process (e.g., syslogd)

- Absolute pathnames of log files (e.g., /var/log/secure.log)

- Names of servers that collect log files

- How long log files are stored

- The names and roles of the staff that read the log files

- Password auditing tools that scan for weak passwords

- Review of firewall rules for unauthorized modification

- How modification of sensitive or critical files is detected

- How audit files are protected

- How denied connections are logged

- Timestamp reliability and how it is ensured

- Who has access to log files

You should include information on system auditing, network auditing, and firewall auditing. To investigate system auditing, find out if your agency is using host-based intrusion detection systems. Find out what events are audited for the various operating systems that are used. Microsoft operating systems are audited differently than UNIX operating systems. Windows 2000 Server and Windows Server 2003 both have configuration settings for Audit Policy. If your information system uses either of these operating systems, describe what the audit settings are in your section on audit. Information on how to configure audit settings for Windows 2000 Servers can be found in the article titled "It's Easy to Secure Windows 2000 Servers, Part 2" (www.intranetjournal.com/articles/200503/ij_03_16_05a.html). Information on auditing Windows Server 2003 can be found at Microsoft's TechNet site (http://technet2.microsoft.com/WindowsServer/en/library/6847e72b-9c47-42ab-b3e3-691addac9f331033.mspx?mfr=true).

How a UNIX system performs auditing depends on what version of UNIX you are using. Each type of UNIX (e.g., Solaris, Linux, OpenBSD, AIX) has audit mechanisms that are somewhat unique.

Since firewalls provide perimeter protection designed to keep unauthorized users out of the production systems that host your C&A infrastructure, firewall auditing deserves special mention. State how your firewall logs are protected from unauthorized modification. Who logged into the firewall last and did they log in from the console or from a remote system? Some firewalls can be administered only from the console and have remote login capabilities disabled. It is worth mentioning if the firewalls are audited directly from the console, or if administrators log into them remotely over the network. It's also possible that firewall logs are reviewed from a central management console. Whatever way your agency uses to review the firewall logs, you should describe it.

Additionally, document the review schedule of the firewall log files. If firewall logs are reviewed only on an as-needed, ad hoc basis, say that. Talk to the security engineers that review the firewall log files and find out what it is that they currently look for when they review these logs. Describe how suspect activity is discovered. Do the administrators have a list of suspect events that they look for or do they just scan through the log files and hope that they will notice the right thing? For example, there are certain suspect events that security administrators sometimes look for such as those listed in Table 19.8.

Table 19.8 Suspicious Events That Are Worth Auditing

Suspicious Event ID	Description
SE 1	Packets that have a source address internal to your network that originate from outside your network.
SE 2	Suspicious outbound connections, e.g., outbound connections that come from a public server on your DMZ.
SE 3	Repeated unsuccessful attempts to connect to a mission critical server or application.
SE 4	Repeated probes to ports that are well-known hacker ports.[1]

SE 5	Similar source ports used to connect to different sockets. An example of this sort of activity is shown here with three connections (now closed):
	    TCP 128.88.41.2:1025 140.216.41.2:80
	CLOSE_WAIT
	    TCP 128.88.41.2:2180 140.216.41.2:80
	CLOSE_WAIT
	    TCP 128.88.41.2:1188 140.216.41.2:80
	CLOSE_WAIT
	(A socket is an IP address plus a port, e.g., 206.208.163.15:80.)

SE 6	Invalid IP addresses that are not in the range of acceptable octets, for example: 295.128.16.0.
SE 7	A **tcpdump** that shows numerous TCP flags set to **S**, which could indicate a SYN flood attack

If your agency uses a Security Enterprise Management system (SEM), sometimes referred to as a Security Information Management (SIM) or Network Behavior Analysis (NBA) system, to look for aberrant network behavior, give an overview of how the system works and what events are configured to issue alarms or alerts. For example, if any of the following commercial products (or products similar to these) are used to generate alerts or alarms, their usage should be discussed:

- ArcSight ESM
- eTrust Security Information Management
- CiscoWorks
- EventGnosis ORION Event Correlation Platform
- Intellitactics Security Manager
- Log Logic LX/ST Appliance
- netForensics nFX OSP
- NetIG Security Manager
- OpenService Security Log Manager
- SenSage Enterprise Security Analytics
- TriGeo Security Information Management
- Q1Labs QRadar

If log files are reviewed only on an ad hoc, as-needed basis and on no particular schedule, you should truthfully document that. Don't describe an elaborate and diligent audit review process if one does not exist for the sake of trying to obtain a positive accreditation on your C&A package. If it is discovered at some later date that you documented review procedures that don't really exist, you could be accused of purposefully misleading auditors.

ISSO Appointment Letter

The *System Security Plan* needs to contain a copy of the signed ISSO (or ISSM) appointment letter. The ISSO appointment letter verifies to the auditors who the person is that is accountable for security of the information systems described in the C&A package and therefore, the ISSO should be named in the appointment letter. The auditors want to be able to hold someone responsible for the information contained in the C&A package and they want to be sure they hold the right person responsible. Since the ISSO letter is usually a signed document, in most cases you will need to include a scanned copy so you can show the signature page. Figure 19.6 shows an example of an ISSO appointment letter.

Figure 19.6 Sample ISSO Appointment Letter

Agency Name Goes Here
Memorandum

Date: September 22, 2006
To: Nancy Morrison, Information System Security Officer
From: James Smith, SAISO
Subject: ISSO Appointment Letter for the Health Information Systems (HIS)

In accordance with the Health Information Systems (HIS) entity-wide Information Technology (IT) Security Program you are being appointed as the HIS Information System Security Officer (ISSO). As the HIS ISSO, you help ensure that all IT security requirements relevant to HIS are implemented and maintained. Your specific responsibilities with regard to HIS and the IT Security Program are:

- Ensure that all requirements prescribed by the <Agency> entity-wide IT Security Program that apply to HIS are appropriately implemented.
- Complete and maintain the Security Plan for the HIS.
- Conduct annual system self-assessments and ensure that periodic risk assessments are accomplished.
- Maintain Certification and Accreditation (C&A) documentation on behalf of the authorizing official.
- Conduct annual recertification of users.
- Ensure that IT security management, operational, and technical controls are incorporated through the system lifecycle.
- Provide guidance for system security acceptance tests.
- Initiate protective or corrective actions.
- Provide assistance in the completion of a waiver request, should one be required.
- Ensure the completion, maintenance, and testing of an HIS Contingency Plan.
- Develop procedures for managing accounts of HIS users.
- Enforce agency IT security policies, standards, and procedures.
- Report security incidents in accordance with <Agency> entity-wide Security Policy.
- Ensure that audit trails are reviewed periodically (e.g., weekly, monthly) and that audit records are archived for future reference.
- Evaluate known threats and vulnerabilities to ascertain if additional safeguards are needed and to brief the authorizing official accordingly.

SIGNATURE INDICATES ACCEPTANCE

I have read the HIS ISSO appointment and fully understand the assigned duties and responsibilities.
Name: Nancy Morrison,
Date: 9/29/06   *Nancy Morrison*

System Security Plan Checklist

Aside from the Self-Assessment questions listed in Chapter 8, use the following checklist to make sure you haven't forgotten anything:

- Are all the management security controls described?
- Are all the operational security controls described?
- Are all the technical security controls described?
- Is the user enrollment and registration process described?
- Have you listed the different user groups and their roles?
- Have you described your Patch Management process?
- Have you described how password aging works?
- Are the password complexity requirements described?
- Is it clear where routers, switches, firewalls, and VPNs are deployed?
- Is there a discussion about what services are allowed through the firewalls?
- Are all protection mechanisms and safeguards named?
- Are schedules documented for when audit and firewall logs are reviewed?
- Are Security Enterprise Management (SEM) systems described?
- What measures have been taken to eliminate critical points of failure?
- Have you documented the audit mechanisms that trace users to actions?
- Is information on session lockouts after periods of inactivity provided?
- Has an account termination process been explained?
- Have both friendly and unfriendly termination procedures been described?
- Is it clear what is done to harden and lockdown the operating systems?

- Is the usage of any PKI systems described?

- Is the usage of any secure file transfer mechanisms documented?

- Have you described how anti-virus products protect the data?

- Are any intrusion detection systems, and how they work, described?

- Are the servers that collect log files named?

- Is it clear how long log files are retained?

- Is it clear what files are considered log files?

- Is there a discussion about intrusion detection systems?

- Has a copy of the ISSO appointment letter been included?

- Is the ISSO appointment letter signed by the ISSO?

Summary

The *System Security Plan* is one of the most important documents in your C&A package. In the *System Security Plan*, you need to discuss and describe all the security controls that safeguard your information system. Management security controls stipulate the rules of the road, provide guidance to staff, and are designed to hold people (including the management team) accountable. Operational security controls stipulate what people should do on a day-to-day basis to keep the information system secure. Technical security controls include descriptions of security mechanisms that are implemented, configured, and installed.

In some cases, there may be overlap or dependent relationships between operational and technical security control. For example, it may make sense to discuss certain aspects of firewalls in both the section on operational and the one on technical controls. In the section on operational controls, you may want to talk about how firewalls are administered. In the technical section, you'll want to talk about how firewalls are configured. It likely won't be disastrous if the evaluation team finds that you have discussed some operational controls in the section on technical controls. It's possible they may ask you to move some of the information from one section to another, but the important thing is that the information is documented somewhere and is informative.

Additional Resources

Various resources that may help you populate your *System Security Plan* with the various sections I have discussed are:

> Danseglio, Mike. *Securing Windows Server 2003*. O'Reilly, November 2004. ISBN: 0596006853.
>
> "Developing a Departmental Security Plan." Rutgers, the State University of New Jersey, May 15, 2006 (http://rusecure.rutgers.edu/security_keys/dept_sec_plan.php).
>
> "FIPS PUB 200 Minimal Security Requirements for Federal Information and Information Systems." Computer Security Division,

Information Technology Lab. National Institute of Standards and Technology, March 2006 (http://csrc.nist.gov/publications/fips/fips200/FIPS-200-final-march.pdf).

Greaves, Sue. "IT Security Zones Baseline Security Requirements." Communications Security Establishment, May 2003 (www.cse-cst.gc.ca/documents/publications/gov-pubs/itsd/itsd02.pdf).

"Guide to the Secure Configuration of Solaris 9." The National Security Agency, July 16, 2004 (www.nsa.gov/snac/os/sunsol_9/I331-007R-2204.pdf).

"Microsoft Solutions for Security and Compliance, Windows Server 2003 Security Guide." The National Security Agency, April 26, 2006 (www.nsa.gov/scan/os/win2003/MSCG-001R-2003.pdf).

Swanson, Marianne, Joan Hash, and Pauline Bowen. "Guide for Developing Security Plans for Federal Information Systems." *NIST Special Publication 800-18, Revision 1.* National Institute of Standards and Technology, February 2006 (http://csrc.nist.gov/publications/nistpubs/800-18-Rev1/sp800-18-Rev1-final.pdf).

Theriault, Marlene, and William Heney. "How to Write an Oracle Security Plan." Johns Hopkins University, October 1998. (http://bbdd.escet.urjc.es/documentos/How%20to%20Write%20an%20Oracle%20Security%20Plan.pdf).

Taylor, Laura. "Understanding IPSec." *Intranet Journal*, June 13, 2002 (www.intranetjournal.com/articles/200206/se_06_13_02a.html).

Notes

1. "Hacker Ports." Relevant Technologies' Security Resource Center. www.relevanttechnologies.com/src_hacker_ports.asp.

Chapter 20

Submitting the C&A Package

"If I see an ending, I can work backward."

—Arthur Miller

Topics in this chapter:

- Structure of Documents

- Who Puts the Package Together?

- Markings and Format

- Signature Pages

- A Word about "Not Applicable" Information

- Submission and Revision

- Defending the Certification Package

- Checklist

Introduction

Ostensibly, like most published works, you could detail a Certification Package to no end and continue adding more details until the additional details detract from the focus. Part of understanding the package preparation process is knowing when to draw the line in the sand and proclaim that the package is finished. Once you have put together your first C&A package, you will soon come to the realization that you could have gone on forever documenting picayune details to no end. In most cases, how far you should go will be determined by a date on the calendar. C&A on all federal information systems has to be done every three years. If the last C&A on a set of systems resulted in a formal accreditation on April 24, 2004, then the next C&A for that group of systems must be completed by April 24, 2007—that means that an Accreditation letter granting Authority to Operate must be in hand by April 24, 2007 whether you started the project three months earlier or six months earlier.

Structure of Documents

In all the documents that are prepared for the C&A package, I have thus far described the different sections that you should be sure to include. In addition to what I have already suggested you include, each of your documents should have the following sections:

- Introduction
- Purpose
- Scope and Applicability
- References, Requirements, and Authorities
- Record of Changes

Each document in the C&A package should include a *Record of Changes* near the beginning of the document. The *Record of Changes* is a history of changes made to the document and should include information about pages that have been updated, change dates, who made the change, and a brief summary of the changes. A sample *Record of Changes* is shown in Table 20.1.

Table 20.1 Example of a *Record of Changes*

Page #	Change Comment	Date of Change	Name
p. 4-6	Changed the release of from 3.2 to 3.3 to reflect a software upgrade.	4/7/06	Glenn Jones
p. 17	Added in discussion about new single sign-on server.	6/10/06	Ellen Frank
p. 18	Update the network diagram to reflect the new single sign-on server.	6/10/06	Ellen Frank

Who Puts the Package Together?

The C&A package usually is submitted in both hard-copy and soft-copy forms. Always insert the hard copy into a binder of some sort—three-ring binders do nicely but be sure to use one that is wide enough to accommodate a large amount of paper. A CD with soft copies of the documents should be inserted into a pocket inside the binder.

Usually a draft package is put together for review before a final package is put together. In some agencies, the document preparation team puts the draft package together and in other agencies, the evaluation team puts the package together after the documents have been submitted to them. The evaluation team makes the decision on who puts the package together. If the evaluation team wants the preparation team to package up the documents, then the preparation team should do so. As far as putting the package together goes, the preparation team should always defer to the evaluation team's guidance. If you're not sure who should put the package together, ask the evaluation team.

Markings and Format

A typical data classification warning that would be suitable for the cover page may read as follows:

> The <Agency Name> **Privileged Information** contained herein is the sole, proprietary, and exclusive property of

<Agency Name> and may only be used by individuals with a
need to know. All information contained herein is privileged
whether such information is in written, graphic, electronic, or
physical form. Those granted limited use to the information
must hold these materials and information in strict confidence. Access to and use of this information by any other
entity or individual is strictly prohibited.

The data classification should be marked on every page. For example, if all
the data is considered Privileged Information, every single page of the
Certification Package should have **Privileged Information** marked on it
either at the header or footer.

Signature Pages

Each C&A document inside the C&A package has to be signed by the
ISSO, the business owner, and members of the business owner's management team and project leaders. Your agency may require signatures from
specific individuals for the different C&A documents. If you're not sure, ask
someone on the evaluation team if there are particular signature requirements. If there are not predefined signature requirements, usually the ISSO
and business owner decide who should review and sign the C&A documents before they are submitted.

Some agencies don't require signatures on the individual C&A documents
though it is certainly more difficult to hold anyone accountable for the contents of the document, and the information security of the systems, without
signatures. Agencies that don't require signatures should move toward
requiring them in the future.

It's sometimes the case that in large agencies, obtaining signatures can be
very time consuming because the documents have to be routed manually
from person to person. Once documents have been signed, you need to scan
in the signature pages to obtain an image file to include on the C&A package
CD. Agencies can expedite the signing process by using SMART documents
and digital signatures. SMART documents are based on Extensible Markup
Language (XML) and can be integrated with digital signature technologies to
use tamper-evident signatures that offer nonrepudiation and verification of

document integrity. Additionally, using XML offers the ability to generate new and updated C&A documents much more expeditiously.

Digital signature technologies and electronic signing pads exist that make signing a Microsoft Word or .pdf file as easy as signing with a pen. Using digital signature products, it is easy to route the document in need of signature from one signatory to another. Signing documents electronically also generates a time-stamped history of the review and approval process. Although most agencies are not using digital signature technologies today, XML digital signatures are the wave of the future and will greatly expedite the sign-off process of C&A documents.

The following vendors offer easy-to-use digital signature solutions:

- Arx (www.arx.com/)
- CIC (www.cic.com)
- DocuSign (www.docusign.com)
- Topaz Systems Inc. (www.topazsystems.com)

Any digital signature solution you put into place for C&A document signing should be thoroughly tested to make sure that signatures are encrypted using FIPS 140-2 compliant algorithms.

A Word about "Not Applicable" Information

When you don't include a particular section in a C&A document or package, even if it is "not applicable," the auditors may come to the conclusion that you forgot it. Including a section and then proclaiming it not applicable shows that you haven't forgotten to include a particular topic. Any item in a document that is not applicable to your information system or major application undergoing C&A should be marked as such. Not forgetting to mark particular sections as not applicable will stave off a lot of questions from the C&A evaluation team.

Submission and Revision

Submit the C&A package according to guidance from the evaluation team. They may want you to e-mail them documents, or upload them into an online library or database. Or it's possible they simply want only the hardcopy in a binder and a CD. Establish a dialogue with the evaluation team so that you can accommodate their preference for package submission. One thing you'll need to find out is how much time the evaluation team requires to review the documents. Be sure to submit them early enough so that you can have an accreditation letter in hand by your required deadline.

Even on a stable group of systems that have had few changes, each time you submit a new C&A package you are opening up yourself to new audit findings. The evaluation team could be an entirely new team that is more stringent on package evaluations than the former team. New requirements may have been put into place by your agency since the last time these general support systems were reviewed. Not all package evaluators do things the same way, and auditors really have the upper hand in whether to be extremely picky or more flexible in interpreting requirements.

Defending the Certification Package

Upon submitting the C&A package, the evaluation team will start reviewing it. The process for evaluating the C&A package is discussed in Chapter 21. Most likely the evaluation team will have questions about various items. They may e-mail questions to the ISSO, or ask the preparation team and ISSO to participate in meetings for the purpose of getting questions answered.

The team that prepares the C&A package should prepare themselves to defend the package. During the evaluation process, the evaluators will have checklists that they fill out while questions are being answered. It's possible that the evaluation team could be in a hurry, and due to this, they may not even read all sections of all documents in your C&A package that you diligently took the time to write. They'll likely ask you questions about items that are clearly answered in your C&A documents. They may even mark down on their checklists certain items as "failures" simply because they did not spend enough time to look for the information in the C&A documents.

If you believe certain items marked as "failures" should not be marked as such, and that the information pertaining to that item is included in the C&A documents, advise the evaluation team what section of what document to look in, and explain to them why you feel the "failure" should be changed to a "pass."

Unquestionably, every item that the evaluation team marks as a failure should be adequately researched by the preparation team. The evaluation team can make mistakes. The evaluation team should give you adequate time to research and comment on their findings. If your package has some failures, that doesn't mean it won't receive a recommendation for accreditation. It is nearly impossible to receive a 100% perfect score on your entire package. If the failure citations given to the package are reasonable, you won't win any points with the evaluators by arguing about these citations. It's very important to address any failure citations professionally and politely. Failure citations are not necessarily a reflection on the folks who put the C&A package together. The preparation team should be documenting the security that already exists. You cannot invent good security controls that don't exist through creative writing.

If the evaluation team does not request to schedule time with the preparation team and ISSO to review the C&A package, it is worth taking the initiative to suggest a get-together to discuss any issues that may arise. The evaluation team should always make time to discuss any issues that they have with the documents. It's not really acceptable for the evaluation team to mark down items as "failures" and not give the ISSO and document preparation team a chance to comment on the issue at hand. Some agencies refer to the discussion between the document preparers and the document evaluators as Comment Resolution sessions.

If the C&A team that prepares the Certification Package does their work diligently and in good faith, it will be second nature to defend any questions posed by the auditors. True leaders are not afraid of the inspection process that a Certification Package goes through. Don't hedge the truth and answer all questions honestly. If you don't know the answer to a question, simply acknowledge that and advise the evaluators that you will be happy to get back to them.

Checklist

Use the following checklist to make sure that you don't forget anything during the submission process:

- Have you ensured that all documents that require signatures have been signed?

- Are all documents included in the C&A package?

- Have you spoken to the evaluation team to obtain specific submission guidance?

- Have you set up a Comment Resolution session to discuss issues?

- Have you researched anything marked as a "failure" to see if the evaluation team made a mistake?

Summary

Once you have submitted the C&A package, you have achieved a major milestone. The package itself is an incredibly valuable suite of documents. Without it, the risks to the systems, networks, and applications would be unknown. The security controls may not be known either. The C&A package is indicative of a security baseline that is far more substantial than one that a simple network scan report can give you. There is so much more to evaluating security than performing a network scan or penetration test.

Additional Resources

The following resources provide information about XML digital signatures that offer improved signing methods for C&A documents:

Downen, Mike, and Shawn Farkas. "Exchange Data More Securely with XML Signatures and Encryption." Microsoft Corporation, November 2004 (http://msdn.microsoft.com/msdnmag/issues/04/11/XMLSignatures/).

Geuer-Pollmann, Christian. "XML Security Page." University of Seigen (www.nue.et-inf.uni-siegen.de/~geuer-pollmann/xml_security.html).

Sanin, Aleksey, Igor Zlatkovic, Tej Arora, Wouter Ketting, and Dmitry Belyavsky. "XML Digital Signature." XMLSec Library (www.aleksey.com/xmlsec/xmldsig.html).

Simon, Ed, Paul Madsen, and Carlisle Adams. "An Introduction to XML Digital Signatures." O'Reilly XML.com, August 8, 2001 (www.xml.com/pub/a/2001/08/08/xmldsig.html).

Sokolowski, Rachael. "SMART Document Version 1.1 Quick Reference Card." Magnolia Technologies, LLC (www.magnoliatech.com/SMARTDoc_QuickRef11.pdf).

Chapter 21

Evaluating the Certification Package for Accreditation

"To give no trust
Is to get no trust."

—Lao-Tzu (sixth century B.C.)

Topics in this chapter:

- **The Security Assessment Report**

- **Checklists for Compliance**

- **Recommendation to Accredit or Not**

- **Accreditation and Authority to Operate**

- **Interim Authority to Operate**

- **Evaluations by an OIG**

- **Evaluations by the GAO**

- **Checklist**

Introduction

Once a final C&A package has been submitted, the evaluation team begins the review process. The person or team of people who evaluate the C&A package should not be the same person or group of people who prepared it. Something that the OIG and GAO will be looking for are instances of the fox guarding the hen house. There needs to be a separation of duties between the folks who prepare the C&A documents and the folks who evaluate them.

The Security Assessment Report

The *Security Assessment Report (SAR)* is a document that is put together by the evaluation team after they have gone through the C&A package with a fine-toothed comb. The *Security Assessment Report* should indicate what audit checks were performed, what passed and what failed, and what the final summary list of vulnerabilities are that the evaluation team found.

The vulnerabilities cited in the SAR may or may not match the vulnerabilities that the C&A preparation team included in the *Business Risk Assessment* or the *System Risk Assessment*. It's possible that the evaluation team may not agree with the vulnerabilities presented to them by the C&A package documents. Or they may agree with the vulnerabilities, but decide to change the risk exposure rating. They may also add on altogether new vulnerabilities based on their findings after performing their compliance audit.

Aside from vulnerabilities, the SAR should include a list of recommended corrective actions. Each vulnerability cited should have recommended corrective action, but there can also be any other type of recommended corrective actions described. *NIST Special Publication 800-37, Guide for the Security Certification and Accreditation of Federal Information Systems*, has further information about the *Security Assessment Report* and can be found at http://csrc.nist.gov/publications/nistpubs/800-37/SP800-37-final.pdf.

Checklists for Compliance

Almost all evaluators of C&A documents have compliance checklists that they use. If you're evaluating a C&A package for the first time, you'll want to either develop your own checklists, or find out if your agency has some that have already been developed. Like the documents in the C&A package, the compliance checklists usually evolve over time, and it is certainly acceptable to update them and refine them as your C&A evaluation team gains more experience.

The compliance checklists should include checks for management controls, operational controls, and technical controls. Each control should have a policy number, security standard, FISMA section citation, or some other guidance that can be referred to as the source of the requirement. Examples of compliance checklists are found in Tables 21.1, 21.2, and 21.3. Note that the examples are not exhaustive, and there may be more compliance checks that are not included in these checklists that your agency will want to take into consideration. The reference to "system" in the compliance checklist refers to all of the systems together that are listed in your C&A package. So if your Hardware and Software Inventory consists of multiple servers and systems, a check for compliance means all of them together—the whole ball of wax. It should never be the case that a compliance check is done on each individual asset listed in the Hardware and Software Inventory.

It is possible that some of the compliance checks will not apply to certain systems and major applications, and those checks should be marked NA (not applicable) when evaluating a package for compliance. For example, if a system does not use encryption keys, there is no need to check to see if encryption keys are FIPS 140-2 compliant.

Some evaluation teams use Yes/No on their compliance checklists and others use Pass/Fail. A Yes is equivalent to a Pass, and using either terminology is considered acceptable. Additionally, some evaluators may elect to include an intermediary rating of Marginal where some aspects of the expected outcome on the compliance check were attained with a small amount of deficiencies noted.

Have the C&A package next to you when filling out the compliance checklists. Be sure to take the time to look through all the information when marking a Pass or Fail. If you have the soft copies of the documents, you can use the search tool to make sure you have found everything related to each audit check. For any audit check that is questionable—you can't decide whether to give it a Pass or Fail—indicate this in some way and meet with the ISSO and the preparation team to obtain clarification. It is okay to ask for more information and more documentation that the preparation team may not have included. However, any ancillary documentation given to you by the preparation team should be documentation that already exists. If you need to speak with systems administrators, database administrators, or security engineers to obtain a better understanding of anything, it is certainly acceptable to ask the ISSO to set up such a meeting.

Compliance Checklist for Management Controls

Table 21.1 Examples of Compliance Checks for Management Controls

ID No.	Description of Audit Check on Management	Yes/No /NA	Comments	Source of Requirement
M-1	During the initiation phase of system development life cycle, were security requirements established?			
M-2	Do the initial security requirements appear to be adequate?			
M-3	At the end of testing in the system develop-ment life cycle, was a System Risk Assessment performed to determine if all security requirements were met?			
M-4	Are the different C&A levels adequately described?			
M-5	Was an assessment conducted based on FIPS 199 to determine the appropriate certification level?			

Continued

Table 21.1 continued Examples of Compliance Checks for Management Controls

ID No.	Description of Audit Check on Management	Yes/No /NA	Comments	Source of Requirement
M-6	Was confidentiality, integrity, and availability taken into consideration when performing the FIPS 199 assessment?			
M-7	Was the C&A level determination process adequately described using possible weights and recommended weights?			
M-8	Were levels of impact taken into consideration when determining the certification level?			
M-9	Were confidentiality levels defined and taken into consideration when determining the certification level?			
M-10	Was the impact of disclosure and a data classification scheme taken into consideration when determining confidentiality levels?			
M-11	Were integrity levels defined and taken into consideration when determining the certification level?			

Continued

Table 21.1 continued Examples of Compliance Checks for Management Controls

ID No.	Description of Audit Check on Management	Yes/No /NA	Comments	Source of Requirement
M-12	Was the level of integrity required and impact of loss taken into consideration when determining the integrity level?			
M-13	Were availability levels defined and taken into consideration when determining the certification level?			
M-14	Was the level of availability required and impact of loss taken into consideration when determining the availability level?			
M-15	Were system attributes' characteristics defined and taken into consideration when determining the certification level?			
M-16	Was the interconnection state taken into consideration when determining the certification level?			
M-17	Was the access state taken into consideration when determining the certification level?			

Continued

Table 21.1 continued Examples of Compliance Checks for Management Controls

ID No.	Description of Audit Check on Management	Yes/No /NA	Comments	Source of Requirement
M-18	Was the accountability state taken into consideration when determining the certification level?			
M-19	Was mission criticality taken into consideration when determining the certification level?			
M-20	Does the certification level appear to have been appropriately calculated?			
M-21	Did the information owner sign an explanatory memo supporting the selection of the certification level?			
M-22	Was the explanatory memo to support the selection of the certification level signed by the Authorizing Official?			
M-23	Is the depth and granularity of the C&A documents commensurate with the established C&A level?			

Continued

Table 21.1 continued Examples of Compliance Checks for Management Controls

ID No.	Description of Audit Check on Management	Yes/No /NA	Comments	Source of Requirement
M-24	Does the Authorizing Official (AO) determine whether to accept a risk, mitigate it, or transfer it based on analysis provided by the ISSO?			
M-25	Was a System Risk Assessment performed after connecting the system to the production network?			
M-26	Was a penetration test or vulnerability assessment scan performed during the System Risk Assessment process?			
M-27	Are System Risk Assessments performed every three years or whenever there is a significant change in configurations or functionality?			
M-28	Is the risk assessment methodology explained in the System Risk Assessment?			
M-29	Does the System Risk Assessment present the risks in an easy-to-follow risk table?			

Continued

Table 21.1 continued Examples of Compliance Checks for Management Controls

ID No.	Description of Audit Check on Management	Yes/No /NA	Comments	Source of Requirement
M-30	Are known vulner-abilities that could be exploited by threats adequately described in the System Risk Assessment?			
M-31	Does the System Risk Assessment take into consideration the likelihood that a vulnerability will be exploited by threats?			
M-32	Does the System Risk Assessment take into consideration the impact that the exploit of vulnerabilities will have on the system?			
M-33	Does the System Risk Assessment adequately determine the risk exposure posed by vulnerabilities?			
M-34	Are recommendations made in the System Risk Assessment on how to handle reported vulnerabilities?			
M-35	Are the recommen-dations in the System Risk Assessment on how to handle reported vulnerabilities acceptable?			

Continued

Table 21.1 continued Examples of Compliance Checks for Management Controls

ID No.	Description of Audit Check on Management	Yes/No /NA	Comments	Source of Requirement
M-36	Was a Business Risk Assessment performed?			
M-37	Does the Business Risk Assessment include a mission map?			
M-38	Does the Business Risk Assessment adequately describe the business mission(s)?			
M-39	Does the Business Risk Assessment include risk statements ("If ..... then.")?			
M-40	Does the Business Risk Assessment include a risk summary table with decisions?			
M-41	Are adequate system life-cycle requirements defined and considered in the System Security Plan?			
M-42	Are security controls for future implementation described in the System Security Plan?			
M-43	Are the security documents that are reviewed by management listed in the System Security Plan?			

Continued

Table 21.1 continued Examples of Compliance Checks for Management Controls

ID No.	Description of Audit Check on Management	Yes/No /NA	Comments	Source of Requirement
M-44	Is the *System Security Plan* reviewed and updated at least once annually to address minor changes?			
M-45	Are Security Self-Assessments conducted on a regular schedule?			
M-46	Do Rules of Behavior exist for the users that describe responsibilities and expected behavior with regard to usage of the system(s)?			
M-47	Do users have to agree (either online or by written signature) to the Rules of Behavior before they are granted access?			
M-48	Are users informed that they will be held accountable for failure to comply with the Rules of Behavior?			
M-49	Are users aware that disciplinary action could occur as a result of failure to comply with the Rules of Behavior?			
M-50	Has a Privacy Impact Assessment been conducted?			

Continued

Table 21.1 continued Examples of Compliance Checks for Management Controls

ID No.	Description of Audit Check on Management	Yes/No /NA	Comments	Source of Requirement
M-51	Have the privacy laws, regulations, and policies that the agency is required to abide by cited in the Privacy Impact Assessment?			
M-52	Has all Personally Identifiable Information (PII) that is taken into consideration described in the Privacy Impact Assessment?			
M-53	Have applications that collect PII been identified in the Privacy Impact Assessment?			
M-54	Is unnecessary PII collected?			
M-55	Does the Privacy Impact Assessment adequately describe what users (and their roles) will have access to PII?			
M-56	Does the Privacy Impact Assessment describe why PII is colleted?			
M-57	Have persistent tracking technologies been adequately identified in the Privacy Impact Assessment?			
M-58	Have risks to PII been identified?			

Continued

Table 21.1 continued Examples of Compliance Checks for Management
Controls

ID No.	Description of Audit Check on Management	Yes/No /NA	Comments	Source of Requirement
M-59	Do the risks to PII that have been identified appear to be credible?			
M-60	Have privacy threats, safeguards, and assets been identified in the Privacy Impact Assessment?			
M-61	Has the purpose of the systems/applications been described in the Privacy Impact Assessment?			
M-62	Has the privacy policy been posted publicly where users can read it?			
M-63	Does the publicly accessible privacy policy disclose for how long PII will be retained/stored?			
M-64	Is a process for the proper decommissioning of PII included in the Privacy Impact Assessment?			
M-65	Has corrective action been applied to POA&M items from prior certifications?			

Continued

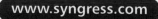

Table 21.1 continued Examples of Compliance Checks for Management Controls

ID No.	Description of Audit Check on Management	Yes/No /NA	Comments	Source of Requirement
M-66	Does all documentation in the C&A package have appropriate markings on each page indicating the disclosure sensitive level of the documents?			
M-67	Has an ST&E been performed on the systems and major applications designated on the Hardware and Software Inventory?			
M-68	Are the procedures used to perform testing documented in the ST&E?			
M-69	Are the security tests indicative of the security requirements?			
M-70	As documented in the ST&E, do expected test results appear to be accurate?			
M-71	As documented in the ST&E, do actual test results appear to be accurate?			
M-72	As documented in the ST&E, is a failure of the security control indicated when expected results are not consistent with actual results?			

Continued

Table 21.1 continued Examples of Compliance Checks for Management Controls

ID No.	Description of Audit Check on Management	Yes/No /NA	Comments	Source of Requirement
M-73	Are the results of all tests performed on the security controls documented in a way that makes it clear as to whether vulnerabilities were discovered or not?			
M-74	Were all security controls tested?			
M-75	Does the ST&E adequately describe the usage of test tools giving tool name and version number?			
M-76	Are members of the test team (and contact information) named in the ST&E?			
M-77	Were tests conducted in a controlled setting?			
M-78	Do all tests documented in the ST&E have a unique test ID number?			
M-79	Are the tests as documented in the ST&E well organized?			
M-80	Has the test environment (hardware platforms, physical location, etc.) been clearly described in the ST&E?			

Continued

Table 21.1 continued Examples of Compliance Checks for Management Controls

ID No.	Description of Audit Check on Management	Yes/No /NA	Comments	Source of Requirement
M-81	Is a copy of a signed ISSO appointment letter included in the System Security Plan?			
M-82	Do all documents in the C&A package have appropriate signatures?			
M-83	Are all pages of all C&A document dated?			
M-84	Do all pages of all C&A documents have the document name listed in the header or footer?			
M-85	Is all documentation restricted to those individuals having a need to know?			

Compliance Checklist for Operational Controls

Table 21.2 Examples of Compliance Checks for Operational Controls

ID No.	Description of Audit Check on Operations	Pass Fail /NA	Comments	Source of Requirement
O-1	Has a Business Impact Assessment been conducted?			
O-2	Does the Business Impact Assessment include estimated recovery times?			

Continued

Table 21.2 continued Examples of Compliance Checks for Operational
Controls

ID No.	Description of Audit Check on Operations	Pass Fail /NA Comments	Source of Requirement
O-3	Does the Business Impact Assessment include relative recovery priorities?		
O-4	Does the Business Impact Assessment include recovery escalation thresholds?		
O-5	Does the Business Impact Assessment include asset tracking numbers?		
O-6	Does the Business Impact Assessment include primary points of contact (phone & e-mail) ?		
O-7	Does the Business Impact Assessment include secondary points of contact (phone & e-mail)?		
O-8	Does the Business Impact Assessment include hardware make and model numbers?		
O-9	Are locations of systems (address, building, room) listed in the Business Impact Assessment?		

Continued

Table 21.2 continued Examples of Compliance Checks for Operational Controls

ID No.	Description of Audit Check on Operations	Pass Fail /NA	Comments	Source of Requirement
O-10	Do the assets listed on the Business Impact Assessment include hostnames and IP addresses?			
O-11	Are system/asset roles listed on the Business Impact Assessment?			
O-12	Has a Contingency Plan been developed?			
O-13	Has the Contingency Plan been adequately tested?			
O-14	Are roles and responsibilities defined in the Contingency Plan?			
O-15	Are staff members (or contactors) associated with all roles and responsibilities designated in the Contingency Plan?			
O-16	Is contact information listed for all staff members named in the Contingency Plan?			
O-17	Do contact lists in the Contingency Plan include a primary and secondary phone number, as well as e-mail address, for each staff member?			

Continued

Table 21.2 continued Examples of Compliance Checks for Operational Controls

ID No.	Description of Audit Check on Operations	Pass Fail /NA	Comments	Source of Requirement
O-18	Do the staff who have been assigned contingency roles and responsibilities have the authority to carry out these tasks?			
O-19	Are procedures for recovering systems (operating systems) included in the Contingency Plan?			
O-20	Is information about where to obtain a configuration guide for hardening the systems (e.g., securing the operating system) included in the Contingency Plan?			
O-21	Are the procedures for recovering systems adequate?			
O-22	Are adequate application recovery procedures included in the Contingency Plan?			
O-23	Are adequate connectivity recovery procedures included in the Contingency Plan?			
O-24	Are adequate key recovery procedures described in the Contingency Plan?			

Continued

Table 21.2 continued Examples of Compliance Checks for Operational Controls

ID No.	Description of Audit Check on Operations	Pass Fail /NA	Comments	Source of Requirement
O-25	Is the off-site storage facility for backup media indicated (with contact information and address) in the Contingency Plan?			
O-26	Are requirements (e.g., facility access cards, PINs) for accessing the off-site storage facility noted in the Contingency Plan?			
O-27	Does the Contingency Plan designate who is authorized to retrieve media from the off-site storage location?			
O-28	Does the Contingency Plan include adequate procedures for how to restore systems from backup media?			
O-29	Are emergency phone numbers for local fire, police, and ambulance services noted in the Contingency Plan?			
O-30	Is notification and activation criteria described in the Contingency Plan?			
O-31	Is the notification and activation criteria adequate?			

Continued

Table 21.2 continued Examples of Compliance Checks for Operational
Controls

ID No.	Description of Audit Check on Operations	Pass Fail /NA	Comments	Source of Requirement
O-32	Has a line of succession been indicated in the Contingency Plan?			
O-33	Are levels of disruption defined in the Contingency Plan?			
O-34	Are all service level agreements (SLAs) documented in the Contingency Plan?			
O-35	Has the logistics coordinator as named in the Contingency Plan been given a copy of the SLAs?			
O-36	Are requirements for temporary power described in the Contingency Plan?			
O-37	Are power recovery procedures described in the Contingency Plan?			
O-38	Are the power recovery procedures adequate?			
O-39	Is an Occupant Evacuation Plan included in the Contingency Plan appendices?			
O-40	Are Standard Operating Procedures included in the Contingency Plan appendices?			

Continued

Table 21.2 continued Examples of Compliance Checks for Operational Controls

ID No.	Description of Audit Check on Operations	Pass Fail /NA	Comments	Source of Requirement
O-41	Has a Configuration Management Plan been developed?			
O-42	Are baselines defined in the Configuration Management Plan?			
O-43	Have adequate baselines been established in the Configuration Management Plan?			
O-44	Has the configuration management system been adequately described?			
O-45	Are roles and responsibilities defined in the Configuration Management Plan?			
O-46	Has the change management process been adequately described in the Configuration Management Plan?			
O-47	Is the change management process acceptable?			
O-48	Is a copy of the Change Management Form depicted in the Configuration Management Plan?			

Continued

Table 21.2 continued Examples of Compliance Checks for Operational Controls

ID No.	Description of Audit Check on Operations	Pass Fail /NA	Comments	Source of Requirement
O-49	Are adequate parameters indicated on the Change Management Form?			
O-50	Are emergency change management procedures documented in the Configuration Management Plan?			
O-51	Are the emergency change management procedures adequate?			
O-52	Are configuration management terms defined in the Configuration Management Plan?			
O-53	Do all documents archived in the configuration management system have a unique ID number?			
O-54	Are appropriate background investigations performed on staff before access is given to systems and applications?			

Continued

Table 21.2 continued Examples of Compliance Checks for Operational Controls

ID No.	Description of Audit Check on Operations	Pass Fail /NA	Comments	Source of Requirement
O-55	Are appropriate background investigations performed on contractors before they are granted access to systems and applications?			
O-56	Do user roles and responsibilities adhere to the principle of separation of duties?			
O-57	Is the principle of least privilege followed when granting access to systems and applications?			
O-58	When an unfriendly termination occurs, is access from systems and applications revoked immediately?			
O-59	When a friendly termination occurs, is access from systems and applications revoked within one day?			
O-60	Are critical points of failure noted in the System Security Plan?			
O-61	Are safeguards in place to mitigate the risk posed by critical points of failure?			

Continued

Table 21.2 continued Examples of Compliance Checks for Operational Controls

ID No.	Description of Audit Check on Operations	Pass Fail /NA Comments	Source of Requirement
O-62	Is there a user enrollment process used for requesting, issuing, and closing user accounts?		
O-63	Are the humidity and temperature of the data center where the systems are housed controlled?		
O-64	Does the data center have an alarm system that alerts appropriate personnel if the temperature and humidity exceeds acceptable levels?		
O-65	Is a fire suppression system installed in the data center where the systems are housed?		
O-66	Does the data center where the systems are housed have an alarm system that alerts appropriate personnel in the event of a fire?		
O-67	Are the systems described in the Hardware and Software Inventory backed up on a regular schedule?		

Continued

Table 21.2 continued Examples of Compliance Checks for Operational Controls

ID No.	Description of Audit Check on Operations	Pass Fail /NA	Comments	Source of Requirement
O-68	Is a copy of the system backup schedule included in the System Security Plan?			
O-69	Are the tools used to perform the backups adequately described in the System Security Plan?			
O-70	Are full backups performed at the minimum of once weekly with incremental backups performed nightly?			
O-71	Does an Incident Response Plan exist?			
O-72	Does the Incident Response Plan include adequate information on roles and responsibilities?			
O-73	Does the Incident Response Plan include a current list of key personnel that fill the roles and responsibilities?			
O-74	Does the Incident Response Plan include a diagram and description of the escalation framework?			

Continued

Table 21.2 continued Examples of Compliance Checks for Operational Controls

ID No.	Description of Audit Check on Operations	Pass Fail /NA	Comments	Source of Requirement
O-75	Does the Incident Response Plan include an adequate description of incident types?			
O-76	Does the Incident Response Plan include information on how to contact the agency CSIRC?			
O-77	Does the Incident Response Plan include an informative section on security forensics?			
O-78	Does the Incident Response Plan include incident handling guidelines?			
O-79	Does the Incident Response Plan include adequate information in incident severity levels?			
O-80	Does the Incident Response Plan include a copy of the a Security Incident Reporting Form?			
O-81	Are members of both the CSIRT and CSIRC teams included in the Incident Response Plan?			
O-82	Does the Incident Response Plan include information on how to report a security incident?			

Table 21.2 continued Examples of Compliance Checks for Operational Controls

ID No.	Description of Audit Check on Operations	Pass Fail /NA Comments	Source of Requirement
O-83	Are safeguards in place to ensure that only authorized individuals can access systems to perform maintenance tasks?		
O-84	Are systems backed up before maintenance tasks are performed?		
O-85	Is a log kept (that includes date and time) of who performs maintenance tasks on which systems?		

Compliance Checklist for Technical Controls

Table 21.3 Examples of Compliance Checks for Technical Controls

ID No.	Description of Audit Check on Technical Controls	Pass / Fail /NA Comments	Source of Requirement
T-1	Does a System Security Plan exist?		
T-2	Does the System Security Plan accurately describe the systems to which it applies?		
T-3	Does the System Security Plan include an adequate description of the system boundaries?		

Continued

Table 21.3 continued Examples of Compliance Checks for Technical Controls

ID No.	Description of Audit Check on Technical Controls	Pass / Fail /NA Comments	Source of Requirement
T-4	Are the procedures for authenticating users (passwords, tokens, biometrics, smart cards, etc.) fully explained in the System Security Plan?		
T-5	Does each user have a unique user ID?		
T-6	Are all user IDs associated with a person?		
T-7	Do all user IDs identify a user to the system, and verify their identity, before the user is allowed to perform any actions on the system?		
T-8	Are all users assigned to groups based on access requirements that comply with the principle of least privilege?		
T-9	Is the display of passwords suppressed on the monitor when users enter their passwords into the system?		
T-10	Are passwords for new users distributed securely?		

Continued

Table 21.3 continued Examples of Compliance Checks for Technical Controls

ID No.	Description of Audit Check on Technical Controls	Pass / Fail /NA	Comments	Source of Requirement
T-11	Are users informed not to share their passwords with others?			
T-12	Are users forced by the system to change their password upon initial activation of their account?			
T-13	Do passwords meet the agency password complexity rules?			
T-14	Do user passwords expire every 90 days?			
T-15	Do **root**, **admin**, all system administration, and all privileged account passwords expire every 30 days?			
T-16	Have all guest and anonymous accounts been removed?			
T-17	Does the system provide a mechanism that notifies the user when a password change is required?			
T-18	Are all passwords stored encrypted and not displayed in clear-text anywhere on the system?			

Continued

Table 21.3 continued Examples of Compliance Checks for Technical Controls

ID No.	Description of Audit Check on Technical Controls	Pass / Fail /NA Comments	Source of Requirement
T-19	Is it certain that passwords are not hard-coded into scripts, software, or applications?		
T-20	Are password auditing tools used to scan for weak passwords?		
T-21	When weak passwords are found are the users with weak passwords required to change their password?		
T-22	Is there a secure process to assist users who have forgotten their passwords?		
T-23	Are all requests for account creation approved by the user's supervisor prior to giving the user access?		
T-24	Are nonactivated accounts removed from the system after 60 days?		
T-25	Are systems configured to lock an account/user ID after 3 consecutive failed logon attempts?		
T-26	Is it possible to trace all system actions to user IDs?		
T-27	Are all logon attempts recorded in an audit log?		

Continued

Table 21.3 continued Examples of Compliance Checks for Technical Controls

ID No.	Description of Audit Check on Technical Controls	Pass / Fail /NA Comments	Source of Requirement
T-28	Do the system/ applications have audit logging capabilities?		
T-29	Is the absolute pathname of all log files used by the system documented in the System Security Plan?		
T-30	Are login records of **root, admin**, and powerful users recorded in audit logs?		
T-31	Are the processes (e.g., **syslogd**) that control auditing noted and adequately discussed in the *System Security Plan*?		
T-32	Does information recorded in audit logs include a date and timestamp?		
T-33	Are all denied connections to servers logged?		
T-34	Are audit logs protected so that read access is limited to only those individuals who are authorized to review audit data?		

Continued

Table 21.3 continued Examples of Compliance Checks for Technical Controls

ID No.	Description of Audit Check on Technical Controls	Pass / Fail /NA Comments	Source of Requirement
T-35	Are safeguards in place to prevent unauthorized alteration of audit logs?		
T-36	Are security audit logs reviewed on a regular schedule?		
T-37	Does the system disconnect a user's session after 30 minutes of inactivity?		
T-38	Is access to security configuration settings restricted to systems administrators?		
T-39	Is an approved logon banner displayed, warning unauthorized users of the consequences of unauthorized access?		
T-40	Does the system prevent concurrent user logins except where operationally required?		
T-41	Do inbound services provide strong authentication using one-time passwords, session passwords, change and response protocols, two-factor authentication, digital signatures, or encryption?		

Continued

Table 21.3 continued Examples of Compliance Checks for Technical Controls

ID No.	Description of Audit Check on Technical Controls	Pass / Fail /NA	Comments	Source of Requirement
T-42	Do all software encryption products have a FIPS 140-2 validation certificate to ensure compliance with correct algorithm implementation?			
T-43	Are all encryption keys securely stored?			
T-44	Does the System Security Plan clearly describe where encryption is used and what is encrypted?			
T-45	Are scripts that are resident on the system secured such that they prevent users from obtaining command level access to the system?			
T-46	Are scripts that are resident on the system secured such that they prevent users from passing a command string to a server through a script?			
T-47	Is perimeter security (firewalls, routers, switches) adequately described in the System Security Plan?			

Continued

Table 21.3 continued Examples of Compliance Checks for Technical
Controls

ID No.	Description of Audit Check on Technical Controls	Pass / Fail /NA Comments	Source of Requirement
T-48	Are there safeguards in place to protect the firewall rules file from unauthorized modification?		
T-49	Are there safeguards in place to protect router ACLs from unauthorized modification?		
T-50	Are firewall logs reviewed on a regular schedule and is the schedule included in the *System Security Plan*?		
T-51	Does the *System Security Plan* make it clear who reviews the firewall logs?		
T-52	Does the *System Security Plan* include information on what open ports and services are required by the system?		
T-53	Does the *System Security Plan* include a topological network map of all the items listed in the Hardware and Software Inventory?		
T-54	Are PKI systems adequately described in the *System Security Plan*?		

Continued

Table 21.3 continued Examples of Compliance Checks for Technical Controls

ID No.	Description of Audit Check on Technical Controls	Pass / Fail /NA	Comments	Source of Requirement
T-55	Are any VPNs used by the system adequately described in the *System Security Plan*?			
T-56	Are all Transport Layer Security (TLS) mechanisms discussed in the System Security Plan?			
T-57	Does the *System Security Plan* make it clear where (on what systems) X.509 certificates are installed?			
T-58	Do all digital certificates used support at the minimum 128 bit encryption?			
T-59	Is the usage of any wireless networks discussed in the *System Security Plan*?			
T-60	Are all wireless network access points noted in the *System Security Plan*?			
T-61	Are all wireless networks adequately secured?			
T-62	Are any secure file transfer methods that are used adequately discussed in the *System Security Plan*?			

Continued

Table 21.3 continued Examples of Compliance Checks for Technical Controls

ID No.	Description of Audit Check on Technical Controls	Pass / Fail /NA Comments	Source of Requirement
T-63	Do all file transfers log the start of transfer time, end of transfer time, what was transferred, and whether the transfer was successful or not?		
T-64	Is the system protected from malware (e.g., viruses, Trojans, worms) by reputable antivirus software?		
T-65	Are antivirus signatures updated regularly?		
T-66	Does the *System Security Plan* discuss how modification of sensitive or critical files is detected?		
T-67	Is the usage of host-based intrusion detection systems adequately discussed in the *System Security Plan*?		
T-68	Is the usage of network-based intrusion detection systems adequately discussed in the *System Security Plan*?		
T-69	Have all intrusion detection systems been tested?		

Continued

Table 21.3 continued Examples of Compliance Checks for Technical Controls

ID No.	Description of Audit Check on Technical Controls	Pass / Fail /NA	Comments	Source of Requirement
T-70	Is information on how the intrusion detection system(s) are configured and set up adequately documented?			
T-71	Are the systems adequately monitored for suspicious activity?			
T-72	Does the *System Security Plan* describe how man-in-the-middle attacks and unlinked session vulnerabilities are mitigated?			
T-73	Does the *System Security Plan* adequately describe how session authenticity is maintained?			
T-74	Does the *System Security Plan* adequately describe how threats to mobile code (ActiveX, JavaScript, Java) are mitigated?			
T-75	Does the *System Security Plan* explain how security patches are tested before they are deployed to production systems?			
T-76	Are security patches applied promptly?			

Continued

Table 21.3 continued Examples of Compliance Checks for Technical Controls

ID No.	Description of Audit Check on Technical Controls	Pass / Fail /NA Comments	Source of Requirement
T-77	Do all remote access capabilities provide strong identification and authentication and protect sensitive information in transit?		
T-78	Are friendly and unfriendly termination procedures adequately described in the *System Security Plan*?		
T-79	Does the system automatically establish encrypted channels (HTTPS, SSL, etc.) for the transmission of sensitive information?		
T-80	Are systems checked for the "SANS Top 20" vulnerabilities on a monthly basis?		
T-82	Is all media sanitized and properly decommissioned before it is disposed of?		
T-82	Are record retention requirements met prior to the disposal and decommissioning of media?		

Table 21.3 continued Examples of Compliance Checks for Technical Controls

ID No.	Description of Audit Check on Technical Controls	Pass / Fail /NA Comments	Source of Requirement
T-83	Are security events monitored by the enterprise Security Information Manage- ment (SIM) system?		
T-84	Are the security events the SIM monitors adequately described in the System Security Plan?		
T-85	Is the ISSO informed of significant security events?		

Recommendation to Accredit or Not

After the evaluation and review of the C&A package documents have been finalized, the evaluation team makes a recommendation on whether the information system or major application described in the C&A package should be accredited or not. The recommendation usually is made to the certifying agent, since the evaluation team usually represents the certifying agent. In most cases, the certifying agent accepts the recommendation of the evaluation team. If the certifying agent ever decides not to accept the recommendation, it means that much faith has been lost in the evaluation team and it might be time for the evaluation team to look for a new job.

The certifying agent may be responsible for the evaluation of the many C&A packages, and therefore, it is often the case that he or she will not have time to read through all of these packages. It is possible, though, that the certifying agent may skim through them and review certain selections of each package. In support of the recommendation made by the evaluation team, the certifying agent will then write an official letter to the authorizing official recommending that the information system or major application described in the C&A package be accredited. A sample recommendation for accreditation letter is illustrated in Figure 21.1.

Accreditation and Authority to Operate

After receiving a copy of the recommendation on whether a C&A package should be accredited or not, the authorizing official writes a letter, known as an Authority to Operate (ATO), to the business owner and ISSO that authorizes the operations of the systems. The ATO is usually not longer than two pages, and will likely mention that there is an expectation that any POA&M items will be adequately reconciled. A sample accreditation letter is illustrated in Figure 21.2.

Interim Authority to Operate

If the C&A package does not pass muster with the evaluation team, but it appears that it is on the right track and has the potential to remediate missing information within a short time period, the business owner may be awarded an Interim Authority to Operate (IATO). All IATOs are awarded with an expiration date assigned to it; most expire after six months. The criteria used for being awarded an IATO vary from agency to agency. Although an IATO is certainly not as desirable as an ATO, it does mean you can continue operating your systems up until the expiration date.

Figure 21.1 Sample Recommendation for Accreditation

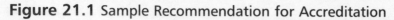

Agency Name Goes Here
Memorandum

Date: October 2, 2006
To: Barbara Tietzel, authorizing official
From: James Allen, certifying agent
Subject: Certification Statement for Dallas Datacenter General Support Systems

A certification review of the Dallas Datacenter General Support Systems has been conducted in accordance with the provisions of the <Agency Name> certification and accreditation program. Certification is the comprehensive testing and evaluation of the technical and nontechnical security controls, features, risks, and safeguards used in support of the accreditation process. Certification establishes the extent to which a particular IT design and implementation meets a specified set of security requirements. The Dallas Datacenter General Support Systems were evaluated for compliance, and meet those federal and <Agency Name> requirements with residual risk remaining as described in the Certification and Accreditation Package developed by Generic Government Contractor dated September 27, 2006.

Based on the residual risk identified in the Certification and Accreditation Package, I recommend that an accreditation be issued for the Dallas Datacenter General Support Systems for a period of no longer than three years, or when a significant change occurs to these systems. The issues on which you plan to take corrective action should be incorporated into a Plan of Actions and Milestones (POA&M), and attached to your accreditation letter.

Barbara Tietzel, authorizing official

        < signature >

cc: *Emily Bramah, Director of IT, Dallas Datacenter*
       William Carroll, ISSO

Figure 21.2 Sample Accreditation Letter

Agency Name Goes Here
Memorandum

Date: October 12, 2006
To: Charles Smith, Chief Information Officer
From: Barbara Tietzel, authorizing official
Subject: Authority to Operate Dallas Datacenter

In accordance with the provisions of <Agency Name> Information Technology Security Policy 4.1 on Certification and Accreditation, I hereby grant full accreditation to the Dallas Datacenter General Support Systems. This accreditation is based on my review of the information provided by 1) the Dallas Datacenter General Support Systems Certification and Accreditation Package prepared by *Generic Security Contractor* dated September 22, 2006 and 2) the *Security Assessment Report* developed by *Generic Security Contractor* on September 29, 2006.

This accreditation is my formal declaration that the Dallas Datacenter General Support System security controls have been properly implemented and is at a satisfactory level of security, commensurate with the known risks, at present. As a result of the certification effort, vulnerabilities that were identified are listed in the Dallas Datacenter General Support Systems Plan of Actions and Milestones (POA&M). The POA&M has been established to track the removal these vulnerabilities which the Director of IT, Dallas Datacenter will implement by the scheduled completion dates identified in the POA&M.

I accept the residual risk from these vulnerabilities in view of the fact that the Dallas Datacenter General Support Systems process low sensitive and unclassified data.

This accreditation is valid for three years from the date of this letter. The Dallas Datacenter General Support Systems will be re-accredited earlier if modifications are implemented that result in significant changes to the system security controls.

Acknowledgement _____
                  <Signature of Charles Smith, CIO>

cc: *Glenda Bramah, Director of IT, Dallas Datacenter*
       William Carroll, ISSO

Evaluations by an OIG

Each agency has an OIG, whose role is to ensure that the agency is complying with all laws. Most agencies usually receive little notice that the OIG is going to be paying a visit. The objective of the OIG is to assess the information security program for compliance with FISMA, and generate a report that documents the results of that evaluation. In accordance with the principles of the Freedom of Information Act (5 U.S.C. 552, as amended by Public Law 104-231), OIG reports are available to the general public.

OIG teams from different agencies will not necessarily assess the information security program in the same way. The reports generated by different OIG teams will not necessarily have the same format and include all the same information. An example of an OIG reports are found at the following URLs:

> EPA OIG Report
> www.epa.gov/oig/reports/2003/epaoigFISMA20031022.pdf
>
> GSA OIG Report
> http://oig.gsa.gov/A050174.pdf
>
> Health and Human Services OIG Report
> http://oig.hhs.gov/oas/reports/cms/180502600.pdf

The inspectors could ask to see just about any type of document related to the information security program. They may ask for a *C&A Handbook*, and they may ask to see 10 randomly selected C&A packages. It's almost impossible to prepare for what they may ask for. The best thing to do is to accommodate them as best as possible and give them everything that they ask to see. They will likely not ask to logon to systems.

One of the best things your agency can do to prepare for a visit from the OIG is to read the OIG report for your agency that was issued the previous year. Look through to see what it is that they asked to review, and what their recommendations were for your agency. They will likely want to know if any action was taken on their prior recommendations.

Evaluations by the GAO

Evaluations and assessments are made by the GAO to verify if the OIG is reporting information correctly. Similar to OIG evaluations, the GAO inspectors could ask to see just about any type of document related to the information security program. Aside from evaluating each agency's C&A program, the GAO will be collecting information to assemble for an annual report to Congress. The 2005 GAO report can be found at http://www.gao.gov/new.items/d05552.pdf.

All GAO inspectors are different, and they may ask for different items to review. Some GAO inspectors are contractors and come from companies that are well versed in computer security. I have seen GAO inspectors ask for items as specific as those listed in Table 21.4. The GAO inspectors may record the date they ask for specific items and the date the items are received. It is best to give them what they want as quickly as possible.

Table 21.4 Real Examples of Items That GAO Inspectors Have Asked For

#	Document Description
1	Listing of the names of security reports generated by the system and the name(s) of the individual(s) responsible for reviewing those reports
2	Printout of **find / -user root –perm 4000 –exec ls –l {} **
3	Printout of **find / -user root –perm 2000 –exec ls –l {} **
4	Printout of the contents of **.rhosts** file
5	Printout of the contents of /etc/security/audit/events file
6	Printout of **host.equiv** file
7	Memorandum of agreements with business partners
8	Copy of AIX security configuration procedures
9	A system-generated list of all users, and user profiles, with access to the system
10	Printout of file access rights (using **ls –l /etc/passwd**)

The GAO inspectors will likely not give the agency much notice before showing up. Every effort should be made to accommodate their requests as expeditiously as possible. The agency should warn ISSOs as soon as it know that GAO inspectors will be arriving so that the ISSOs can make themselves available to answer any questions.

Checklist

Use the following checklist to make sure evaluations are done carefully:

- Has an audit checklist been developed for management controls?

- Has an audit checklist been developed for operational controls?

- Has an audit checklist been developed for technical controls?

- Do the audit checks adequately check for compliance with confidentiality, integrity, and availability security policies?

- Does the *Security Assessment Report* include a final list of vulnerabilities and corrective action?

Summary

Evaluating a C&A package is a big undertaking. Many evaluation teams don't leave enough time for reading through the information-rich C&A documents that were so thoughtfully prepared. The evaluation team should treat the preparation team and ISSO with professionalism and respect and avoid having the evaluation process degenerate into a squabbling affair. The evaluation team, through its recommendations, has an opportunity to make a difference by pointing out vulnerabilities that may have been missed by the preparation team and ISSO. Though most C&A packages don't usually obtain a perfect score on all audit checks, that doesn't mean that the package and systems are not worthy of accreditation. Recommendations on whether to accredit a group of systems (or not) should be made very thoughtfully, with justifications behind every recommendation.

## Chapter 22

Addressing C&A Findings

"I don't believe in failure. It is not failure if you enjoyed the process."

—Oprah Winfrey

Topics in this chapter:

- POA&Ms

- Development and Approval

- POA&M Elements

- A Word to the Wise

- Checklist

Introduction

Understanding how to resolve the reported vulnerabilities is the final step in the C&A process.

POA&Ms

Whether you receive full Accreditation and an Authority to Operate (ATO), or an Interim Authority to Operate (IATO), you will be required to correct weaknesses related to your security controls. If you were awarded an IATO, there will likely be far more weaknesses that you'll need to correct than if you were awarded an ATO. The weaknesses need to be identified and described in a document known as the Plan of Action & Milestones (POA&M). The POA&M represents the ISSO's to-do list and typically needs to be approved by the evaluation team that evaluated the C&A package before they send in the recommendation for accreditation.

The objective of the POA&M is to have all the vulnerabilities and below-standard security controls identified and listed in one consolidated document. The POA&M is the final output of the certification and accreditation process and is where OIG and GAO are going to look to determine what your plans are to reduce the risks to your systems going forward.

Development and Approval

Typically the POA&M is created by the ISSO. However, the ISSO may delegate this task to a staff member or contractor. There should be a separation of duties between whoever develops the POA&M and the folks who will be required to implement the corrective action requirements. Once your POA&M is complete, it needs to be approved. The ISSO should submit the POA&M to the evaluation team that made the recommendation for accreditation who will review it, and then send it to the authorizing official.

Sometimes some of the mitigation activities will be nothing more than updating software or installing the latest patches at little to no cost to the organization. Other mitigation activities could cost thousands of dollars and need upper level management approval for the funds. You should make sure that the authorizing official has seen and approved the POA&M—that way, when you request the money to complete the tasks there should be no problems getting the funding.

POA&M Elements

A POA&M is typically put together in tabular format and includes information about the cited weakness or vulnerability, milestones, and cost. You should make sure the following information is included in each POA&M:

- **ID No.** A unique number used by the organization to track mitigation activities.

- **Weakness** Include a description of the weakness identified by the annual program review, OIG, or GAO audit.

- **Severity** High, Moderate, or Low.

- **POC** Include contact information for the office and/or organization that the agency will hold responsible for resolving the weakness.

- **Resources Required** List the estimated funding and resources required to resolve the weakness. Include the anticipated source of funding (e.g., within the department or as a part of a cross-cutting security infrastructure program). Include whether a reallocation of base resources or a request for new funding is anticipated. This column should also identify other nonfunding obstacles and challenges to resolving the weakness (e.g., lack of personnel or expertise, development of new system to replace insecure legacy system, etc.). To determine resource costs for employees, use the latest agency average salary and benefit hourly rate, then multiply the rate by the number of hours. Remember, this is just an estimate.

- **Projected Completion Date** Identify the date for resolving the weakness. Typically the projected completion date cannot be changed. If a weakness is resolved before or after the projected completion date, you should show the actual completion date in the status column.

- **Milestones with Completion Dates** Identify specific requirements to correct the weakness and include completion dates.

- **Identified in C&A evaluation or other review?** State how the weakness was identified (e.g., Security Assessment Report, OIG audit, GAO audit, etc.). If the weakness that is identified is reportable to the OIG, include the specific language and/or law from the pertinent audit report.

- **Status?Ongoing or Completed** Completed should be used only when a weakness has been fully resolved and the corrective action has been validated. For canceled milestones, update the Status column to say Completed with the date, and give a brief explanation in the Comments column.

- **Comments** Include a Comments column to record additional status.

Table 22.1 shows an example of a POA&M.

Table 22.1 An Example of a POA&M

ID No.	Weakness	Severity	Point of Contact	Resources Required	Projected Completion Date	Milestones with Completion Dates	Identified in C&A evaluation or other review?	Status
1	No IDS System installed in the environment	Moderate	Timothy Toms 111-222-3333	2 techs / 80 hours System costs $10,000.00 Total Cost: $26,000	12/15/06	Order Servers 10/15/06 Order Software 10/15/06 Build out system 11/15/06 Test system 12/10/06	Identified during C&A Process	On-Going
2	Windows 2000 PCs do not have the latest patches	Moderate	Harold Barns 111-333-2222	1 techs / 80 hours cost $8000.00	11/15/06	Download all patches 10/30/06 Test patches 11/10/06	Identified during C&A Process	On-Going
3	No Configuration Management Plan for system	Low	Alice Jackson 222-111-3333	2 techs / 80 hours System costs $16,000	12/1/06	Develop Configuration Management Plan	Identified during C&A Process	On-Going
4	Settings on Telnet port 25 on numerous servers are not sufficiently restrictive to prevent e-mail masquerading	High	James Wilson 111-222-3333	Not applicable	9/15/06	9/15/06	Identified during C&A process	Transferred to ISSO in department G73

A Word to the Wise

Now the C&A Package is complete. It has been delivered and approved by the evaluation team and you have an Authority to Operate in hand. Good job to everybody involved! It was a long hard road, and the job is done . . . or is it? Unfortunately it's often the case that once the C&A package has been completed, the organization sticks the POA&M on a shelf and forgets about the C&A process. The next year when the evaluation team comes around to obtain updates for FISMA reporting, it can create a big worriment to find out the status of the mitigation activities. In some cases, the mitigation activities may have never even been started and there may be no way to complete them before the end of the reporting period. Such scenarios defeat the purpose of the entire C&A process.

The point of C&A is to assess and document the security of your systems, identify vulnerabilities in your systems, and mitigate those vulnerabilities to improve the security posture. Don't waste all the hard work and effort that you and your colleagues put into the C&A process by not tracking and following up on the mitigation activities. If you track, follow up on, and validate that the mitigation activities are being completed, the next year, reporting will be an easy task. You'll know the status of the activities, your systems will be more secure, and your work will have made a difference.

Checklist

Use the following checklist to make sure you don't forget anything when developing your POA&M:

- Are all system weaknesses identified and listed?
- Does each system weakness have at least one corresponding milestone?
- Does the mitigation strategy information include a scheduled completion date?
- Does each milestone have a projected completion date?
- Does the mitigation strategy information include a Point of Contact?

- Are changes to milestones identified and listed?

- Does the weakness identified include a source (e.g., package evaluation)?

- Is the status of the identified weakness indicated?

- Does the mitigation strategy information include the required financial resources?

Summary

The findings that result from the evaluation of the C&A package should be turned into action items. ISSOs use a Plan of Action & Milestones (POA&M) document to summarize and track the action items. In subsequent audits, the evaluation team, OIG, and GAO may investigate to find out if corrective actions were applied to all security weaknesses. Addressing the findings that result from the C&A process is key to getting the value out of all the time and resources that were put into the security certification and accreditation process. Following through on POA&M action items is imperative to improving the secure posture of your systems.

## Chapter 23

Improving Your Federal Computer Security Report Card Scores

"Excellent firms don't believe in excellence—
only in constant improvement and constant
change."

—Tom Peters

Topics in this chapter:

- Elements of the Report Card

- Actions for Improvement

- Trends

Introduction

Each year, every agency has the opportunity to improve its annual Federal Computer Security Report Card. Aside from being audited by their own OIG and then by the GAO, agencies are required to self-report FISMA and privacy information annually. The White House Office of Management and Budget gives specific instructions on how to prepare and submit your agency's FISMA information. An overview for agencies to use on how to self-report their FISMA information is listed in memorandum M-05-15 available at www.whitehouse.gov/omb/memoranda/fy2005/m05-15.html.

Detailed self-reporting instructions are available at www.whitehouse.gov/omb/memoranda/fy2005/m05-15_att.pdf.

The Excel template into which you enter your FISMA information is available at www.whitehouse.gov/omb/inforeg/fisma/FY05_FISMA_reporting_template_CIO.xls.

Agency Inspector Generals are required to file their own report on their agency based on the subset of systems and documents that they review when they come on site for audits.

Elements of the Report Card

Each agency receives a roll-up score based on the consummate score from the agency's bureaus and their respective departments. Every year the report card grade changes. If your agency scored well last year, that doesn't necessarily mean they will score well in subsequent years. Each year, the self-reporting templates that contain the roll-up scores all change somewhat. Last year, the self-reporting template put emphasis in the following areas:

- Number of systems certified and accredited (including contractor systems)
- Configuration management
- Security policies and procedures
- Security training and awareness
- Number of security incidents reported

- Incident detection capabilities
- Implementation of security controls

Although the emphasis may change from year to year, it is unlikely that it will change in its entirety. Therefore, it behooves all agencies to review the emphasis from the prior year.

Actions for Improvement

To improve your report card, it will take a team effort that needs to be driven from the top down. Your CIO, SAISO, and all authorizing officials will need to do some homework before developing an action plan for improvement. First, you'll need to read the annual OMB report to Congress and make note of any negative citations about your agency. You'll need to read the OIG report developed by your own inspectors and make note of the deficiencies that your inspectors found in your agency. Additionally, you'll need to read the information security report about your agency published by GAO. Your agency CIO (with the assistance of the SAISO) should look for trends in these reports and make a comprehensive list of your agency's deficiencies. Finally, you'll need to do some research on any security incidents that may have occurred, particularly security incidents that received public media scrutiny. In doing background research on your deficiencies, look for trends cited in the different reports.

Once a list of the agency's deficiencies have been put together, the CIO should create an internal Corrective Action Plan for improving FISMA Scores, and make it a point to disseminate the plan to all ISSOs and other information security staff. CIOs and SAISOs should advise their agency or bureau to put more focus in the deficient areas. The CIOs and SAISOs should ask the assistance of the C&A evaluation teams to work through the Corrective Action Plan for improving FISMA Scores with the ISSOs. The evaluation team should put more emphasis on deficient areas for all C&A packages that they evaluate. C&A package evaluation teams can help ISSOs achieve a higher level of compliance by informing them up front where they should focus their efforts. CIOs should require that the evaluation team check in with ISSOs on a regular basis to make sure that they have the latest templates, information security policies, and C&A requirements.

A CIO cannot improve the agency's scores alone. It takes a team. It is imperative that the CIO communicate the desire and expectation for improvement throughout all the information security avenues of the agency. Agency CIOs need to hold bureau CIOs accountable, who in turn need to hold business owners and ISSOs accountable.

Streamlining the C&A process by using online signatures and XML-based SMART documents that interact directly with databases and monitoring systems will ultimately speed up C&A activities. Creating an in-house C&A portal can also improve communications and provide valuable resources for helping your agency understand C&A requirements.

Trends

Recent trends have shown that the following areas often are consistently neglected:

- Contingency Plans are not tested
- Mitigation activities listed in POA&Ms are left undone
- Not all systems are certified and accredited
- Contractor systems connected to agency networks are not certified and accredited

Summary

It is possible to improve your annual Federal Computer Security Report Card, but it requires systematic diligence driven from the top down. In summary, paying attention to the following areas should help all agencies make improvements:

- Do research on OMB, OIG, and GAO reports to find your agency's deficiencies

- Summarize the deficiencies and create a FISMA Corrective Action Plan

- Distribute the FISMA Corrective Action Plan to staff

- Communicate the desire and expectation of improvement

- Allocate a bigger security budget to security areas that receive the lowest scores

- If need be, hire contractors to help out the in-house staff

- Refine your *C&A Handbook* and update your templates regularly

- Have the evaluation team check in with ISSOs on a regular basis

- Require signatures on all C&A documents so that staff can be held accountable

- Ensure that all production systems and applications are certified and accredited

- Streamline the C&A process and automate reporting activities as much as possible

Chapter 24

Resources

The following resources may help you better understand Certification and Accreditation:

- *Certification and Accreditation 101*
  www.intranetjournal.com/articles/200406/ij_06_23_04a.html

- *Clinger-Cohen Act of 1996*
  http://akss.dau.mil/DAG/Guidebook/IG_c7.8.asp

- *Computer Fraud and Abuse Act of 1986*
  http://cio.doe.gov/Documents/CFA.HTM

- *Computer Security Act of 1987*
  www.epic.org/crypto/csa/csa.html

- *Critical Infrastructure Protection, GAO-01-1168T*
  www.gao.gov/new.items/d011168t.pdf

- *Director of Central Intelligence Directive 6/3, Protecting Sensitive Compartmented Information Within Information Systems – Policy*
  www.fas.org/irp/offdocs/DCID_6-3_20Policy.htm

- *Director of Central Intelligence Directive 6/3, Protecting Sensitive Compartmented Information Within Information Systems – Manual*
  www.fas.org/irp/offdocs/DCID_6-3_20Manual.htm

- *DoD Information Technology Security Certification & Accreditation Process (DITSCAP)*
  http://iase.disa.mil/ditscap/

- *Department of Homeland Security, National Response Plan,* December 2004
  www.dhs.gov/interweb/assetlibrary/NRP_FullText.pdf

- *E-Government Act of 2002*
  www.whitehouse.gov/omb/egov/g-4-act.html

- *Federal Information Processing Standards (FIPS) Publication 199, Standards for the Security Categorization of Federal Information and Information Systems*
  http://csrc.nist.gov/publications/fips/fips199/FIPS-PUB-199-final.pdf

- *Federal Information Processing Standards (FIPS) Publication 200, Minimum Security Requirements for Federal Information and Information Systems*
  http://csrc.nist.gov/publications/fips/fips200/FIPS-200-final-march.pdf

- *Federal Information Technology Security Assessment Framework*
  www.cio.gov/archive/federal_it_security_assessment_framework.html

- *Federal Manager's Financial Integrity Act of 1982*
  www.whitehouse.gov/omb/financial/fmfia1982.html

- *Federal Preparedness Circular 65, July 1999*
  www.usaid.gov/policy/ads/100/fpc65899.pdf

- *Homeland Security Presidential Directive (HSPD-7)*
  www.whitehouse.gov/news/releases/2003/12/20031217-5.html

- *National Information Assurance Certification and Accreditation Process*
  www.nstissc.gov/Assets/pdf/nstissi_1000.pdf
  National Response Plan, December 2004
  www.dhs.gov/interweb/assetlibrary/NRPbaseplan.pdf

- *NIST Special Publication 800-37, Guide for the Security Certification and Accreditation of Federal Information Systems*
  http://csrc.nist.gov/publications/nistpubs/800-37/SP800-37-final.pdf

- *Office of Management and Budget (OMB), Circular A-130, Appendix III*
  www.whitehouse.gov/omb/circulars/a130/a130appendix_iii.html
  Presidential Decision Directive 63, Critical Infrastructure Protection
  www.fas.org/irp/offdocs/pdd-63.htm

- *The Privacy Act of 1974*
  www.usdoj.gov/oip/privstat.htm

Acronyms

AIS	Automated Information Systems
ALE	Annual Loss Expectancy
ARO	Annualized Rate of Occurrence
ATO	Authority to Operate
BIA	Business Impact Assessment
CER	Cross-over Error Rate
CIO	Chief Information Officer
C&A	Certification and Accreditation
CMT	Cryptographic Module Testing
CMVP	Cryptographic Module Validation Program
CSIRC	Computer Security Incidence Response Center
DAA	Designated Approving Authority
DCID	Director of Central Intelligence Directive
DISA	Defense Information Systems Agency
DITSCAP	Defense Information Technology Systems Certification and Accreditation Process
DoD	Department of Defense
FAR	False Acceptance Rate
FEMA	Federal Emergency Management Agency
FIPS	Federal Information Processing Standard
FISMA	Federal Information Security Management Act
FRR	False Reject Rate
FTA	Failure to Acquire
FTE	Failure to Enroll
GAO	Government Accountability Office
HIPAA	Health Insurance Portability and Accountability Act
IATO	Interim Authority to Operate
IG	Inspector General
IT	Information Technology
LAFE	Local Annual Frequency Estimate
NIACAP	National Information Assurance Certification and Accreditation

	Process
NIST	National Institute of Standards and Technology
NSTISSC	National Security Telecommunications and Information Systems Security Committee
OIG	Office of Inspector General
OMB	Office of Management and Budget
PDA	Personal Digital Assistant
POA&M	Plan of Action & Milestones
RBAC	Role-based Access Control
SAFE	Standard Annual Frequency Estimate
SAISO	Senior Agency Information Security Officer
SBU	Sensitive But Unclassified
SLE	Single Loss Expectancy
ST&E	Security Test & Evaluation

Appendix A:

FISMA

TITLE III—INFORMATION SECURITY

SEC. 301. INFORMATION SECURITY.

(a) SHORT TITLE.—This title may be cited as the "Federal Information Security Management Act of 2002".

(b) INFORMATION SECURITY.—

(1) IN GENERAL.—Chapter 35 of title 44, United States Code, is amended by adding at the end the following new subchapter:

"SUBCHAPTER III—INFORMATION SECURITY

"§ 3541. Purposes

"The purposes of this subchapter are to—

"(1) provide a comprehensive framework for ensuring the effectiveness of information security controls over information resources that support Federal operations and assets;

"(2) recognize the highly networked nature of the current Federal computing environment and provide effective governmentwide management and oversight of the related information security risks, including coordination of information security efforts throughout the civilian, national security, and law enforcement communities;

"(3) provide for development and maintenance of minimum controls required to protect Federal information and information systems;

"(4) provide a mechanism for improved oversight of Federal agency information security programs;

"(5) acknowledge that commercially developed information security products offer advanced, dynamic, robust, and effective information security solutions, reflecting market solutions for the protection of critical information infrastructures important to the national defense and economic security of the nation that are designed, built, and operated by the private sector; and

"(6) recognize that the selection of specific technical hardware and software information security solutions should be left to individual agencies from among commercially developed products.

"§ 3542. Definitions

"(a) IN GENERAL.—Except as provided under subsection (b), the definitions under section 3502 shall apply to this subchapter.

"(b) ADDITIONAL DEFINITIONS.—As used in this subchapter:

"(1) The term 'information security' means protecting information and information systems from unauthorized access, use, disclosure, disruption, modification, or destruction in order to provide—

"(A) Integrity, which means guarding against improper information modification or destruction, and includes ensuring information nonrepudiation and authenticity;

"(B) Confidentiality, which means preserving authorized restrictions on access and disclosure, including means for protecting personal privacy and proprietary information; and

"(C) Availability, which means ensuring timely and reliable access to and use of information.

"(2)(A) The term 'national security system' means any information system (including any telecommunications system) used or operated by an agency or by a contractor of an agency, or other organization on behalf of an agency—

"(i) the function, operation, or use of which—

"(I) involves intelligence activities;

"(II) involves cryptologic activities related to national security;

"(III) involves command and control of military forces;

"(IV) involves equipment that is an integral part of a weapon or weapons system; or

"(V) subject to subparagraph (B), is critical to the direct fulfillment of military or intelligence missions; or

"(ii) is protected at all times by procedures established for information that have been specifically authorized under criteria established by an Executive order or an Act of

Congress to be kept classified in the interest of national defense or foreign policy.

"(B) Subparagraph (A)(i)(V) does not include a system that is to be used for routine administrative and business applications (including payroll, finance, logistics, and personnel management applications).

"(3) The term 'information technology' has the meaning given that term in section 11101 of title

40.

"§ 3543. Authority and functions of the Director

"(a) IN GENERAL.—The Director shall oversee agency information security policies and practices, including—

"(1) developing and overseeing the implementation of policies, principles, standards, and guidelines on information security, including through ensuring timely agency adoption of and compliance with standards promulgated under section 11331 of title 40;

"(2) requiring agencies, consistent with the standards promulgated under such section 11331 and the requirements of this subchapter, to identify and provide information security protections commensurate with the risk and magnitude of the harm resulting from the unauthorized access, use, disclosure, disruption, modification, or destruction of—

"(A) information collected or maintained by or on behalf of an agency; or

"(B) information systems used or operated by an agency or by a contractor of an agency or other organization on behalf of an agency;

"(3) coordinating the development of standards and guidelines under section 20 of the National Institute of Standards and Technology Act (15 U.S.C. 278g–3) with agencies and offices operating or exercising control of national security systems (including the National Security Agency) to assure, to the maximum extent feasible, that such standards and guidelines are complementary with standards and guidelines developed for national security systems;

"(4) overseeing agency compliance with the requirements of this subchapter, including through any authorized action under section 11303 of title 40, to enforce accountability for compliance with such requirements;

"(5) reviewing at least annually, and approving or disapproving, agency information security programs required under section 3544(b);

"(6) coordinating information security policies and procedures with related information resources management policies and procedures;

"(7) overseeing the operation of the Federal information security incident center required under section 3546; and "(8) reporting to Congress no later than March 1 of each year on agency compliance with the requirements of this subchapter, including—

"(A) a summary of the findings of evaluations required by section 3545;

"(B) an assessment of the development, promulgation, and adoption of, and compliance with, standards developed under section 20 of the National Institute of Standards and Technology Act (15

U.S.C. 278g-3) and promulgated under section 11331 of title 40;

"(C) significant deficiencies in agency information security practices;

"(D) planned remedial action to address such deficiencies; and

"(E) a summary of, and the views of the Director on, the report prepared by the National Institute of Standards and Technology under section 20(d)(10) of the National Institute of Standards and Technology Act (15 U.S.C. 278g–3).

"(b) NATIONAL SECURITY SYSTEMS.—Except for the authorities described in paragraphs (4) and (8) of subsection (a), the authorities of the Director under this section shall not apply to national security systems.

"(c) DEPARTMENT OF DEFENSE AND CENTRAL INTELLIGENCE

AGENCY SYSTEMS.—(1) The authorities of the Director described in paragraphs (1) and (2) of subsection (a) shall be delegated to the Secretary of Defense in the case of systems described in paragraph (2) and to the Director of Central Intelligence in the case of systems described in paragraph (3).

"(2) The systems described in this paragraph are systems that are operated by the Department of Defense, a contractor of the Department of Defense, or another entity on behalf of the Department of Defense that processes any information the unauthorized access, use, disclosure, disruption, modification, or destruction of which would have a debilitating impact on the mission of the Department of Defense.

"(3) The systems described in this paragraph are systems that are operated by the Central Intelligence Agency, a contractor of the Central Intelligence Agency, or another entity on behalf of the Central Intelligence Agency that processes any information the unauthorized access, use, disclosure, disruption, modification, or destruction of which would have a debilitating impact on the mission of the Central Intelligence Agency.

"§ 3544. Federal agency responsibilities

"(a) IN GENERAL.—The head of each agency shall—

"(1) be responsible for—

"(A) providing information security protections commensurate with the risk and magnitude of the harm resulting from unauthorized access, use, disclosure, disruption, modification, or destruction of—

"(i) information collected or maintained by or on behalf of the agency; and "(ii) information systems used or operated by an agency or by a contractor of an agency or other organization on behalf of an agency;

"(B) complying with the requirements of this subchapter and related policies, procedures, standards, and guidelines, including—

"(i) information security standards promulgated under section 11331 of title 40; and

"(ii) information security standards and guidelines for national security systems issued in accordance with law and as directed by the President; and

"(C) ensuring that information security management processes are integrated with agency strategic and operational planning processes;

"(2) ensure that senior agency officials provide information security for the information and information systems that support the operations and assets under their control, including through—

"(A) assessing the risk and magnitude of the harm that could result from the unauthorized access, use, disclosure, disruption, modification, or destruction of such information or information systems;

"(B) determining the levels of information security appropriate to protect such information and information systems in accordance with standards promulgated under section 11331 of title 40, for information security classifications and related requirements;

"(C) implementing policies and procedures to cost-effectively reduce risks to an acceptable level; and

"(D) periodically testing and evaluating information security controls and techniques to ensure that they are effectively implemented;

"(3) delegate to the agency Chief Information Officer established under section 3506 (or comparable official in an agency not covered by such section) the authority to ensure compliance with the requirements imposed on the agency under this subchapter, including—

"(A) designating a senior agency information security officer who shall—

"(i) carry out the Chief Information Officer's responsibilities under this section;

"(ii) possess professional qualifications, including training and experience, required to administer the functions described under this section;

"(iii) have information security duties as that official's primary duty; and "(iv) head an office with the mission and resources to assist in ensuring agency compliance with this section;

"(B) developing and maintaining an agencywide information security program as required by subsection

(b);

"(C) developing and maintaining information security policies, procedures, and control techniques to address all applicable requirements, including those issued under section

3543 of this title, and section 11331 of title 40;

"(D) training and overseeing personnel with significant responsibilities for information security with respect to such responsibilities; and

"(E) assisting senior agency officials concerning their responsibilities under paragraph (2);

"(4) ensure that the agency has trained personnel sufficient to assist the agency in complying with the requirements of this subchapter and related policies, procedures, standards, and guidelines; and

"(5) ensure that the agency Chief Information Officer, in coordination with other senior agency officials, reports annually to the agency head on the effectiveness of the agency information security program, including progress of remedial actions.

"(b) AGENCY PROGRAM.—Each agency shall develop, document, and implement an agency-wide information security program, approved by the Director under section 3543(a)(5), to provide

information security for the information and information systems that support the operations and assets of the agency, including those provided or managed by another agency, contractor, or other source, that includes—

"(1) periodic assessments of the risk and magnitude of the harm that could result from the unauthorized access, use, disclosure, disruption, modification, or destruction of information and information systems that support the operations and assets of the agency;

"(2) policies and procedures that—

"(A) are based on the risk assessments required by paragraph (1);

"(B) cost-effectively reduce information security risks to an acceptable level;

"(C) ensure that information security is addressed throughout the life cycle of each agency information system; and

"(D) ensure compliance with—

"(i) the requirements of this subchapter;

"(ii) policies and procedures as may be prescribed by the Director, and information security standards promulgated under section 11331 of title 40;

"(iii) minimally acceptable system configuration requirements, as determined by the agency; and

"(iv) any other applicable requirements, including standards and guidelines for national security systems issued in accordance with law and as directed by the

President;

"(3) subordinate plans for providing adequate information security for networks, facilities, and systems or groups of information systems, as appropriate;

"(4) security awareness training to inform personnel, including contractors and other users of information systems that support the operations and assets of the agency, of—

"(A) information security risks associated with their activities; and

"(B) their responsibilities in complying with agency policies and procedures designed to reduce these risks; "(5) periodic testing and evaluation of the effectiveness of information security policies, procedures, and practices, to be performed with a frequency depending on risk, but no less than annually, of which such testing—

"(A) shall include testing of management, operational, and technical controls of every information system identified in the inventory required under section 3505(c); and

"(B) may include testing relied on in a evaluation under section 3545;

"(6) a process for planning, implementing, evaluating, and documenting remedial action to address any deficiencies in the information security policies, procedures, and practices of the agency;

"(7) procedures for detecting, reporting, and responding to security incidents, consistent with standards and guidelines issued pursuant to section 3546(b), including—

"(A) mitigating risks associated with such incidents before substantial damage is done;

"(B) notifying and consulting with the Federal information security incident center referred to in section 3546; and

"(C) notifying and consulting with, as appropriate—

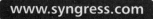

"(i) law enforcement agencies and relevant Offices of Inspector General;

"(ii) an office designated by the President for any incident involving a national security system; and

"(iii) any other agency or office, in accordance with law or as directed by the President; and

"(8) plans and procedures to ensure continuity of operations for information systems that support the operations and assets of the agency.

"(c) AGENCY REPORTING.—Each agency shall—

"(1) report annually to the Director, the Committees on Government Reform and Science of the House of Representatives, the Committees on Governmental Affairs and Commerce, Science, and Transportation of the Senate, the appropriate authorization and appropriations committees of Congress, and the Comptroller General on the adequacy and effectiveness of information security policies, procedures, and practices, and compliance with the requirements of this subchapter, including compliance with each requirement of subsection (b);

"(2) address the adequacy and effectiveness of information security policies, procedures, and practices in plans and reports relating to—

"(A) annual agency budgets;

"(B) information resources management under subchapter 1 of this chapter;

"(C) information technology management under subtitle III of title 40;

"(D) program performance under sections 1105 and 1115 through 1119 of title 31, and sections 2801 and 2805 of title 39;

"(E) financial management under chapter 9 of title 31, and the Chief Financial Officers Act of 1990 (31 U.S.C. 501 note; Public Law 101–576) (and the amendments made by that Act);

"(F) financial management systems under the Federal Financial Management Improvement Act (31 U.S.C. 3512 note); and

"(G) internal accounting and administrative controls under section 3512 of title 31, (known as the 'Federal Managers Financial Integrity Act'); and

"(3) report any significant deficiency in a policy, procedure, or practice identified under paragraph (1) or (2)—

"(A) as a material weakness in reporting under section 3512 of title 31; and

"(B) if relating to financial management systems, as an instance of a lack of substantial compliance under the Federal Financial Management Improvement Act (31 U.S.C. 3512 note).

"(d) PERFORMANCE PLAN.—(1) In addition to the requirements of subsection (c), each agency, in consultation with the Director, shall include as part of the performance plan required under section 1115 of title 31 a description of—

"(A) the time periods, and

"(B) the resources, including budget, staffing, and training, that are necessary to implement the program required under subsection (b).

"(2) The description under paragraph (1) shall be based on the risk assessments required under subsection (b)(2)(1).

"(e) PUBLIC NOTICE AND COMMENT.—Each agency shall provide the public with timely notice and opportunities for comment on proposed information security policies and procedures to the extent that such policies and procedures affect communication with the public.

"§ 3545. Annual independent evaluation

"(a) IN GENERAL.—(1) Each year each agency shall have performed an independent evaluation of the information security program and practices of that agency to determine the effectiveness of such program and practices.

"(2) Each evaluation under this section shall include—

"(A) testing of the effectiveness of information security policies, procedures, and practices of a representative subset of the agency's information systems;

"(B) an assessment (made on the basis of the results of the testing) of compliance with—

"(i) the requirements of this subchapter; and

"(ii) related information security policies, procedures, standards, and guidelines; and

"(C) separate presentations, as appropriate, regarding information security relating to national security systems.

"(b) INDEPENDENT AUDITOR.—Subject to subsection (c)—

"(1) for each agency with an Inspector General appointed under the Inspector General Act of 1978, the annual evaluation required by this section shall be performed by the Inspector

General or by an independent external auditor, as determined by the Inspector General of the agency; and

"(2) for each agency to which paragraph (1) does not apply, the head of the agency shall engage an independent external auditor to perform the evaluation.

"(c) NATIONAL SECURITY SYSTEMS.—For each agency operating or exercising control of a national security system, that portion of the evaluation required by this section directly relating to a national security system shall be performed—

"(1) only by an entity designated by the agency head; and

"(2) in such a manner as to ensure appropriate protection for information associated with any information security vulnerability in such system commensurate with the risk and in accordance with all applicable laws.

"(d) EXISTING EVALUATIONS.—The evaluation required by this section may be based in whole or in part on an audit, evaluation, or report relating to programs or practices of the applicable agency.

"(e) AGENCY REPORTING.—(1) Each year, not later than such date established by the Director, the head of each agency shall submit to the Director the results of the evaluation required under this section.

"(2) To the extent an evaluation required under this section directly relates to a national security system, the evaluation results submitted to the Director shall contain only a summary and assessment of that portion of the evaluation directly relating to a national security system.

"(f) PROTECTION OF INFORMATION.—Agencies and evaluators shall take appropriate steps to ensure the protection of information which, if disclosed, may adversely affect information security. Such protections shall be commensurate with the risk and comply with all applicable laws and regulations.

"(g) OMB REPORTS TO CONGRESS.—(1) The Director shall summarize the results of the evaluations conducted under this section in the report to Congress required under section 3543(a)(8).

"(2) The Director's report to Congress under this subsection shall summarize information regarding information security relating to national security systems in such a manner as to ensure appropriate protection for information associated with any information security vulnerability in such system commensurate with the risk and in accordance with all applicable laws.

"(3) Evaluations and any other descriptions of information systems under the authority and control of the Director of Central Intelligence or of National Foreign Intelligence Programs systems under the authority and control of the Secretary of Defense shall be made available to Congress only through the appropriate oversight committees of Congress, in accordance with applicable laws.

"(h) COMPTROLLER GENERAL.—The Comptroller General shall periodically evaluate and report to Congress on—

"(1) the adequacy and effectiveness of agency information security policies and practices; and

"(2) implementation of the requirements of this subchapter.

"§ 3546. Federal information security incident center

"(a) IN GENERAL.—The Director shall ensure the operation of a central Federal information security incident center to—

"(1) provide timely technical assistance to operators of agency information systems regarding security incidents, including guidance on detecting and handling information security incidents;

"(2) compile and analyze information about incidents that threaten information security;

"(3) inform operators of agency information systems about current and potential information security threats, and vulnerabilities; and

"(4) consult with the National Institute of Standards and Technology, agencies or offices operating or exercising control of national security systems (including the National Security Agency), and such other agencies or offices in accordance with law and as directed by the President regarding information security incidents and related matters.

"(b) NATIONAL SECURITY SYSTEMS.—Each agency operating or exercising control of a national security system shall share information about information security incidents, threats, and vulnerabilities with the Federal information security incident center to the extent consistent with standards and guidelines for national security systems, issued in accordance with law and as directed by the President.

"§ 3547. National security systems

"The head of each agency operating or exercising control of a national security system shall be responsible for ensuring that the agency—

"(1) provides information security protections commensurate with the risk and magnitude of the harm resulting from the unauthorized access, use, disclosure, disruption, modification, or destruction of the information contained in such system;

"(2) implements information security policies and practices as required by standards and guidelines for national security systems, issued in accordance with law and as directed by the President; and
"(3) complies with the requirements of this subchapter.

"§ 3548. Authorization of appropriations

"There are authorized to be appropriated to carry out the provisions of this subchapter such sums as may be necessary for each of fiscal years 2003 through 2007.

"§ 3549. Effect on existing law

"Nothing in this subchapter, section 11331 of title 40, or section 20 of the National Standards and Technology Act (15 U.S.C. 278g–

3) may be construed as affecting the authority of the President, the Office of Management and Budget or the Director thereof, the National Institute of Standards and Technology, or the head of any agency, with respect to the authorized use or disclosure of information, including with regard to the protection of personal privacy under section 552a of title 5, the disclosure of information under section 552 of title 5, the management and disposition of records under chapters 29, 31, or 33 of title 44, the management of information resources under subchapter I of chapter 35 of this title, or the disclosure of information to the Congress or the Comptroller General of the United States. While this subchapter is in effect, subchapter II of this chapter shall not apply.".

(2) CLERICAL AMENDMENT.—The table of sections at the beginning of such chapter 35 is amended by adding at the end the following:

"SUBCHAPTER III—INFORMATION SECURITY

"Sec.

"3541. Purposes.

"3542. Definitions.

"3543. Authority and functions of the Director.

"3544. Federal agency responsibilities.

"3545. Annual independent evaluation.

"3546. Federal information security incident center.

"3547. National security systems.

"3548. Authorization of appropriations.

"3549. Effect on existing law.".

(c) INFORMATION SECURITY RESPONSIBILITIES OF CERTAIN AGENCIES.

—

(1) NATIONAL SECURITY RESPONSIBILITIES.—(A) Nothing in this Act (including any amendment made by this Act) shall supersede any authority of the Secretary of Defense, the Director of Central Intelligence, or other agency head, as authorized by law and as directed by the President, with regard to the operation, control, or management of national security systems, as defined by section 3542(b)(2) of title 44, United States Code.

(B) Section 2224 of title 10, United States Code, is amended—

(i) in subsection (b), by striking "(b) OBJECTIVES AND MINIMUM REQUIREMENTS.—(1)" and inserting "(b) OBJECTIVES OF THE PROGRAM.—";

(ii) in subsection (b), by striking paragraph (2); and

(iii) in subsection (c), in the matter preceding paragraph

(1), by inserting ", including through compliance with subchapter III of chapter 35 of title 44" after "infrastructure".

(2) ATOMIC ENERGY ACT OF 1954.—Nothing in this Act shall supersede any requirement made by or under the Atomic Energy Act of 1954 (42 U.S.C. 2011 et seq.). Restricted data or formerly restricted data shall be handled, protected, classified, downgraded, and declassified in conformity with the Atomic Energy Act of 1954 (42 U.S.C. 2011 et seq.).

SEC. 302. MANAGEMENT OF INFORMATION TECHNOLOGY.

(a) IN GENERAL.—Section 11331 of title 40, United States Code, is amended to read as follows:

"§ 11331. Responsibilities for Federal information systems standards

"(a) STANDARDS AND GUIDELINES.—

"(1) AUTHORITY TO PRESCRIBE.—Except as provided under paragraph (2), the Secretary of Commerce shall, on the basis of standards and guidelines developed by the National Institute of Standards and Technology pursuant to paragraphs (2) and

(3) of section 20(a) of the National Institute of Standards and Technology Act (15 U.S.C. 278g–3(a)), prescribe standards and guidelines pertaining to Federal information systems.

"(2) NATIONAL SECURITY SYSTEMS.—Standards and guidelines for national security systems (as defined under this section) shall be developed, prescribed, enforced, and overseen as otherwise authorized by law and as directed by the President.

"(b) MANDATORY REQUIREMENTS.—

"(1) AUTHORITY TO MAKE MANDATORY.—Except as provided under paragraph (2), the

Secretary shall make standards prescribed under subsection (a)(1) compulsory and binding to the extent determined necessary by the Secretary to improve the efficiency of operation or security of Federal information systems.

"(2) REQUIRED MANDATORY STANDARDS.—(A) Standards prescribed under subsection (a)(1) shall include information security standards that—

"(i) provide minimum information security requirements as determined under section 20(b) of the National Institute of Standards and Technology Act (15 U.S.C. 278g– 3(b)); and

"(ii) are otherwise necessary to improve the security of Federal information and information systems.

"(B) Information security standards described in subparagraph

(A) shall be compulsory and binding.

"(c) AUTHORITY TO DISAPPROVE OR MODIFY.—The President may disapprove or modify the standards and guidelines referred to in subsection (a)(1) if the President determines such action to be in the public interest. The President's authority to disapprove or modify such standards and guidelines may not be delegated. Notice of such disapproval or modification shall be published promptly in the Federal Register. Upon receiving notice of such disapproval or modification, the Secretary of Commerce shall immediately rescind or modify such standards or guidelines as directed by the President.

"(d) EXERCISE OF AUTHORITY.—To ensure fiscal and policy consistency, the Secretary shall exercise the authority conferred by this section subject to direction by the President and in coordination with the Director of the Office of Management and Budget.

"(e) APPLICATION OF MORE STRINGENT STANDARDS.—The head of an executive agency may employ standards for the cost-effective information security for information systems within or under the supervision of that agency that are more stringent than the standards the Secretary prescribes under this section if the more stringent standards—

"(1) contain at least the applicable standards made compulsory and binding by the Secretary; and

"(2) are otherwise consistent with policies and guidelines issued under section 3543 of title 44.

"(f) DECISIONS ON PROMULGATION OF STANDARDS.—The decision by the Secretary regarding the promulgation of any standard under this section shall occur not later than 6 months after the submission of the proposed standard to the Secretary by the National Institute of Standards and Technology, as provided under section 20 of the National Institute of Standards and Technology Act (15 U.S.C. 278g–3).

"(g) DEFINITIONS.—In this section:

"(1) FEDERAL INFORMATION SYSTEM.—The term 'Federal information system' means an information system used or operated by an executive agency, by a contractor of an executive agency, or by another organization on behalf of an executive agency.

"(2) INFORMATION SECURITY.—The term 'information security' has the meaning given that term in section 3542(b)(1) of title 44.

"(3) NATIONAL SECURITY SYSTEM.—The term 'national security system' has the meaning given that term in section 3542(b)(2) of title 44.".

(b) CLERICAL AMENDMENT.—The item relating to section 11331 in the table of sections at the beginning of chapter 113 of such title is amended to read as follows:

"11331. Responsibilities for Federal information systems standards."

SEC. 303. NATIONAL INSTITUTE OF STANDARDS AND TECHNOLOGY.

Section 20 of the National Institute of Standards and Technology Act (15 U.S.C. 278g–3), is amended by striking the text and inserting the following:

"(a) IN GENERAL.—The Institute shall—

"(1) have the mission of developing standards, guidelines, and associated methods and techniques for information systems;

"(2) develop standards and guidelines, including minimum requirements, for information systems used or operated by an agency or by a contractor of an agency or other organization on behalf of an agency, other than national security systems (as defined in section 3542(b)(2) of title 44, United States Code); and

"(3) develop standards and guidelines, including minimum requirements, for providing adequate information security for all agency operations and assets, but such standards and guidelines shall not apply to national security systems.

"(b) MINIMUM REQUIREMENTS FOR STANDARDS AND GUIDELINES.

—The standards and guidelines required by subsection (a) shall include, at a minimum—

"(1)(A) standards to be used by all agencies to categorize all information and information systems collected or maintained by or on behalf of each agency based on the objectives of providing appropriate levels of information security according to a range of risk levels;

"(B) guidelines recommending the types of information and information systems to be included in each such category; and

"(C) minimum information security requirements for information and information systems in each such category;

"(2) a definition of and guidelines concerning detection and handling of information security incidents; and

"(3) guidelines developed in conjunction with the Department of Defense, including the National Security Agency, for identifying an information system as a national security system consistent with applicable requirements for national security systems, issued in accordance with law and as directed by the President.

"(c) DEVELOPMENT OF STANDARDS AND GUIDELINES.—In developing standards and guidelines required by subsections (a) and

(b), the Institute shall—

"(1) consult with other agencies and offices and the private sector (including the Director of the Office of Management and Budget, the Departments of Defense and Energy, the National Security Agency, the General Accounting Office, and the Secretary of Homeland Security) to assure—

"(A) use of appropriate information security policies, procedures, and techniques, in order to improve information security and avoid unnecessary and costly duplication of effort; and

"(B) that such standards and guidelines are complementary with standards and guidelines employed for the protection of national security systems and information contained in such systems;

"(2) provide the public with an opportunity to comment on proposed standards and guidelines;

"(3) submit to the Secretary of Commerce for promulgation under section 11331 of title 40, United States Code—

"(A) standards, as required under subsection (b)(1)(A), no later than 12 months after the date of the enactment of this section; and

"(B) minimum information security requirements for each category, as required under subsection (b)(1)(C), no later than 36 months after the date of the enactment of this section;

"(4) issue guidelines as required under subsection (b)(1)(B), no later than 18 months after the date of the enactment of this section;

"(5) to the maximum extent practicable, ensure that such standards and guidelines do not require the use or procurement of specific products, including any specific hardware or software;

"(6) to the maximum extent practicable, ensure that such standards and guidelines provide for sufficient flexibility to permit alternative solutions to provide equivalent levels of protection for identified information security risks; and

"(7) to the maximum extent practicable, use flexible, performance-based standards and guidelines that permit the use of off-the-shelf commercially developed information security products.

"(d) INFORMATION SECURITY FUNCTIONS.—The Institute shall—

"(1) submit standards developed pursuant to subsection

(a), along with recommendations as to the extent to which these should be made compulsory and binding, to the Secretary of Commerce for promulgation under section 11331 of title

40, United States Code;

"(2) provide technical assistance to agencies, upon request, regarding—

"(A) compliance with the standards and guidelines developed under subsection (a);

"(B) detecting and handling information security incidents; and

"(C) information security policies, procedures, and practices;

"(3) conduct research, as needed, to determine the nature and extent of information security vulnerabilities and techniques for providing cost-effective information security;

"(4) develop and periodically revise performance indicators and measures for agency information security policies and practices;

"(5) evaluate private sector information security policies and practices and commercially available information technologies to assess potential application by agencies to strengthen information security;

"(6) assist the private sector, upon request, in using and applying the results of activities under this section;

"(7) evaluate security policies and practices developed for national security systems to assess potential application by agencies to strengthen information security;

"(8) periodically assess the effectiveness of standards and guidelines developed under this section and undertake revisions as appropriate;

"(9) solicit and consider the recommendations of the Information Security and Privacy Advisory Board, established by section 21, regarding standards and guidelines developed under subsection (a) and submit such recommendations to the Secretary of Commerce with such standards submitted to the Secretary; and

"(10) prepare an annual public report on activities undertaken in the previous year, and planned for the coming year, to carry out responsibilities under this section.

"(e) DEFINITIONS.—As used in this section—

"(1) the term 'agency' has the same meaning as provided in section 3502(1) of title 44, United States Code;

"(2) the term 'information security' has the same meaning as provided in section 3542(b)(1) of such title;

"(3) the term 'information system' has the same meaning as provided in section 3502(8) of such title;

"(4) the term 'information technology' has the same meaning as provided in section 11101 of title 40, United States Code; and

"(5) the term 'national security system' has the same meaning as provided in section 3542(b)(2) of title 44, United States Code.

"(f) AUTHORIZATION OF APPROPRIATIONS.—There are authorized to be appropriated to the Secretary of Commerce $20,000,000 for each of fiscal years 2003, 2004, 2005, 2006, and 2007 to enable the National Institute of Standards and Technology to carry out the provisions of this section."

SEC. 304. INFORMATION SECURITY AND PRIVACY ADVISORY BOARD.

Section 21 of the National Institute of Standards and Technology

Act (15 U.S.C. 278g–4), is amended—

(1) in subsection (a), by striking "Computer System Security and Privacy Advisory Board" and inserting "Information Security and Privacy Advisory Board";

(2) in subsection (a)(1), by striking "computer or telecommunications" and inserting "information technology";

(3) in subsection (a)(2)—

(A) by striking "computer or telecommunications technology" and inserting "information technology"; and

(B) by striking "computer or telecommunications equipment" and inserting "information technology";

(4) in subsection (a)(3)—

(A) by striking "computer systems" and inserting "information system"; and

(B) by striking "computer systems security" and inserting "information security";

(5) in subsection (b)(1) by striking "computer systems security" and inserting "information security";

(6) in subsection (b) by striking paragraph (2) and inserting the following:

"(2) to advise the Institute, the Secretary of Commerce, and the Director of the Office of Management and Budget on information security and privacy issues pertaining to Federal

Government information systems, including through review of proposed standards and guidelines developed under section 20; and";

(7) in subsection (b)(3) by inserting "annually" after "report";

(8) by inserting after subsection (e) the following new subsection: "(f) The Board shall hold meetings at such locations and at such time and place as determined by a majority of the Board.";

(9) by redesignating subsections (f) and (g) as subsections (g) and (h), respectively; and

(10) by striking subsection (h), as redesignated by paragraph (9), and inserting the following: "(h) As used in this section, the terms 'information system' and 'information technology' have the meanings given in section

20.'"

SEC. 305. TECHNICAL AND CONFORMING AMENDMENTS.

(a) COMPUTER SECURITY ACT.—Section 11332 of title 40, United States Code, and the item relating to that section in the table of sections for chapter 113 of such title, are repealed.

(b) FLOYD D. SPENCE NATIONAL DEFENSE AUTHORIZATION ACT FOR FISCAL YEAR 2001.—The Floyd D. Spence National Defense Authorization Act for Fiscal Year 2001 (Public Law 106–398) is amended by striking section 1062 (44 U.S.C. 3531 note).

(c) PAPERWORK REDUCTION ACT.—(1) Section 3504(g) of title 44, United States Code, is amended—

(A) by adding "and" at the end of paragraph (1);

(B) in paragraph (2)—

(i) by striking "sections 11331 and 11332(b) and (c) of title 40" and inserting "section 11331 of title 40 and subchapter II of this chapter"; and

(ii) by striking "; and" and inserting a period; and

(C) by striking paragraph (3).

(2) Section 3505 of such title is amended by adding at the end—

"(c) INVENTORY OF MAJOR INFORMATION SYSTEMS.—(1) The head of each agency shall develop and maintain an inventory of major information systems (including major national security systems) operated by or under the control of such agency.

"(2) The identification of information systems in an inventory under this subsection shall include an identification of the interfaces between each such system and all other systems or networks, including those not operated by or under the control of the agency.

"(3) Such inventory shall be—

"(A) updated at least annually;

"(B) made available to the Comptroller General; and

"(C) used to support information resources management, including—

"(i) preparation and maintenance of the inventory of information resources under section 3506(b)(4);

"(ii) information technology planning, budgeting, acquisition, and management under section 3506(h), subtitle III of title 40, and related laws and guidance;

"(iii) monitoring, testing, and evaluation of information security controls under subchapter II;

"(iv) preparation of the index of major information systems required under section 552(g) of title 5, United States Code; and

"(v) preparation of information system inventories required for records management under chapters 21, 29, 31, and 33.

"(4) The Director shall issue guidance for and oversee the implementation of the requirements of this subsection."

(3) Section 3506(g) of such title is amended—

(A) by adding "and" at the end of paragraph (1);

(B) in paragraph (2)—

(i) by striking "section 11332 of title 40" and inserting "subchapter II of this chapter"; and

(ii) by striking "; and" and inserting a period; and

(C) by striking paragraph (3).

Appendix B

OMB Circular A-130: Appendix III

Security of Federal Automated Information Resources

A. Requirements.

1. Purpose
This Appendix establishes a minimum set of controls to be included in Federal automated information security programs; assigns Federal agency responsibilities for the security of automated information; and links agency automated information security programs and agency management control systems established in accordance with OMB Circular No. A-123. The Appendix revises procedures formerly contained in Appendix III to OMB Circular No. A-130 (50 FR 52730; December 24, 1985), and incorporates requirements of the Computer Security Act of 1987 (P.L. 100-235) and responsibilities assigned in applicable national security directives.

2. Definitions

The term:

a.   "adequate security" means security commensurate with the risk and magnitude of the harm resulting from the loss, misuse, or unauthorized access to or modification of information. This includes assuring that systems and applications used by the agency operate effectively and provide appropriate Confidentiality, Integrity, and Availability, through the use of cost-effective management, personnel, operational, and technical controls.

b.   "application" means the use of information resources (information and information technology) to satisfy a specific set of user requirements.

c.   "general support system" or "system" means an interconnected set of information resources under the same direct management control which shares common functionality. A system normally includes hardware, software, information, data, applications, communications, and people. A system can be, for example, a local area network (LAN) including smart terminals that supports a branch office, an agency-wide backbone, a communications network, a departmental data processing center including its operating system and utilities, a tactical radio network, or a shared information processing service organization (IPSO).

d.   "major application" means an application that requires special attention to security due to the risk and magnitude of the harm resulting from the loss, misuse, or unauthorized access to or modification of the information in the application. Note: All Federal applications require some level of protection. Certain applications, because of the information in them, however, require special management oversight and should be treated as major. Adequate security for other applications should be provided by security of the systems in which they operate.

3. Automated Information Security Programs. Agencies shall implement and maintain a program to assure that adequate security is provided for all agency information collected, processed, transmitted, stored, or disseminated in general support systems and

major applications.

Each agency's program shall implement policies, standards and procedures which are consistent with government-wide policies, standards, and procedures issued by the Office of Management and Budget, the Department of Commerce, the General Services Administration and the Office of Personnel Management (OPM). Different or more stringent requirements for securing national security information should be incorporated into agency programs as required by appropriate national security directives. At a minimum, agency programs shall include the following controls in their general support systems and major applications:

a. Controls for general support systems.

1) Assign Responsibility for Security. Assign responsibility for security in each system to an individual knowledgeable in the information technology used in the system and in providing security for such technology.

2) System Security Plan. Plan for adequate security of each general support system as part of the organization's information resources management (IRM) planning process. The security plan shall be consistent with guidance issued by the National Institute of Standards and Technology (NIST). Independent advice and comment on the security plan shall be solicited prior to the plan's implementation. A summary of the security plans shall be incorporated into the strategic IRM plan required by the Paperwork Reduction Act (44 U.S.C. Chapter 35) and Section 8(b) of this circular. Security plans shall include:

a) Rules of the System. Establish a set of rules of behavior concerning use of, security in, and the acceptable level of risk for, the system. The rules shall be based on the needs of the various users of the system. The security required by the rules shall be only as stringent as necessary to provide adequate security for information in the system. Such rules shall clearly delineate responsibilities and expected behavior of all individuals with access to the system. They shall also include appropriate limits on interconnections to other systems and shall define service provision and restoration priorities. Finally, they shall be clear about the consequences of behavior not consistent with the rules.

b) Training. Ensure that all individuals are appropriately trained in how to fulfill their security responsibilities before allowing them access to the system. Such training shall assure that employees are versed in the rules of the system, be consistent with guidance issued by NIST and OPM, and apprise them about available assistance and technical security products and techniques. Behavior consistent with the rules of the system and periodic refresher training shall be required for continued access to the system.

c) Personnel Controls. Screen individuals who are authorized to bypass significant technical and operational security controls of the system commensurate with the risk and magnitude of harm they could cause. Such screening shall occur prior to an individual being authorized to bypass controls and periodically thereafter.

d) Incident Response Capability. Ensure that there is a capability to provide help to users when a security incident occurs in the system and to share information concerning common vulnerabilities and threats. This capability shall share information with other organizations, consistent with NIST coordination, and should assist the agency in pursuing appropriate legal action, consistent with Department of Justice guidance.

e) Continuity of Support. Establish and periodically test the capability to continue providing service within a system based upon the needs and priorities of the participants of the system.

f) Technical Security. Ensure that cost-effective security products and techniques are appropriately used within the system.

g) System Interconnection. Obtain written management authorization, based upon the acceptance of risk to the system, prior to connecting with other systems. Where connection is authorized, controls shall be established which are consistent with the rules of the system and in accordance with guidance from NIST.

3) Review of Security Controls. Review the security controls in each system when significant modifications are made to the system, but at least every three years. The scope and frequency of the review should be commensurate with the acceptable level of risk for the system. Depending on the potential risk and magnitude of harm that could occur, consider identifying a deficiency pursuant to OMB Circular No. A-123, "Management Accountability and Control" and the Federal Managers' Financial Integrity Act (FMFIA), if there is no assignment of security responsibility, no security plan, or no authorization to process for a system.

4) Authorize Processing. Ensure that a management official authorizes in writing the use of each general support system based on implementation of its security plan before beginning or significantly changing processing in the system. Use of the system shall be re-authorized at least every three years.

b.   Controls for Major Applications.

1) Assign Responsibility for Security. Assign responsibility for security of each major application to a management official knowledgeable in the nature of the information and process supported by the application and in the management, personnel, operational, and technical controls used to protect it. This official

shall assure that effective security products and techniques are appropriately used in the application and shall be contacted when a security incident occurs concerning the application.

2) Application Security Plan. Plan for the adequate security of each major application, taking into account the security of all systems in which the application will operate. The plan shall be consistent with guidance issued by NIST. Advice and comment on the plan shall be solicited from the official responsible for security in the primary system in which the application will operate prior to the plan's implementation. A summary of the security plans shall be incorporated into the strategic IRM plan required by the Paperwork Reduction Act. Application security plans shall include:

> a) Application Rules. Establish a set of rules concerning use of and behavior within the application. The rules shall be as stringent as necessary to provide adequate security for the application and the information in it. Such rules shall clearly delineate responsibilities and expected behavior of all individuals with access to the application. In addition, the rules shall be clear about the consequences of behavior not consistent with the rules.

> b) Specialized Training. Before allowing individuals access to the application, ensure that all individuals receive specialized training focused on their responsibilities and the application rules. This may be in addition to the training required for access to a system. Such training may vary from a notification at the time of access (e.g., for members of the public using an information retrieval application) to formal training (e.g., for an employee that works with a high-risk application).

> c) Personnel Security. Incorporate controls such as separation of duties, least privilege and individual accountability into the application and application rules as appropriate. In cases where such controls cannot adequately protect the application or information in it, screen individuals commensurate with the risk and magnitude of the harm they could cause. Such screening shall be done prior to the individuals' being authorized to access the application and periodically thereafter.

> d) Contingency Planning. Establish and periodically test the capability to perform the agency function supported by the application in the event of failure of its automated support.

> e) Technical Controls. Ensure that appropriate security controls are specified, designed into, tested, and accepted in the application in accordance with appropriate guidance issued by NIST.

> f) Information Sharing. Ensure that information shared from the

application is protected appropriately, comparable to the protection provided when information is within the application.

g) Public Access Controls. Where an agency's application promotes or permits public access, additional security controls shall be added to protect the Integrity of the application and the confidence the public has in the application. Such controls shall include segregating information made directly accessible to the public from official agency records.

3) Review of Application Controls. Perform an independent review or audit of the security controls in each application at least every three years. Consider identifying a deficiency pursuant to OMB Circular No. A-123, "Management Accountability and Control" and the Federal Managers' Financial Integrity Act if there is no assignment of responsibility for security, no security plan, or no authorization to process for the application.

4) Authorize Processing. Ensure that a management official authorizes in writing use of the application by confirming that its security plan as implemented adequately secures the application. Results of the most recent review or audit of controls shall be a factor in management authorizations. The application must be authorized prior to operating and re-authorized at least every three years thereafter. Management authorization implies accepting the risk of each system used by the application.

4. Assignment of Responsibilities

a.   Department of Commerce. The Secretary of Commerce shall:

1) Develop and issue appropriate standards and guidance for the security of sensitive information in Federal computer systems.

2) Review and update guidelines for training in computer security awareness and accepted computer security practice, with assistance from OPM.

3) Provide agencies guidance for security planning to assist in their development of application and system security plans.

4) Provide guidance and assistance, as appropriate, to agencies concerning cost-effective controls when interconnecting with other systems.

5) Coordinate agency incident response activities to promote sharing of incident response information and related vulnerabilities.

6) Evaluate new information technologies to assess their security vulnerabilities, with technical assistance from the Department of Defense, and apprise Federal agencies of such vulnerabilities as soon as they are known.

b. Department of Defense. The Secretary of Defense shall:

1) Provide appropriate technical advice and assistance (including work products) to the Department of Commerce.

2) Assist the Department of Commerce in evaluating the vulnerabilities of emerging information technologies.

c. Department of Justice. The Attorney General shall:

1) Provide appropriate guidance to agencies on legal remedies regarding security incidents and ways to report and work with law enforcement concerning such incidents.

2) Pursue appropriate legal actions when security incidents occur.

d. General Services Administration. The Administrator of General Services shall:

1) Provide guidance to agencies on addressing security considerations when acquiring automated data processing equipment (as defined in section 111(a)(2) of the Federal Property and Administrative Services Act of 1949, as amended).

2) Facilitate the development of contract vehicles for agencies to use in the acquisition of cost-effective security products and services (e.g., back-up services).

3) Provide appropriate security services to meet the needs of Federal agencies to the extent that such services are cost-effective.

e. Office of Personnel Management. The Director of the Office of Personnel Management shall:

1) Assure that its regulations concerning computer security training for Federal civilian employees are effective.

2) Assist the Department of Commerce in updating and maintaining guidelines for training in computer security awareness and accepted computer security practice.

f. Security Policy Board. The Security Policy Board shall coordinate the activities of the Federal government regarding the security of information technology that processes classified information in accordance with applicable national security directives;

5. Correction of Deficiencies and Reports

a.   Correction of Deficiencies. Agencies shall correct deficiencies which are identified through the reviews of security for systems and major applications described above.

b.   Reports on Deficiencies. In accordance with OMB Circular No. A-123, "Management Accountability and Control", if a deficiency in controls is judged by the agency head to be material when weighed against other agency deficiencies, it shall be included in the annual FMFIA report. Less significant deficiencies shall be reported and progress on corrective actions tracked at the appropriate agency level.

c.   Summaries of Security Plans. Agencies shall include a summary of their system security plans and major application plans in the strategic plan required by the Paperwork Reduction Act (44 U.S.C. 3506).

B. Descriptive Information.

The following descriptive language is explanatory. It is included to assist in understanding the requirements of the Appendix.

The Appendix re-orients the Federal computer security program to better respond to a rapidly changing technological environment. It establishes government-wide responsibilities for Federal computer security and requires Federal agencies to adopt a minimum set of management controls. These management controls are directed at individual information technology users in order to reflect the distributed nature of today's technology.

For security to be most effective, the controls must be part of day-to-day operations. This is best accomplished by planning for security not as a separate activity, but as an integral part of overall planning.

"Adequate security" is defined as "security commensurate with the risk and magnitude of harm resulting from the loss, misuse, or unauthorized access to or modification of information." This definition explicitly emphasizes the risk-based policy for cost-effective security established by the Computer Security Act.

The Appendix no longer requires the preparation of formal risk analyses. In the past, substantial resources have been expended doing complex analyses of specific risks to systems, with limited tangible benefit in terms of improved security for the systems. Rather than continue to try to precisely measure risk, security efforts are better served by generally assessing risks and taking actions to manage them. While formal risk analyses need not be performed, the need to determine adequate security will require that a risk-based approach be used. This risk assessment approach should include a consideration of the major factors in risk management: the value of the system or application, threats, vulnerabilities, and the effectiveness of current or proposed safeguards. Additional guidance on effective risk assessment is available in "An Introduction to Computer Security: The NIST Handbook" (March 16, 1995).

Discussion of the Appendix's Major Provisions. The following discussion is provided to aid reviewers in understanding the changes in emphasis in the Appendix.

Automated Information Security Programs. Agencies are required to establish controls to assure adequate security for all information processed, transmitted, or stored in Federal automated information systems. This Appendix emphasizes management controls affecting individual users of information technology. Technical and operational controls support management controls. To be effective, all must interrelate. For example, authentication of individual users is an important management control, for which password protection is a technical control. However, password protection will only be effective if both a strong technology is employed, and it is managed to assure that it is used correctly. Four controls are set forth: assigning responsibility for security, security planning, periodic review of security controls, and management authorization. The Appendix requires that these management controls be applied in two areas of management responsibility: one for general support systems and one for major applications.

The terms "general support system" and "major application" were used in OMB Bulletins Nos. 88-16 and 90-08. A general support system is "an interconnected set of information resources under the same direct management control which shares common functionality." Such a system can be, for example, a local area network (LAN) including smart terminals that supports a branch office, an agency-wide backbone, a communications network, a departmental data processing enter including its operating system and utilities, a tactical radio network, or a shared information processing service organization. Normally, the purpose of a general support system is to provide processing or communications support.

A major application is a use of information and information technology to satisfy a specific set of user requirements that requires special management attention to security due to the risk and magnitude of harm resulting from the loss, misuse or unauthorized access to or modification of the information in the application. All applications require some level of security, and adequate security for most of them should be provided by security of the general support systems in which they operate. However, certain applications, because of the nature of the information in them, require special management oversight and should be treated as major. Agencies are expected to exercise management judgement in determining which of their applications are major.

The focus of OMB Bulletins Nos. 88-16 and 90-08 was on identifying and securing both general support systems and applications which contained sensitive information. The Appendix requires the establishment of security controls in all general support systems, under the presumption that all contain some sensitive information, and focuses extra security controls on a limited number of particularly high-risk or major applications.

    a.   General Support Systems. The following controls are required in all general support systems:

        1) Assign Responsibility for Security. For each system, an individual should be a focal point for assuring there is adequate security within the system, including ways to prevent, detect, and recover from security problems. That responsibility

should be assigned in writing to an individual trained in the technology used in the system and in providing security for such technology, including the management of security controls such as user identification and authentication.

2) Security Plan. The Computer Security Act requires that security plans be developed for all Federal computer systems that contain sensitive information. Given the expansion of distributed processing since passage of the Act, the presumption in the Appendix is that all general support systems contain some sensitive information which requires protection to assure its Integrity, Availability, or Confidentiality, and therefore all systems require security plans.

Previous guidance on security planning was contained in OMB Bulletin No. 90-08. This Appendix supersedes OMB Bulletin 90-08 and expands the coverage of security plans from Bulletin 90-08 to include rules of individual behavior as well as technical security. Consistent with OMB Bulletin 90-08, the Appendix directs NIST to update and expand security planning guidance and issue it as a Federal Information Processing Standard (FIPS). In the interim, agencies should continue to use the Appendix of OMB Bulletin No. 90-08 as guidance for the technical portion of their security plans.

The Appendix continues the requirement that independent advice and comment on the security plan for each system be sought. The intent of this requirement is to improve the plans, foster communication between managers of different systems, and promote the sharing of security expertise.

This Appendix also continues the requirement from the Computer Security Act that summaries of security plans be included in agency strategic information resources management plans. OMB will provide additional guidance about the contents of those strategic plans, pursuant to the Paperwork Reduction Act of 1995.
The following specific security controls should be included in the security plan for a general support system:

a)   Rules. An important new requirement for security plans is the establishment of a set of rules of behavior for individual users of each general support system. These rules should clearly delineate responsibilities of and expectations for all individuals with access to the system. They should be consistent with system-specific policy as described in "An Introduction to Computer Security: The NIST Handbook" (March 16, 1995). In addition, they should state the consequences of non-compliance. The rules should be in writing and will form the basis for security awareness and training.

The development of rules for a system must take into consideration the needs of all parties who use the system. Rules should be as stringent as necessary to provide adequate security. Therefore, the acceptable level of risk for the system must be established and should form the basis for determining the rules.

Rules should cover such matters as work at home, dial-in access, connection to the Internet, use of copyrighted works, unofficial use of government equipment, the assignment and limitation of system privileges, and individual accountability. Often rules should reflect technical security controls in the system. For example, rules regarding password use should be consistent with technical password features in the system. Rules may be enforced through administrative sanctions specifically related to the system (e.g. loss of system privileges) or through more general sanctions as are imposed for violating other rules of conduct. In addition, the rules should specifically address restoration of service as a concern of all users of the system.

b) Training. The Computer Security Act requires Federal agencies to provide for the mandatory periodic training in computer security awareness and accepted computer security practice of all employees who are involved with the management, use or operation of a Federal computer system within or under the supervision of the Federal agency. This includes contractors as well as employees of the agency. Access provided to members of the public should be constrained by controls in the applications through which access is allowed, and training should be within the context of those controls. The Appendix enforces such mandatory training by requiring its completion prior to granting access to the system. Each new user of a general support system in some sense introduces a risk to all other users. Therefore, each user should be versed in acceptable behavior — the rules of the system — before being allowed to use the system. Training should also inform the individual how to get help in the event of difficulty with using or security of the system.

Training should be tailored to what a user needs to know to use the system securely, given the nature of that use. Training may be presented in stages, for example as more access is granted. In some cases, the training should be in the form of classroom instruction. In other cases, interactive computer sessions or well-written and understandable brochures may be sufficient, depending on the risk and magnitude of harm.

Over time, attention to security tends to dissipate. In addition, changes to a system may necessitate a change in the rules or user procedures. Therefore, individuals should periodically have refresher training to assure that they continue to understand and abide by the applicable rules.

To assist agencies, the Appendix requires NIST, with assistance from the Office of Personnel Management (OPM), to update its existing guidance. It also proposes that OPM assure that its rules for computer security training for Federal civilian employees are effective.

c) Personnel Controls. It has long been recognized that the greatest harm has come from authorized individuals engaged in improper activities, whether intentional or accidental. In every general support system, a number of technical, operational, and management controls are used to prevent and detect harm. Such controls include individual accountability, "least privilege," and separation of duties.

Individual accountability consists of holding someone responsible for his or her actions. In a general support system, accountability is normally accomplished by identifying and authenticating users of the system and subsequently tracing actions on the system to the user who initiated them. This may be done, for example, by looking for patterns of behavior by users.

Least privilege is the practice of restricting a user's access (to data files, to processing capability, or to peripherals) or type of access (read, write, execute, delete) to the minimum necessary to perform his or her job.

Separation of duties is the practice of dividing the steps in a critical function among different individuals. For example, one system programmer can create a critical piece of operating system code, while another authorizes its implementation. Such a control keeps a single individual from subverting a critical process.

Nevertheless, in some instances, individuals may be given the ability to bypass some significant technical and operational controls in order to perform system administration and maintenance functions (e.g., LAN administrators or systems programmers). Screening such individuals in positions of trust will supplement technical, operational, and management controls, particularly where the risk and magnitude of harm is high.

d) Incident Response Capability. Security incidents, whether caused by viruses, hackers, or software bugs, are becoming more common. When faced with a security incident, an agency should be able to respond in a manner that both protects its own information and helps to protect the information of others who might be affected by the incident. To address this concern, agencies should establish formal incident response mechanisms. Awareness and training for individuals with access to the system should include how to use the system's incident response capability.

To be fully effective, incident handling must also include sharing information concerning common vulnerabilities and threats with those in other systems and other agencies. The Appendix directs agencies to effectuate such sharing, and tasks NIST to coordinate those agency activities government-wide.

The Appendix also directs the Department of Justice to provide appropriate guidance on pursuing legal remedies in the case of serious incidents.

e) Continuity of Support. Inevitably, there will be service interruptions. Agency plans should assure that there is an ability to recover and provide service sufficient to meet the minimal needs of users of the system. Manual procedures are generally NOT a viable back-up option. When automated support is not available, many functions of the organization will effectively cease. Therefore, it is important to take cost-effective steps to manage any disruption of service.

Decisions on the level of service needed at any particular time and on priorities in service restoration should be made in consultation with the users of the system and incorporated in the system rules. Experience has shown that recovery plans that are periodically tested are substantially more viable than those that are not. Moreover, untested plans may actually create a false sense of security.

f) Technical Security. Agencies should assure that each system appropriately uses effective security products and techniques, consistent with standards and guidance from NIST. Often such techniques will correspond with system rules of behavior, such as in the proper use of password protection.

The Appendix directs NIST to continue to issue computer security guidance to assist agencies in planning for and using technical security products and techniques. Until such guidance is issued, however, the planning guidance included in OMB Bulletin 90-08 can assist in determining techniques for effective security in a system and in addressing technical controls in the security plan.

g) System Interconnection. In order for a community to effectively manage risk, it must control access to and from other systems. The degree of such control should be established in the rules of the system and all participants should be made aware of any limitations on outside access. Technical controls to accomplish this should be put in place in accordance with guidance issued by NIST.

There are varying degrees of how connected a system is. For example, some systems will choose to isolate themselves, others will restrict access such as allowing only e-mail connections or remote access only with sophisticated authentication, and others will be fully open. The management decision to interconnect should be based on the Availability and use of technical and non-technical safeguards and consistent with the acceptable level of risk defined in the system rules.

3) Review of Security Controls. The security of a system will degrade over time, as the technology evolves and as people and procedures change. Reviews should assure that management, operational, personnel, and technical controls are functioning effectively. Security controls may be reviewed by an independent audit or a self review. The type and rigor of review or audit should be commensurate with the acceptable level of risk that is established in the rules for the system and the likelihood of learning useful information to improve security. Technical tools such as virus scanners, vulnerability assessment products (which look for known security problems, configuration errors, and the installation of the latest patches), and penetration testing can assist in the on-going review of different facets of systems. However, these tools are no substitute for a formal management review at least every three years. Indeed, for some high-risk systems with rapidly changing technology, three years will be too long.

Depending upon the risk and magnitude of harm that could result, weaknesses identified during the review of security controls should be reported as deficiencies in accordance with OMB Circular No. A-123, "Management Accountability and Control" and the Federal Managers' Financial Integrity Act. In particular, if a basic management control such as assignment of responsibility, a workable security plan, or management authorization are missing, then consideration should be given to identifying a deficiency.

4) Authorize Processing. The authorization of a system to process information, granted by a management official, provides an important quality control (some agencies refer to this authorization as accreditation). By authorizing processing in a system, a manager accepts the risk associated with it. Authorization is not a decision that should be made by the security staff.

Both the security official and the authorizing management official have security responsibilities. In general, the security official is closer to the day-to-day operation of the system and will direct or perform security tasks. The authorizing official will normally have general responsibility for the organization supported by the system. Management authorization should be based on an assessment of management, operational, and technical controls. Since the security plan establishes the security controls, it should form the basis for the authorization, supplemented by more specific studies as needed. In addition, the periodic review of controls should also contribute to future authorizations. Some agencies perform "certification reviews" of their systems periodically. These formal technical evaluations lead to a management accreditation, or "authorization to process." Such certifications (such as those using the methodology in FIPS Pub 102 "Guideline for Computer Security Certification and Accreditation") can provide useful information to assist management in authorizing a system, particularly when combined with a review of the broad behavioral controls envisioned in the security plan required by the Appendix.

Re-authorization should occur prior to a significant change in processing, but at least every three years. It should be done more often where there is a high risk and potential magnitude of harm.

> b.   Controls in Major Applications. Certain applications require special management attention due to the risk and magnitude of harm that could occur. For such applications, the controls of the support system(s) in which they operate are likely to be insufficient. Therefore, additional controls specific to the application are required. Since the function of applications is the direct manipulation and use of information, controls for securing applications should emphasize protection of information and the way it is manipulated.

1) Assign Responsibility for Security. By definition, major applications are high risk and require special management attention. Major applications usually support a single agency function and often are supported by more than one general support system. It is important, therefore, that an individual be assigned responsibility in writing to assure that the particular application has adequate security. To be effective, this individual should be knowledgeable in the information and process supported by the application and in the management, personnel, operational, and technical controls used to protect the application.

2) Application Security Plans. Security for each major application should be addressed by a security plan specific to the application. The plan should include controls specific to protecting information and should be developed from the application manager's perspective. To assist in assuring its viability, the plan should be provided to the manager of the primary support system which the application uses for advice and comment. This recognizes the critical dependence of the security of major applications on the underlying support systems they use. Summaries of application security plans should be included in strategic information resource management plans in accordance with this Circular.

> a) Application Rules. Rules of behavior should be established which delineate the responsibilities and expected behavior of all individuals with access to the application. The rules should state the consequences of inconsistent behavior. Often the rules will be associated with technical controls implemented in the application. Such rules should include, for example, limitations on changing data, searching databases, or divulging information.

> b) Specialized Training. Training is required for all individuals given access to the application, including members of the public. It should vary depending on the type of access

allowed and the risk that access represents to the security of the application and information in it. This training will be in addition to that required for access to a support system.

c) Personnel Security. For most major applications, management controls such as individual accountability requirements, separation of duties enforced by access controls, or limitations on the processing privileges of individuals, are generally more cost-effective personnel security controls than background screening. Such controls should be implemented as both technical controls and as application rules. For example, technical controls to ensure individual accountability, such as looking for patterns of user behavior, are most effective if users are aware that there is such a technical control. If adequate audit or access controls (through both technical and non-technical methods) cannot be established, then it may be cost-effective to screen personnel, commensurate with the risk and magnitude of harm they could cause. The change in emphasis on screening in the Appendix should not affect background screening deemed necessary because of other duties that an individual may perform.

d) Contingency Planning. Normally the Federal mission supported by a major application is critically dependent on the application. Manual processing is generally NOT a viable back-up option. Managers should plan for how they will perform their mission and/or recover from the loss of existing application support, whether the loss is due to the inability of the application to function or a general support system failure. Experience has demonstrated that testing a contingency plan significantly improves its viability. Indeed, untested plans or plans not tested for a long period of time may create a false sense of ability to recover in a timely manner.

e) Technical Controls. Technical security controls, for example tests to filter invalid entries, should be built into each application. Often these controls will correspond with the rules of behavior for the application. Under the previous Appendix, application security was focused on the process by which sensitive, custom applications were developed. While that process is not addressed in detail in this Appendix, it remains an effective method for assuring that security controls are built into applications. Additionally, the technical security controls defined in OMB Bulletin No. 90-08 will continue, until that guidance is replaced by NIST's security planning guidance.

f) Information Sharing. Assure that information which is shared with Federal organizations, State and local governments, and the private sector is appropriately protected comparable to the protection provided when the information is within the application. Controls on the information may stay the same or vary when the information is shared with another entity. For example, the primary user of the information may require a high level of Availability while the secondary user does not, and can therefore relax some of the controls designed to maintain the Availability of the information. At the same time, however, the information shared may require a level of Confidentiality that should be extended to the secondary user. This normally requires notification and agreement to protect the information prior to its being shared.

g) Public Access Controls. Permitting public access to a Federal application is an important method of improving information exchange with the public. At the same time, it introduces risks to the Federal application. To mitigate these risks, additional controls should be in place as appropriate. These controls are in addition to controls such as "firewalls" that are put in place for security of the general support system.

In general, it is more difficult to apply conventional controls to public access systems, because many of the users of the system may not be subject to individual accountability policies. In addition, public access systems may be a target for mischief because of their higher visibility and published access methods.

Official records need to be protected against loss or alteration. Official records in electronic form are particularly susceptible since they can be relatively easy to change or destroy. Therefore, official records should be segregated from information made directly accessible to the public. There are different ways to segregate records. Some agencies and organizations are creating dedicated information dissemination systems (such as bulletin boards or World Wide Web servers) to support this function. These systems can be on the outside of secure gateways which protect internal agency records from outside access.

In order to secure applications that allow direct public access, conventional techniques such as least privilege (limiting the processing capability as well as access to data) and Integrity assurances (such as checking for viruses, clearly labeling the age of data, or periodically spot checking data) should also be used. Additional guidance on securing public access systems is available from NIST Computer Systems Laboratory Bulletin "Security Issues in Public Access Systems" (May, 1993).

3) Review of Application Controls. At least every three years, an independent review or audit of the security controls for each major application should be performed. Because of the higher risk involved in major applications, the review or audit should be independent of the manager responsible for the application. Such reviews should verify that responsibility for the security of the application has been assigned, that a viable security plan for the application is in place, and that a manager has authorized the processing of the application. A deficiency in any of these controls should be considered a deficiency pursuant to the Federal Manager's Financial Integrity Act and OMB Circular No. A-123, "Management Accountability and Control."

The review envisioned here is different from the system test and certification process required in the current Appendix. That process, however, remains useful for assuring that technical security features are built into custom-developed software applications. While the controls in that process are not specifically called for in this Appendix, they remain in Bulletin No. 90-08, and are recommended in appropriate circumstances as technical controls.

4) Authorize Processing. A major application should be authorized by the management official responsible for the function supported by the application at least every three years, but more often where the risk and magnitude of harm is high. The intent of this requirement is to assure that the senior official whose mission will be adversely affected

by security weaknesses in the application periodically assesses and accepts the risk of operating the application. The authorization should be based on the application security plan and any review(s) performed on the application. It should also take into account the risks from the general support systems used by the application.

4. Assignment of Responsibilities. The Appendix assigns government-wide responsibilities to agencies that are consistent with their missions and the Computer Security Act.

a.   Department of Commerce. The Department of Commerce, through NIST, is assigned the following responsibilities consistent with the Computer Security Act.

1) Develop and issue security standards and guidance.

2) Review and update, with assistance from OPM, the guidelines for security training issued in 1988 pursuant to the Computer Security Act to assure they are effective.

3) Replace and update the technical planning guidance in the appendix to OMB Bulletin 90-08 This should include guidance on effective risk-based security absent a formal risk analysis.

4) Provide agencies with guidance and assistance concerning effective controls for systems when interconnecting with other systems, including the Internet. Such guidance on, for example, so-called "firewalls" is becoming widely available and is critical to agencies as they consider how to interconnect their communications capabilities.

5) Coordinate agency incident response activities. Coordination of agency incident response activities should address both threats and vulnerabilities as well as improve the ability of the Federal government for rapid and effective cooperation in response to serious security breaches.

6) Assess security vulnerabilities in new information technologies and apprise Federal agencies of such vulnerabilities. The intent of this new requirement is to help agencies understand the security implications of technology before they purchase and field it. In the past, there have been too many instances where agencies have acquired and implemented technology, then found out about vulnerabilities in the technology and had to retrofit security measures. This activity is intended to help avoid such difficulties in the future.

b.   Department of Defense. The Department, through the National Security Agency, should provide technical advice and assistance to NIST, including work products such as technical security guidelines, which NIST can draw upon for developing standards and guidelines for protecting sensitive information in Federal computers.

Also, the Department, through the National Security Agency, should assist NIST in evaluating vulnerabilities in emerging technologies. Such vulnerabilities may present a risk to national security information as well as to unclassified information.

c.   Department of Justice. The Department of Justice should provide appropriate guidance to Federal agencies on legal remedies available to them when serious security incidents occur. Such guidance should include ways to report incidents and cooperate with law enforcement.

In addition, the Department should pursue appropriate legal actions on behalf of the Federal government when serious security incidents occur.

d.   General Services Administration. The General Services Administration should provide agencies guidance for addressing security considerations when acquiring information technology products or services. This continues the current requirement.

In addition, where cost-effective to do so, GSA should establish government-wide contract vehicles for agencies to use to acquire certain security services. Such vehicles already exist for providing system back-up support and conducting security analyses. GSA should also provide appropriate security services to assist Federal agencies to the extent that provision of such services is cost-effective. This includes providing, in conjunction with the Department of Defense and the Department of Commerce, appropriate services which support Federal use of the National Information Infrastructure (e.g., use of digital signature technology).

e.   Office of Personnel Management. In accordance with the Computer Security Act, OPM should review its regulations concerning computer security training and assure that they are effective.

In addition, OPM should assist the Department of Commerce in the review and update of its computer security awareness and training guidelines. OPM worked closely with NIST in developing the current guidelines and should work with NIST in revising those guidelines.

f.   Security Policy Board. The Security Policy Board is assigned responsibility for national security policy coordination in accordance with the appropriate Presidential directive. This includes policy for the security of information technology used to process classified information.

Circular A-130 and this Appendix do not apply to information technology that supports certain critical national security missions, as defined in 44 U.S.C. 3502(9) and 10 U.S.C. 2315. Policy and procedural requirements for the security of national security systems (telecommunications and information systems that contain classified information or that support those critical national security missions (44 U.S.C. 3502(9) and 10 U.S.C. 2315)) is assigned to the Department of Defense pursuant to Presidential directive. The Circular clarifies that information classified for national security purposes should also be handled in accordance with appropriate national security directives. Where classified information is required to be protected by more stringent security requirements, those requirements should be followed rather than the requirements of this Appendix.

5. Reports. The Appendix requires agencies to provide two reports to OMB:

The first is a requirement that agencies report security deficiencies and material weaknesses within their FMFIA reporting mechanisms as defined by OMB Circular No. A-

123, "Management Accountability and Control," and take corrective actions in accordance with that directive.

The second, defined by the Computer Security Act, requires that a summary of agency security plans be included in the information resources management plan required by the Paperwork Reduction Act.

Appendix C

FIPS 199

FIPS PUB 199

FEDERAL INFORMATION PROCESSING STANDARDS PUBLICATION

Standards for Security Categorization of Federal Information and Information Systems

Computer Security Division
Information Technology Laboratory
National Institute of Standards and Technology
Gaithersburg, MD 20899–8900

February 2004

U.S. DEPARTMENT OF COMMERCE
Donald L. Evans, Secretary

TECHNOLOGY ADMINISTRATION
Phillip J. Bond, Under Secretary for Technology

NATIONAL INSTITUTE OF STANDARDS AND TECHNOLOGY
Arden L. Bement, Jr., Director

FOREWORD

The Federal Information Processing Standards Publication Series of the National Institute of Standards and Technology (NIST) is the official series of publications relating to standards and guidelines adopted and promulgated under the provisions of Section 5131 of the Information Technology Management Reform Act of 1996 (Public Law 104-106) and the Federal Information Security Management Act of 2002 (Public Law 107-347). These mandates have given the Secretary of Commerce and NIST important responsibilities for improving the utilization and management of computer and related telecommunications systems in the federal government. The NIST, through its Information Technology Laboratory, provides leadership, technical guidance, and coordination of government efforts in the development of standards and guidelines in these areas.

Comments concerning Federal Information Processing Standards Publications are welcomed and should be addressed to the Director, Information Technology Laboratory, National Institute of Standards and Technology, 100 Bureau Drive, Stop 8900, Gaithersburg, MD 20899-8900.

— SUSAN ZEVIN, ACTING DIRECTOR

INFORMATION TECHNOLOGY LABORATORY ii

AUTHORITY

Federal Information Processing Standards Publications (FIPS PUBS) are issued by the National Institute of Standards and Technology (NIST) after approval by the Secretary of Commerce pursuant to Section 5131 of the Information Technology Management Reform Act of 1996 (Public Law 104-106) and the Federal Information Security Management Act of 2002 (Public Law 107-347).

TABLE OF CONTENTS

1 PURPOSE

The E-Government Act of 2002 (Public Law 107-347), passed by the one hundred and seventh Congress and signed into law by the President in December 2002, recognized the importance of information security to the economic and national security interests of the United States. Title III of the E-Government Act, entitled the Federal Information Security Management Act of 2002 (FISMA), tasked NIST with responsibilities for standards and guidelines, including the development of:

Standards to be used by all federal agencies to categorize all information and information systems collected or maintained by or on behalf of each agency based on the objectives of providing appropriate levels of information security according to a range of risk levels;

Guidelines recommending the types of information and information systems to be included in each category; and

Minimum information security requirements (i.e., management, operational, and technical controls), for information and information systems in each such category.

FIPS Publication 199 addresses the first task cited—to develop standards for categorizing information and information systems. Security categorization standards for information and information systems provide a common framework and understanding for expressing security that, for the federal government, promotes: (i) effective management and oversight of information security programs, including the coordination of information security efforts throughout the civilian, national security, emergency preparedness, homeland security, and law enforcement communities; and (ii) consistent reporting to the Office of Management and Budget (OMB) and Congress on the adequacy and effectiveness of information security policies, procedures, and practices. Subsequent NIST standards and guidelines will address the second and third tasks cited.

2 APPLICABILITY

These standards shall apply to: (i) all information within the federal government other than that information that has been determined pursuant to Executive Order 12958, as amended by Executive Order 13292, or any predecessor order, or by the Atomic Energy Act of 1954, as amended, to require protection against unauthorized disclosure and is marked to indicate its classified status; and (ii) all federal information systems other than those information systems designated as national security systems as defined in 44 United States Code Section 3542(b)(2). Agency officials shall use the security categorizations described in FIPS Publication 199 whenever there is a federal requirement to provide such a categorization of information or information systems. Additional security designators may be developed and used at agency discretion. State, local, and tribal governments as well as private sector organizations comprising the critical infrastructure of the United States may consider the use of these standards as appropriate. These standards are effective upon approval by the Secretary of Commerce.

3 CATEGORIZATION OF INFORMATION AND INFORMATION SYSTEMS

This publication establishes security categories for both information[1] and information systems. The security categories are based on the potential impact on an organization should certain events occur which jeopardize the information and information systems needed by the organization to accomplish its assigned mission, protect its assets, fulfill its legal responsibilities, maintain its day-to-day functions, and protect individuals. Security categories are to be used in conjunction with vulnerability and threat information in assessing the risk to an organization.

[1] Information is categorized according to its *information type*. An information type is a specific category of information (e.g., privacy, medical, proprietary, financial, investigative, contractor sensitive, security management) defined by an organization or, in some instances, by a specific law, Executive Order, directive, policy, or regulation.

Security Objectives

The FISMA defines three security objectives for information and information systems:

CONFIDENTIALITY

"Preserving authorized restrictions on information access and disclosure, including means for protecting personal privacy and proprietary information…" [44 U.S.C., Sec. 3542] A loss of *Confidentiality* is the unauthorized disclosure of information.

INTEGRITY

"Guarding against improper information modification or destruction, and includes ensuring information non-repudiation and authenticity…" [44 U.S.C., Sec. 3542] A loss of *Integrity* is the unauthorized modification or destruction of information.

AVAILABILITY

"Ensuring timely and reliable access to and use of information…" [44 U.S.C., SEC. 3542] A loss of *Availability* is the disruption of access to or use of information or an information system.

Potential Impact on Organizations and Individuals

FIPS Publication 199 defines three levels of *potential impact* on organizations or individuals should there be a breach of security (i.e., a loss of Confidentiality, Integrity, or Availability). The application of these definitions must take place within the context of each organization and the overall national interest.

The *potential impact* is **LOW** if—

– The loss of Confidentiality, Integrity, or Availability could be expected to have a **limited** adverse effect on organizational operations, organizational assets, or individuals.[2]

AMPLIFICATION: A limited adverse effect means that, for example, the loss of Confidentiality, Integrity, or Availability might: (i) cause a degradation in mission capability to an extent and duration that the organization is able to perform its primary functions, but the effectiveness of the functions is noticeably reduced; (ii) result in minor damage to organizational assets; (iii) result in minor financial loss; or (iv) result in minor harm to individuals.

The *potential impact* is **MODERATE** if—

– The loss of Confidentiality, Integrity, or Availability could be expected to have a **serious** adverse effect on organizational operations, organizational assets, or individuals.

AMPLIFICATION: A serious adverse effect means that, for example, the loss of Confidentiality, Integrity, or Availability might: (i) cause a significant degradation in mission capability to an extent and duration that the organization is able to perform its primary functions, but the effectiveness of the functions is significantly reduced; (ii) result in significant damage to organizational assets; (iii) result in significant financial loss; or (iv) result in significant harm to individuals that does not involve loss of life or serious life threatening injuries.

[2] Adverse effects on individuals may include, but are not limited to, loss of the privacy to which individuals are entitled under law.

The *potential impact* is **HIGH** if—

– The loss of Confidentiality, Integrity, or Availability could be expected to have a **severe or catastrophic** adverse effect on organizational operations, organizational assets, or individuals.

AMPLIFICATION: A severe or catastrophic adverse effect means that, for example, the loss of Confidentiality, Integrity, or Availability might: (i) cause a severe degradation in or loss of mission capability to an extent and duration that the organization is not able to perform one or more of its primary functions; (ii) result in major damage to organizational assets; (iii) result in major financial loss; or (iv) result in severe or catastrophic harm to individuals involving loss of life or serious life threatening injuries.

Security Categorization Applied to Information Types

The security category of an information type can be associated with both user information and system information[3] and can be applicable to information in either electronic or non-electronic form. It can also be used as input in considering the appropriate security category of an information system (see description of security categories for information systems below). Establishing an appropriate security category of an information type essentially requires determining the *potential impact* for each security objective associated with the particular information type.

The generalized format for expressing the security category, SC, of an information type is:

SC information type = {(**Confidentiality**, *impact*), (**Integrity**, *impact*), (**Availability**, *impact*)},

where the acceptable values for potential impact are LOW, MODERATE, HIGH, or NOT APPLICABLE.[4]

EXAMPLE 1: An organization managing *public information* on its web server determines that there is no potential impact from a loss of Confidentiality (i.e., Confidentiality requirements are not applicable), a moderate potential impact from a loss of Integrity, and a moderate potential impact from a loss of Availability. The resulting security category, SC, of this information type is expressed as:

SC public information = {(**Confidentiality**, NA), (**Integrity**, MODERATE), (**Availability**, MODERATE)}.

EXAMPLE 2: A law enforcement organization managing extremely sensitive *investigative information* determines that the potential impact from a loss of Confidentiality is high, the potential impact from a loss of Integrity is moderate, and the potential impact from a loss of Availability is moderate. The resulting security category, SC, of this information type is expressed as:

SC investigative information = {(**Confidentiality**, HIGH), (**Integrity**, MODERATE), (**Availability**, MODERATE)}.

EXAMPLE 3: A financial organization managing routine *administrative information* (not privacy-related information) determines that the potential impact from a loss of Confidentiality is low, the potential impact from a loss of Integrity is low, and the potential impact from a loss of Availability is low. The resulting security category, SC, of this information type is expressed as:

SC administrative information = {(**Confidentiality**, LOW), (**Integrity**, LOW), (**Availability**, LOW)}.

3 System information (e.g., network routing tables, password files, and cryptographic key management information) must be protected at a level commensurate with the most critical or sensitive user information being processed, stored, or transmitted by the information system to ensure Confidentiality, Integrity, and Availability.
4 The potential impact value of *not applicable* only applies to the security objective of Confidentiality.

Security Categorization Applied to Information Systems

Determining the security category of an information system requires slightly more analysis and must consider the security categories of all information types resident on the information system. For an information system, the potential impact values assigned to the respective security objectives (Confidentiality, Integrity, Availability) shall be the highest values (i.e., high water mark) from among those security categories that have been determined for each type of information resident on the information system.[5]

The generalized format for expressing the security category, SC, of an information system is:

SC information system = {(**Confidentiality**, *impact*), (**Integrity**, *impact*), (**Availability**, *impact*)},

where the acceptable values for potential impact are LOW, MODERATE, or HIGH.

Note that the value of *not applicable* cannot be assigned to any security objective in the context of establishing a security category for an information system. This is in recognition that there is a low minimum potential impact (i.e., low water mark) on the loss of Confidentiality, Integrity, and Availability for an information system due to the fundamental requirement to protect the system-level processing functions and information critical to the operation of the information system.

EXAMPLE 4: An information system used for large acquisitions in a contracting organization contains both sensitive, pre-solicitation phase contract information and routine administrative information. The management within the contracting organization determines that: (i) for the sensitive contract information, the potential impact from a loss of Confidentiality is moderate, the potential impact from a loss of Integrity is moderate, and the potential impact from a loss of Availability is low; and (ii) for the routine administrative information (non-privacy-related information), the potential impact from a loss of Confidentiality is low, the potential impact from a loss of Integrity is low, and the potential impact from a loss of Availability is low. The resulting security categories, SC, of these information types are expressed as:

SC contract information = {(**Confidentiality**, MODERATE), (**Integrity**, MODERATE), (**Availability**, LOW)},

and

SC administrative information = {(**Confidentiality**, LOW), (**Integrity**, LOW), (**Availability**, LOW)}.

The resulting security category of the information system is expressed as:

SC acquisition system = {(**Confidentiality**, MODERATE), (**Integrity**, MODERATE), (**Availability**, LOW)},

representing the high water mark or maximum potential impact values for each security objective from the information types resident on the acquisition system.

[5] It is recognized that information systems are composed of both programs and information. Programs in execution within an information system (i.e., system processes) facilitate the processing, storage, and transmission of information and are necessary for the organization to conduct its essential mission-related functions and operations. These system processing functions also require protection and could be subject to security categorization as well. However, in the interest of simplification, it is assumed that the security categorization of all information types associated with the information system provide an appropriate *worst case* potential impact for the overall information system—thereby obviating the need to consider the system processes in the security

categorization of the information system.

EXAMPLE 5: A power plant contains a SCADA (supervisory control and data acquisition) system controlling the distribution of electric power for a large military installation. The SCADA system contains both real-time sensor data and routine administrative information. The management at the power plant determines that: (i) for the sensor data being acquired by the SCADA system, there is no potential impact from a loss of Confidentiality, a high potential impact from a loss of Integrity, and a high potential impact from a loss of Availability; and (ii) for the administrative information being processed by the system, there is a low potential impact from a loss of Confidentiality, a low potential impact from a loss of Integrity, and a low potential impact from a loss of Availability. The resulting security categories, SC, of these information types are expressed as:

SC sensor data = {(**Confidentiality**, NA), (**Integrity**, HIGH), (**Availability**, HIGH)},

and

SC administrative information = {(**Confidentiality**, LOW), (**Integrity**, LOW), (**Availability**, LOW)}.

The resulting security category of the information system is initially expressed as:

SC SCADA system = {(**Confidentiality**, LOW), (**Integrity**, HIGH), (**Availability**, HIGH)},

representing the high water mark or maximum potential impact values for each security objective from the information types resident on the SCADA system. The management at the power plant chooses to increase the potential impact from a loss of Confidentiality from low to moderate reflecting a more realistic view of the potential impact on the information system should there be a security breach due to the unauthorized disclosure of system-level information or processing functions. The final security category of the information system is expressed as:

SC SCADA system = {(**Confidentiality**, MODERATE), (**Integrity**, HIGH), (**Availability**, HIGH)}.

Table 1 summarizes the potential impact definitions for each security objective—Confidentiality, Integrity, and Availability.

POTENTIAL IMPACT

Security Objective	LOW	MODERATE	HIGH
Confidentiality Preserving authorized restrictions on information access and disclosure, including means for protecting personal privacy and proprietary information. [44 U.S.C., SEC 3542]	The unauthorized disclosure of information could be expected to have a **limited** adverse effect on organizational assets, or individuals.	The unauthorized disclosure of information could be expected to have a **serious** adverse affect on organizational operations, organizational assets, or individuals.	The unauthorized disclosure of information could be expected to have a **severe or catastrophic** adverse effect on organizational operations, organizational assets, or individuals.
Integrity Guarding against improper information modification or destruction, and includes erasing information non-repudiation and authenticity. [44 U.S.C., SEC 3542]	The unauthorized modification or destruction of information could be expected to have a **limited** adverse effect on organizational operations, organizational assets, or individuals.	The unauthorized modification or destruction of information could be expected to have a **serious** adverse effect on organizational operations, organizational assets, or individuals.	The unauthorized modification or destruction of information could be expected to have a **severe or catastrophic** adverse effect on organizational operations, organizational assets, or individuals.
Availability Ensuring timely and reliable access to and use of information. [44 U.S.C., SEC 3542]	The disruption of access to or use of information or an information system could be expected to have a **limited** adverse effect on organizational operations, organizational assets, or individuals.	The disruption of access to or use of information or an information system could be expected to have a **serious** adverse effect on organizational assets, or individuals.	The disruption of access to or use of information or an information system could be expected to have a **severe or catastrophic** adverse effect on organizational operations, organizational assets, or individuals.

APPENDIX A TERMS AND DEFINITIONS

AVAILABILITY: Ensuring timely and reliable access to and use of information. [44 U.S.C., SEC. 3542]

CONFIDENTIALITY: Preserving authorized restrictions on information access and disclosure, including means for protecting personal privacy and proprietary information. [44 U.S.C., SEC. 3542]

EXECUTIVE AGENCY: An executive department specified in 5 U.S.C., SEC. 101; a military department specified in 5 U.S.C., SEC. 102; an independent establishment as defined in 5 U.S.C., SEC. 104(1); and a wholly owned Government corporation fully subject to the provisions of 31 U.S.C., CHAPTER 91. [41 U.S.C., SEC. 403]

FEDERAL INFORMATION SYSTEM: An information system used or operated by an executive agency, by a contractor of an executive agency, or by another organization on behalf of an executive agency. [40 U.S.C., SEC. 11331]

INFORMATION: An instance of an information type.

INFORMATION RESOURCES: Information and related resources, such as personnel, equipment, funds, and information technology. [44 U.S.C., SEC. 3502]

INFORMATION SECURITY: The protection of information and information systems from unauthorized access, use, disclosure, disruption, modification, or destruction in order to provide Confidentiality, Integrity, and Availability. [44 U.S.C., SEC. 3542]

INFORMATION SYSTEM: A discrete set of information resources organized for the collection, processing, maintenance, use, sharing, dissemination, or disposition of information. [44 U.S.C., SEC. 3502]

INFORMATION TECHNOLOGY: Any equipment or interconnected system or subsystem of equipment that is used in the automatic acquisition, storage, manipulation, management, movement, control, display, switching, interchange, transmission, or reception of data or information by the executive agency. For purposes of the preceding sentence, equipment is used by an executive agency if the equipment is used by the executive agency directly or is used by a contractor under a contract with the executive agency which: (i) requires the use of such equipment; or (ii) requires the use, to a significant extent, of such equipment in the performance of a service or the furnishing of a product. The term information technology includes computers, ancillary equipment, software, firmware and similar procedures, services (including support services), and related resources. [40 U.S.C., SEC. 1401]

INFORMATION TYPE: A specific category of information (e.g., privacy, medical, proprietary, financial, investigative, contractor sensitive, security management), defined by an organization, or in some instances, by a specific law, Executive Order, directive, policy, or regulation.

INTEGRITY: Guarding against improper information modification or destruction, and includes ensuring information non-repudiation and authenticity. [44 U.S.C., SEC. 3542]

NATIONAL SECURITY SYSTEM: Any information system (including any telecommunications system) used or operated by an agency or by a contractor of an agency, or other organization on behalf of an agency— (i) the function, operation, or use of which involves intelligence activities; involves cryptologic activities related to national security; involves command and control of military forces; involves equipment that is an integral part of a weapon or weapons system; or is critical to the direct fulfillment of military or intelligence missions (excluding a system that is to be used for routine administrative and business applications, for example, pay-roll, finance, logistics, and personnel management applications); or, (ii) is protected at all times by procedures established for information that have been specifically authorized under criteria established by an Executive Order or an Act of Congress to be kept classified in the interest of national defense or foreign policy. [44 U.S.C., SEC. 3542]

SECURITY CATEGORY: The characterization of information or an information system based on an assessment of the potential impact that a loss of Confidentiality, Integrity, or Availability of such information or information system would have on organizational operations, organizational assets, or individuals.

SECURITY CONTROLS: The management, operational, and technical controls (i.e., safeguards or countermeasures) prescribed for an information system to protect the Confidentiality, Integrity, and Availability of the system and its information.

SECURITY OBJECTIVE: Confidentiality, Integrity, or Availability.

REFERENCES

[1]   Privacy Act of 1974 (Public Law 93-579), September 1975.

[2]   Paperwork Reduction Act of 1995 (Public Law 104-13), May 1995.

[3]   OMB Circular A-130, Transmittal Memorandum #4, *Management of Federal Information Resources*, November 2000.

[4]   Information Technology Management Reform Act of 1996 (Public Law 104- 1 0 6), August 1996.

[5]   Federal Information Security Management Act of 2002 (Public Law 107-347), December 2002.

Index